PORT CITY

RAILWAY EXPRESS AGENCY INC

3:52 PM)(20-800)

SAN FRANCISCO, CALIF.

PORT CITY

The History and
Transformation of the
Port of San Francisco,
1848–2010

MICHAEL R. CORBETT

Introduction by
MIKE BUHLER AND JAY TURNBULL

San Francisco Architectural Heritage

CONTENTS

7   Acknowledgments

10   Foreword
MONIQUE MOYER

12   Introduction
MIKE BUHLER AND JAY TURNBULL

---

34   The Port Landscape and the City

54   Commerce

76   The Board of State Harbor Commissioners

92   Ships, Rails, and Trucks

106   Tenants and Workers

122   Engineering

144   Architecture and Planning

162   Epilogue: The Port Since 1969

174   Catalogue

220   Appendix: The Chief Engineer and the Engineering Department

---

226   Notes

234   Bibliography

241   Index

247   Photograph and Reproduction Credits

ACKNOWLEDGMENTS

The publication of this book has been made possible by generous contributions from:

Plant Construction Company, LP
The Historic Preservation Fund
  Committee, City and County
  of San Francisco
San Francisco Waterfront Partners,
  LLC

The Bland Family Foundation
The Acacia Foundation
Anne and Jay Turnbull
Linda Jo Fitz
Julie Chase
Barbara and Ron Kaufman

San Francisco Architectural Heritage would also like to thank the following members of the book committee for their dedication and guidance during the compilation of this book:

Scott Haskins, *Chair*
Mike Buhler
Alice Ross Carey
Charles Edwin Chase
Julie Chase
Linda Jo Fitz

Jack Gold
Nancy Goldenberg
Charles R. Olson
Gee Gee Platt
Jay Turnbull

The book committee would like to recognize the contributions of San Francisco Architectural Heritage staff Leiasa Beckham, William C. Beutner, Constance Farrell, Barbara Roldan, and Dana Talise.

When I began research on the history of the port of San Francisco in 2003, I quickly learned that there were already several good books and other studies on the subject. In the last two years, two more books have been published and two others may be finished by the time this book is available. These cover the span of years of the American-era port from 1848 to the present, and they address many aspects of the port's history. Many have focused on the early history; there are also books on Mission Bay, the Ferry Building, Fisherman's Wharf, shipping companies and international connections, sailors, waterfront labor, the administration of the port, the port since 1950, and the Belt Railroad.

Particularly notable among these are John Haskell Kemble's *San Francisco Bay: Pictorial History* (1957), a rich collection of photographs assembled and interpreted by a scholar of West Coast ports; Nancy Olmsted's *Vanished Waters: A History of San Francisco's Mission Bay* (1986) and *The Ferry Building* (1998), focused studies by a longtime historian of the port; Albert Shumate's *South Park and Rincon Hill* (1988), a neighborhood history tied to the early decades of the port; Alessandro Baccari Jr.'s *San Francisco's Fisherman's Wharf* (2006), a rich collection of photographs; James P. Delgado's *Gold Rush Port: The Maritime Archeology of San Francisco's Waterfront* (2009), the first of two volumes drawing on archeological studies; and Wayne Bonnett's *San Francisco, Gateway to the Pacific* (2010), an illustrated history of shipping companies and international connections. Bill Kaufman is writing a history of the Belt Railroad. Jasper Rubin, a geography professor at San Francisco State University, has almost completed a history of the port since 1950; his manuscript was critical to my understanding of that period. Among numerous more obscure sources, one has achieved cult status among students of the port—Gerald Dow's 1973 master's thesis at San Francisco State, "Bay Fill in San Francisco: A History of Change."

What is the subject of this book? With so many histories of the port, why write another one? In writing this book I have tried to answer questions that others haven't asked. Why does San Francisco's waterfront—the port—look the way it does? And what is the relationship of the development of the port to the rest of the city?

The short answer to the first question is that the character and appearance of this unique part of the city are the result of the interaction of various historical forces, such as those related to engineering, administration, architecture and planning, social factors, politics, labor, economics and trade, business, and transportation. This book addresses these subjects while seeking to understand how they influenced the physical history of the port. There are still books to be written about many of the individual topics.

So this book is different from other histories of the port in two ways: it attempts to look at the whole history of the port, rather than at specific eras or themes; and it selects those aspects of the port's history that created the twentieth-century port, much of which survives. A similar effort was made once before, by the Northern California Writers' Project of the Works Progress Administration, but it died with the beginning of World War II. The initial outlines and collections of materials are stored at the State Archives.

The key sources for this book are the various publications of the Board of State Harbor Commissioners, especially the biennial reports from 1864 to 1940. These reports typically include maps, drawings, photographs, tables of shipping data, lists of construction contracts, and reports by the chief engineer, the attorney, and the board itself.

The first draft of much of this book was written in 2003–2005 as a report on the Port of San Francisco Embarcadero Historic District, a nomination to the National Register of Historic Places. The district, which stretches from Pier 45 to Pier 48 along the Embarcadero, was listed in the National Register on May 12, 2006.

The long process of producing that nomination was the result of a collaboration of many people. The project was conducted by the URS Corporation for the Port of San Francisco. Denise Bradley and Des Garner managed the project for URS. Mark Paez managed the project for the port. In addition to me as lead author, Marjorie Dobkin wrote the sections on labor and Bill Kostura wrote much of the history and description of the piers and other structures. Their sections of the National Register nomination served as the starting point for parallel sections in this book.

A committee at San Francisco Architectural Heritage—led by Scott Haskins and including

Mike Buhler, Alice Carey, Charles Edwin Chase, Julie Chase, Linda Jo Fitz, Jack Gold, Nancy Goldenberg, Charles Olson, Gee Gee Platt, and Jay Turnbull—has guided this book.

The first steps in the enormous task of finding photographs and other images for the book were taken by interns Christina LaLanne, Anna Corbett, and Roxan Schwettmann. In the research and search for images we had help from Herb Lingl at Aerial Archives; Lorna Kirwan and Susan Snyder at the Bancroft Library, University of California, Berkeley; Frank Cresci at the Bay Area Longshoremen's Memorial Association; Debra Kaufman and Mary Morganti at the California Historical Society; Debra Bowen at the California State Archives; Rodney Palmer and Eric Milstein at the California State Lands Commission; Kathleen Correia at the California State Library; Kathryn Santos at the California State Railroad Museum; Miranda Hambro and Waverly Lowell at the Environmental Design Archives, University of California, Berkeley; John Harder; Peter J. Blodgett, Mario Einaudi, and Juan Gomez at the Huntington Library in San Marino; Bradley Cook at Indiana University; Robin Walker at the International Longshore and Warehouse Union; Ted Miles and Ed Le Blanc at the Maritime Museum; Jim Flack at the Mechanics Institute; Nikki Braunton and Sarah Williams at the Museum of London; John M. Cahoon at the Natural History Museum, Los Angeles; Michael Morenzini at the New York City Municipal Archives; Jill Slaight at the New York Historical Society; Julie Takata at the San Francisco Airport Museums; Susan Backman at the San Francisco Museum of Modern Art; Susan Goldstein, Mike Levy, Christina Moretta, and Jeff Thomas at the San Francisco Public Library; Elizabeth Han at Skidmore, Owings & Merrill; Patricia Keats and Elizabeth Young at the Society of California Pioneers; and Moira A. Fitzgerald at Yale University.

Many people helped with research questions and conversations, including Noreen Ambrose, Bruce Anderson, Alessandro Baccari Jr., Bill Beutner, Rachel Brahinsky, Gray Brechin, Bob Cherny, John Corbett, Jim Delgado, Gary Goss, Cris Hart, Allan Jacobs, Bill Kaufman, Tim Kelley, Max Kirkeberg, Bridget Maley, Woody Minor, Nancy Olmsted, Ron Rioux, Dave Roth, Elisa Skaggs, Chris VerPlanck, and Sally Woodbridge. Several people read all or part of the manuscript—Brad Benson, Jim Delgado, Mary Hardy, Mark Paez, and Jasper Rubin.

The team that produced the book includes Elisa Urbanelli, editor and project manager; Robin Weiss, designer; Ezra Cattan, photographer; Leiasa Beckham, photo coordinator; Leslie Ann Dutcher, photo permissions; Mark Woodworth, proofreader; and Susan Burke, indexer. Brian Vahey did the word processing of the manuscript.

MICHAEL CORBETT

For consenting to be interviewed concerning the port, our thanks go to Chris Meany of Wilson Meany Sullivan, Simon Snellgrove of Pacific Waterfront Partners, Robert Cherny of San Francisco State University, and Brian McWilliams of the International Longshore and Warehouse Union. For advice concerning labor history, we thank Tim Kelley, former president of the San Francisco Landmarks Preservation Advisory Board and consulting historian. For research and drafting of the introductory text, architectural historian Jonathan Lammers provided invaluable help. Graphic designer Emily Hung Wilson and historian Rebecca Fogel diligently prepared the introductory illustrations.

JAY TURNBULL

Piers at Union and Green streets, Fisherman's Wharf, before 1900

FOREWORD

The Port of San Francisco is honored that San Francisco Architectural Heritage chose to highlight the history of the city's waterfront as the sequel to its 1979 publication *Splendid Survivors*, the definitive reference for the architectural history of downtown.

In the last decade, the San Francisco waterfront has undergone a transformation that centers on a renewed appreciation of its significant maritime historic resources. Many of these sites are now open to the public. Visitors, especially those arriving by water, cannot help but visually and physically experience the uniqueness of the port's expansive finger piers, artifacts of a bygone era. You don't have to be a historian to be enthralled by the dramatic, Beaux-Arts style buildings set against the backdrop of the bay, Alcatraz and Treasure islands, and the Bay Bridge. People from around the world are captivated by the port's distinctive and internationally renowned collection of historic piers and the iconic Ferry Building.

There has always been a strong element of waterfront nostalgia and pride within the port. However, the creation of the Embarcadero Historic District has fundamentally changed how the port, its governmental partners, and stakeholders embrace and experience the waterfront. The formal recognition of this rare and distinct collection of architectural treasures is in large part a product of Heritage's efforts. Over the years, the organization has strived to raise public awareness of and appreciation for how the waterfront's development has shaped the birth and identity of San Francisco.

That process continues to evolve. *Port City* tells the story of how the Board of State Harbor Commissioners governed the planning, development, and management of the waterfront since 1863. Stretching for three miles from Fisherman's Wharf to China Basin, the simple but grand piers, warehouses, bulkhead buildings, and maritime support structures, along with the Ferry Building, were the economic hub of the city through World War II. In the decades that followed, the Embarcadero waterfront gradually lost its luster and sense of purpose, until the 1989 Loma Prieta earthquake triggered the demolition of the Embarcadero Freeway and revealed these resources in a very different light.

In the intervening years, the upland rail yards and warehouse districts were redeveloped to accommodate the expansion of downtown San Francisco. Projects focused on new businesses, residential neighborhoods, and a different population and culture. In this altered setting, the surviving historic waterfront structures became precious again. In the late 1990s and early 2000s,

Rail spur on Pier 26

Heritage was instrumental in working with the community and regulators to bring about the nomination and listing of the Port of San Francisco Embarcadero Historic District in the National Register of Historic Places. Due to the extraordinary talents and scholarly research of historians Michael Corbett, Marjorie Dobkin, and William Kostura (who authored the nomination report) and Port Planning staff members Diane Oshima and Mark Paez, we are all the beneficiaries of the fascinating account of events and historic photographs in *Port City*.

Today's Port Commission is the descendent of the Board of State Harbor Commissioners. The challenges the board faced during the port's early development and operation are an essential part of its story and continue to shape the historic waterfront today. Most notable is the organizational structure that has required—and continues to require—the port to be economically self-sufficient with limited access to outside funding. This has necessitated constant adaptations and innovation to keep the port solvent, to maintain its business base and relevancy to the city, and to withstand the considerable forces of nature. The historical achievements of the Board of State Harbor Commissioners provide a long-term perspective that inspires the Port Commission today as it continues to navigate the economic and regulatory realities of waterfront development in the twenty-first century.

Indeed, the power of San Francisco's waterfront history inspires greatness and innovation as the port plans its future. The preservation of the Ferry Building and Piers 1 through 5 is among our proudest achievements. This is not only because these historic resources have a new lease on life; they also have played a key role in fostering a renaissance of the waterfront as a civic gathering place. These resources were rehabilitated in accordance with the Secretary of the Interior's Standards for the Treatment of Historic Properties, allowing for financial and regulatory benefits that were fundamental to their successful completion. The Federal Historic Rehabilitation Tax Credit Program has been an essential tool for the port's development partners to make these public-private rehabilitation projects possible.

The piers and bulkhead buildings are marvels of architecture and engineering, but they are more than one hundred years old. The port faces a two-billion-dollar, and growing, need for capital to provide basic maintenance and repair of its waterfront and its aging infrastructure—both historic and non-historic. In an active political environment, it is a daunting task to fund historic preservation projects in addition to maritime business and other public trust objectives, to achieve environmental sustainability goals, and to respond to public demand for more waterfront open space and transportation improvements.

Thus it is incumbent upon the port, the city government, and those who love the waterfront to form partnerships and share creative strategies that honor this rich and storied part of San Francisco. The port enjoys this collaborative partnership with San Francisco Architectural Heritage, and we look forward to working together to address the challenges and attain even greater achievements along the waterfront.

MONIQUE MOYER
Executive Director, Port of San Francisco

INTRODUCTION

MIKE BUHLER AND JAY TURNBULL

San Francisco Architectural Heritage (Heritage) was founded in 1971 to stem the increasingly rapid destruction of the city's unique architectural legacy. In the four decades since, the organization has proactively and vigilantly safeguarded that legacy. Heritage was instrumental in establishing the framework of preservation protections that has allowed the city's downtown to evolve and flourish without sacrificing its distinct character. From Mission Dolores to the Transamerica Pyramid, and from the Painted Ladies to the Ferry Building, San Francisco's diverse landmarks—old and new, architectural and cultural—draw visitors from around the world and fuel the city's creative and economic vitality.

Today it is easy to take such things for granted, to assume that San Franciscans have always recognized the inherent value of protecting the places that make this city unique. Not so. Heritage came into existence in the wake of the redevelopment frenzy of the 1950s and 1960s, when entire neighborhoods were being leveled in the name of "urban renewal." The city had no comprehensive inventory of historic resources, and the Landmarks Preservation Ordinance was still in its infancy. Looking back, the upstart organization had a remarkably swift and dramatic impact, not only staving off threats to individual buildings but also presciently surveying large swaths of the city to inform future planning efforts. Although the preservation community has certainly come a long way, the need for vigilance continues in the face of ever more complex and nuanced threats to the city's historic built environment.

Over the past four decades, Heritage has scored many successes and suffered some heartbreaking losses. In the early 1970s, urban renewal policies galvanized the local preservation community. The possibility of saving Victorian houses slated for demolition in the Western Addition precipitated the formation of Heritage, which stepped in to rescue twelve structures in the largest building-moving project in the history of San Francisco. In partnership with the Redevelopment Agency and the Landmarks Board, Heritage acted as a clearinghouse to match the transported Victorians with public-spirited investors willing to rehabilitate them. Although relocation is not considered a preferred preservation solution today, the Western Addition project showed the Redevelopment Agency that Heritage was serious, prompting the agency to think in terms of rehabilitation rather than demolition. Good press coverage gave the fledgling organization high visibility and won public support for its efforts.

In 1973, while still in the process of rescuing the Victorians in the Western Addition, Heritage was entrusted with caring for one of its own. The Haas-Lilienthal House, a pristine 1886 Victorian mansion with most of its contents intact, was given to Heritage by members of the prominent Haas and Lilienthal families. Today, it serves myriad functions: as a house museum; as a popular venue for meetings, lectures, and social events; and as Heritage's administrative office, library, and archive. Through a variety of activities, including Heritage Hikes for schoolchildren, the house is the centerpiece of Heritage's education program and has become a powerful exemplar of responsible stewardship.

SPLENDID SURVIVORS

The 1970s were a time of emerging awareness of the value of historic preservation across the nation. In the wake of passage of the National Historic Preservation Act of 1966, state and local historic preservation offices, review boards, and commissions were established, and federal aid to cities was tied to requirements for local historic-resource surveys and land-use plans. In 1967, San Francisco enacted a Landmarks Preservation Ordinance as Article 10 of the city's Planning Code. The following year, the Junior League of San Francisco commissioned the book *Here Today*, based on its influential early survey of twenty-five hundred historic buildings throughout San Francisco, San Mateo, and Marin counties.[1] And between 1974 and 1976, the San Francisco Planning Department conducted a preliminary architectural inventory of the city's building stock.

San Francisco was entering what would become the greatest downtown building boom since the post-1906 reconstruction, with new development threatening many important historic structures. Preservation battles over buildings that did not have landmark status were generally lost, most notoriously the City of Paris department store on Union Square. (The Beaux-Arts icon was demolished in 1981 after a four-year legal battle and a petition signed by sixty thousand citizens protesting the building's destruction.) Realizing that fighting many individual battles would prove ineffective in the long run, Heritage embarked on an unprecedented effort to develop a comprehensive preservation strategy in place of piecemeal efforts to save threatened downtown historic buildings.

In 1975, Heritage commissioned an intensive architectural survey of downtown San Francisco. Prepared by Charles Hall Page & Associates under the direction of architectural historian Michael Corbett, the results were published in 1979 as the acclaimed book *Splendid Survivors: San Francisco's Downtown Architectural*

The Haas-Lilienthal House, built in 1886, is now the headquarters of San Francisco Architectural Heritage.

In the early 1970s, Victorian houses in the Western Addition were moved in order to save them from demolition.

Heritage. It was one of the first such inventories compiled anywhere in the country.

The *Splendid Survivors* survey became the authoritative guide used by the city to define significant historic buildings in its pioneering 1985 Downtown Plan. Heralded as a model for cities throughout the country, the Downtown Plan rated historic resources and created incentives for their protection. It mandated retention of 248 significant buildings, encouraged protection of nearly 200 others, and established six conservation districts to preserve the scale and character of significant groupings of historic structures. Decades later, the organization San Francisco Planning and Urban Research (SPUR) observed: "The success of the downtown plan is illustrated by its influence on other cities and by the fact that San Francisco continues to have one of the best downtowns in the country."[2]

Building on the success of *Splendid Survivors*, Heritage continued to canvass the city and expand upon its downtown survey. The organization, and others, went on to conduct surveys of the Van Ness Corridor, South of Market, North of Market, the Civic Center, Chinatown, the Northeast Waterfront, and the Inner Richmond.

Areas surveyed within San Francisco

PORT CITY

Much like the genesis of the Downtown Plan, the nomination of the Port of San Francisco Embarcadero Historic District to the National Register of Historic Places was borne out of piecemeal threats to the port's historic infrastructure. Alarmed by early planning policies that called for the removal of historic buildings to open up views to the bay, in the late 1990s Heritage joined Port staff and a Port committee of waterfront stakeholders to explore the possibility of a National Register nomination. Port leadership eventually embraced historic designation—and the tax incentives that can flow from it—as essential to waterfront revitalization efforts. Funded by the Port and authored by Michael Corbett, Marjorie Dobkin, PhD, and William Kostura, the five-hundred-page nomination is the most definitive history of San Francisco's waterfront to date and qualified a three-mile area for designation as a National Register historic district in 2006.

Ever since the publication of *Splendid Survivors*, Heritage has sought to follow it with a worthy companion volume. Corbett's documentation for the Port's nomination as a National Register historic district offered a comprehensive body of work similar to the survey that underlies *Splendid Survivors*. Certainly, the waterfront boasts one of the richest and most compelling collections of historic resources anywhere in the city. Like its predecessor, *Port City* will advance Heritage's ongoing mission to increase community awareness of and involvement in architectural preservation, planning, and urban design. Heritage raised money for writing, editing, and publication costs from San Francisco's Historic Preservation Fund Committee, foundations, firms, and individuals to exhibit the extensive body of research through this book project. To each of these entities that have made *Port City* possible, we extend our profound thanks.

Piers 35, 33, and 31 seen from Telegraph Hill

"THE HARBOR OF HARBORS"

It is worth remembering that what is now called San Francisco Bay was the locus of movement patterns, food gathering, and tribal communities long before Europeans settled here. Early Spanish explorers immediately grasped the value of such a vast, protected anchorage. Pedro Font, chronicler of Juan Bautista de Anza's expedition in 1776, hailed the bay as "a marvel of nature" and "the harbor of harbors," noting, "It has the best advantages to founding in it a most beautiful city."[3] In his chapter on commerce at the port of San Francisco, Corbett chronicles the waterfront's rapid transformation from a few wharves to a world-class port, beginning in 1849 with the Gold Rush.

The port of San Francisco has followed a pattern of development, expansion, abandonment, and renewal typical among historic urban waterfronts. Ports like San Francisco's begin when the activities of arrival, transfer of goods, resupply, refitting, and departure literally constitute the community. They expand when new forms of communication and transportation append themselves to shipping. Buildings push up against the waterfront; increasingly larger vessels require deeper water and longer piers to accommodate changing maritime technologies and markets. Ultimately, the space required for modern shipping and freight handling forces port activities to migrate to more remote and expansive locations,

Arthur Frank Mathews, *Discovery of the Bay of San Francisco by Portola*, oil on canvas, 1896

separating the port from the city it brought into being. Finally, the old urban waterfront is abandoned by shipping and industry, and it becomes ripe for reinvention. Following this trajectory, the Port of San Francisco's transformation to accommodate new uses has been an ongoing endeavor since the decline of break-bulk cargo began in the late 1950s.

PROMISE AND CHALLENGE

As an idea, as a complex of political and economic influences, as an institution, and as a force within the community, the Port of San Francisco is much more than piers, wharves, transit sheds, bulkhead buildings, and seawall. It controls property that is at once the site of our proudest history and the locus of new development. San Francisco boasts the most intact early-twentieth-century finger-pier waterfront in the country. This high degree of authenticity has proven to be both an asset and a liability. While the port's historic character remains largely intact, much of its infrastructure is in disrepair. It contains promise and challenge.

Over the past decade, a powerful and synergistic partnership between the private and public sectors has reenergized sections of the historic port, heralding its transformation into a mixed-use destination that attracts residents and visitors alike for both business and recreation. The 1991 removal of the earthquake-damaged Embarcadero Freeway, which had long been a barrier between downtown and the bay, precipitated waterfront revitalization efforts. Perhaps

nothing better epitomizes the renaissance of San Francisco's port today than the spectacular 2003 rehabilitation of the landmark Ferry Building and its teeming, jostling Saturday farmers' market. Immediately to the north, the adaptive reuse of Piers 1, 1½, 3, and 5 extended the revitalization of the Northeast Waterfront.

But replicating these successes elsewhere at the Port has proven difficult. Preservation initiatives have been hampered by a cauldron of complex economics, planning issues, environmental contamination, political infighting, seismic deficiencies, and environmental-justice issues. A position paper adopted by SPUR in 2007 asks, "Can the waterfront be saved?"

> San Franciscans face hard choices at the Port. Compared to the Ferry Building and other recently completed high-profile projects, the future challenges facing the Port are far more formidable, and time is not on the Port's side. The costs of repairing, seismically upgrading and redeveloping the Port's iconic but rapidly deteriorating finger piers are staggering. Significant public investment above and beyond what could be generated from proposed development will be needed, and sources of funding will have to be found. Painful priorities will have to be set [and] the numerous regulations to which the Port is subject . . . will have to be revisited. Hard choices will have to be made—and made soon.[4]

In 2010, with an economic downturn persisting and competition for public funds intense, these challenges are more daunting than ever.

Although developers experienced in port-rehabilitation projects have different points of view, they echo some common themes. When asked if the Port of San Francisco will be able to maintain the level of rehabilitation seen at the Ferry Building, one replied: "It is *not* possible to continue such development, with the constraints now imposed by the Port and various other regulatory agencies. The many agencies impose conflicting objectives and make such projects difficult to achieve. There are the physical costs of development. There are different roles and jurisdictional responsibilities. Market realities make it economically challenging to be able to reach compromises, build new alliances, and

Port lands within San Francisco in 2010, with the historic district noted in red

to balance otherwise competing goals."[5] Labor experts concur: "In a sense the Port can never succeed. It does not control its own tax base. It has no guaranteed revenue. It is saddled with a crumbling infrastructure for which, when the city reacquired the Port in 1969, the state took no responsibility. The tragedy for maritime use at the Port is that you can prevail over particular issues hundreds of times but you only get to lose once and then what you fought for is gone forever."[6]

Lest the picture seem hopelessly bleak, these same observers remain inspired by the tremendous potential of the waterfront. "It's not land,

it's a pier," said one, "but it is a magic space, particularly when it commands a view."[7] Another is unconcerned about conflicting objectives, noting that they ensure there is adequate discussion of any initiative and that weaker proposals wither away automatically, even though hard lessons may be learned in the process. They point to other ports that provide important lessons for San Francisco, such as Sydney, Vancouver, New York, Seattle, and East London. Indeed, most cities that have waterfronts are in some stage of reclaiming them, and the literature is full of studies and ambitious master plans.

The rehabilitated Car-Ferry Head House at Pier 43

LESSONS LEARNED

Based on the experiences of other cities, their successes and failures, a certain amount of consensus has been achieved in defining the overall character of desirable waterfront development. The first imperative is public access to the water with easy connections to the city core. Most planners acknowledge the need to blend "anchors," such as museums and recreational facilities, with commercial and residential development. A diversity of functions is critical: otherwise, the waterfront may become dependent solely on the flow of occasional visitors. Preserving a sense of place is also important. The most convincing plans combine a multiplicity of uses with the preservation of tangible reminders of the area's historic maritime identity.

SYDNEY

The experience of Sydney, Australia, is reminiscent of San Francisco's, while highlighting the need for a consensus-based, comprehensive vision. Although Sydney's political culture places a premium on cooperative planning, the jumble of various consent bodies with jurisdiction over waterfront development has resulted in projects that are isolated by arbitrary political boundaries rather than integrated with the city as a whole. For example, the 134-acre Darling Harbour redevelopment—though successful in terms of visitation—suffers from lack of integration with existing city streets; instead, one reaches it by a freeway that encircles it and cuts it off from the city. Darling Harbour also relies almost exclusively on retail and entertainment facilities, and it has no residential component.

VANCOUVER

By contrast, the city of Vancouver, Canada, has placed residential housing at the heart of its waterfront plans. The catalyst for the city's shoreline renewal was Expo '86, a world's fair that was built over 204 acres of reclaimed industrial land. The property was later sold to a consortium of developers, who were subject to stringent land-use controls that required new construction to incorporate continuous walking paths, community centers, parks, and social housing. In addition, existing city streets were extended to improve connections with the city core. Over time, these same planning principles have been repeated at other industrial sites and continue to guide the city's overall development strategy.

Perhaps the most notable aspect of Vancouver's waterfront development is that it wholly rejected suburban models of development and instead was geared to promote a specific type of lifestyle—a walkable urban community rather than one structured around free-flowing traffic and reliant on the automobile. In this sense, Vancouver and San Francisco share many similarities in emphasizing development geared to people rather than to cars. However, some critics have blamed Vancouver's repetition of slender residential towers for creating a monotonous consistency that is divorced from the cultural context. Unlike San Francisco, Vancouver's wholesale clearance of former industrial areas did not prioritize preservation of historic infrastructure. Thus, the challenge in San Francisco is to find ways to treat the port's historic spaces and buildings—the "markers" of the city's maritime past—as resources worthy of adaptation and reuse, and not as a burdensome legacy.

Sydney's Darling Harbour

Vancouver's redeveloped waterfront

New York's waterfront, before and after the loss of its finger piers

NEW YORK

New York City also once had an impressive collection of finger piers, but, like San Francisco, it has struggled with the costs of maintenance and the ability to bring economically viable reuse projects to fruition. Vocal citizen opposition to large-scale development initiatives, such as the failed Westway and Riverwalk developments, has meant that most projects proposed today are smaller in scale—and often incorporate parkland or recreational facilities as a prominent feature. Perhaps most emblematic is Hudson River Park, which consists of several segments incorporating everything from soccer fields and kayaking facilities to the USS *Intrepid* Sea-Air-Space Museum. Toward its southern end, Hudson River Park connects to the Chelsea Piers, once the destination for luxury ocean liners of the White Star and Cunard lines. The piers were redeveloped during the 1990s into a successful dining and sports complex, but almost none of the original historic fabric was retained. Similarly, the renovated finger piers of the nearby New York Passenger Ship Terminal, which handle nearly nine hundred thousand passengers a year, bear little resemblance to their 1930s origins.

One of the most recent and intriguing adaptive-reuse projects is the High Line, a landscaped linear greenway developed atop a 1930s elevated freight railway at Manhattan's western edge. Despite its popularity, one need only look down from the High Line to be able to compare the redeveloped Chelsea project with less well-utilized piers. Given the intense demand for waterfront land in the city, as well as the enormous costs associated with rehabilitation, many historic port facilities could eventually be lost. In order to succeed, future preservation projects will likely require some form of public-private partnership—and substantial political will.

SAN FRANCISCO

As these case studies demonstrate, creative solutions abound for reimagining urban waterfronts as vehicles for economic development, community recreation, and civic engagement. They also serve as cautionary tales. Attempting to duplicate these efforts could lead to what one author describes as "uniformization on an international scale, not only of some construction standards but also of organizational methods, spatial typologies, and architectural forms, thus generating a monotonous sense of déjà vu."[8] Undoubtedly, the one universal truth that can be gleaned from

San Francisco

other port cities is the need for broad public support of waterfront development initiatives.

Taken as a whole, the inescapable conclusion is that San Francisco must craft its own unique vision for the future of the port. We must work together to build on the city's past innovation with pioneering projects at Ghirardelli Square and the Cannery in the 1960s and, more recently, in the Northeast Waterfront Historic District. The Port of San Francisco has demonstrated resourcefulness and foresight in identifying new sources of revenue, leveraging rehabilitation tax credits, and championing creative reuse of its facilities. Certainly, most would agree that reuniting the city with its waterfront through the demolition of the Embarcadero Freeway and the rehabilitation of the Ferry Building is one of San Francisco's greatest successes in a generation.

To realize similar successes in the future will require compromises by both development and preservation interests. Development plans have little chance of success unless they are designed to accommodate compatible uses and public access. The city needs to establish clear guidelines for what is and what is not acceptable on the waterfront. For its part, Heritage must exercise leadership in forging a collective vision for the next phase in the evolution of the city's historic waterfront. By lending expertise to identify sensitive solutions, advocating for rehabilitation incentives, and building consensus among divergent interest groups, the preservation community will continue to be an essential partner in the revitalization of the waterfront. Based on its longstanding advocacy for the city's historic resources, Heritage brings credibility and legitimacy to the citywide discussion about the future of the port. By contributing to a much more thorough understanding of the port's architectural and historical legacy—and acknowledging the challenges it poses—*Port City* will enhance Heritage's credibility to convene stakeholders, bridge competing views, and foster a unified vision for waterfront development.

In this vein, San Francisco should be able to inaugurate a new period of prosperity at the port—one that provides jobs and recreation for its residents while retaining and celebrating the unique and tangible reminders of its past. The buildings and spaces that constitute the port are at the very root of the city's identity and are more than deserving of a prominent role in the city's ongoing evolution.

NOTES

Opposite: View north along the Embarcadero from the foot of Market Street, circa 1940

1. The findings of the *Here Today* survey were formally adopted by the San Francisco Board of Supervisors on May 11, 1970, as Resolution No. 268-70.

2. *Vision of a Place: A Guide to the San Francisco General Plan* (San Francisco: San Francisco Planning and Urban Research, 2002), 56.

3. Pedro Font, *Complete Diary of Anza's California Expeditions* (1776), quoted in Stephen Vincent, ed., *O California!* (San Francisco: Beaux-Arts Publishers, 1989).

4. San Francisco Planning and Urban Research Association, "Hard Choices at the Port of San Francisco: Can the Waterfront Be Saved?" June 20, 2007, 1.

5. Christopher Meany, principal, Wilson Meany Sullivan, interview, May 6, 2010.

6. Brian McWilliams, International Longshore and Warehouse Union, interview, May 13, 2010.

7. Simon Snellgrove, principal, Pacific Waterfront Partners, interview, April 30, 2010.

8. Richard Marshall, "Connection to the Waterfront," in *Waterfronts in Post-industrial Cities* (London and New York: Spon Press, 2001), 48.

Opposite top: View from Potrero Hill

Opposite bottom: Aerial view, circa 1920

Top: Pier 35

Middle: Aquatic Park

Bottom: View from Hyde Street Pier toward the California Fruit Canners Association warehouse

HILLS BROS COFFEE

Above: View from Pier 26

Opposite top: Pier 40

Opposite bottom: Pier 46B, Refrigerated Products Terminal, 1932

Top: Containers at Pier 96

Bottom: Pacific Coast Steel Corporation buildings at Pier 70

Opposite: View from Telegraph Hill, circa 1936, showing Piers 23, 19, and 17

View north on East Street (later the Embarcadero) from Folsom Street, circa 1901–1906.

THE PORT LANDSCAPE AND THE CITY

The port of San Francisco is a complex entity that has always connected the waterfront to the larger city beyond. When we envision the port we think first of the berths of ships—the places where ships are loaded and unloaded. In broader terms, the port is also the area that was controlled by the Board of State Harbor Commissioners (BSHC), a corridor of land and water that runs along the waterfront from Fisherman's Wharf at the northern and eastern edges of the city to the San Mateo County line, including the two-hundred-foot-wide Embarcadero and the seawall lots on the west side of the Embarcadero, both created by fill behind the seawall, as well as the extensive wharves and associated facilities at China Basin, Islais Creek, and India Basin. The port also encompasses the Belt Railroad that runs along the Embarcadero and onto the piers, the rail yards on many of the seawall lots, and the yards and spurs that extend beyond the land owned by the Port of San Francisco into city streets and onto privately and publicly owned land.

Business generated by the port played a substantial role in the development of San Francisco's skyline, especially in the 1910s and 1920s, and extended beyond downtown into industrial and residential districts of the city.

North Point in 1855, before Telegraph Hill was quarried and fill extended the shoreline. This view evokes the early term *city front* for the edge of the city, used when people frequently experienced the city from the water. As the importance of that experience diminished over time, the term *waterfront* became more common.

The port's gently curving outer boundary is defined by the Pier Head Line, a demarcation established by the U.S. Army Corps of Engineers, beyond which no pier or other structure may be built. The Pier Head Line was first established at six hundred feet from the shore and was extended to eight hundred feet from the shore as the size of ships increased. The angling of Pier 45 to the waterfront was a way of building a pier longer than eight hundred feet that stayed within the Pier Head Line.

The port is most irregular on its inner boundary, where the seawall lots meet the preexisting waterfront of the city. Prior to the erection of the current seawall, which was built in stages from 1878 to 1915, the waterfront was a jagged edge, the result of the filling of water lots within extensions of the street grid beyond the shoreline. These lots were filled behind sheet pilings and, for short stretches, behind an earlier version of the seawall. The port controls a corridor of water between the waterfront, or Bulkhead Line, and the federally defined Pier Head Line from Van Ness Avenue to the San Mateo County border.

The area controlled by the Port of San Francisco is also intermittent along the waterfront, extending continuously except for gaps that have remained in the jurisdiction of others for most of its history. These gaps are at Potrero Point (known as Pier 70 since 1982, when it was acquired by the port), Hunters Point, and Fort Mason. Potrero Point was first developed by private industry; Hunters Point was sparsely developed until it was taken over by the U.S. Navy in World War II; and Fort Mason was an Army facility. In addition, the waterfront below Hunters Point, adjoining South Basin, was filled and developed with Navy housing.

The port is distinguished from the rest of the city by its ownership, but it is also defined by the character of its landscape—by the types of structures built there, by its abundance of open space, and by the presence of water as well as land. The seawalls; the wharves and piers; the railroad tracks, yards, car ferries, and engine house; the cranes, pile drivers, dredges, and other mobile working machinery; the berths between the piers; the two-hundred-foot-wide Embarcadero; the seawall lots inshore of the Embarcadero; and the imposing architecture of the facades of the bulkhead buildings: together these features created a visually distinctive part of the city. The open character of the port is in contrast to the densely built-up city that starts at the edge of the port property; portions of the city side of that boundary have been called the "city front" for the wall it presents to the more open area of the port.

If the legal entity known as the Port of San Francisco is a specific area along the waterfront, more broadly speaking, the port is a much larger part of the city that contributes to the operation and business of the waterfront. If any city might justifiably have been called Port City, it was San Francisco for its first hundred years. The port did not grow so much to serve the city as the other way around. The port first developed to serve the mining and agricultural economy of a vast part of California, and the city grew in the beginning largely to serve that same economy, via the port.

Specifically, because of the port, railroads were established in San Francisco: the port's own Belt Railroad, the Southern Pacific, the Santa Fe, the Western Pacific, and the Northwestern Pacific. Warehouses and manufacturing plants were located on the various rail lines and spurs, where they were linked to the piers along the waterfront. Power and fuel facilities were located on the waterfront to serve

BIRDS EYE VIEW OF THE **EASTERN PORTION** OF SAN FRANCISCO CAL.
COPYRIGHTED AND ISSUED NOV. 1892, BY **BALDWIN & HAMMOND** REAL ESTATE AGENTS 10 MONTGOMERY ST.
Showing the Potrero District North of Nevada Street and East of Potrero Avenue.
PROPERTY OF THE REAL ESTATE AND DEVELOPMENT COMPANY, SHADED THUS,

REFERENCE.
1-CITY HALL.
2-CHRONICLE BUILDING.
3-CROCKER "
4-MILLS "
5-PALACE HOTEL.
6-S.P. DEPOT.
7-UNION IRON WORKS.
8-PACIFIC ROLLING MILLS

REFERENCE.
9-GAS WORKS
10-CALIFORNIA SUGAR REFINERY.
11-ROPE WALK.
12-MISSION ROCK, WAREHOUSES.
13-JACKSON PARK.
14-BUENA VISTA PARK.
15-OFFICE OF REAL ESTATE
AND DEVELOPMENT CO.

the ships at the port, nearby industries and businesses, and the homes of workers. The city brought streets, sewers, and water to the waterfront and allowed Belt Railroad spurs to run in its streets when the railroad extended beyond the Embarcadero and the seawall lots. Much of downtown San Francisco was built up with offices for shipping companies, commission merchants, marine insurance businesses, and a wide variety of companies whose business was tied to the port. These commercial areas did not represent separate economies and activities; rather, they were part of a large integrated economy whose core was the port. The port and the city were enmeshed in a seamless web of economics and activities every day, with people, vehicles, goods, money, and communications moving back and forth, day and night, for most of San Francisco's history.

THE IMPACT OF RAILROADS AT THE WATERFRONT
Railroads first came to the port and big industry to the waterfront in anticipation of the 1869 completion of the transcontinental railroad. Indeed, the BSHC was established in the same year— 1863—that work began on the transcontinental

The completion of the transcontinental railroad in 1869, with a line around San Francisco Bay and up the peninsula to the port, led to the first substantial development of the southern waterfront. The industries concentrated at Potrero Point, the enclosure and filling of Mission Bay, and warehouses on Mission Rock are seen in this 1892 bird's-eye view.

railroad, representing the interdependence of the two. Large-scale industrial development began in 1866 at Potrero Point with the establishment of Pacific Rolling Mills. The first dry dock, which was the first significant development at Hunters Point, was built in 1868. Seeing the demand for waterfront property, the state passed the Tidelands Act in 1868 and established the Board of Tidelands Commissioners to survey and auction tidelands not previously sold. As a result, by 1871, thirty acres south of China Basin and west of Third Street was sold to two railroads, the Central Pacific and the Western Pacific—both of which would end up in the hands of the Southern Pacific—on the condition that each establish a "San Francisco terminus." At the terminus would be yards, a roundhouse, and shops.

In addition, Central Pacific and its successor Southern Pacific bought many blocks north of China Basin, where it built yards, a station on the south side of Townsend Street east of Fourth Street, and general offices in a three-story brick building at the northeast corner of Townsend and Fourth streets. Of particular symbolic importance was Southern Pacific's 1870 purchase of Tichenor's Ways, a shipbuilding and repair facility on Steamboat Point at the foot of Second Street near its later intersection with Townsend Street. This brought the Southern

Pacific Railroad to the waterfront, a position it would hold for decades until section 13A of the seawall, an extension of the engineer T. J. Arnold's seawall plan of 1878, was completed in 1924, the last section of the seawall north of China Basin. The dominance of Southern Pacific in the South Beach area of the waterfront was enhanced by its control of the Pacific Mail Steamship Company, whose facilities were at the foot of First Street.

Just as Central Pacific-Southern Pacific was the first private railroad on the waterfront, it was the only railroad that connected San Francisco by land to the rest of the United States, running down the San Francisco Peninsula to San Jose and up the east side of the bay to the main transcontinental line at Niles. The other railroads were connected to main lines only by water—via car ferries across San Francisco Bay.

The second railroad on the waterfront was the Belt Railroad of the BSHC. Built in phases starting in 1890, it was initially located several blocks north of Market Street, at the far end of the port from the area served by the Southern Pacific. The first section of the port's railroad picked up railcars from the car ferry at the foot of Lombard Street and in the beginning served yards and warehouses between Broadway and Taylor Street. Only with the victory in 1910 of

This 1859 view shows the rock seawall along Front Street from Vallejo to Union streets, one of only two built segments of an early seawall designed in a zigzag alignment. The plan caused silting and was abandoned.

This 1881 drawing from *Harper's Weekly* shows the gently curving alignment of the redesigned seawall, built from 1878 to 1915 and later extended, before construction of the bulkhead wharf made it possible for ships to unload directly onto the shore.

With the creation of land behind the new seawall, the port's property was an irregular corridor of open space that was occupied by the Embarcadero and rail yards in the seawall lots between the water and the warehouses and businesses of the city front. This view from the 1930s extends across Seawall Lot 5 to the Harbor Warehouses and Piers 39, 37, and 35.

reform politicians who opposed the power of the Southern Pacific was the Belt Railroad extended south of Market Street into what had been considered Southern Pacific territory. In 1913, the north and south sections of the Belt Railroad were joined across the foot of Market Street in front of the Ferry Building. In the following year, the railroad was extended through a new tunnel to the west side of Fort Mason and the Harbor View section of the waterfront that was being developed for the Panama-Pacific International Exposition (PPIE). Following the exposition, the Belt Railroad was extended in 1917 to its ultimate northern terminus at the Presidio. At the other end of the port, in 1933 the Belt Railroad was extended south of China Basin for the first time, across a new Third Street Bridge. Because extensive rail lines south of China Basin were already in place, in part the Belt Railroad used Santa Fe and Western Pacific tracks to reach its own rail spurs to the piers.

The second major private railroad, the Atchison, Topeka, and Santa Fe (known as the Santa Fe), began service in San Francisco in 1900. It was promoted and supported to provide competition to the Southern Pacific. In 1895, the Santa Fe had taken over the tidelands that the old Western Pacific had acquired in 1868 south of China Basin. Then, under an agreement with the BSHC, the railroad built the seawall from China Basin to El Dorado Street, one block above Sixteenth Street, and made major improvements over many years. The Santa Fe constructed a car-ferry terminal at the northeast corner of this property, connecting San Francisco to its main yards and shops in Point Richmond. Parallel to the waterfront, the company established a secondary yard linked to Piers 48, 50, and 52, as well as to Pier 54, which it built in 1911 under a special act of the legislature.

The Northwestern Pacific (NWP) Railroad, formed in 1907 out of several smaller railroads that ran up the coast to Humboldt County, operated a car ferry to San Francisco from its main yards and shops in Tiburon. At its peak in the 1940s, the NWP leased two rail yards in seawall lots from the BSHC and operated a passenger ferry from Sausalito.

The last private railroad to establish facilities in San Francisco was the Western Pacific (not related to the earlier Western Pacific Railroad that was taken over by Southern Pacific), another

Right: Potrero Point, one of the few projections of private property within the zone of the publicly owned waterfront, was a creation of the confluence of ships and railroads at the port of San Francisco. The densest concentration of heavy industry in the West, it was bordered by housing for workers, as shown in this 1892 photograph.

Below: This view from the 1930s shows Southern Pacific Railroad's vast holdings on both sides of Channel Street, just west of its original terminus on San Francisco Bay, including the six-story China Basin Building, wooden freight sheds, rail yards for freight and passengers, and the passenger depot at the southwest corner of Third and Townsend streets.

important competitor of Southern Pacific's. Western Pacific began its operation from Salt Lake City to Oakland in 1909, with car-ferry service across the bay to terminals near the foot of Army Street (now Cesar Chavez Street) and at Pier 36. From its car ferry at Army Street, a Western Pacific line ran west to Iowa Street, then diagonally across the Potrero district to yards along Brannan Street from Seventh to Eighth streets and to spurs nearby. The Western Pacific also leased rail yards in seawall lots from the BSHC, but it built its principal yards and shops across the bay in Oakland.

Other railroads—including the Napa Valley, the Sacramento Northern, and the Petaluma & Santa Rosa—served the port through ferries, car ferries, and the Belt Railroad, but none of them had any yards or other facilities in San Francisco.

These railroads provided the means for extending the business of the port beyond its boundaries. The railroads picked up and delivered railcars full of goods, shuttling between car-ferry terminals and piers to warehouses, factories, and other industrial plants. The spurs of the various railroads served a broad range of destinations.

WAREHOUSES AND INDUSTRIES
SERVED BY THE RAILROADS

The first warehouses, used during the Gold Rush, were converted ships, which were soon accompanied by buildings on piles over water lots in Yerba Buena Cove. These early structures were followed by those built on landfill as the water lots were made into permanent parts of the city. Before the arrival of the railroads, the best location for a warehouse was at the edge of the waterfront, as close as possible to the berths of the ships. Two surviving examples from this era—the Gibbs warehouses on Front Street flanking Vallejo—faced the water when they were constructed but lost their prime position as more fill extended the edge of the city into the bay. These were two-story brick structures on standard city lots, much smaller than warehouses built a few years later. They were made for the general cargo of the day: commodities, hardware, and dry goods that were imported because they were not produced in California.

The location of pre-railroad industries

followed the same pattern. Tubbs Cordage Works, which made rope, long a necessity of sailing ships and cargo handling, was established just south of Potrero Point in 1856. Tubbs's rope walk—a traditional type of building for making rope in which long strands of hemp or other material were laid out and twisted—was fourteen-hundred feet long by forty-five feet wide and was built at an angle to the city's grid, projecting into the bay.

Another pre-railroad industry was the Pioneer Woolen Mill, founded in North Beach in 1858. Its principal building of 1862 was taken over by the D. Ghirardelli Company and is now part of Ghirardelli Square. Like Tubbs Cordage, the Pioneer Woolen Mill was built at the water's edge without regard for the grid. One of the earliest factories in California, the mill was conceived to capture the market previously held by importers of wool by using the abundant wool available in California. In this way it represented a pattern that would be followed by many other port-dependent industries—manufacturing and processing California's natural and agricultural resources for local and distant markets.

With the arrival of the railroads, industries were established or relocated following a new

The first railroad at the port was the Central Pacific, the predecessor of the Southern Pacific. It met the warehouses and wharves of the Pacific Mail Steamship Company in 1869 near what is now Second and Townsend streets, shown here in the early 1870s. This private outpost lost its water frontage in 1909, when the port finally built the seawall and filled behind it, landlocking the Southern Pacific.

Top: Car ferries were long an essential link in the system that brought freight cars from the Southern Pacific, Santa Fe, Western Pacific, and Northwestern Pacific railheads across the bay to car-ferry slips at the port, where they were moved by Belt Railroad locomotives to piers or warehouses.

Middle: Rail spurs and yards—like this Western Pacific yard at Seventh and Brannan streets in 1929—connected the port to warehouses and industrial sites in scattered neighborhoods such as North Beach, South of Market, the Mission District, and the Potrero.

Bottom: Before the railroads, warehouses and industrial plants were located adjacent to the berths of ships, like Cowell's Wharf of 1853 at Battery between Union and Filbert streets, shown here about 1870. Some—abandoned ships altered for the purpose—were in the water, others were in unfilled water lots, and still others were at the edge of the shore.

pattern, and some of these enterprises were much larger than their predecessors. The densest concentration of heavy industry stimulated by the railroad occurred at Potrero Point, with the appearance of Pacific Rolling Mills in 1866, a large gas works of the San Francisco Gas and Electric Company in 1872, the California Sugar Refining Company in 1881, Union Iron Works in 1883 (relocated from First and Mission streets), and the Arctic Oil Works of the Pacific Steam Whaling Company by 1884. By 1899, the California Barrel Company had built a factory and the Southern Pacific Railroad had set up cattle corrals in the area.

The industries of Potrero Point had their own private wharves, but they were also served by spurs of the Southern Pacific Railroad. Like an octopus with its eight tentacles—Frank Norris titled his novel exposing the unfair practices of the Southern Pacific *The Octopus*—that company monopolized San Francisco rail traffic for decades, in part by the tentacles of its spurs. Few warehouses or other industries would be built in the city from 1869 to 1910 that were not on a Southern Pacific spur. Until the seawall was built and the seawall lots behind it were filled, the railroad could control its own access to the waterfront.

Along with Potrero Point, in the late 1860s and early 1870s industry also concentrated around Steamboat Point, where First and Second streets terminated at the shoreline of Mission Bay, more or less along Townsend Street. (The BSHC had not yet exercised control of this section of the waterfront.) Southern Pacific's spurs on these streets served the dispersed facilities of the Pacific Mail Steamship Company, including the Oriental Warehouse. Within a few blocks, in 1899 Southern Pacific also served the California Car Works of J. M. Hammond & Company, a stone yard of the McGilvray Stone Company, the Pacific Oil and Lead Works, the bottling works of the Buffalo Brewing Company, and the Union Ice Company, to name a few.

With the railroad linking the port to warehouses and industrial plants, there was no longer an advantage in being located next to the water. Indeed, as long as it was on a rail spur, the specific location of an industrial plant made little difference, except that sites further from the water were less congested and less

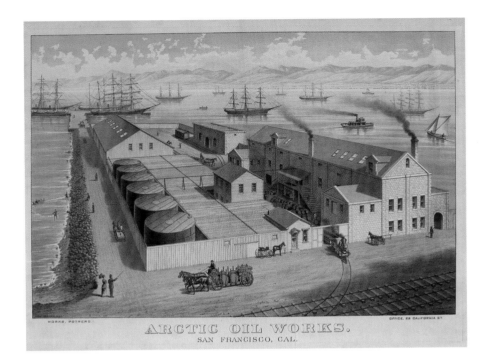

ARCTIC OIL WORKS.
SAN FRANCISCO, CAL.

Left: Even after the railroads came, a few major industrial sites were located adjacent to the water on their own wharves, such as the Arctic Oil Works. Established near Potrero Point in 1883, it was the principal storage and processing plant for whale oil during the years when San Francisco was the world's leading port for that product.

Below: The port's seawall lots were mostly given over to rail yards of the Belt Railroad and leased to private railroads. Seawall Lot 7, leased to the Western Pacific Railroad, is shown here across the Embarcadero from Piers 31 and 29 in 1931.

expensive. Thus, by 1906, new concentrations of industrial sites began to be developed in San Francisco along Southern Pacific rail spurs. For example, in 1899, a number of warehouses and other businesses many blocks inland on Townsend, between Fourth and Fifth streets, were all served by Southern Pacific spurs. These included the agricultural implement warehouses of the Deere Implement Company and Baker & Hamilton, Warehouse No. 6 of the Overland Freight Transfer Company for beer and general merchandise, and Warehouses Nos. 24 and 25 of W. P. Fuller & Company for oils and turpentine. Similar businesses were located along this corridor as far west as Seventh Street.[1]

By 1899, another cluster of industries was located on Southern Pacific spurs that extended from the main line where it curved from Eighth to Division streets (now called Showplace Square). Among them were a plant of the

National Ice Company, a Tesla Coal Company yard, the Pork Packing House of Roth, Blum & Company, the Potrero Chemical Works of Stauffer Chemical Company, a Market Street Railway Company power house, a terra-cotta storage yard of Gladding McBean, a supply depot for the Pacific Coast Telegraph Company, and the Pacific Sheet Metal Works.

In the 1910s, Southern Pacific built spurs north on Second Street to Folsom Street and up Beale and Spear streets to Mission Street. This stimulated the construction on Second Street of one of the densest warehouse and industrial districts,[2] which included the Blinn Estate Warehouse (1912) at the southeast corner of Brannan Street, the Crane Company Building at the southwest corner of Brannan Street, two Schmidt Lithograph buildings (1907–1938) at the northeast corner of Bryant Street, the General Electric Company Warehouse (1916) at 355–367

Bryant Street, the D. N. & E. Walter Co. furniture and carpet warehouse at the southeast corner of Bryant Street, the Moore Investment Company buildings between Brannan and Townsend streets for pipe and steel manufacturing and storage, and the Tobacco Company of California warehouse at the southwest corner of South Park Avenue.

Another feverish period of industrial construction in the Second Street vicinity was reported in the *San Francisco Chronicle* in the 1920s: "The demand for spur track locations in this district is increasing because of its convenience to docks and railroads."[3] This produced many more warehouses and industrial buildings, most of them large, reinforced concrete structures. Among these were the Hawley Terminal Building (1924) at 274 Brannan Street, the Ondawa Building (1920) at the southwest corner of Bryant and Rincon streets, the Kohler Company Building (1923) for plumbing supplies at the northwest corner of Second Street and South Park Avenue, the Los Angeles Soap Company Warehouse (1923) at the northeast corner of Second and Bryant streets, and three buildings on Second Street between Brannan and Townsend streets: the Crane Company Warehouse (1927) for plumbing supplies, the U.S. Radiator Company Building (1926), and the B.F. Goodrich Rubber Company office and warehouse (1923).

By 1914, Southern Pacific spurs along Harrison Street had stimulated the development of another cluster of industries, including the Long Syrup Refining Company, a yard of the City Street Improvement Company, a storage yard for the Steiger Terra Cotta & Pottery Works, a planing mill of the Inlaid Floor Company, a warehouse of the Blue & Gold Bottling Company, a machine shop of the Pelton Water Wheel Company, a mattress factory of the Crescent Feather Company,

After the earthquake and fire of 1906, the old warehouse district below Telegraph Hill, shown here in a view down Greenwich Street to Pier 23 before 1926, was largely rebuilt with more specialized storage facilities—cold storage warehouses for meat, eggs, produce, and ice making.

Left to right: San Francisco port officials and business leaders believed that the opening of the Panama Canal in 1914 would bring unprecedented prosperity to San Francisco, which would become to the Pacific Ocean what New York had been to the Atlantic. The Matson Navigation Company's headquarters on Market Street, seen here in 1932, was a rich expression of that hope.

The Dollar Steamship Line was one of the principal San Francisco–based shipping companies of the twentieth century. By the time of this 1947 photograph, the company occupied the Robert, R. Stanley, and J. Harold Dollar buildings, all clustered in this central downtown block.

The flat, filled area of Yerba Buena Cove along California Street east of Montgomery Street was built up after 1906 with a mix of small buildings for port-related businesses like ship chandlers and medium-size offices—such as the Marine, Welch, and Newhall buildings seen on the right—for shipping companies, marine insurance, and commission merchants.

Above, left to right: The businesses of the port—shipping companies, drayage companies, marine insurance, commission merchants, and many others—occupied nearby offices, especially in the filled area of Yerba Buena Cove, shown in this 1926 view of the north side of California Street west of Market. The Marvin and St. Clair buildings of 1908 are both still standing.

This 1920s view of the heart of downtown San Francisco, looking east from Montgomery down California to Market Street, is dominated by buildings associated with the business of the port, including the Merchants Exchange, the Dollar buildings, the Alaska Commercial Building, the Newhall Building, and the Southern Pacific Building at the end of the street.

and a Ford Motor Company assembly plant.

Although the Belt Railroad began operating its first section north of Market Street in 1890, it had little impact on the type or density of industrialization until after 1900. San Francisco's original warehouse district was located between the waterfront and Telegraph Hill because of its proximity to the earliest landing places of ships. The warehouses of the 1850s and 1860s that filled up this area were typically small brick buildings for general cargo, with limited capacity and limited utility for the requirements of increasingly specialized goods. This early waterfront stayed largely intact with few new developments—a warehouse of the City Warehouse Company (1900), the Italian Swiss Colony Warehouse (1903), and the W. P. Fuller & Company glass warehouse and mirror factory (1905) were exceptions—until 1906.

The Belt Railroad's principal impact in its first fifteen years was to prompt the development of grain warehouses, corrals, and lumberyards in seawall lots, along the bulkhead wharf, and on the heads of piers. The reconstruction of damaged and destroyed buildings after the 1906 earthquake along with an expanded infrastructure of rail spurs from the Embarcadero resulted in a widespread modernization of the northeastern waterfront. Shortly, the advent of north–south spurs on Davis, Front, and Kearny streets and east–west spurs on Vallejo, Green, Union, Filbert, Greenwich, Lombard, Chestnut, and Francisco streets was accompanied by an associated increase in the scale of industrial development. By that time, there was also development further west along the North Point line and the Jefferson Street spur. Thus, after 1906, the few surviving buildings were joined by new structures and businesses that depended on rail connections to the waterfront and that reflected changing ways of doing business in an evolving economy.

A key new development, based on improvements in ice making and cold storage, was dependent on rapid rail connections in the area. A cold-storage district emerged in the old warehouse district below Telegraph Hill (now part of the Northeast Waterfront Historic District) to serve two divergent industries—California's growing export business in fruits and vegetables and a changing meat industry in which meat could be kept longer than a day or two after slaughtering. The Swift & Company meatpacking plant, the Armour & Company Meat Packing Plant, and the Cudahy Meat Packing Plant, all branches of Chicago companies; the National Ice & Cold Storage Company plant, described as the largest ice plant in California; and a complex of warehouses for the Merchant's Ice and Cold Storage Company appeared between 1906 and 1914.

The beginning of Santa Fe Railway service south of China Basin in 1900 stimulated the location of several new industrial plants in

The 1908 Alaska Commercial Building was the most richly decorated of the port-related buildings of its era. Its carved granite details such as walruses, icicles, and sea serpents represented the environment of the north Pacific fur-seal business. At the right across California Street is the J. Harold Dollar Building, a shipping-company office.

Although the Southern Pacific Company's influence over the port declined after 1910, the design and siting of this new 1916 headquarters was symbolically powerful. With its belvedere and references to Italian Renaissance palaces, its location terminating the view down prestigious California Street, and its conspicuous position across from the Ferry Building headquarters of the Board of State Harbor Commissioners, the building asserted the company's continuing role at the port and in San Francisco, as well as its ambitions for the future.

clusters along its spurs. On the line along Illinois Street, parallel to the waterfront, spurs served the Indian Refining Company Oil Warehouse, Somers & Company Grain Warehouse, a warehouse and machine shop of the Westinghouse Electric & Manufacturing Company, and the Barneson & Hibberd Warehouse Company complex. Where this spur turned toward the waterfront on Twenty-Third Street, it served the California Barrel Company and the Western Sugar Refining Company. Among these companies, at least two were connected to Adolph B. Spreckels, who was instrumental in bringing the Santa Fe Railway to San Francisco; one of his business partners owned Barneson & Hibberd, and the Spreckels family owned Western Sugar Refining.

A second industrial cluster on Santa Fe spurs was in the vicinity of Indiana and Eighteenth streets, including the heavy hardware warehouse of Berger & Carter Company, a warehouse of the A. L. Young Machinery Company, a stove and tinware warehouse of W. F. Boardman Company, and a stove warehouse of Mangrum & Otter.

The Western Pacific, which began operation in 1910, had spawned only a few industries

on its spurs by the time of the 1913 Sanborn map, in a cluster around its rail yards at Eighth and Brannan streets. Among these were the Schlesinger & Bender Wine Warehouse, the J. I. Case Threshing Machine Company, and a California Coal Company yard. This cluster grew gradually, with the greatest increase in the years just before World War II, which saw the arrival of a Standard Brands coffee roasting plant in 1937 and a large complex for Safeway Stores—including a truck freight terminal, and two steel-frame warehouses—in 1941.

Prior to World War I, an extension of the Belt Railroad generated new industrial sites and clusters. By 1916, a spur along Spear Street from the Embarcadero to the block between Howard and Mission streets reached almost to the back door of the Southern Pacific Building, a symbol of the ascendance of the public port after decades of private dominance.

PORT-RELATED OFFICES

If the railroads and the industries they served extended the physical work of the port into utilitarian districts of the city, much of the business of the port was conducted downtown. Commission merchants, insurance companies, shipping companies and agents, and the administrative offices of railroads, drayage companies, warehouse companies, power and fuel providers, suppliers of lumber and building materials, construction companies, and every kind of manufacturing company—whether local or based elsewhere—were housed in downtown offices.

While the warehouses and industrial plants were generally utilitarian in character, their downtown offices were in buildings that were architecturally embellished to provide an attractive public image for customers and clients. The largest companies at the port had their own headquarters, some of which incorporated nautical or other symbols to represent their businesses. Others occupied quarters in general office buildings with various tenants. The greatest concentration of port-related businesses was in the vicinity of lower Market, California, and Sansome streets, a short walking distance from the offices of the BSHC in the Ferry Building and from the waterfront offices on the piers along the Embarcadero. This area of landfill was originally Yerba Buena Cove, and is the same area where many of the first shipping businesses were located.

The largest port-related businesses were those of the shipping companies. When office space was scarce right after the earthquake and fire of 1906, businesses occupied any space they could find. Many moved into the first large buildings to reopen—generally those that were damaged and rebuilt rather than new structures—including the Flood, Monadnock, Spreckels, and Merchants Exchange buildings. Of these, the Merchants Exchange, established in 1849, was one of the oldest institutions in the city tied to the port. Each of its buildings has had a rooftop belvedere; the first of these were used to communicate by semaphore and telegraph with incoming ships. This feature was retained in the 1903 building, which was rebuilt in 1907 and still stands, symbolically representing its original function. Commodities were exchanged in the building's trading hall, which is decorated with maritime-themed murals.

Quickly, however, new buildings opened after the earthquake and were filled with shipping companies, commission merchants, and related businesses. Among those still standing in 2010, the Boyd Estate Building at the northwest corner of California and Davis streets, built by a shipping family in 1907, provided "offices for shipping and marine agencies."[4] Later that same year, the Marine Building, at the northeast corner of California and Front streets, was occupied by a coffee importer and other trading companies, as well as the Robert Dollar steamship line. In 1908, at 244–256 California Street, the Welch Building opened on the same site it had occupied since about 1880 as the headquarters of Welch & Company, shipping and commission merchants with business in China, Japan, the Philippines, Hawaii, and throughout the British Empire. The largest and most lavish of buildings in this first wave of post-earthquake development was the Alaska Commercial Building, erected in 1908 at the northeast corner of California and Sansome streets, where the company had been previously. The Alaska

This 1939 view from the tenth-floor executive offices of the Southern Pacific Building takes in the Ferry Building, which housed the offices of the Board of State Harbor Commissioners on the second floor below the tower, as well as the piers and rail yards to the north and south where Southern Pacific was one of the most powerful presences.

Commercial Company, which dominated the fur seal trade in the north Pacific in the 1880s and 1890s, had a fleet of ships; it also built communities for its workers and operated salmon canneries to feed them. Carved granite and cast terra-cotta figures of walruses, polar bears, sea serpents wound around tridents, sea monsters, seashells, fish, icicles, and a heavy nautical rope represented the company's tools, the raw materials it sought, the environment in which it worked, and the gods who supplied the riches and guided the venture.

Soon, other new buildings catered to the same kinds of tenants. Erected in 1910, the Newhall Building of H. M. Newhall & Company, at 260 California Street, was largely occupied by shipping companies, commission merchants, insurance agents, import-export firms, and canned goods companies. That same year, the five-story Robert Dollar Building, which served as the headquarters of a local steamship company, rose diagonally across the intersection of California and Battery streets. The Orient Building, opened in 1912 at 330–332 Pine Street, housed the local headquarters of a large New York shipping company, W. R. Grace & Company, and the offices of Sperry Flour, a major dealer in grain with facilities near the waterfront.

The largest and most spectacular office buildings appeared after the 1914 opening of the Panama Canal, when San Francisco business leaders and investors expected a huge boom that they believed would turn the city into the dominant world port. As New York had been the primary port when international trade was dominated by traffic across the Atlantic between Europe and the United States, so the port of San Francisco would rise to prominence in the near future when the focus of world trade shifted to the Pacific. The companies that stood to gain the most in wealth and power from the growth of the port—shipping companies and railroads— built new headquarters that would physically accommodate future expansion and symbolically represent the place of these companies in the new order.

Planning and construction of these headquarters began after the Panama Canal opened and, after a delay caused by World War I, continued into the early 1920s. Each of these buildings was named for the company that developed it and was much larger than what the company needed, providing space to grow while enhancing its public image. In the meantime, it generated rental income from other tenants.

In 1916, construction began on the new Southern Pacific Building. The company had been in its own building amid railroad yards and warehouses on Townsend Street from the 1870s to 1906. After the earthquake it moved to the Merchants Exchange Building, a location that placed it among the city's business elite during a period when its dominance was challenged politically and threatened by new competitors. As the site for its new headquarters, the company chose lower Market Street, almost directly across the Embarcadero from the symbolic and administrative headquarters of the port, the Ferry Building. Earlier plans for a rail terminal at this location were abandoned by the time that work on the building began. The site faced the route of the Market Street Railway (formerly owned by Southern Pacific) and was in view of the company's fleet of ferries at the Ferry Building and its railcars being shuttled along the Embarcadero by the Belt Railroad.

Southern Pacific planned a massive ten-story structure that loomed over the Ferry Building and could be seen from great distances across the water and around San Francisco. Company officers in their top-floor suites literally looked down on the Ferry Building offices of the BSHC, enjoying a panoramic view of the Embarcadero from its midpoint that the three commissioners themselves might envy. Furthermore, by virtue of its size, location, and design, this building was the most conspicuous structure to be seen by anyone leaving the Ferry Building, including thousands of daily commuters.

The San Francisco architects Bliss & Faville based the building's design on that by their previous employers, McKim, Mead & White of New York, for the 1906 headquarters of the Gorham Company, a competitor of Tiffany & Company. Both designs drew from Italian Renaissance sources.

Later in 1916, construction began at the southwest corner of Market and Second streets on a twelve-story headquarters for the Atchison, Topeka, and Santa Fe Railway. Called the Santa Fe Building, it accommodated ticket sales and executive offices in a conspicuous downtown

location that was also convenient via Second Street to the Santa Fe yards and shops south of China Basin. Second Street had been the principal route from downtown offices to the meeting of rail and port facilities at Steamboat Point since it was cut through Rincon Hill in 1869.

The third major railroad, Western Pacific, announced plans for a headquarters in 1916 but did not execute them. After renting offices in the Mills Building, in 1920 the company took over an existing building at 526 Mission Street.

The first of the large shipping companies to enhance its presence in response to the Panama Canal boom was the San Francisco–based Dollar Steamship Company, "the main U.S. steamship company in the transpacific trade between the two world wars."[5] In 1920 it expanded and remodeled the 1910 Robert Dollar Building at the southwest corner of California and Battery streets. *Architect and Engineer* described the building, designed by Charles McCall, as having "interest and dignity worthy to represent one of our foremost steamship companies." It was embellished with "appropriate symbols—the house flag, marine life, and ship details."[6]

The most lavish and impressive of the shipping company buildings was the Matson Building (1921), at the southwest corner of Market and Main streets. The Matson Navigation Company was engaged primarily in carrying sugar cane from Hawaii to the mainland. Its San Francisco headquarters was built to provide offices for Hawaii's "big five" sugar companies and other Hawaiian businesses. According to a

Above: Cheap wooden boarding houses with ground-floor saloons were built for sailors just outside the district where fireproof construction was required, such as this row on the east side of Steuart Street between Folsom and Howard, shown in 1913.

Opposite: The 1917 headquarters building of the Santa Fe Railway was located on a prominent site, just up Market Street from the Ferry Building and at the beginning of Second Street, the most direct route from the business center to the southern waterfront after it was cut through Rincon Hill in 1869.

Unions for sailors, longshoremen,
teamsters, pile drivers, and other
waterfront workers rented offices in
ordinary buildings scattered as far
from the port as the Mission District
and the Tenderloin until after the
1934 strike. Subsequently, many built
their own halls, such as this magnificent 1950 building for the Sailors
Union of the Pacific on Rincon Hill, at
Harrison and First streets.

1923 newspaper critique, the building's "white
exterior . . . [and] cool sea-green trim" were
enlivened by nautical symbols, including a
Viking ship, "its sails spread by the wind that
blows around the world. Terra cotta decorations
of conventionalized tridents, ship's lines, sea
shells, fish and bas-relief plaques of the *Maui*
and *Matsonia* tell the observant student of architecture that here is a building devoted to ocean
transportation." The top of the building culmi-
nates in an iron pineapple.[7]

The last of the major shipping company buildings of the Panama Canal boom was the Balfour
Building (1920) at the southwest corner of
California and Sansome streets. Balfour, Guthrie
& Company, established in San Francisco in 1869
as an affiliate of a Liverpool company, operated
ships, sold marine insurance, developed land,

and invested in a range of California businesses.

In addition to these major buildings, there
were many minor buildings downtown and
along the waterfront that played an essential part
in the everyday life of the port. Many of these
faced the port's property or were within a block
or two of the port, in the area referred to as the
"city front." Some provided services and supplies to the port and its tenants, such as ship
chandlers, ship stores, shipwrights, and caulkers,
especially on California and Sansome streets.
A business that fit into this category but was
exceptional in size was the Wells Fargo Express,
whose eight-story building of 1902, enlarged and
rebuilt in 1907, stood at the corner of Mission
and Second streets. This key location was eight
blocks from a building on the bulkhead wharf
at the foot of Mission Street that the business

leased from the BSHC, and eight blocks from China Basin and the concentration of businesses in that area.

Saloons, restaurants, cheap hotels, houses of prostitution, dance halls, and other businesses near the port catered to a partly itinerant workforce of single men—sailors, seamen, and laborers who also traveled to seasonal work in agriculture and factories. Until 1917, when prostitution was brought under control in the neighborhood, the most infamous district for vice in the waterfront was the Barbary Coast on Pacific Avenue.

In addition to the many businesses and commercial enterprises, various institutions and organizations had outposts in the area of the port. The 1853 U.S. Marine Hospital at Rincon Point provided services to seamen. (Southern Pacific opened its own hospital for employees in 1908 on Fell Street facing the Panhandle, halfway across the city from the waterfront.) Numerous missions associated with various churches and other charities provided spiritual and material assistance to those in need. An example of a building of this type was the Seamen's Institute at 240–242 Steuart Street, built in 1907 and demolished in 1997. In 1924, the Army-Navy YMCA (now the Harbor Court Hotel) was built on the Embarcadero at Howard Street.

Early on, labor organizations were often housed in rented quarters near the port. For example, the Audiffred Building accommodated labor groups from the time of its construction in 1889 until it was damaged by fire in 1978 and subsequently remodeled. After 1906, these groups also occupied 113 Steuart Street next door. In the 1920s and 1930s the Workmen's Educational Association met in Albion Hall, on Albion Street in the Inner Mission, where some of the early organizing took place among longshoremen that led to the General Strike of 1934.[8]

With the strengthening of the labor movement as a result of the 1934 strike, unions built their own headquarters and facilities. Chief among these was the Sailors Union of the Pacific (1950) at 450 Harrison Street, a spacious and grand hiring hall comparable to the public spaces of the business elite (e.g., the Merchants Exchange) and the port itself (the Ferry Building). Others followed, erecting buildings that were characterized by striking modern designs and artwork:

the Marine Firemen's Union (1957) at 240 Second Street, the International Longshore and Warehouse Union (1959) at 400 North Point Street, and the National Maritime Union (1966) at 91 Drumm Street.

Finally, the port's workers lived throughout the city and commuted to their jobs by foot, public transit, or automobile. The laboring class came from neighborhoods near the port: North Beach, South of Market, Dog Patch, and Bay View. Clerical and office workers might have come from the Tenderloin, the Western Addition, and the Mission District. Executives lived in Pacific Heights, Presidio Heights, and St. Francis Wood. As the largest employment sector in San Francisco over many decades, workers at all levels connected the world of the port to the larger city on a daily basis.

Port workers were served by a variety of medical, social, and religious institutions, such as the 1924 Army-Navy YMCA on the Embarcadero, shown here in the late 1940s.

COMMERCE

Long before the port began to develop, San Francisco Bay was considered "one of the finest natural harbors in the world"—a sentiment expressed repeatedly by people with varying perspectives in every period of the port's history, from the earliest explorers and visitors. In the Mexican and early American periods, food for the small Euro-American population was produced locally, and trade consisted of an exchange with Boston merchants of California hides and tallow for clothing, hardware, and other daily necessities. There were numerous small landings around the bay and on the rivers that fed into the bay, close to the ranches where the hides were produced. San Francisco was the largest of the potential cities in the area; however, before gold was discovered in 1848, only minor port facilities were located there: four rudimentary wharves between Clarke's Point (near the foot of Broadway) and Sacramento Street, none of which extended to deep water.

This view across the warehouses below Telegraph Hill and the Produce District was taken on March 31, 1906, three weeks before the earthquake of April 18. At that time, the port and the adjacent parts of the city were a dense, rough, industrial area that served the city's businesses, with few amenities and little beautification.

Before the Gold Rush, the natural shape and depth of Yerba Buena Cove were not yet diminished by landfill. The cove filled an arc from Clarke's Point, just out of view on the left side of this 1847 drawing (near Broadway and Front Street), to Rincon Point (near Harrison and Spear streets) in the center of the drawing. Today the area of the cove is the heart of downtown San Francisco.

In 1849, hundreds of ships brought tens of thousands of people to California in search of gold. After disembarking from these ships, these voyagers traveled by river and then overland to the mines. A port was suddenly an essential link in the system. Furthermore, with inadequate amounts of food produced in California and no local sources to supply the miners with equipment, provisions and supplies had to be brought in ships and stored until they were needed. According to the geographer James E. Vance Jr., "The men who came to dig for gold were entrepreneurs, not farmers, so their economic existence depended upon the presence of a warehouse kept filled by full-time merchants."[1]

In the absence of roads, rivers provided the means of travel and transport to landings near the mines. The oceangoing ships that entered San Francisco Bay were too big to travel up the rivers. Passengers and cargo had to be transferred to smaller vessels for the trips inland. (The process of transferring goods from one vessel to another in order to facilitate delivery to an ultimate destination is called *transshipment*.) As Vance explains, this process happened in San Francisco because, as had occurred for centuries in Europe, "In a water-based transportation system, it is advantageous to bring inland navigation as close to the sea as possible." San Francisco, with its deep water off Yerba Buena Cove and its location just inside the Golden Gate, emerged almost overnight as the principal port in San Francisco Bay, fulfilling a very particular purpose in the economic development of California from the Gold Rush to the completion of the transcontinental railroad in 1869.[2]

In the early 1850s, the warehouses that were essential to the functioning of the port were first established in the water lots of the tidelands in and around Yerba Buena Cove. At the time, only some of the lots were on filled land. As the port flourished in the 1850s and 1860s, the warehouse district developed in two separate areas for different purposes: "Trade in perishable goods tended to stick to the wharfhead location, while the activities of wholesalers whose goods could be stocked for some time, and whose trade practices called for the salesman to visit the customer rather than the customer come to the wholesaler, were shifted to the area south of Market Street by the 1870s."[3] In other words,

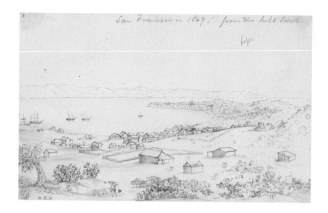

the Produce District grew up near the first piers, between Broadway and Market Street, where produce could be quickly received and delivered to nearby businesses. The wholesale district emerged farther from the first piers but close to that part of the city that the railroads—at that time under construction—would serve.

Housing for workers at the port and in the warehouse districts was built up immediately inland of these areas. Almost all port workers were males who lived in cheap hotels and boarding houses within walking distance of the waterfront. Some, including married workers, lived in flats. In this early period of the port's history, long-standing patterns of commerce and development were established.

San Francisco was not only the junction of oceangoing and river traffic but also the focus of extensive traffic on the bay. A variety of small boats and ferries, first used to bring agricultural products to the city from landings around the bay, soon carried thousands of passengers daily, most of them commuters who worked in the city. The prevalence of water traffic and the construction over water in the 1850s of the most active commercial section of the city led at least one observer to characterize San Francisco as "a Venice."[4]

While the initial impetus for the port was to bring goods to California from other places, the demands of the growing state quickly gave rise to manufacturing plants and other industries. These enterprises were first developed along San Francisco's waterfront and were important to both the physical expansion of the port and the increase in the port's business. The first notable manufacturing plant was the Union Shovel Works, later Union Iron Works, located at First and Mission streets in 1851. As Vance explains, "This concern proved a bellwether of San Francisco industry, being the first of a flock of mining machinery and equipment factories that made the city the world center of this trade by 1875. Long after the California Gold Rush had slowed to a plodding pace, San Francisco continued to supply the capital goods for expansion of mining in Australia and South Africa."[5] Manufacturing plants were located on or near the waterfront south of Market Street, north of Broadway, and along North Beach close to piers built for receiving raw materials and shipping out finished products.

All of this activity had immediately impressive results. According to the historians Robert W. Cherny and William Issel, in 1852–1853, "only three cities . . . could claim a larger share of the nation's foreign commerce." And by 1861, "San Francisco's harbor ranked sixth among U.S. ports in total freight handled."[6] In this same era San Francisco's population grew spectacularly from fewer than 1,000 in 1848, to 34,776 in 1852, to 149,473 in 1870.

The early period in the port's development was also marked by administrative chaos, inadequate piers and wharves, and the deficiencies of a poorly maintained harbor, all of which posed serious threats to the commercial future of the port. To correct these conditions, in 1863 the state of California took control of the port from the city and created the Board of State Harbor Commissioners (BSHC). Among the board's first efforts to improve the physical conditions of the port, following four years of litigation brought by private property owners, was the design and construction of the initial seawall in 1867.

The establishment of the port of San Francisco as a state responsibility, accomplished with the support of interests outside of the city, is a testament to the significance of the port to the commerce of the entire state at that time. Abetted by the stabilizing influence of the BSHC, by 1866–1867 business was booming; according to a later report by the board, "The tonnage of vessels arriving in San Francisco from foreign and eastern ports exceeded 426,000."[7]

STIMULUS OF THE PORT
FROM THE TRANSCONTINENTAL RAILROAD

The next phase in the commercial history of the port was inaugurated by the completion in 1869 of the transcontinental railroad. Because the railroad ended at Vallejo and Oakland, on the continental side of the bay, it provided a substantial boost to business at the ports of those cities and introduced a major long-term complication in the commercial operations of the port of San Francisco—the need to transfer rail cargo to various types of vessels for the trip across the bay to San Francisco. Without this extra step and the costs it entailed, the port of San Francisco could

By 1851, the transformation of Yerba Buena Cove was well under way. A fleet of abandoned ships was occupied as warehouses and hotels, city streets were extended into the water as wharves, and the shoreline was moving outward on new landfill, creating a dense neighborhood of port-related buildings.

not have sustained its position as the dominant port in the region.

In the short term, the railroad depressed the economy of California. In San Francisco, improvement of the port stopped, including work on the seawall. In 1869–1870, "The tonnage of vessels arriving dropped precipitously to 176,000."[8] However, within a few years, the port recovered and continued its dramatic growth. As a report by the State Senate later declared, "If one were to name the most vigorous period in the early maritime history of San Francisco Bay, it would undoubtedly be during the 1870s and 1880s—a period when trade was relatively unhampered by restrictions and when shipping through the Golden Gate flourished."[9] In 1880, when the tonnage was estimated at 3,350,000,[10] the United States census described San Francisco, with 233,959 people, as "the commercial metropolis of the Pacific Coast." At that time, the city "handled 99 per cent of all merchandise imported to and 83 per cent of all exports from three Pacific Coast states, and produced 60 per cent of all manufactured goods in the region."[11] With the intersection of rail and ship transportation at the port, San Francisco was the nexus of voluminous business from eastern and foreign ports and from the city's "tributary region." "From throughout the West, commerce flowed to San Francisco: minerals from the mountains, wheat and other agricultural products from the central valleys of California, hay and timber from the north."[12] According to the U.S. Army Corps of Engineers, "The port became the distributing center of goods for consumption in the rapidly developing western territory, and when the transcontinental railroads were completed, its functions were increased to include the concentration of cargoes for shipment to the Orient and other parts of the world."[13]

One effect of the presence of railroads during this period was the creation in the region of "specialized ports," which were characterized by the handling of only one commodity. Whereas San Francisco was always a general cargo port, with no single type of cargo predominating, railroads made it possible to bring shipping facilities closer to the site of production or processing of some items—rather than to the traditional place of transshipment in San Francisco. The

most notable early example was Port Costa, a generic name for a series of ship landings along the Carquinez Strait, where wheat was brought by rail in the 1870s and 1880s. As described by Vance, "Carquinez Strait served as the site for the world's great grain port in an alignment along the south shore between Martinez on the east and what is now Crockett on the west."[14] This had the effect of diminishing the volume of shipments that might otherwise have gone through San Francisco and represented the first challenge to the city's dominance as a port. A local study in 1886 recognized that San Francisco could not compete with this development.[15]

While the port of San Francisco remained the preeminent port in the West for many more years, about 1890 other competing ports began to emerge, notably those of Seattle, Portland, and Tacoma. In that year, San Francisco's tonnage dropped to 2,540,000. By 1900, tonnage in San Francisco had increased to 6,013,680, and the city was still recognized as the "Metropolis of the West."[16]

MODERNIZATION AND PLANNING FOR BENEFITS FROM THE PANAMA CANAL

The next stage in the history of the port began around 1900, when a number of circumstances prompted an intense period of analysis, projection, and planning by both the BSHC and outside interests. Confronted with unusually high tonnage from 1899 to 1901, the facilities of the port and warehouses in adjacent districts were inadequate for the requirements of commerce. One account described the situation succinctly:

> Docks had been built by the commissioners primarily for transit on goods moving eastward. Now, industrialization laid the groundwork for independent West Coast commerce, and the waterfront became congested. Moreover, ships increased in size. Docks built for sailing vessels that had discharged about 300 tons of cargo daily were wholly inadequate for steamers that unloaded more than 750 tons a day. . . . Users of the harbor felt its inadequacies severely.[17]

At the same time, the ports in Washington and Oregon were continuing to grow. New specialized ports were developed around San Francisco Bay and along the lower Sacramento River, including facilities for Ideal Portland Cement in Redwood City, C & H Sugar in

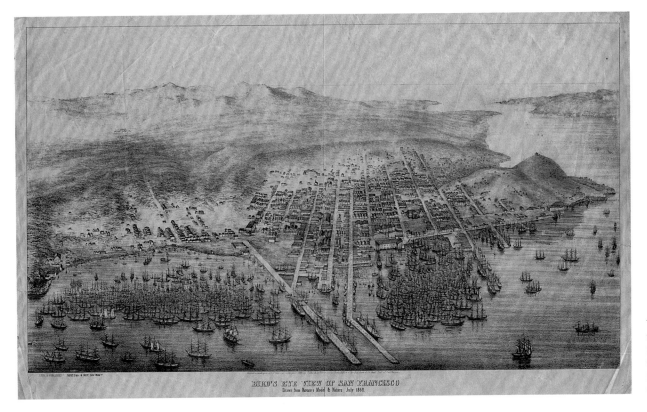

BIRD'S EYE VIEW OF SAN FRANCISCO
Drawn from Messer's Model & Nature July 1852.

This bird's-eye view from 1852 shows the encroachment of wharves and landfill on Yerba Buena Cove and the temporary presence of two coves, one below Market Street and one above Commercial Street.

LOMBARD, NORTH POINT and GREENWICH DOCKS,
SAN FRANCISCO.
SHIPS GREAT REPUBLIC, HURRICANE and ZENOBIA DISCHARGING.

Before the arrival of the railroads, warehouses were built as close as possible to the water to facilitate the movement of cargo between ships and warehouses. This 1857 view looks up Sansome Street to the North Point and Greenwich wharves, the northern extent of the contiguous port at that time.

Crockett, Union Oil in Oleum, Shell Oil in Martinez, Standard Oil in Point Richmond, and Columbia Steel in Pittsburg. Most threatening of all to the future dominance of the San Francisco port were the efforts being made by Los Angeles, San Diego, and other cities to attract the huge new business in anticipation of the opening of the Panama Canal.

With all of these concerns on the minds of the port's principal managers and users, the damage done by the earthquake in 1906 stimulated plans for modernizing and improving the port. Within three years, several reports presented arguments and technical information for this initiative, including one by Walter Bartnett, who wrote, "The development of commerce on the Pacific will in a few years mean more to the state than all her mineral wealth. To enable her merchants to attract this commerce to her ports and to handle it as it should be handled, the idea has become general that it is essential that the harbors of the State be improved—improved in a comprehensive and permanent way suited to the volume and character of the commerce

impending."[18] Bartnett was among the first of many writers to advocate for the creation of a single administration for all Bay Area ports. Other reports by Marsden Manson (former chief engineer of the port), the San Francisco Chamber of Commerce, the Counties Committee of the California Promotion Committee, and the Federated Harbor Users Association all supported the urgent modernization of the port.[19] Despite the loudly voiced concern, however, improvements were slow because of the requirement that they be financed by annual revenues.

Nevertheless, tonnage in 1910 climbed to 7,324,577, while the city's population increased to 416,912. In that year, the BSHC reported, "The commerce of the port of San Francisco is steadily increasing with acceleration that will become greater and greater with the opening of the Panama Canal and the inevitable growth of trade in the Pacific Ocean. San Francisco possesses all of the prime requisites of a great seaport except ample docking facilities."[20]

More specifically, the board stated, "Lumber, mineral oil, wine and general merchandise are

This circa 1855–1860 view looking north from Rincon Point, across what was originally the center of Yerba Buena Cove, shows flat areas where filling had begun, water lots articulated by wooden piers, ships still used as buildings, and recently built waterfront industry that was soon to be landlocked.

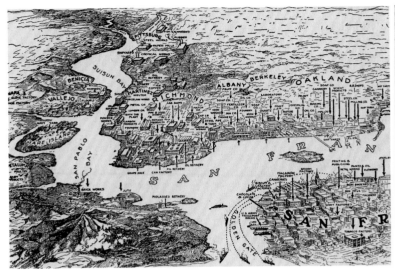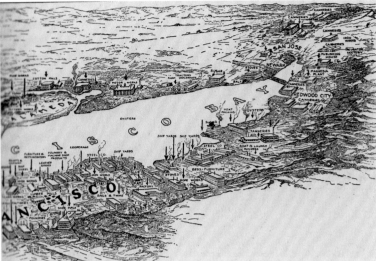

at present the principal articles of trade handled over the state wharves."[21] A map accompanying the biennial report for 1910–1912 showed a long grain shed on the waterfront roughly between Kearny and Montgomery streets and cattle corrals adjacent to the grain shed between Sansome and Battery streets. The biennial report for 1912–1914 noted that construction had begun on Pier 15 "designed for coal bunker use."[22] Thus, in the period when construction of the modern port was just beginning, facilities along the Embarcadero accommodated a wide range of cargoes, including live animals, bulk grains, and break-bulk cargo.

As the opening of the Panama Canal got closer, many became increasingly excited about its impact on commerce. In a paper presented to the American Society of Civil Engineers on November 20, 1912, H. M. Chittenden began, "Since the days of Magellan, imaginative minds have pictured the Pacific Ocean as the future home of the world's commerce."[23] As the port of New York dominated North American trade across the Atlantic, local boosters hoped that San Francisco would dominate North American trade across the Pacific, and more detached observers expected San Francisco Bay ports collectively to play that role. San Francisco's port had been compared to New York's since at least 1875.[24] Acknowledging that business at the port of New York was ten times that of San Francisco, the German city planner Werner Hegemann saw great promise in San Francisco Bay, writing in a 1915 report that it had "the necessary physical characteristics to compare favorably some

day with the harbor of New York."[25] The opening of the Panama Canal appeared to present the opportunity for the port of San Francisco to grow enormously. In his paper on the "Ports of the Pacific," Chittenden looked at all of them and concluded, "It is now time and for a long while will so remain, that San Francisco Bay is far and away the most important port on the Coast."[26]

Reporting in 1916, the BSHC wrote, "The Panama Canal was thrown open to ships of limited draught in July, 1914, and within less than a year thereafter to the largest ships, and it was especially gratifying that the large new business so confidently expected began to materialize almost immediately. . . . The harbor was completely ready for the canal opening, and the march of improvement and expansion has been kept fully abreast of the increasing demand for new berths." However, "The Great European War measurably halted this development, a number of the steamers familiar in this port having been soon drafted to other lines of trade by the war's demands."[27] For the unexpectedly long duration of World War I, growth of the port was inhibited. In 1920, tonnage rose modestly to 7,685,402.

Still, expectations remained high. The BSHC continued to seek to improve conditions for commerce:

The board has for some time past been considering the advisability of having additional warehouses adjacent to the water front and of having such warehouses under the jurisdiction of the board so as to permit of the storage of cargoes, the movement of which is unduly delayed. It has finally been decided to proceed

As San Francisco grew, the port served four areas of trade—inland, coastal, intercoastal, and across the oceans. This 1921 view from the Chamber of Commerce shows the cities, industrial sites, and agricultural landings of the inland trade around the bay and up the rivers to Sacramento, Stockton, and elsewhere.

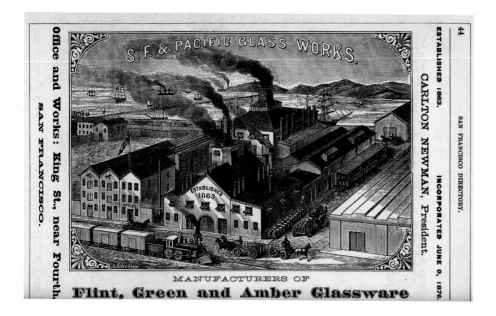

With the arrival of the railroads, individual industries were built to facilitate the transfer of material between railroads and ships. The San Francisco and Pacific Glass Works, shown here in 1883, was located on King Street near Fourth, in the first area served by the Southern Pacific Railroad.

In 1906, the Ferry Building was the most prominent feature of the city, an expression of the role of the port at that time. The silhouettes of the Humboldt Bank tower, the Merchants Exchange, and the Fairmont Hotel indicate the growing skyline and the emergence of important new elements of the local economy.

with the construction of the first of what may eventually be a chain of publicly owned modern storage warehouses. The first unit will be located on a portion of Seawall Lot 4 and the corner of Bay and Kearny streets and the Embarcadero. It will be a reinforced concrete building six stories in height, with an area on each floor of about 21,000 square feet. It will be served by the Belt Railroad and will be equipped with elevators, hoists, chutes, etc.[28]

By far the most ambitious proposal in this era was a highly complex and sophisticated plan for the new tidelands, known as Islais Creek and India Basin, acquired in 1918. This proposal would have almost doubled the facilities and capacity of the port by replicating the northern waterfront in the south, with improvements responding to new technology. The India Basin–Islais Creek plan was practically a new

city, with a grid of streets oriented to the waterfront for maximum efficiency of traffic movement and a marginal street one hundred feet wide (the Embarcadero is two hundred feet wide). Alleys in the grid would have three rail spurs each to serve the warehouses and factories in each block. Nine large piers would extend from the waterfront, along with transit sheds, rail spurs, bulkhead sheds, and warehouses on the bulkhead wharf and an elevated sidewalk above the piers. Rail yards, an engine house, and a car-ferry terminal were also included in the plan. Islais Creek would be lined with wharves for coal, lumber, and other bulk materials.

Little was done in the immediate aftermath of the plan. A new Vegetable Oil Station was built on the south side of Islais Creek. Apart from the improvement by the Santa Fe Railway on port land south of China Basin, this represented the first significant development by the BSHC on the southern waterfront. The overall plan was never realized. In the 1960s and 1970s, the area was largely developed but in a completely different way.

According to planning historian Mel Scott, "World War I . . . limited the commercial use of the Panama Canal and reduced maritime trade, so that the West Coast did not benefit appreciably from the opening of the new intercoastal route until the early twenties."[29] Even after the war ended, the board reported, "a great deal of shipping was diverted from San Francisco to eastern ports,"[30] and referred to "the business depression which overshadowed the entire shipping world following the world war."[31]

PROSPERITY AND DISAPPOINTMENT IN THE 1920S

In 1922, the first year of recovery from the wartime slump, tonnage at the port of San Francisco increased sharply to 14,837,609. Although this would remain the highest tonnage until World War II, through 1931 the figures remained substantially higher than before. While the 1920s were prosperous years at the port, the relative position of San Francisco among West Coast ports changed during the decade. According to a 1927 report by the U.S. Army Corps of Engineers, "San Francisco has generally handled a larger volume of the general import and export trade than any of its competitors, although in recent years the values have been less than at Seattle,

because of the large silk movements through the latter port, and the total tonnage has been less than at Los Angeles, because of the heavy shipments of petroleum from southern California."[32]

Thus, beginning in the 1920s, the strength of the port of San Francisco took a different form, becoming increasingly a break-bulk port predominated by general cargo. Efforts to build up trade in bulk commodities had yielded limited success, as in the case of the recently built vegetable oil plant. According to a BSHC report, "Following the decline in the vegetable oil trade through this port it was decided to convert the oil terminal at Islais Creek into an export grain terminal."[33] This terminal primarily served an important local need, but it did not operate at anywhere near the scale of the grain warehouses along the Carquinez Strait. By mid-1926, the last of six coal bunkers (large storage bins) had been removed from the waterfront.[34] They were superseded by oil-bunkering facilities, first built in 1911–1912. These were used mostly for activity around the port and were not part of an export industry, as at Point Richmond, for example. Bulk commodities were important to the port, but they did not dominate.

One important new source of growth in trade came from the emergence of new industries linked to the port by the Belt Railroad. These included a gravel company, several warehouses, and "the Southern Pacific Co. automobile station at North Point and Leavenworth Streets."[35]

In the biennial report of 1924–1926, the president of the BSHC wrote an enthusiastic sketch of conditions at the port:

The Port of San Francisco is the industrial and commercial center of the Pacific Ocean. It is the great American hub of trade on the Pacific and, in direct proportion as the development of this coast has unfolded, so have the facilities of this great harbor been developed to meet without stint every requirement.

The Port of San Francisco serves a greatly diversified area. This may be best visualized when we realize that this service includes all of northern and central California (which comprises three-fourths of the state), all of Nevada and, when San Francisco's association with the Orient and overseas Pacific ports are considered, the entire country.

This is the only combined river and bay port on the Pacific [he neglects to mention Oakland and Portland]. Two giant rivers tap the inland empire (which is larger than all the states of New England) and San Francisco Bay is the only outlet for this vast territory. This is not only the "Gateway to the Orient" but also to these rich interior valleys which hold the bulk of the wealth of the State of California. . . .

San Francisco boasts of well balanced cargoes including canned fruits and vegetables, dried fruits, cotton, leather, autos, minerals, coffee, sugar, copra, tea, fibres, tin, nitrates, peanuts, crab meat, gunnies, manufactured machinery and general merchandise and other articles too numerous to recount.

It is not the total tonnage alone that must be considered as the real test of value to a city and port. The value of the tonnage handled in this port is second only to that of New York, and each year the total value, proportionate to tonnage, continues to increase.

Agricultural landings that ringed the bay, like this one in southern Alameda County, supplied San Francisco with hay for horses, milk, eggs, meat, wheat, barley, potatoes, fruits, and vegetables. Eventually the busy traffic of small vessels was put out of business by trucks that more easily carried these products from farms to centralized rail and ferry stops.

It is most significant that, as each anniversary rolls around, a greater percentage of the ship cargoes sent forth from the Port of San Francisco consists of merchandise and products produced either on land within the shipping limits of the port or else is produced within the plants and factories situated in the bay area.[36]

San Francisco's prosperity at the time was linked to that of the wider region: "For the Pacific Coast as a whole, the peak period occurred about the mid and late 1920s. Owing to enormous volume in the coastwise and intercoastal trades, both vessel and cargo tonnage of San Francisco Bay reached heights never anticipated during the 1880s."[37]

Despite its prosperity in the 1920s, San Francisco failed to emerge, like New York on the Atlantic Coast, as the dominant port on the Pacific Coast. As Gerald Nash explains, "Competition from other ports, failure of the expected Far East trade to materialize, and the agricultural depression all impeded the harbor's growth."[38] Another factor was the failure to provide sufficient facilities. For the old reason that the funding of port improvements was incremental, San Francisco did not keep up with demand. For example, after the canned- and dried-fruit business increased during World War I, congestion at the San Francisco port caused it to move to Oakland, providing an important boost to that port. In 1922 and 1923, the problem was "especially severe."[39]

THE GREAT DEPRESSION: STABILITY FROM TRADE IN GENERAL CARGO AND NEW TYPES OF BUSINESS

The effects of the Great Depression of the 1930s were not felt dramatically at first. At the end of the biennium 1930–1932, San Francisco retained its second-place rank to New York among United States ports. However, tonnage and revenues had dropped, and there was a "considerable

Top: The promise of San Francisco's transformation with new business from the opening of the Panama Canal was the catalyst for intensive reconstruction of port facilities in the 1910s, including Pier 29 and its bulkhead wharf, seen in this 1916 view. The ornamental fronts on the new bulkhead buildings could not disguise the rough working landscape of the era, including a grain elevator on the waterfront and a PG&E gasworks with its giant gasholder.

Bottom: As doubts increased about San Francisco's destiny to be a leading world port, in 1923 the Chamber of Commerce promoted the port as the Strategic Center of World Trade in this butterfly map by B. J. S. Cahill.

decrease" in activity on the Belt Railroad.[40] When the same trend continued in the next two years, the commissioners considered it "imperative that the board institute operating economies in order to balance expenditures with revenues."[41] However, from 1932 to the end of the decade, annual tonnage, which was between 6,000,000 and 7,000,000, was far less than it had been in 1931 and similar to tonnage levels in the 1910s.

Because other ports suffered declining activity at the same time, San Francisco maintained its second-place status among United States ports in the value of its cargo. (Official statistics maintained by the U.S. Customs Service and the Corps of Engineers listed tonnage each year, but in its biennial summaries, the BSHC stressed a secondary statistic on the value of cargo that placed the port of San Francisco in a more favorable light.) As overall business declined, new efforts to generate business yielded results. Among these, several are particularly notable.

The oil-bunkering business flourished. Six oil companies maintained "storage and bunkering facilities" along the waterfront and "by

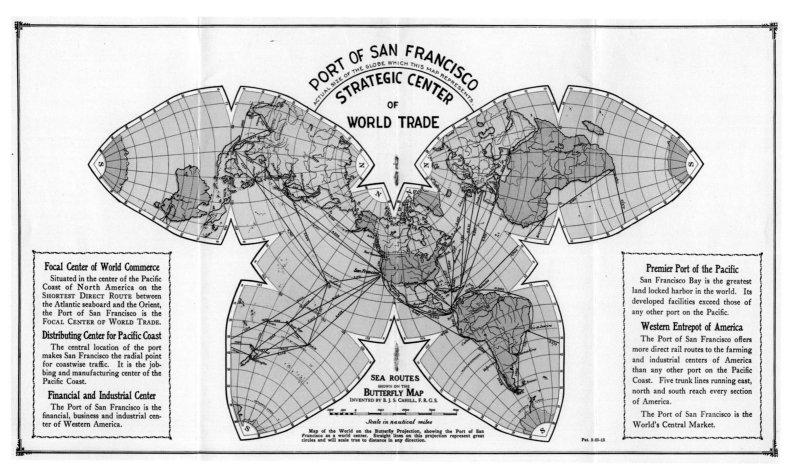

PORT OF SAN FRANCISCO
ACTUAL SIZE OF THE GLOBE WHICH THIS MAP REPRESENTS
STRATEGIC CENTER
OF
WORLD TRADE

SEA ROUTES
SHOWN ON THE
BUTTERFLY MAP
INVENTED BY B. J. S. CAHILL, F. R. G. S.

Scale in nautical miles

Map of the World on the Butterfly Projection, showing the Port of San Francisco as a world center. Straight lines on this projection represent great circles and will scale true to distance in any direction.

Pat. 2-25-13

Focal Center of World Commerce

Situated in the center of the Pacific Coast of North America on the SHORTEST DIRECT ROUTE between the Atlantic seaboard and the Orient, the Port of San Francisco is the FOCAL CENTER OF WORLD TRADE.

Distributing Center for Pacific Coast

The central location of the port makes San Francisco the radial point for coastwise traffic. It is the jobbing and manufacturing center of the Pacific Coast.

Financial and Industrial Center

The Port of San Francisco is the financial, business and industrial center of Western America.

Premier Port of the Pacific

San Francisco Bay is the greatest land locked harbor in the world. Its developed facilities exceed those of any other port on the Pacific.

Western Entrepot of America

The Port of San Francisco offers more direct rail routes to the farming and industrial centers of America than any other port on the Pacific Coast. Five trunk lines running east, north and south reach every section of America.

The Port of San Francisco is the World's Central Market.

barge at shipside" to supply ships and water-front machinery of all kinds.[42] An "automobile unloading platform" was established in an existing automobile station at a spur of the Belt Railroad on North Point Street "for the purpose of unloading new automobiles for the account of San Francisco dealers."[43] Most extensive were various facilities for fresh fruits and vegetables. In 1938, the BSHC declared, "A "sizeable foreign business . . . has developed in the last six or seven years for northern California deciduous fresh fruits, due largely to precooling facilities of the State Refrigeration Terminal in the Port of San Francisco, and 'reefer' ships that deliver luscious pears, apples, plums, and grapes from the inland valleys contiguous to San Francisco to cities on the European Continent or ports in the Far East."[44] The principal facility for this business was the State Products Terminal Building on the north side of China Basin; the State Shipside Refrigeration Terminal occupied the second floor. Facilities for related products were established or improved: for bananas at Channel and Fourth streets on the south side of China Basin,

for copra (dried coconut meat) at Pier 84, and for vegetable oils and grains at Islais Creek.

Focusing on foreign trade, a particular strength of the port, efforts were initiated to establish a Foreign Trade Zone at the port of San Francisco in the mid-1930s. Following the passage of the federal Foreign Trade Zone Act in 1934, the BSHC began planning and lobbying to designate Pier 45 as such a zone, whose "essential function . . . is to facilitate transshipment and reconsignment trade."[45] That is, it would allow transshipment to take place and destinations of goods to be changed at a lower cost than would normally apply.

In addition to gaining stability through generalized trade, the port began to benefit from long-term efforts by many in the Bay Area to attract military facilities, particularly the Pacific headquarters of the reorganized Navy. In 1931, Pier 14 was assigned to the Navy. For the biennium 1932–1934, the chief wharfinger reported, "This port enjoys the unique distinction of berthing at piers, U.S. Navy ships of the super-dreadnaught class" and that this represented

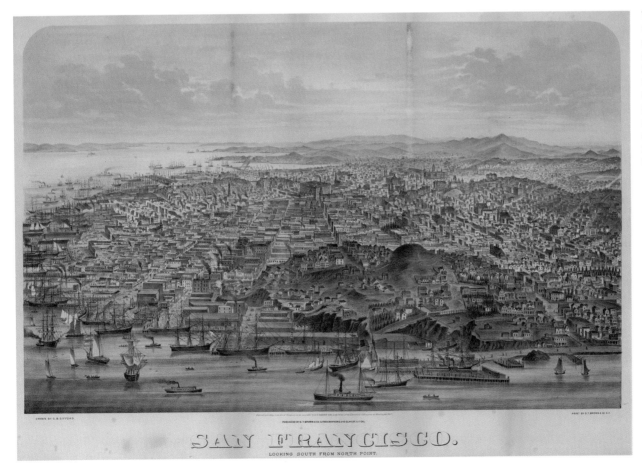

This view in 1877, just before construction began on the new seawall, shows the zigzag waterfront of wharves and piers aligned with the streets and the original pattern of development on the north waterfront, where no rail lines had yet been built. The skyline of the city consisted mostly of factory smokestacks, church steeples, and a few roof towers on hotels and commercial buildings.

SAN FRANCISCO.

LOOKING SOUTH FROM NORTH POINT.

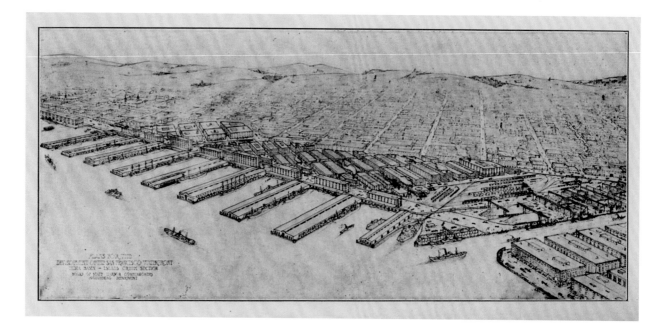

The India Basin-Islais Creek plan of 1918 illustrated the port's proposal for a massive doubling of its capacity south of China Basin to meet the anticipated increase in trade from the Panama Canal. This new industrial city included larger piers and berths for larger ships, as well as dozens of reinforced concrete warehouses, all linked by an extensive network of rail spurs—and all built by the port on its own property.

"operations not essentially related to usual port activities."[46] By mid-1938, San Francisco Bay had been designated "the fleet's principal West Coast repair and supply base," featuring "the mammoth Hunters Point dry dock," large enough for the repair of "modern battleships."[47] Two years later, the BSHC reported that it had "made assignments of some of its piers for the sole use of the Army and the Navy. Greater amounts of cargo are going onto other piers for shipment to America's far flung possessions in the Pacific, Hawaii, Guam, the Philippines, and Samoa."[48]

At the end of the Depression, the port of San Francisco was the second largest port in the United States in the value of its cargo.[49] In relation to others, its business was unusually stable: "The foreign and domestic cargo story of the Port of San Francisco is so general and diversified in actual summation as to be bewildering in detail. Cargo passing over its piers runs into a vast array of commodities imported and exported, inbound and outbound, foreign and intercoastally, as to make up a well balanced trade of staggering collective value."[50] The diminished volume of traditional commerce at the end of the Depression was at least partly made up by military activity.

WORLD WAR II: MILITARY BUSINESS AND THE PEAK OF ACTIVITY

Business at the port was severely disrupted by World War II. From a civilian commercial port, San Francisco was transformed into a port whose primary function was to supply personnel and materials for the military. While the purpose was different during the war, the activity was the same—loading and unloading ships with people and general cargo. Thus, San Francisco remained, in essence, a commercial port, but one that was dominated by a single client, the military: "During World War II . . . the port came largely under federal jurisdiction. Virtually all of its facilities were devoted to the war effort in the Pacific."[51]

Even before the country officially declared war in December 1941, the military had a considerable presence at the port of San Francisco. At first, during the 1930s, the BSHC leased various piers and other facilities to the military without any central coordination. In December 1940, the *San Francisco Chronicle* reported that the port was being "pressed by the army, navy, and marines for additional waterfront facilities." The port responded by assigning "pier 45 to the army and three buildings along Islais Creek to the navy." Local officials were concerned that "any further allocation of space may result in congestion and a possible loss of business to the port in the future."[52]

In a meeting with the BSHC, representatives of the Army and shipping interests discussed the Army's request for more space. The port objected to the Army's desire to use the transit sheds for long-term storage, which would remove them

from port use. Steamship companies were concerned that if they lost their piers, "they would be unable to fulfill their obligations both to the commercial shippers and to the Procurement Division of the Federal Government." In particular, the commissioners pointed out the types of difficulties they faced: "San Francisco is the center of the coffee industry for the Western United States. . . . Coffee represents a substantial portion of the commerce of the Port of San Francisco and a vital industry in the City. . . . The coffee movement is just beginning for the season and it is a duty of the Board to provide satisfactory

facilities for the expeditious handling of this and other commodities in order that they will not be diverted to other ports."[53] Altogether, the minutes of this meeting reveal the serious disruption to the normal activities of the port caused by the military takeover.

Most of the port came under the control of the San Francisco Port of Embarkation, which "had the responsibility of delivering men and supplies the length and breadth of the Pacific."[54] It had a long history in San Francisco, beginning "with the completion of three piers and two permanent storehouses in 1912" at Fort Mason, which

In 1907, downtown offices were just beginning to rise above the low, utilitarian buildings of the industrial waterfront.

became "both an army general depot and the docking area for the Army Transport service."[55] The port of San Francisco was connected to what were then called the Army Transport Docks at Fort Mason in 1914 by the construction of a tunnel that extended the Belt Railroad. In 1932, the Army Transport Docks became the San Francisco Port of Embarkation. The War Department's Army Transportation Corps operated the Ports of Embarkation, which, by the end of the war, included Boston, Hampton Roads, Los Angeles, New York, Seattle, and San Francisco.

In 1940 the San Francisco Port of Embarkation began planning for expanded facilities in

In 1938, the port was at its point of maximum development and the downtown was full of office towers serving a new type of worker and a new corporate economy.

Oakland's Outer Harbor, eventually the Oakland Army Base. From February to October 1941, the San Francisco Port of Embarkation looked intensively for more space in other cities, including San Diego, Los Angeles, Seattle, and Portland, which were established as sub-ports of San Francisco and were later run independently. In northern California, the San Francisco Port of Embarkation controlled all or parts of the following: Fort McDowell, the Embarcadero piers in San Francisco, the Oakland Army Base, the Alameda Air Force Intransit Depot on the Alameda piers (probably a facility of the Army Air Corps, not the Air Force, which was not established until after the war), the Emeryville Ordinance Shops, the Richmond Parr Terminals, the Benicia Piers at the Benicia Arsenal, Camp Stoneman, the Stockton piers, the Humboldt Bay piers, the Animal Depot and other agencies at the Presidio of San Francisco, and Hamilton Field.

The port of San Francisco was used for transporting both cargo and troops, serving as "the funnel through which a large majority of Pacific troops were passed."[56] The military commandeered Piers 7 and 45 before July 1941 for troop movements. Piers 17, 20, 24, 25, and 90 were taken over in 1941; Piers 37, 39, and 41 in January 1942; and Pier 19 in December 1942—all apparently for U.S. Army cargo. In 1942, the Army was given 7,048 square feet in the Ferry

Changing technologies are evident in this view north on East Street (later the Embarcadero) from Folsom Street, taken circa 1901–1906. Horse-drawn wagons carried loads between ships and warehouses, and tall coal loaders supplied fuel to steamships. The U.S. Army transport ship, visible on the right, is an indication of the military presence at the port that began with the Spanish-American War.

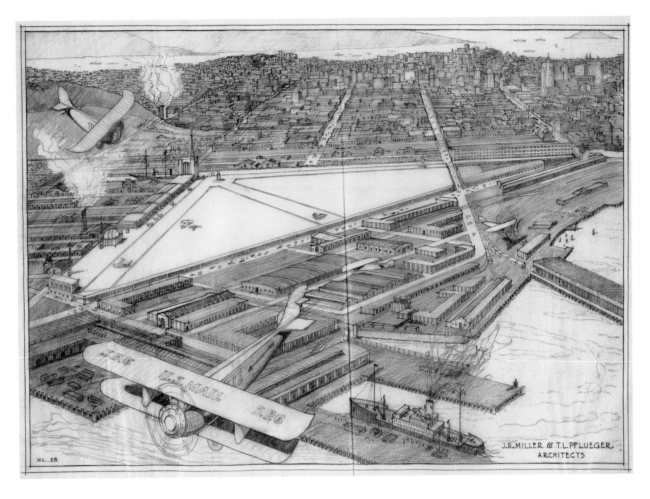

In the scramble to stay competitive with other rapidly growing West Coast ports, San Francisco port planners and engineers considered ways to integrate air transport with rail lines and ships, as shown in this circa 1928 "Bird's Eye View of the Proposed China Basin Airport" by the architects J. R. Miller and T. L. Pflueger.

Building and space at Fisherman's Wharf. In December 1944, Pier 15 was enlisted for returning troops. Piers 25, 29, 35, and 90 were used only temporarily because of their insufficient rail tracks and water depths. The U.S. Navy took control of Pier 54 in 1940 or 1941, Piers 22 and 50 in 1941, and Piers 27, 31, 33, and 48 in 1942. The Navy was also given office space in the Ferry Building in 1941. An unknown branch of the government occupied Pier 56 in 1940. The Army Air Corps took over Piers 90 and 92 in 1942.

The San Francisco Port of Embarkation's need for piers was inseparable from the need for warehouse space wherever it could be found. Even before the war, the military was concerned with storage space for "'critical and strategic' national defense materials," such as hemp, wool, rubber, and tin, and a proposal was made to build temporary warehouses on port property along the Embarcadero.[57] According to the scholars James W. Hamilton and William J. Bolce Jr., "Both Oakland and Embarcadero operations suffered at the outset from a lack of space on the piers and of warehouse space near them, from having little or no rail or motor equipment facilities for relaying troops and freight from trains and warehouses to shipside, and from a shortage of expert personnel."[58]

Near the end of the war, the *San Francisco Chronicle* described conditions at the port: "At present, the ten-mile waterfront has been taken over almost exclusively by the Federal Government. Ships in the harbor have more than doubled in volume and the port boasts more embarkation than any other similar area in the world, . . . Before the war more than 50 major steamship companies were represented at San Francisco piers. Today, the finest ships reconverted for war use the harbor as a major port of call."[59] The reason behind so much activity at the port at that time was explained by the Army: "Army cargo ships being loaded at the time of the Japanese surrender were part of the great fleet which would have supported the Allied invasion of Japan."[60]

When the war ended, the Army summarized

The tanks in this 1919 view represent two important developments of the period: the switch from coal to fuel oil in steamships and persistent efforts by the port to attract and develop new types of money-generating business—in this case, tropical vegetable oils linked by pipelines to Piers 42, 44, and 46A across the Embarcadero. The photograph was taken from the current site of the San Francisco Giants' ballpark.

"the Bay Area's role as the supply and transportation center for the Pacific War . . . the San Francisco Port of Embarkation, in 45 months of war, shipped 1,644,243 soldiers and 23,589,446 ship tons of cargo to the Pacific theaters. Those figures established the Bay Area as the second greatest war port in the United States, and with the continuation of the flow of supplies for Pacific forces, San Francisco tonnage may eventually pass that of New York. . . . For brief periods following Pearl Harbor, and during the last months of the war, San Francisco was the world's greatest harbor." While this statement pertains to the entire San Francisco Port of Embarkation—primarily the Bay Area at the end of the war—nearly all of the troops and 34.5 percent of the cargo were shipped from the port of

San Francisco itself. A proportionate number of the 39,000 employees, not including longshoremen, worked on the San Francisco waterfront during this period.[61]

AFTER WORLD WAR II: SHARP DECLINE IN PORT ACTIVITY
After the war ended in August 1945, the work of the port of San Francisco within the San Francisco Port of Embarkation continued until well into 1946. While the port tried to plan for a return to normal civilian use, General Homer M. Groninger, commander of the San Francisco Port of Embarkation, said "he could not predict when such companies as Matson would again control their great white fleets. He declined to predict, also, when the Army would relinquish control of its many San Francisco facilities."[62] In this

The military was an important user of the port during World War I and the dominant tenant during World War II, when port operations reached their peak of capacity. Here, soldiers are on their way home after the war.

Building on long-time strengths, the port of San Francisco was the third port in the country to operate a Foreign Trade Zone, adopting special U.S. government rules that facilitated foreign trade. Here, European cars sit in the Foreign Trade Zone facility at Pier 45 in 1953.

uncertain climate, the port began preparing for the future. On March 11, 1945, the *San Francisco Chronicle* reported:

> Between three and four million dollars have been allocated by the State Board of Harbor Commissioners for San Francisco to make the city's waterfront the finest in the world, as soon as hostilities cease and materials are available. . . . A survey is now in progress outlining necessary modernization and increasing the size of several piers among the 46 jutting into the waters of San Francisco Bay. Size will increase up to 100 feet in width and several hundred feet in length and will accommodate the largest ships afloat.[63]

In 1946, the port announced a twenty-million-dollar modernization program that would take more than twenty years, beginning

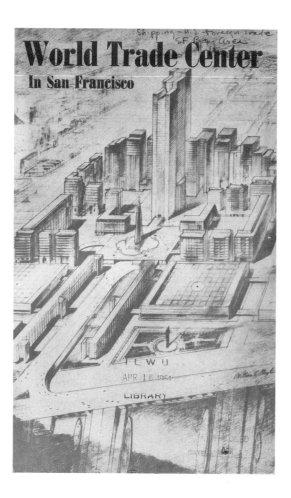

In San Francisco

The establishment of a World Trade Center at the port after World War II was another tool for promoting foreign trade. This 1951 proposal, designed by William Gladstone Merchant, would have replaced the little-used Ferry Building with a modern World Trade Center.

with improvements along Islais Creek. The largest development under this program, designed for the new scale of commercial shipping operations, was the twenty-acre, six-million-dollar Mission Rock Terminal at Pier 50 to accommodate four ships, transit sheds, and connections to rail and trucks. In 1950–1952, Piers 30 and 32 south of the Bay Bridge were combined into a single "quay-type terminal," similar to Pier 50 but not as big, with a new open wharf between the piers for trucks. In 1955–1956, Piers 15 and 17 on the north waterfront were joined in a similar manner. These upgrades may have prolonged the maritime use of the piers, but they did not reverse the loss of shipping at the port.

These changes could not keep up with improvements in other West Coast ports, notably those of Oakland, Los Angeles, and Seattle. For "the 5-year period 1946–1950, the total waterborne commerce passing through the Port of San Francisco averaged 4,835,717 short tons annually,"[64] which was slightly more than the tonnage reported in 1909. A 1949 article in the

San Francisco Chronicle stated, "San Francisco's maritime health is not robust."[65] In 1950, the U.S. Army Corps of Engineers lowered its assessment of the port of San Francisco, calling it "one of the key ports on the Pacific Coast"[66]—the first time it was not described as the coast's leading port.

Although its tonnage was down and its relative position among other ports was weakened, San Francisco maintained stability in the nature of its commerce. In 1951, the Board of Engineers for Rivers and Harbors declared, "San Francisco is primarily a general cargo port, and diversified commodities make-up a well-balanced trade. . . . Non-metallic minerals was the principal commodity classification, accounting for about 46 per cent; vegetable food products, approximately 20 per cent; metals and manufactures, 7 per cent; and the remainder was composed of textile fibers and manufactures, wood and paper, inedible vegetable products, and animals and animal products."[67]

Building on another old strength, the port sought to establish a Foreign Trade Zone, an effort that began in the late 1930s, and a World Trade Center. Foreign Trade Zone No. 3, the third in the United States after New York and New Orleans, was created at Pier 45 after World War II. When it opened in June 1948, the port optimistically characterized its importance: "The establishment of this facility is the Pacific Coast's most useful contribution toward promoting and expediting international commerce since the opening of the Panama Canal."[68] A World Trade Center was a type of organization that emerged just before World War II to promote and facilitate international trade. In San Francisco, an attempt to boost the port resulted in the formation of a new state agency, the San Francisco World Trade Center Authority, in 1947. Working with the port, in 1948 a joint proposal was made to demolish the Ferry Building (little used since the bridges opened and put the ferries out of business) and replace it with a new World Trade Center that would consist of a complex of modern structures and plazas around a high central tower. Public objections and practical obstacles to such a radical change led to a redesign that put a scaled-down version in the remodeled north end of the Ferry Building. When it opened in 1956, the World Trade Center was a combination office building, conference center, and exhibit hall intended to promote California products in world markets.

Despite these endeavors, the port suffered three straight years in the 1950s in which its revenues did not meet its operating costs. Then, in 1956, revenues exceeded operating costs. According to one newspaper headline, San Francisco reestablished itself as the "leading port on the Pacific Coast." The good times were short lived, however—1959 was described in another headline as the "worst year since 1903."[69]

A port plan for Fisherman's Wharf prepared by John S. Bolles and Ernest Born in 1961 included provisions to maintain the fishing fleet and support facilities while radically redesigning the adjacent waterfront for commercial purposes. This also failed.

Even in its weakest years, the port continued to play a significant role in San Francisco's economy. The *California Blue Book* of 1961 estimated that the port of San Francisco "supports the income and livelihood of one-third of San Francisco's population."[70] According to a study in the mid-1960s, "It is estimated that close to 12 percent of the total work force of San Francisco is supported by the activity directly and indirectly associated with the port"[71]— approximately twenty-three thousand jobs.

For all of its efforts, in the 1960s the port of San Francisco could not keep up with the new facilities at the port of Oakland, nor could San Francisco compete with Oakland's geographical advantages. The use of larger ships required larger wharves, which were more easily built on the spacious waterfront in Oakland, an area that had been expanded by the military filling tidelands during World War II and was enhanced by increased dredging by the U.S. Army Corps of Engineers. Oakland's new wharves were equipped with the latest technologies for cargo handling, which only heightened their superiority. Shippers in Oakland connected directly with the railroads and did not require the extra step of transferring cargo across the bay. Finally, when containerization was rapidly adopted on a large scale in the late 1960s, Oakland was the second largest container port in the world,[72] and San Francisco's business was falling.

Fisherman's Wharf in 1940, with the gasholder and the Crabmen's Protective Association in the background.

THE BOARD OF
STATE HARBOR COMMISSIONERS

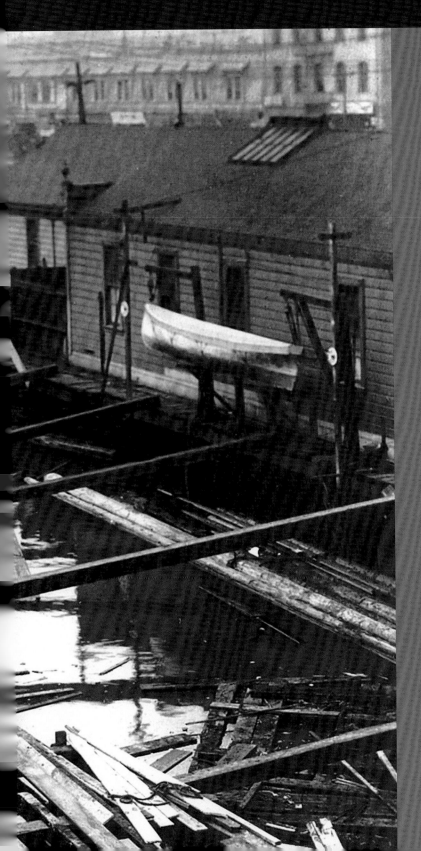

For most of its history, the port of San Francisco was in the hands of a state agency —the Board of State Harbor Commissioners (BSHC). The port's operation, the expansion of its property, its development as an important commercial and transportation hub, its accommodation of the needs of shipping companies and numerous types of waterfront labor, the design and construction of its great variety of physical facilities, and its architectural image were all the purview of this administrative body.

The Board of State Harbor Commissioners (BSHC) was responsible for building, maintaining, and operating the port from 1863 to 1969. Its most enduring work was planning and constructing the seawall, shown here in Section 9 just south of the Ferry Building in 1909–1910. When the seawall was finished, the water seen on the right was filled to create the Embarcadero and seawall lots.

The BSHC does not represent the only governmental effort to regulate and support the port's development. The City and County of San Francisco, the state of California, and the federal government all participated in substantial ways at varying times.

In the early years, the city appointed a harbor master and two dock masters in a largely symbolic display of municipal authority at the port. Throughout the history of the port, the city's bureaucracy oversaw many utilitarian functions: the maintenance of sewers that emptied into the bay after passing through landfill and the seawall, the delivery of water and electricity to the port, the issuance of building permits, the regulation of Belt Railroad spurs on city streets, and transit service. The Harbor Police Station, long located at the northeast corner of Drumm and Commercial streets, patrolled the high-crime zone of the waterfront. The most visible city presence was the Fire Department, which maintained fireboats at Pier 33½ and Pier 22½, where the station still stands.

Apart from the BSHC, many other state entities were involved with the port. The Boards of Pilot Examiners and Pilot Commissioners regulated the Bar Pilots, a state agency. The Board of Tide Land Commissioners surveyed and sold much of the waterfront in 1869–1870. The welfare of workers was the concern of the Board of Sailor Boarding House Commissioners, the Board of Industrial Relations, and the Industrial Accident Commission. The Railroad Commissioners regulated the rail industry. The Port Wardens were concerned with "any vessel arriving in distress, or which has sustained damage or injury at sea."[1] The Agriculture Building housed numerous divisions of the Department of Agriculture, which was concerned with agricultural products passing through the port.

At the federal level, the government was widely involved in matters associated with navigation, with commerce between the states and foreign countries, and with the safety of ships. The Army Corps of Engineers has been concerned with navigation since 1867.[2] In the early days, one of its principal functions was blowing up rocks in the bay. The Lighthouse Service, established in 1850, built lighthouses in the Golden Gate and up and down the Pacific Coast. Ships were monitored by the Inspector

of Boilers of Steam Vessels and the Inspector of Hulls, Steam, and Sail Vessels, succeeded by the Inspector of Steam and Sail Vessels and the Merchant Marine Inspectors of the Coast Guard. The Coast Guard was responsible for policing the waters and for providing aids to navigation: fog horns, fog bells, buoys, and lightships. The Customs Service collected tariffs and had its own Barge Office at Fisherman's Wharf from which it could approach and board ships in the bay or U.S. waters. The Customhouse and the Appraiser's Warehouse behind it accommodated many of the federal offices with concerns at the port. After 1878, a Quarantine Station for persons with communicable diseases addressed the safety of the population. Likewise, the Bureau of Entomology and Plant Quarantine was located with similar state offices in the Agriculture Building.

Overlapping concerns of commerce and the military were handled by the Shipping Board, established in 1917 and succeeded by the Maritime Commission. The Shipping Board regulated commercial ships and their routes, marine insurance, shipping rates, and port facilities.

Yet other federal functions were carried out by an array of programs. The Marine Hospital provided care for seamen beginning in 1852. The Bureau of Immigration controlled foreign immigration, especially from China. The Railroad Administration nationalized the railroads from 1917 to 1920. And the U.S. Post Office, an important user of the port from the beginning, became a tenant there in 1884.

These many involvements by all levels of government—incompletely represented here—required integration with the port itself. Viewed together with commercial operations and other interests, they suggest the complexity of the building and operation of the port, sometimes said to be "almost like a city."[3]

EARLY DEVELOPMENT OF THE PORT
The early development of the port of San Francisco was chaotic, shaped by weak governmental authority and the self-interests of real-estate speculators, merchants, and ship owners. At first, under the jurisdiction of the state—California claimed its tidelands in the state constitution—the shallow tidelands of Yerba Buena Cove were surveyed and water

On an official map of the city prepared in 1851 by William M. Eddy, known as the Eddy Red Line Map, an inner red line indicates the original shoreline of the city. Beyond the line are surveyed water lots, most of which were sold to private owners and filled. The water lots terminate at the Jurisdiction Line between city and state authority, beyond which piers could extend six hundred feet.

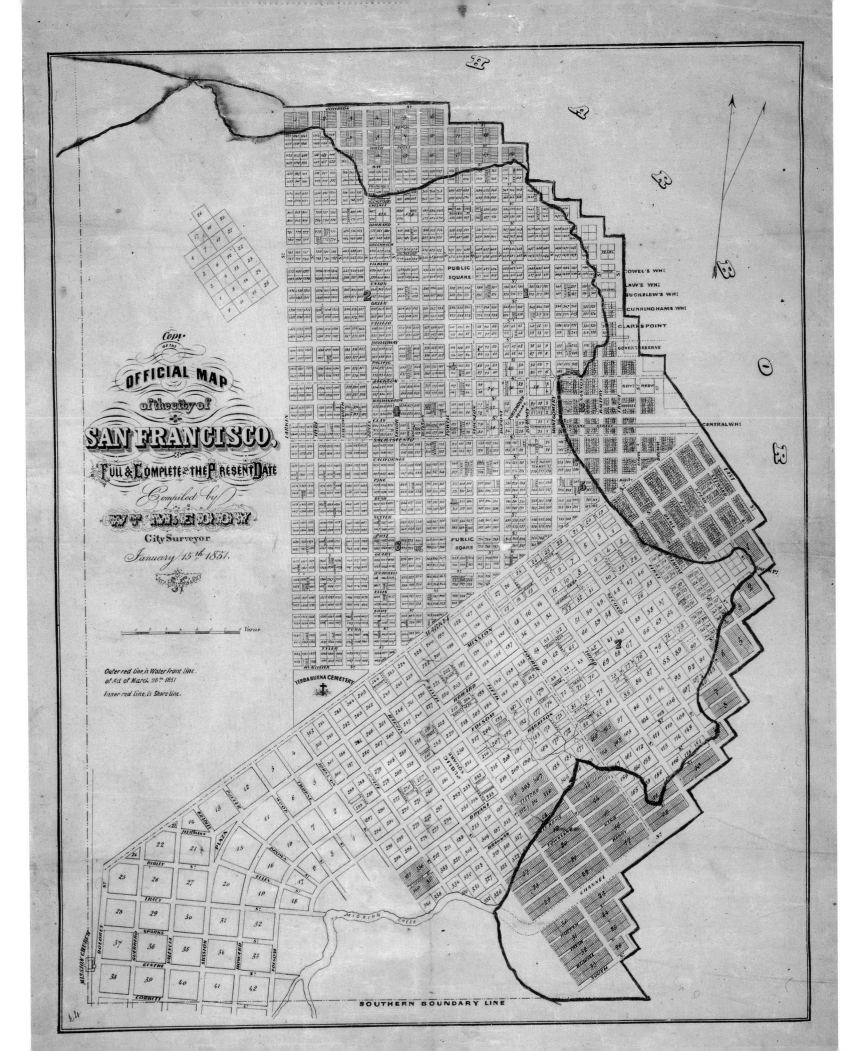

Copy
OF THE

OFFICIAL MAP

of the city of

SAN FRANCISCO,

Full & Complete to the Present Date

Compiled by

Wm M. EDDY

City Surveyor

January 15th 1851.

Outer red line, is Water front line
of Act of March 26th 1851

Inner red line, is Shore line.

YERBA BUENA CEMETERY

SOUTHERN BOUNDARY LINE

MISSION CREEK

MISSION CHURCH

COWEL'S WH.
LAW'S WH.
BUCKELEW'S WH.
CUNINGHAM'S WH.
CLARK'S POINT
GOVT. RESERVE
GOVT. RESV.
CENTRAL WH.

PUBLIC SQUARE

PUBLIC SQUARE

In this panorama made in 1853, the chaos of San Francisco's early waterfront, before it was taken over by the BSHC, is apparent. This view north from Rincon Hill across Yerba Buena Cove captures a ragged shoreline of wharves and piers, the uncoordinated demarcation of water lots, and laid-up ships used as warehouses and for other purposes.

lots were sold to private interests. According to Edward Morphy's 1923 history of the port, "Work was vigorously pushed, and in October 1850, an aggregate of 6,000 feet of new wharves had been constructed by various companies and individuals at an outlay computed at $1,000,000."[4]

Also in 1850, jurisdiction over the waterfront was transferred from the state to the city of San Francisco. The city was "empowered to construct wharves at the ends of all streets" as extensions of the street alignments, "not to exceed 200 yards beyond the present outside line of the beach and water lots."[5] Because the street grid met the irregular line of the waterfront in two different directions—at right angles to one another—an orthogonal grid of wharves was developed over the tidelands. The privately owned water lots within this grid were filled with sand and rock to make new ground, sometimes contained by sheet piling or other structures and sometimes spilling out in all directions.

The city's attempts to control and benefit from development of the port were ineffectual. As the historian Gerald Nash explains the situation:

Many portions of San Francisco Bay were left to shoaling and silting in the 1850s and became increasingly unnavigable. Sunken wrecks, rocks, and other obstructions made large areas of the harbor dangerous for shipping, and threatened to diminish the flow of traffic. At the same time a number of individuals during this period built unauthorized wharves along the waterfront, often jutting far into the bay, thus further adding to difficulties of navigation. In 1853 a committee of the California Legislature investigated the situation and scored "the irregular and predatory manner in which the . . . waterfront is now being extended by capricious enterprise." It noted that some plan of physical development of the harbor was absolutely essential lest the dockage was to be utterly ruined, to the great injury of the city's commerce.[6]

In spite of these conditions, in 1853, the city of San Francisco granted ten-year leases to numerous private interests for the construction and operation of wharves and piers. During the period of the leases, conditions only got worse; the need for a seawall, in particular, became more acute. With the leases due to expire in 1863 and no sign that the situation at the port would improve, the state took jurisdiction of the port from the city.

On April 24, 1863, the state's "Act to Provide for Improvement and Protection of Wharves, Docks, and Waterfront in the City and Harbor of San Francisco" was signed, establishing the BSHC to administer and develop the port. The board was created with three commissioners, each with a four-year term: one was elected

statewide, one was chosen by the legislature, and one was chosen by the city of San Francisco. After a scandal in 1872, they were appointed by the governor to serve overlapping terms, and starting in 1911, they served at the pleasure of the governor. The BSHC met once a week. Because its members were barred from having direct connections to shipping interests in San Francisco Bay, many came to the position with neither an understanding of the port nor applicable experience. In a doctoral dissertation on the history of the administration of the waterfront, Lamberta Voget characterized the job of the harbor commissioners as "finding an equilibrium between political stresses and the demands of business efficiency."[7]

Over the years, most members of the BSHC were politically well-connected insiders, and many had links to the Southern Pacific Railroad, especially before the reform administration was elected in 1910. Among those more widely known were men representing a diverse range of experience and points of view. Jasper O'Farrell, a civil engineer on the board from 1870 to 1873, had been the surveyor general of Alta California for the Mexican government and had created the first extended professional plan for the city of San Francisco in 1847. Washington Bartlett (not to be confused with Washington A. Bartlett, first alcalde of San Francisco) served on the board in 1871, was mayor of San Francisco from 1883 to 1887 with the support of Christopher Buckley (the Blind Boss), and was governor of California in 1887 when he died.[8] Frank McCoppin, who served as mayor from 1867 to 1869, opposed the influence of the Central Pacific Railroad before

he was a harbor commissioner in 1879–1880 and again in 1886–1887. Henry J. Crocker, wealthy owner of the H. J. Crocker printing and publishing business, lost the 1903 mayor's election to the Union Labor Party candidate Eugene Schmitz and served as a harbor commissioner from 1907 to 1909. Marshall Hale, owner of one of the largest San Francisco department stores, Hale Brothers, served as president of the board during its most intense era of reform in 1911–1912.

For its first four years, the BSHC was immobilized by litigation in a diffused effort by private interests to retain their wharves and other waterfront property. After that, the board was able to proceed with the development of the port, beginning in 1867 with the initial phases of a seawall and related landfill. From that time forward, every improvement at the port was made under the administration of the BSHC. In addition to the seawall, during the nineteenth century, the board oversaw the design and construction of numerous wharves and piers, as well as the Ferry Building; the first phase of the Belt Railroad; and the maintenance of all of these facilities. According to W. V. Stafford, at one time the president of the BSHC and a knowledgeable writer about the port, the beginning of construction of the second seawall in 1878 "may be considered as marking the commencement of the permanent harbor of San Francisco."[9]

ROLE OF THE U.S. GOVERNMENT

With the establishment of the BSHC, the state and federal governments contributed to the development of the port in their areas of jurisdiction. As plans for the new seawall were under

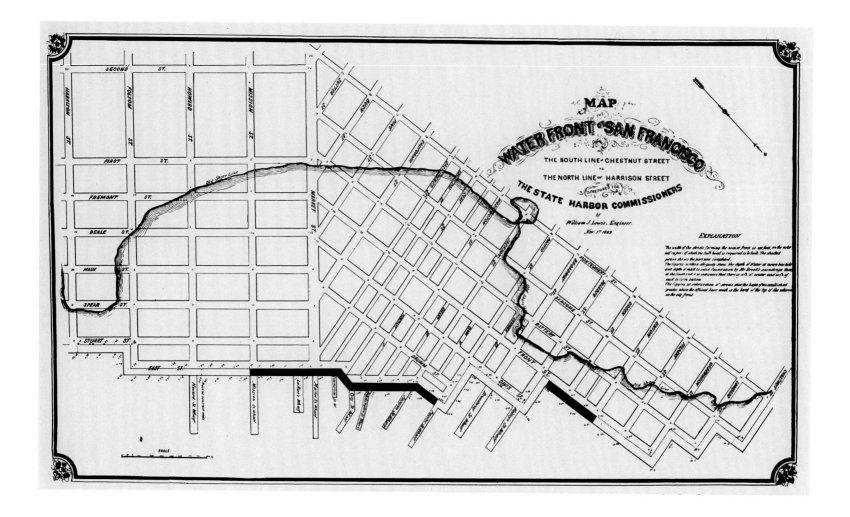

The BSHC first began building a seawall in 1867 along two segments of the Jurisdiction Line, shown on this map. Work on this seawall stopped permanently in 1869 for both engineering and financial reasons. With this seawall, the only land the port would own was a zigzag street 160 feet wide along the Jurisdiction Line.

way, "harbor lines" were adopted by the state legislature on February 28, 1876. These were two curving, parallel lines: a Bulkhead Line, behind which would be landfill; and a Pier Head Line six hundred feet out into the bay from the bulkhead line, the farthest point allowed for construction of piers or other features. In 1888, the U.S. Army Corps of Engineers, addressing the federal government's responsibility for navigable waters, adopted "substantially the same" harbor lines.[10] In 1901 and 1903, at the request of the BSHC, the Corps of Engineers extended the Pier Head Line another two hundred feet, making it eight hundred feet from the Bulkhead Line as far south as Mission Rock, near where Pier 50 would later be built.[11] In each case, the landfill behind the Bulkhead Line was to a level defined as "city base"—("The 'City Base' . . . was the height above mean high water arranged by the original surveyors as the height of the city foreshore")— by the City and County of San Francisco.[12]

In the nineteenth and early twentieth centuries, the U.S. Army Corps of Engineers also performed two other important functions in regard to the port of San Francisco. First of all, it blew up rocks that were hazards to navigation. One rock had a particularly direct relationship to the port—Mission Rock off of Pier 50. And secondly, it dredged sand bars to maintain a clear channel through the Golden Gate.

The U.S. Post Office was long an important tenant of the port; it occupied dedicated facilities built by the BSHC. In 1896, the Post Office moved into its own pier and distinctive building just south of the Ferry Building. Designed in the Romanesque Revival style, the building was replaced in 1915 by a new Embarcadero Post Office in the style of a Renaissance palazzo, which was still distinctive but more in keeping with other port buildings. The postal service moved out in 1925, and in 1933 the building was taken over by the state Department of

Agriculture. It has been known ever since as the Agriculture Building.

ORGANIZATION AND EVOLUTION OF THE
BOARD OF STATE HARBOR COMMISSIONERS

When it was established in 1863, the BSHC was empowered to rent offices at a maximum of fifty dollars per month and to pay salaries to the three commissioners, a secretary, and a wharfinger.[13] The early history of the staff is not well known. California established an eight-hour workday in 1863, the same year that the board was founded. While state employees may have adhered to the rule, the contractors commissioned by the BSHC to perform much of the day-to-day work did not apply it in practice, according to an 1886 report on "the condition of the laborers employed by contractors on the seawall."[14]

Until it moved to the Ferry Building in 1898, the BSHC occupied rented quarters in a series of ordinary, small brick buildings on Montgomery and California streets. Its first office, from 1863 to 1867, was in the A. B. McCreery Building, a four-story structure at the northeast corner of Montgomery and Pine streets.[15] From 1868 through 1874 it leased the second floor of a two-story building at 414 Montgomery Street. The small size of this building, which occupied the front half of a twenty-five-foot lot, indicates that the BSHC had a limited number of administrative employees at that time. In 1875–1876, it was located at the northeast corner of Montgomery and Jackson streets in the ground-floor banking space of what had been the Bank of Lucas Turner & Company.[16] Then, from 1877 to 1898, it was on an upper floor at 10 California Street.

In 1899—the first year for which a list of employees is available—the BSHC's new Ferry Building offices were occupied by no more than two dozen central office workers, including three commissioners, two secretaries, a statistician, a bookkeeper, three members of the engineering department, and an attorney. Of nearly two hundred employees in total, most appear to have been located on the wharves, including the chief wharfinger and nineteen assistants; fifteen collectors; twenty-two pile drivers; twenty-eight operators of tugs and dredges; twenty-eight carpenters, patchers, and painters to perform "urgent repairs"; eight machinists, electricians, inspectors, and plumbers; nineteen workers

The first office of the BSHC, from 1863 to 1867, was in the A. B. McCreery Building at the northeast corner of Pine and Montgomery streets, several blocks from the waterfront.

The BSHC's second office, from 1868 to 1874, was upstairs at 414 Montgomery Street. At that time the board required space for only the three commissioners and the secretary, who met once a week.

After a year in the ground-floor office space of the Bank of Lucas Turner & Co. at the northeast corner of Montgomery and Jackson streets, in a building that is still standing, the BSHC moved for the first time to a location near the waterfront, at 10 California Street, which it occupied from 1877 to 1898.

EAST STREET, SHOWING BELT LINE R.R. AND SHIPPING.   MAY 11, 1906.

TURRILL & MILLER, OFF. PHOTO.
THE CALIFORNIA PROMOTION COMMITTEE

The first section of the Belt Railroad was built by the BSHC in 1889–1890 on the north waterfront. Taken less than a month after the earthquake of April 18, 1906, this photograph, looking north from Broadway, shows the Belt Railroad fully operating on the Embarcadero and in the seawall lots.

on the Belt Railroad; thirty-five sweepers, watchmen, boatmen, cartmen, sprinklers, and policemen; and thirteen janitors for the Ferry Building.[17]

Under state law, the operations of the staff and the improvements to the port's facilities were to be paid for by the annual revenues of the port. These revenues—including tariffs; rents on wharf space, the Ferry Building, and seawall lots; and Belt Railroad switching fees—fluctuated with activity at the port. On the one hand, this

unpredictability resulted in funding problems when major expenditures were necessary, as in the case with the construction of the seawall, which was drawn out over thirty-five years. On the other hand, the BSHC was able to boast that the port never cost the taxpayers a cent. Rather, it generated an enormous business that benefited the economy of the state.

An important exception to the use of revenues to cover the port's expenses was the issuance of bonds on infrequent occasions. The first use of bonds occurred in 1891, when six hundred thousand dollars were approved for the Ferry Building. When this amount proved inadequate, the BSHC finished the project with revenue money. In 1903, two million dollars were issued for the San Francisco Seawall Fund. In 1909, nine million dollars went to the Second Seawall Fund, and one million dollars allowed the purchase of India Basin. In 1913, ten million dollars were authorized for the Third Seawall Fund.

During the early history of the port, the only other source of funds was the one hundred thousand dollars made available immediately after the earthquake of 1906 "from the general state fund for the reconstruction and repair of the waterfront." In 1907, the state lent the BSHC an additional quarter million dollars for earthquake repairs.[18]

Along with the physical modernization of the port that began in the early twentieth century, the staff of the BSHC also underwent changes. Up to 1909, the list of state employees in the *California Blue Book* included the political affiliation of the staff's white-collar members— almost all of whom were Republicans. Following the victory of Governor Hiram Johnson on a Progressive platform, the 1911 *California Blue Book* omitted political affiliations of employees.

The report of the first BSHC appointed by Governor Johnson, during the biennium of 1910–1912, was written in an uncharacteristically bold tone. According to the report, the governor promised in his campaign "to destroy the illegitimate influences of the Southern Pacific Company in California politics"[19]—including its sway over the BSHC. By 1868, the Central Pacific Railroad "had already established political control of the state board of harbor commissioners."[20] Among "the evil effects of Southern Pacific control" was "the habitual appointment of harbor employees, especially of the higher grades, from political retainers, very frequently of delegates to State conventions, who secured their positions in the harbor employ in exchange for their convention votes."[21] During an earlier effort at cleaning house in 1897, E. L. Colnon, president of the BSHC, had eliminated many jobs, explaining, "The jobs are accounted about the best of the many sinecures on the front."[22] The BSHC reported how it remedied this favoritism:

Obviously the quickest method of removing Southern Pacific influence from harbor affairs was to discharge such employees, especially those at the heads of departments, as owed their positions, and therefore paid their allegiance, to the Southern Pacific "machine." And this has been done with gratifying improvement in the personnel of the force and the conduct of the harbor business. Not all of the employees were of this class, but many of the most important were, and such were discharged. Devotion to public interests has thus been substituted for responsiveness to private interests.[23]

For the future, the commissioners advocated civil-service reform, which was adopted as state law on August 10, 1913: "The harbor force should be organized, selected, and operated on business principles under the merit system, and utterly in disregard of politics."[24]

The number of employees of the BSHC grew substantially in this period, from fewer than 200 in 1899 to 285 in 1907[25] and 373 in 1911.[26] In 1912, the *San Francisco Call* criticized the "Johnson political machine" under which "the payroll has nearly doubled . . . and there is nothing to show for it in the way of work" except votes.[27] One factor in the growth of the staff was the long-term trend away from the use of contract labor by the port's various departments and toward the adoption of "day laborers." "The Board, on recommendation of its engineering department, has substituted the day-labor system in place of the contract system in many classes of repair and other work, with the result, according to the engineering department, of much better and cheaper work."[28] *Day labor* is defined as "Work executed at a given rate per day, as distinguished from that paid for by the piece or contracted for at a given total figure. Day's work is especially advantageous where quality is of greater importance than time or cost in money."[29] Contrary to the implication of their label, day laborers were listed as part of the staff of the BSHC and thus inflated the number of employees. According to Voget, "By 1911, the contract system seems to have been abandoned."[30]

The top positions on the staff of the BSHC were the secretary, the chief wharfinger, and the chief engineer, all of whom were paid the same annual salary, which was the same as that

This aerial view of San Francisco on May 28, 1906, a month after the earthquake and fire, highlights the good condition of the port in contrast to the devastation almost everywhere else. The port played a major role during the emergency and the subsequent recovery of the city. The port's piers and wharves were in full use and its Belt Railroad was running, and a dense cluster of privately owned warehouses around Rincon Hill was standing.

of two of the three commissioners, not including the president. Among these, the secretary was an administrative position attached to the three commissioners. In 1918, a woman was appointed to a two-year term as secretary: "Miss Hilda Gohrman, the new secretary of the State Harbor Commissioners, enjoys the privilege of being the first woman to hold a state position of

this kind."[31] The chief wharfinger was supported by an assistant chief wharfinger and numerous wharfingers and collectors. "The Wharfingers Department controls the vessel operations and the berthing of vessels along the seventeen miles of berthing space available, and charges and collects the dockage for the use of this space; controls all of the pier areas, over 169 acres, and

BEAR PHOTO S.F. 399

allots it to cargo operations in rotation, so that there is seldom any pier area unused; collects the tolls on all cargo and demurrage charges when cargo remains on the piers beyond the free period."[32] The chief engineer was responsible for both maintenance and new construction of port facilities. (See the Appendix on page 220 for additional information on the office of the chief engineer.)

The BSHC provided the leadership for the development of the port in the early twentieth century. According to Morphy, "Up to the time of the fire of 1906, most of the improvements essayed were only temporary. With the reconstruction of San Francisco, however, came the real development of the waterfront."[33]

A chief responsibility of the BSHC was maintenance of its facilities: wharves, piers, berths between piers, transit sheds, roads, and railroads. This post-1938 photograph from Union Street shows work on the Belt Railroad tracks on spurs leading to Seawall Lot 10.

Maintenance work of the BSHC included continual dredging of channels and berths. This 1926 view shows dredging of Channel Street west of Fourth Street.

Commenting on that period, W. V. Stafford, president of the BSHC, wrote that the port's facilities were inadequate and that "it is the purpose of the Board of State Harbor Commissioners to improve and develop, to the extent of its financial ability, the port facilities of San Francisco, along modern lines, until this port shall in this respect compare favorably with any of the great seaports of the world."[34] These goals of the BSHC were realized in the construction of the piers, the reconstruction of the bulkhead wharf, the completion of the final sections of the seawall between 1908 and 1938, and the expansion of the port and the Belt Railroad into new areas.

MEASURING THE SUCCESS OF THE BOARD OF STATE HARBOR COMMISSIONERS

When Edward Morphy wrote his history of the port in the early 1920s, he believed that the port was at a turning point, having come through a series of crises, most recently "the epochal incidents of the opening of the Panama Canal and the simultaneous outbreak of the World War." The port, preparing "intelligently to meet the explosion assured by the development of trade on the Pacific," had arrived at this moment because of the existence of the BSHC and its sound organization and actions. First of all, "by its steady policy of meeting expenses out of revenues, and involving the state in no new taxation to meet any emergency, the

Board of State Harbor Commissioners weathered all difficulties and preserved intact save for increasements of the great property that is now constituted in the water front and the Belt Railroad of San Francisco." Secondly, in relation to all other American ports, San Francisco had "exceptional modern facilities" developed by the BSHC "without imposing a dollar of taxation upon the community." Furthermore, the operation was notable for "the efficiency that had been achieved in the equipment and control of this great seaport. . . . The port of San Francisco is the only port in the United States wherein all activities are coordinated and harmonized under single control." According to Morphy, "This achievement, admittedly the work of many years, was rendered possible solely by the fact that its Harbor Commissioners, through the succeeding generations, not only had behind them the credit of the State of California but also were in a position to rise superior to the narrow influences of local politics."[35]

Writing twenty years later about the period up to 1930, Lamberta Voget, the other principal historian of the early decades of the port, echoed Morphy's view with a somewhat different emphasis. Voget considered it significant that the port's early success was due to its establishment not for the local interests of one city but for the wider community of California. "That the waterfront of San Francisco consisted of land legally created in its entirety by the state through legislative action and physically filled in under the auspices of the harbor commissioners gave to it a unique position among U.S. harbors—it was in reality a *state* harbor."[36] In relation to other United States ports, Voget said of San Francisco:

> The Board of State Harbor Commissioners has been a pioneer in providing a centralized system of public administration which had full control over all waterfront properties including the Belt Line. Whereas other ports in the United States have suffered at the hands of private transportation companies and other interests that crowded along their shore lands the waterfront at San Francisco, in spite of railroad influence in state politics and the strategic location of the peninsular city, has remained under public control and has been physically developed along plans envisaged as early as 1873. It has had a carefully defined schedule of charges that enabled the port to be wholly self-supporting. It has given a measure of satisfaction to port patrons. Indeed, San Francisco has been the most important port on the Pacific Coast, it has ranked high among American ports in general, and its administration has elicited the commendation of impartial critics.[37]

The port of San Francisco was almost alone among major North American ports to be entirely under the control of a single public agency.

The success of the port of San Francisco under the BSHC led smaller ports to adopt similar boards. The BSHC for the ports of Eureka and San Diego were established by 1896.[38] Jurisdiction over these ports and the port of San Jose was transferred to the state Division of Ports by 1928.[39]

The port of Los Angeles, which was never under state control, was formally organized by the city in 1907 under the administration of the Board of Harbor Commissioners. The other principal California ports—Long Beach, Sacramento, Stockton, Oakland, Redwood City, and Richmond—did not develop substantially until later and followed different administrative models.

The influence of the BSHC was also felt through the participation of its staff in professional organizations, notably the American Association of Port Authorities and its Pacific Coast Associates, as well as the California Association of Port Authorities. Several chief engineers of the BSHC routinely participated in meetings of these groups. In 1936, chief engineer Frank G. White was president of the American Association of Port Authorities and chaired its annual meeting in San Francisco. Regular participation in these organizations also kept San Francisco's engineering staff and administrators informed about new ideas and technologies for ports.

EFFECTIVE ADMINISTRATION: 1920S TO 1940S

The BSHC managed an operation that concerned shipping companies, merchants, railroads, labor, and the general public. As the issues facing the port grew more complex, this independent state agency turned to outsiders for advice. In 1918, while World War I was diminishing activity and development at the port, the BSHC invited "some fifty or more representatives of the ship owners and merchants, for the purpose of discussing affairs generally affecting the welfare of the port."[40] In the biennium of 1918–1920, this affiliation grew into the Advisory Committee to the BSHC. The Advisory Committee's twenty members represented importers and exporters, ship owners and operators, railroad employees, stevedores, warehousemen, draymen, and the

Damage to piers, aprons, and dolphins from collisions with ships demanded constant attention from the maintenance employees of the BSHC. In this view north toward Pier 1, engineers inspect a slip behind the Ferry Building that was damaged by a ferryboat.

Chamber of Commerce.[41] In various forms, this advisory group remained in place for many years.

In the 1920s, the port staff continued to increase. In 1923, Morphy reported that there were 450 employees;[42] three years later, there were 490.[43] The growth in the staff in this period was partly a function of new job categories, including a business solicitor, a traffic manager, and a materials testing department.[44] Within a few years, the job of the traffic manager warranted a whole department. The testing department was established to perform the essential task of testing building materials, such as cement, which was an important function as the port turned increasingly to reinforced

The Wharfingers Department of the BSHC represented the board on the wharves and piers, allocating berths to incoming ships, assessing charges, and collecting payment from shipping companies. The chief wharfinger was located in these buildings on the bulkhead wharf north of the Ferry Building from 1909 until 1919, when the building on the left was moved to Pier 29 as offices for the Belt Railroad.

concrete construction. It grew steadily as its availability and usefulness became better known, and it was made available to all state agencies except the highway department. The staff also grew because of the upkeep needed on the aging piers, especially on the north waterfront: "On account of the increased age of the structures along the water front, their maintenance has required the employment of a larger number of mechanics in all lines," notably pile drivers, top men, carpenters, roofers, and sheet-metal workers.[45]

Despite the prosperity of the 1920s, the

replacement of old wooden piers by modern concrete structures proceeded slowly. The ten-million-dollar bond issue of 1913 was not depleted until the late 1920s. In 1930, a new bond issue of the same amount was approved, along with a plan for the replacement of the remaining wooden piers on the waterfront with "nine modern concrete piers capable of docking the largest liner afloat"[46] accounting for all of the piers between Lombard Street and the Ferry Building. The slow development of new facilities was a principal cause of recurring efforts by San Francisco interests to transfer control of the port to the city.[47]

As the port began to feel the effects of the Depression in diminished activity, the BSHC responded in different ways. Less than a year after the stock market crashed, the biennial report of 1928–1930 showed 480 employees, ten fewer than in 1926. By this time, the port was forced to take severe measures, adopting a plan that "provided for reducing the time of employees, thus spreading employment among as many as possible. . . . The employees have shown a laudable spirit of cheerful cooperation and consideration for their fellow employees in this respect, accepting a four and five-day week, and in some instances a three-day week with a corresponding reduction in income without protest."[48]

The 1930 bond issue did not sell well. Beginning in 1936, the port sought money from the federal Public Works Administration (PWA). The PWA paid 45 percent of construction costs and by the middle of 1940 had granted $926,143 for port of San Francisco projects, including Piers 9, 19, 35, and 37.[49]

DECLINE OF THE BOARD OF STATE HARBOR COMMISSIONERS

During World War II, the BSHC was occupied with facilitating military use of port property. After the war, it became apparent that the fundamental structure of the agency was no longer effective. According to a critical historical study of the issue by Gerald Nash, "In the post World War II era many weaknesses of state management reappeared in stronger measure, . . . San Francisco was losing business to other Pacific ports and also to other forms of transportation." Following studies in 1953 and 1959, "It was clear by 1960 that the structure of state harbor

administration required a thorough reorganization." By that time, there was a "different
configuration of interests" than had given rise
to and sustained the BSHC, a state agency with
limited flexibility in administrative and financial
matters. Most of all, the growth of competition
from other Bay Area ports, especially Oakland,
which had geographical advantages of space
and access to both rail and truck transportation
routes, presented challenges that the BSHC could
not meet.[50]

As an interim measure, on September 11,
1957, the three-member BSHC was increased to
a five-member entity called the San Francisco
Port Authority, still a state agency. On February
7, 1969, state control over the port was transferred to the San Francisco Port Commission,
a new city agency. Ironically, it was about this
time that the port entered its biggest crisis, represented by the surprisingly rapid adoption of
containerized shipping and the emergence of the
port of Oakland as a major container port.

After the extension of the Belt
Railroad past the Ferry Building
in 1913, the BSHC had increased
responsibilities for managing traffic
and public safety while maintaining
efficient rail and port operations.

SHIPS, RAILS, AND TRUCKS

During the nineteenth century, there was no consistent order to the location of businesses along the waterfront. Ferries were the exception. The 1875 Ferry House, the immediate precursor to the Ferry Building, stood specifically at the foot of Market Street so that ferry passengers could transfer conveniently to horse-car lines that funneled to that point via the city's main artery.

The three iconic buildings in this 1922 photograph—the Ferry Building tower, the Southern Pacific Building, and the Matson Building—represent the Board of State Harbor Commissioners, the railroads, and the shipping companies, respectively, three of the principal operators at the port.

Top: The focal point of transportation at the port was the Ferry Building, from its completion in 1898 until the opening of the Bay Bridge in 1936. Ferryboats, streetcars turning at the foot of Market Street, pedestrians crossing the Embarcadero on the viaduct, motor vehicles passing under the streetcar turnaround, and the Belt Railroad all converge at the Ferry Building in this 1936 view.

Bottom: Horse-drawn conveyances driven by teamsters were a principal means of moving goods at the port until long after the introduction of motor vehicles. This photograph was taken at China Basin in 1904.

As the port was rebuilt in the twentieth century, the port's managers imposed order on the piers: "Pier assignments have been rearranged, to bring together in convenient locations ships engaged in the same character of business."[1] In other words, inland shipping service was located closest to the Ferry Building; coastwise, intercoastal, and foreign services were successively distant from it. As before, the heaviest passenger traffic occurred between the ferries and the transportation on Market Street, whose horse-car lines were joined by horse-drawn omnibuses and succeeded by cable cars and streetcars. Eventually, 8,500 streetcars a week would turn around in front of the Ferry Building.

Shipping companies performed the various classifications of service: inland, coastwise, intercoastal, and foreign. The companies with the most business occupied entire piers and functioned as the operators of those piers, which made them responsible for any docked ships— usually their own and often those of others with which they had prior arrangements. The state's wharfingers were responsible for assigning arriving ships to berths, and although ships were generally sent to their company's piers, congestion or other special circumstances could cause ships to be sent to the piers of unrelated companies.

Once cargo was unloaded onto a pier, it had to be transshipped to a place of storage or to a final destination. In the earliest years of the port, human- or animal-powered carts and wagons accomplished this task. When the Board of State Harbor Commissioners (BSHC) took control of the port in 1863, it charged shippers with tariffs that were structured to encourage the quick removal of cargo from piers and the rapid departure of ships from berths. Imposed by the chief wharfinger and his deputies, these fees were known as *tolls* (charges for the passage of passengers or goods over a wharf; also *wharfage*), *demurrage* (charges for cargo or vehicles remaining on a wharf or pier longer than the minimal time allowed by payment of the toll), and *dockage* (charges for use of a berth by a vessel). These tariffs were a source of income for the port and an incentive for efficient loading and unloading of cargo. While various forms of land transportation were essential to the functioning of the port, the port itself was fundamentally a place

for ships. Many shipping companies maintained offices in the bulkhead buildings at the front of the piers, as well as downtown. As modernization of the port's facilities began in 1908, these companies made an active and formalized contribution to the design of wharves, piers, and cargo-handling equipment.

To accommodate various types of vessels, the BSHC built and rebuilt a system of wharves and piers. These varied in dimension, proportion, and length depending on the types of ships to be served as well as the availability of land transportation and cargo-handling technology. From the early days of the port to the mid-twentieth century, as ships became longer and larger, so piers were redesigned to be longer and wider. By 1900, almost all piers were built with long sheds to shelter cargo that was in transit. The suitability of the piers to the kinds of ships that used them was essential to efficient operations, and efficient operations were essential to the commercial success of the port.

WATERBORNE TRANSPORTATION

From the beginning, San Francisco's port has been the nexus of transportation in the city. Like all ports, San Francisco's was built first of all to serve ships, but at the same time it needed to interact with various forms of transportation in order to move cargo and passengers to and from other sites. Because of the geography of the region, San Francisco's transportation system long remained focused at the port. Unlike Chicago, for example, which began as a port and was transformed by the railroads, San Francisco remained primarily a port city, even with the development of connections to major long-distance rail lines and a substantial local rail infrastructure.

The port of San Francisco developed with facilities to serve a variety of types of vessels, including ferryboats, riverboats, oceangoing vessels, sailing ships, steamships, motor ships, barges, car ferries, car floats, freighters, and passenger ships. Wind-powered vessels were classified as ships, barks, barkentines, brigs, schooners, and sloops. Steamships were classified as ocean steamers or as bay and river steamers.[2]

In addition to the ferries that crossed the bay, the vessels that called in San Francisco were classified as coastwise (serving the Pacific Coast ports of the United States), inland (serving bay and river ports, including Stockton, Sacramento, Oakland, Redwood City, Richmond, and Vallejo), intercoastal (serving East and Gulf Coast ports

This 1910 view of Pier 36 juxtaposes old and new technologies: sailing ships, whose era was ending, and modern, industrial-era pier construction, which entailed using reinforced concrete and incorporating a terminal for railcar transfers.

This 1933 view of Pier 40 shows a functioning, modern pier of that era, including steamships equipped with cranes for loading and unloading, railcars on the aprons to carry cargo to or from nearby warehouses, and a transit shed for temporary storage of goods in the process of transshipment.

of the United States), and foreign (serving ports outside of the United States). Numerous types of smaller vessels, including tug boats, pilot boats, fireboats, lighters, launches, coal and oil bunkers (barges equipped with fuel-storage bins or tanks), dredges, and pile-driving rigs, performed work in and around the port.

Over time, the number, the mode of operation, and the type of vessels at the port changed. However, it is difficult to chart these changes because of the different ways shipping statistics were recorded. One of the most fundamental developments was the steady increase in size of oceangoing vessels after the mid-nineteenth century. This was in large part a function of the shift from wind power to steam power—a transition that took more than fifty years. For steam-powered ships, another change took place in the conversion from coal to oil, a process that was fully under way in 1910–1912 when the first tanks for fuel oil were built on port property.[3] Some small vessels, such as launches, ran on gasoline by the mid-1920s. In 1912 and 1913, the port of San Francisco was visited for the first time by a large steam-powered passenger ship, *The Cleveland*, a "mighty cruise liner—one of the type that circles the globe with hundreds of tourists."[4] By the mid-1920s, ships of this sort came routinely to San Francisco and required facilities to serve them.

The number of vessels that called fluctuated. In the biennium of 1910–1912, 1,472 vessels (not including barges and lighters) docked in San Francisco, many of them several times. The BSHC recorded 787 vessels in 1924 and 1,053 vessels in 1926.

LAND TRANSPORTATION

It was in the interest of both the shipping companies and the BSHC to move cargo quickly to and from the waterfront. Accordingly, there was constant pressure to facilitate and improve the means of land transportation.

When the engineer T. J. Arnold addressed the problems of the original seawall in 1873 he proposed a continuous, curving two-hundred-foot-wide thoroughfare along the waterfront in place of the zigzag pattern caused by the way the grid of streets then under construction met the waterfront at a diagonal. After the BSHC adopted this plan in 1878, East Street was built gradually as sections of the seawall were finished. The new design substantially shortened the distances needed to haul cargo along the waterfront, especially between the piers and warehouses in the two wholesale districts, and it established a busy working area that, together with the seawall lots, was integral to the overall operations of the port, providing the space needed to move cargo and to hold it temporarily while ships entered and left. The name East Street was changed to the Embarcadero in 1909, though as late as 1921 the city directory still listed some businesses on East Street. After it was finally completed, one of the harbor commissioners described it as a "marginal street belting the entire harbor. This street is now used as a great thoroughfare of the city over which passes thousands upon thousands of tons of merchandise to and from all piers."[5] In the beginning, teamsters and drayage companies were organized to haul cargo between the waterfront and destinations in San Francisco and down the peninsula. Gradually, the role of horse-drawn conveyances was taken over by rail and motor-vehicle transportation.

SOUTHERN PACIFIC AND OTHER RAILROADS

When the San Francisco and San Jose Railroad— the city's first rail line—was completed in January 1864, it stopped many blocks short of the waterfront. In the East Bay, the San Francisco and Oakland Ferry Railroad (from central Oakland to the Oakland Wharf) was completed in September 1863, the San Francisco and Alameda Railroad in 1864, and the Central Pacific Railroad (the transcontinental railroad) in 1869. These provided important linkages to the San Francisco waterfront but no rail lines at the port itself.

The first Southern Pacific Railroad headquarters was located near its places of operation rather than downtown with the offices of other large companies. Built about 1872 at the northeast corner of Fourth and Townsend streets, it stood across the street from a simple wooden passenger depot and rail yards, and a few blocks from its car-ferry facilities.

Belt Railroad locomotives, which had a wide turning radius, moved freight cars between piers and warehouses. This photograph from the 1920s shows a train leaving Pier 41 and the gasworks at Powell and Jefferson streets.

Left: In this 1941 view south from Green Street along the portion of the Embarcadero allocated to the Belt Railroad, Pier 11 is on the left and freight cars of the Western Pacific are temporarily stored in Seawall Lot 12 on the right.

Middle: Belt Railroad access to the piers was designed in various ways. Early tracks brought the locomotive into the center of the transit shed; all others led only to the side aprons, such as at Pier 24, where the tracks passed through the arch and out through the sides.

Right: Rail cars were loaded and unloaded from car floats by means of ramps that were raised and lowered according to the tide by hoisting mechanisms. This Santa Fe car ferry, whose hoisting tower was across China Basin from Pier 46A, shuttled between San Francisco and its East Bay terminal in Point Richmond from 1900 until after World War II.

The first rail service at the port was established in 1872 when the Central Pacific Railroad, the predecessor of the Southern Pacific, built a car-ferry terminal at the foot of Second Street. Tracks ran from this terminal to the Central Pacific rail yards a block to the southwest, between Townsend and Berry streets. With these facilities, Central Pacific railcars were brought by ferry from the terminus of the transcontinental line in Oakland to the port of San Francisco and the nearby rail yards almost twenty years before any other railroad operated at the port. By 1885, these facilities were all part of the Southern Pacific Railroad. Not only was Southern Pacific located in this area, but so also were the facilities of the Pacific Mail Steamship Company, with which Southern Pacific negotiated a series of secret contracts fixing freight rates beginning in 1871. The railroad came to control the steamship company and eventually dominated the southern part of the port to such an extent that the area above China Basin, despite its public ownership, was known as Southern Pacific territory. The same company also had extensive facilities on the northern waterfront, including the Davis Street Wharf at Davis and Vallejo streets. In 1875, while retaining the Davis Street Wharf for other purposes, Central Pacific ferries began operating out of the new Ferry House at the foot of Market Street. In addition to the names of the destinations of ferryboats and passenger lines, the initials "C.P.R.R." (for Central Pacific Railroad) appeared boldly on the building. In the early 1880s the California Steam Navigation Company,

owned by the Central Pacific, provided service from a wharf at Davis Street and Broadway to bay and river ports.

In 1911, after taking office as governor of California on a Progressive platform, Hiram Johnson appointed new harbor commissioners who set about to remove the influence of the Southern Pacific company at the port:

> Nowhere in the administrative branch of the state government was the malign influence of that dominating corporation more conspicuously illustrated than in the condition and management of the San Francisco harbor. For over forty years, with infrequent intervals, not long enough to effect much of a reform, the Southern Pacific practically owned and operated the waterfront, and used it as a piece of private business property for the advancement of its own political and business interests.[6]

Even after this reform, the planner Werner Hegemann wrote in 1915 that the Belt Railroad "gives . . . physical connection with only one single track line [Southern Pacific]. All other trunk lines have to connect by water, i.e., by the expensive system of car floating."[7]

Apart from short-lived construction rail lines—such as the steam paddy that filled the tidelands with sand from leveled hills from 1852 to 1873, and the line that carried quarried stone for the foundations of the new City Hall from the waterfront to the City Hall Reservation near Eighth and Market streets in 1871—no other railroads served the port of San Francisco until the 1890s. In 1900, there was a Santa Fe Railway wharf at Main Street for freight barges connecting to the new transcontinental line in Oakland. And ten years later, improvements were made to accommodate car ferries from the new Western Pacific transcontinental line in Richmond.

BELT RAILROAD

As part of his original conception for the port when he developed his proposal for the new seawall, in 1873 T. J. Arnold recommended a railroad along East Street (later the Embarcadero) that would link the piers to the nearby ware-houses. It was not until 1889 that the BSHC approved a plan for the construction of the Belt Railroad, which the board would own and operate. At its peak of operation, the Belt Railroad was a whole system that included rail spurs, the main lines in the Embarcadero, car-ferry slips along the waterfront, rail yards in the seawall lots, eight locomotives (original steam locomotives were replaced by diesel locomotives by the 1950s), an office (now called Pier 29 Annex), a roundhouse across the Embarcadero from the office, a connection to the Southern Pacific

To accommodate its various users, the Embarcadero was divided into a paved zone for motor vehicles, a zone of basalt-block paving for horse traffic, and a track zone for the Belt Railroad. This 1926 view north includes Pier 11 on the right and the tower of a Sperry Flour warehouse in the distance, at the northeast corner of Sansome and Green streets.

With the big increase in truck traffic after the opening of the Bay Bridge in 1936, patterns of land use along the Embarcadero and in the seawall lots underwent major changes. In this 1948 view, trucks stand and load in Seawall Lot 16, across from Pier 7. In the early part of the twentieth century, this lot was the site of the Free Public Market.

A vehicular subway under the streetcar turnaround opened in 1925. Here, a low flatbed truck, adapted for easy loading on the piers, enters the subway.

Responding to both the requirements of larger ships and the increasing use of trucks, a new type of pier was introduced. These so-called quay-type piers either were adapted from existing structures, such as Pier 15–17, shown here in 1957 shortly after its completion, or were built new, such as Piers 45, 48, and 50.

Railroad line on Townsend Street, and spurs to numerous commercial warehouses inland from the waterfront, both north and south of Market Street.

The locomotives pulled railcars owned by commercial railroad companies. This made it possible to load and unload ships at the piers and to efficiently transport the cargo between the piers and the warehouses.

Construction of the Belt Railroad occurred in phases beginning in 1890, "starting from the old freight ferry slip at the foot of Lombard Street and running thence to Powell Street on the west side and Pacific Street on the southeast. Its total length was about a mile and it was a three-rail track, so that narrow gauge cars could be hauled as well as standard gauge. The rails were light and the pavement between the rails was planked."[8] The railroad was gradually extended as sections of the seawall and its associated thoroughfare were completed, and as money became available.

With the construction of the Belt Railroad, connections to the commercial railroads on the Oakland side of the bay were established via "car ferry transfer . . . at the foot of Lombard Street."[9] The system allowed cargo to be "unloaded from the ship's side in San Francisco, trucked into the waiting freight car and switched off on a railroad journey to Mexico or New York without further transfer."[10] According to the historian Gerald Nash, this had a radical effect: "The Belt Railroad made it possible to ship directly to and from San Francisco without unloading for the trip across the bay, and this altered the whole pattern of freight movements in the area."[11] Rail yards were built in the seawall lots to hold empty railcars.

Initially, the Belt Railroad served only the piers north of Market Street. Then, "early in 1910 construction was commenced on the Belt Railroad south of Market Street, beginning at a point near the foot of Spear Street and running southerly along East Street to the vicinity of the Pacific Mail docks (piers 42 and 44)."[12] This new section of the Belt Railroad was connected to rail spurs on each of several new piers: Piers 34, 36, 38, 40, 42, and 44. The BSHC reported in 1910: "Pier 36 is built with a ferry car slip on the outer end, and is now giving service to all of the railroads for the exchange of cars."[13]

When the Belt Railroad was built, the design of piers and transit sheds was modified to accommodate both the weight of the railcars and locomotives and also the different operations involved in moving goods between railcars and ships. At first, rail spurs ran down the center of the piers, inside the transit sheds. After about 1910, the spurs were built on the aprons, outside the transit sheds. In both cases, doorways had to be large enough to accommodate locomotives, which often passed through the bulkhead buildings to the aprons alongside the transit sheds. The wide turning radius needed by the

railcars in order to make the curve between the Embarcadero and the piers was an unavoidable factor in building the tracks of the rail spurs.

The two sections of the Belt Railroad, north and south of Market Street, operated separately until January 27, 1913, when they were connected. Around the same time, construction was begun on two new car-ferry slips at Powell and Mason streets; in the biennium of 1928–1930, one of them was removed and its hoisting tower rebuilt at the end of Pier 45, then nearing completion. They allowed for linkage to the Southern Pacific, Western Pacific, and Santa Fe rail lines in Oakland and Richmond; the San Francisco, Napa, and Calistoga Railroad in Vallejo; and the Northwestern Pacific Railroad in Sausalito.

By the time of this 1953 photograph, truck traffic on the Embarcadero was dominated by passenger traffic, a mix of port workers, businessmen, and leisure drivers, the latter of which were observed as far back as the mid-1920s.

The car-ferry slips, the expanding Belt Railroad yards on the seawall lots, and the links to commercial rail yards on both sides of China Basin established a complete system of rail-to-port connections.

About 1900, the Santa Fe Railway operated a car-ferry slip at the southeast corner of China Basin, where the basin meets the bay. Prior to 1906, the Southern Pacific Railroad established its car-ferry slip between the foot of El Dorado Street and Sixteenth Street. By 1922, the Western Pacific Railroad ran a car-ferry slip at the foot

of Twenty-Fifth Street. And sometime after July 1948, the Santa Fe Railway began operation of a second car-ferry slip at Pier 52. These slips were all taken out of service between 1966 and the early 1980s. Of this group, only a portion of the second Santa Fe slip survives—the hoisting tower at Pier 52.

Along with rail lines and car-ferry facilities, the Belt Railroad built rail yards on the seawall lots inshore of the Embarcadero. By 1918, nine hundred cars could be accommodated in these yards. Among many such statements, the BSHC wrote in 1914: "Few harbor improvements are more sought by all ports than the bringing of ship and railroad car close together, side by side if possible, so as to promote dispatch and cheapness in transferring freight";[14] and, in 1916: "San Francisco undoubtedly now has the most complete harbor belt line railroad switching system in the country."[15]

In 1914, to support military efforts related to the war in Europe, a tunnel was built to extend

the Belt Railroad to Fort Mason. From there it was easy to lengthen it still farther to the site of the Panama-Pacific International Exposition, then under construction. In 1917, the railroad was extended to the Presidio. By the early 1920s, the Belt Railroad had fifty-four miles of track.

Three years after the north and south sections of the Belt Railroad were joined, the BSHC boasted:

> By these constructions and extensions, a continuous belt railroad switching system, adequately equipped, is now in full and successful operation around the whole active harbor front of San Francisco, from the United States transport docks on the north and west to Channel street on the south. It is a tremendous gain to the harbor, and its real advantages only become properly estimated when it is recollected than even such a great seaport as New York has no harbor belt line.[16]

The Belt Railroad required a large staff, all employees of the BSHC. Job categories included clerks, engineers, firemen, yardmasters, foremen, and switchmen. The number of employees fluctuated. In 1938, between peaks of employment in the 1920s and the 1940s, there were 150 employees of the Belt Railroad.

Work around the railroad was dangerous for anyone who got in the way of moving cars. Settlements for injuries and deaths were frequently discussed in the attorney's section of the BSHC's biennial reports—always denying the board's responsibility. There appear to have been fewer accidents after the establishment of the Industrial Accident Commission in 1911.

MOTOR VEHICLES

Around the time that the port's rail system reached maturity with the connection of the Belt Railroad across Market Street, accommodations began to be made for a new form of land transportation. With the "general adoption of the auto truck,"[17] a new design for pier aprons was introduced to support their heavier loads. By 1916, a section of the Embarcadero from Bay Street to a point between Stockton and Powell streets was paved with smooth asphalt "to accommodate the enormously increased automobile travel."[18] Smooth surfaces provided more comfortable rides for motor vehicles, whereas basalt-block paving provided better traction for horse-drawn

Beginning in the 1920s, the arrival and departure of passenger liners brought intense periods of traffic congestion that inhibited the movement of goods along the Embarcadero. In this 1930s view, cars queue up for a passenger liner at Pier 37. Piers 39 and 41 are visible in the distance. The Otis Elevator Building and a PG&E gasholder are on the left.

vehicles. A program was begun to divide the Embarcadero into three zones that were generally parallel to the seawall: rail tracks for the Belt Railroad, basalt-block paving for horse-drawn vehicles, and asphalt paving for automobiles and trucks.

The convergence of the Belt Railroad, the municipal railway, and pedestrian traffic in front of the Ferry Building; the emergence and rapid increase of motor-vehicle traffic along the entire Embarcadero; and the increase in all kinds of traffic except for that of horse-drawn vehicles—which continued to be used nonetheless—created new problems that called for various solutions. In the biennium of 1918–1920, the BSHC established a new position of traffic manager to deal with these issues. To separate pedestrians from other forms of traffic, "a viaduct extending from the second floor of the Ferry Building, across the Embarcadero to the west side of the street"[19] was begun in 1918 and opened on May 17, 1919. At the time, the BSHC intended "to build a second viaduct on the south

side of the building,"[20] but this was never done. On September 6, 1923, plans were adopted for "a vehicular subway under the ferry street car loop to divert such travel from the Market Street crossing on The Embarcadero and make the thoroughfare safe for many thousands of pedestrians."[21] This was completed on May 2, 1925.

In the biennium of 1930–1932, the last sections of the Embarcadero were paved with asphalt, creating "a continuous smooth thoroughfare from the channel to Taylor Street."[22] From the 1920s to the 1950s, "Movement between ship and warehouse [was] usually affected by truck and the special type of low-slung trucks in use [provided] the most convenient means of handling merchandise."[23] This type of truck may have become popular in part because of a local manufacturing plant— the Doane Motor Truck Company, established at Third and Perry streets in 1917. Improved conditions for motor vehicles were associated with an increase in traffic accidents and in the use of heavy trucks. For the first time, the BSHC noted

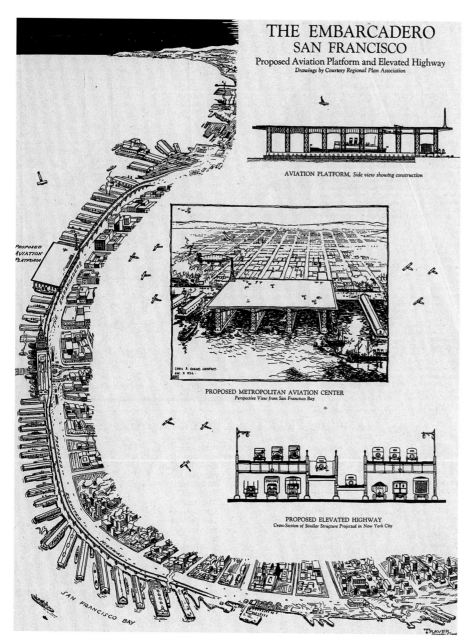

THE EMBARCADERO
SAN FRANCISCO
Proposed Aviation Platform and Elevated Highway
Drawings by Courtesy Regional Plan Association

AVIATION PLATFORM, *Side view showing construction*

PROPOSED METROPOLITAN AVIATION CENTER
Perspective View from San Francisco Bay

PROPOSED ELEVATED HIGHWAY
Cross-Section of Similar Structure Projected in New York City

This 1926 proposal by architect Lewis Hobart was an attempt to integrate new forms of transportation with existing port operations that had developed to link ships with railroads. Loosely following the Burnham Plan of 1905, and anticipating the Embarcadero Freeway, Hobart proposed an elevated highway. In addition, from Pier 24 to Pier 32, he suggested an Aviation Platform for dirigibles and small planes.

substantial non-port use of the working thoroughfare. In 1922, an automobile-ferry line began running between Hyde Street and Sausalito, and five years later, a new automobile-ferry terminal was opened at Hyde Street, feeding traffic from Marin County and Berkeley onto the Embarcadero. As the BSHC reported, "In the past few years, the Embarcadero has become an artery for private pleasure vehicles."[24]

In the 1930s, the opening of the Bay Bridge and the Golden Gate Bridge had a profound effect on the port's complex overlapping and interdependent transportation systems. In anticipation, the BSHC noted, "Modern highways are developing a very important form of transportation in the way of motor passenger bus and truck transport service."[25] Bulkhead-connector buildings and wider wharves for quay-type piers were built to accommodate trucks. If the commissioners were concerned about the changes the bridges would bring, there was little they could do about it, even though the Bay Bridge was built partly on the port's property and required the port's approval. In the biennium when the bridges opened (the Bay Bridge on November 12, 1936; the Golden Gate Bridge on May 27, 1937) the changes were immediate: "Today much of the port's inbound and outbound waterborne cargo is moved to and from the docks by trucks using the bridges."[26] At that time there were "more than thirty common carrier truck lines"[27] serving the port of San Francisco. The opening of the bridges resulted in a decrease in Belt Railroad traffic, ferry traffic, and some shipping: "The loss in the inland waterway trade is attributable principally to the completion of the San Francisco-Oakland Bay Bridge and the Golden Gate Bridge which caused the discontinuance of extensive ferryboat services and deprived the port of large waterborne tonnage movements." As a related effect, "The loss in coastwise trade was caused by rail and truck carrier competition."[28] The loss of ferry traffic was also expected to diminish the need for ferryboat facilities, allowing for "replacement of ferry slips in the immediate Ferry Building area with cargo piers, giving the port still more berthing space for deep water ships."[29] In this way, the BSHC looked at the new role of trucks

as providing an opportunity to relieve shipping congestion.

When the electrified trains of the Southern Pacific and the Key System began operating over the Bay Bridge in January 1939, ferry service to the East Bay was discontinued. This left the Ferry Building without its principal reason for being, and consideration was given to using it as either a bus terminal or a steamship terminal.

The introduction of Bay Bridge trains could not stop the general trend toward still greater dependence on motor vehicles. The width of the Embarcadero continued to be used as a working area, which, the commissioners noted, "permits orderly and rapid trucking."[30] This trend accelerated after World War II. In 1957, the port reported, "About 75 percent of the Port's inbound and outbound cargo moves to and from piers by truck. More than 10,000 Western and transcontinental trucking firms are involved."[31] By mid-1940, the increase in truck traffic and an even larger increase in automobile traffic— from commuters driving to work—had led to the establishment of a new Traffic Department and an organized effort to accommodate automobile parking by "grading, cleaning, and surfacing of the Embarcadero sea wall lots to provide free public automobile parking."[32] In 1948, the first parking meters were installed along the

Embarcadero, and by 1958 the little-used rail yards on the seawall lots were converted to parking lots.

When the elevated Embarcadero Freeway was built on port property—a long stretch of the Embarcadero and several seawall lots—it displaced parking, turning areas for trucks, and tracks and yards of the Belt Railroad. The first section of the freeway was finished in 1956. The freeway was completed in late 1958 and opened in February 1959. At about the same time, the trains were taken off the Bay Bridge, which further increased the use of motor vehicles.

Left: Plans for the Embarcadero Freeway in the mid-1950s were accompanied by proposals for alternative designs, such as this idea by Vernon DeMars and Theodore Osmundson, an architect and a landscape architect.

Right: Once the freeway design by the State Highway Department was approved, proposals like this one were made to try to ameliorate the visual and environmental blight it brought to the Ferry Building. Improving the rest of the waterfront was ignored.

The completion of the Embarcadero Freeway in 1959 was only one of many major changes in the area of the port. This 1965 view from Golden Gateway Center, which replaced much of the Produce District, shows the rest of the neighborhood in the process of being cleared to make way for the Embarcadero Center.

TENANTS AND WORKERS

358.- SHIPPING SCENE ON THE WHARF - SAN FRANCISCO, C

E very day during its busy years the port of San Francisco was swarmed with people: the five hundred employees of the Board of State Harbor Commissioners (BSHC); clerks and officials of the shipping companies that rented offices in the bulkhead buildings; managers, foremen, and skilled workers in the construction companies engaged in the constant building, repair, and rebuilding of the port's structures; sailors and longshoremen loading and unloading ships; teamsters and drivers hauling cargo and materials to and from the port; and a fluctuating number of laborers doing the hard physical work of the port—on the ships and piers, on the streets and seawall lots, and on the Belt Railroad. On top of this, by far, the largest number of people were the thousands of ship and ferry passengers who passed through the port each day, most coming and going on streetcars that terminated at the Ferry Building.

This busy 1907 scene at the Howard Street Wharf shows the key steps in the process of cargo handling during that era. Break-bulk cargo (boxes of canned salmon) is being unloaded from a ship in a sling that is loaded by seamen and powered by a steam donkey. Then boxes on the wharf are loaded by longshoremen onto flatbed wagons and hauled away by teamsters. On the left is a large coal loader.

Most of the work at the port was physical labor, much of it hard and dangerous. Sailors lacked basic rights and worked in virtual slavery, subject to corporal punishment and imprisonment for desertion. The term *shanghai*, referring to the kidnapping of men to serve on sailing vessels, symbolizes the sailors' lot; it was reputedly coined in San Francisco in the early 1850s.[1] Not until the passage of the La Follette Seamen's Act in 1915 were sailors emancipated, but even then their working conditions generally remained harsh.

Land-based workers suffered hardships in other ways. There was little recourse for the victims or their families following the frequent accidents in which workers were injured or killed until the establishment of the California Industrial Accident Board in 1911 and compulsory insurance for workers in 1913. The newspapers were full of stories of injuries and deaths like that of John Dugan Jr., who "was killed in November 1891, by being caught under a heavy gate which fell from the shed situated on section 4 of the seawall"[2] and "P. H. Brandt, a longshoreman who lives on Castro Street, [who] fell down the hold of the bark *Fresno*, lying at Fremont-street wharf, . . . fracturing his left shoulder and bruising his back and left hip. He lies at the receiving hospital."[3]

The typical response of the port's legal department was expressed without specifics. For example, attorney James H. Budd commented in 1902: "Several accidents occurring on the Belt Railroad have required my presence before the

Of the many people at the port every day, the largest number were members of the public making connections between city transit systems and commuter ferries or passenger lines. This photograph was taken at 5:20 p.m. on March 2, 1915.

coroner, or in court, to the end that the interests of the State and Board be protected. The accidents were shown to have been without negligence on part of the Board and to have occurred under circumstances exempting the State from liability."[4]

Over time, the dangers and hardships of waterfront work were ameliorated in two ways— by advances in cargo-handling technology and by the organization of labor.

CARGO HANDLING

Improvements in cargo-handling technology were a mixed blessing to workers. New machinery and systems lessened the burden of backbreaking work even when they were no less dangerous than the old ways. But they also resulted in a need for fewer workers.

The most basic work at the port was the loading and unloading of ships and the movement of cargo into transit sheds and away from the piers to warehouses or other destinations.[5] The process of moving cargo changed over time, often in small steps. For most of its history, San Francisco was a break-bulk port. Cargo was broken up into units—barrels, sacks, or boxes—that could be handled by one man or a few men in teams. Notoriously, one man traditionally handled sugar in three-hundred-pound bags. Until World War I,

most cargo in San Francisco was moved between piers and ships by means of winches and booms or derricks in rope slings, "the old piece of hoisting equipment, taking some burden off the back," according to Otto Hagel, a longshoreman and historian.[6] The first winches were powered by human or animal power. Following the invention in 1881 of the steam donkey, a small portable engine that could be moved as needed, these machines were used on the piers. In 1920, the port first provided electricity to the piers for "electric cargo handling machinery."[7]

For many years, sling loads were pulled from a ship and lowered onto the pier apron. There, the sling was opened and its contents sorted. Hand trucks making multiple trips delivered the goods to designated areas in the transit shed, where they were piled according to the hand or stage system, a standard method of organizing unloaded cargo. This process was simplified by the introduction of the four-wheel platform hand truck in 1907. With this conveyance, the sling was placed directly on a truck that the longshoreman pulled into the shed, saving many trips. At the same time, the sling board was introduced; this protected the cargo in a sling and made it possible to move larger loads.

Roy MacElwee, a prolific authority on waterfront facilities, and Thomas R. Taylor described

Above: Employees of a contractor hired by the port are shown here constructing a section of the bulkhead wharf, building forms, setting rebar, and pouring concrete. In the background is an ever-present pile-driving rig.

Opposite: Pile drivers, known as pile butts, pose in front of a pile-driving rig at ferry slip no. 3 behind the Ferry Building in 1911. The moveable wooden derrick provided a frame for a steam hammer that loudly pounded concrete piles into the mud to serve as a structural foundation.

work on the waterfront just before the rapid changes that occurred in the 1920s: "The stevedore's gang for each hatch unloading usually consists of 23 longshoremen, six in the 'hold,' five sailormen on deck and twelve men on the pier." A stevedore and his gang were supervised by a chief or boss stevedore, who had long experience as a longshoreman and was an expert on loading ships: "Ships have their own individuality and do not carry their loads alike. [The boss stevedore] is assisted by the ship's officers, who also acquire an intimate knowledge of how a cargo can best be stowed on their own particular vessel. The ship must be loaded to capacity so as to avoid waste of carrying space, and yet it must not be loaded below the safe-load line or in such a manner as to strain hull or expose cargo to damage."[8]

The gangs described here were, in fact, made up of two groups: seamen attached to the ship and longshoremen under the direction of a stevedoring company based in the port. In 1919, the United States Railroad Administration standardized these relationships, so that seamen who worked on the ships were responsible for moving cargo between the ships and the pier aprons, and longshoremen were responsible for moving cargo between the pier aprons and the transit sheds, railcars, or trucks.[9]

A timekeeper and sometimes a tallyman employed by the BSHC monitored the gangs on the piers. These workers kept track of the time each longshoreman spent on the pier, paid the longshoremen with cash in pay envelopes, and reported accidents. "It requires a clear head to be a timekeeper, as he has to charge labor time against forty-eight different items (in the cost accounting of [one] company . . .)."[10]

While each pier had a timekeeper, areas of the port were assigned to a single wharfinger. The wharfinger was an officer of the BSHC and represented the port at the piers, which were rented to shipping companies. The wharfinger had final responsibility for assigning ships to piers and assessed fees due to the port for the use of a pier by a ship—wharfage, dockage, and demurrage.

During the first eighty-five years of the port's history, the longshoreman's day began early in the morning with a gathering of workers hoping to be hired for the day. Known as the shape-up, this gathering took place at various piers and, after it opened in 1898, in front of the Ferry Building. The shape-up was a long, degrading ritual—lasting up to two hours—that occurred every day regardless of the weather. Workers never knew if they would be hired. No one was paid until the work began. And the process was corrupted by bribes and favoritism.

The shape-up began when a gang boss, an employee of a stevedoring company hired by a shipping company, faced the crowd of waiting men. The historian Boris Stern described a typical shape-up in 1932:

> But the eyes of all men in the "shape" are fastened upon every move of the hiring foreman who either calls out the men by their names or walks slowly along the "shape" pointing with his finger at a man here in the first row, at another man in the second row, and perhaps still a third man in the last row. A few seconds later he picks a whole group of five or more men who are standing together and sends them to the gate where they give their names to the clerk and receive the brass number which entitles them to work on the pier. . . . When the picking is finished, the men who were unfortunate enough to be left behind, sullenly and sadly move away from the pier only to return several hours later in the hope of being more successful in the next "shape."[11]

DRIVING CONCRETE PILES IN SLIP 3   SEPT. 23RD 1911.

One of the perennial cargoes at the port for most of its history was lumber. This pre-1912 view shows one of several lumberyards along China Basin.

Longshoremen with hand trucks load a ferry on the Sacramento River with boxes of potatoes bound for San Francisco.

Longshoremen, who loaded ships, worked in groups called gangs under the direction of a stevedore.

Gangs of seamen handled cargo on ships. This 1946 view of a gang in the hold includes black workers, who were commonly excluded from hiring before the 1934 strike.

A great victory of the 1934 longshoremen's strike was the elimination of the shape-up and its replacement by a hiring hall.

This partial portrait of work at the port only looks at one arena of activity, albeit a central and well-recognized kind of work. In addition, railroad workers and teamsters hauled cargo to commercial warehouses, where it was handled by warehousemen, or to the rail yards of commercial railroads. Clerks recorded the movements of cargo. Pile drivers built the bulkhead wharf and the piers; carpenters, metal workers, electricians, painters, and others built the transit sheds, bulkhead buildings, and other buildings on the waterfront. Because maintenance is a particular problem in the exposed conditions on the waterfront, these laborers also had an essential role in the unending maintenance of buildings and structures at the port. Similarly, laborers built and repaired the ships that came to the port. Shipbuilders and repair workers

included shipwrights, coppersmiths and other metal tradesmen, riggers, caulkers, ship painters, and ship scalers.

THE ORGANIZATION OF LABOR

The hardships of work at the port were also mitigated as a result of the organization of labor. This was not a steady progression but instead involved many swings of the pendulum.

In the first twenty years of port activity, chronic labor shortages produced extremely high wages. Even within this period, however, unstable conditions lead to fluctuating wages, deflation, and unemployment. This instability stimulated the formation of unions and other labor organizations on the waterfront and elsewhere in San Francisco. According to labor historian David Selvin, "Nearly all trades in San Francisco organized during the 1850s: teamsters, draymen, lightermen, riggers, and stevedores in 1851; . . . shipwrights, carpenters, and caulkers in 1853." In conjunction with strikes in 1851 and 1853, the first longshoremen's union in San Francisco, the Riggers' and Stevedores' Association, was formed. From 1863 to 1866, the San Francisco Trades Union served as an umbrella organization for unions and labor interests. As a result of these efforts, the eight-hour day was adopted for various waterfront trades.[12]

The arrival of the transcontinental railroad in 1869 ushered in a new era of hard times for workers by lowering prices and ending the labor shortage in California. The labor movement collapsed, unions folded, and the eight-hour day was abandoned. The economic nadir of this period began with the failure of the Bank of California in 1875. By 1877 a large number of unemployed white workers in all trades turned against the Chinese and those who employed them, including two of the key businesses at the port—the Central Pacific Railroad, which was built largely by Chinese workers, and the Pacific

For most of its history, San Francisco was a break-bulk port—its primary cargoes were broken down into units that one man could carry or maneuver, such as barrels, bales, sacks, or boxes. This view of the interior of a transit shed is from the 1920s.

Mail Steamship Company, whose ships were the principal means by which Chinese workers came to San Francisco.

As economic conditions improved, labor at the port and elsewhere renewed its efforts to organize. A federation of labor unions called the Trades Assembly was formed in 1878. Frank Roney, a founder of the Seamen's Protective Union in 1880, took over the Trades Assembly and used it as a base for organizing unions in a variety of areas, many of which included waterfront workers. One group, the wharf builders, was organized in 1883 and advocated for nine-hour days. In 1886, there was a mass meeting of waterfront unions: the Coast Seamen's Union, the Steamshipmen's Protective Union, the Steamship Sailor's Union, the Marine Firemen's Union, the Shipwrights' Union, the Ship Joiners' and Carpenters' Union, the Lumberman's Protective Association, the Stevedores' Protective Association, the Steamship Stevedores' Union, the Riggers' Association, and the Wharf Builders' Union. In 1888, the Federated Council of Wharf and Wave Unions was established; however, in 1890, an effort to join all maritime unions in one organization failed.[13]

Many of these unions were short-lived. Most occupied rented quarters on private land near the waterfront—in the so-called city front. For example, in the 1890s the Sailors' Union of the Pacific, Marine Engineers, Masters and Pilots, Pile Drivers, and other maritime unions rented space in the Audiffred Building at the foot of Mission Street, just inshore of the boundary of the port property.

As labor organized, so did employers. In 1893, efforts of the Ship Owners Association to lower wages and monitor workers with a "grade book" culminated in the deaths of eight seamen from an explosion, blamed on striking workers.[14] This was only a prelude to a contest in 1901 between waterfront workers and employers, the first with significant repercussions beyond the San Francisco waterfront. Attempts by the Employers Association to weaken labor were resisted by the City Front Federation, which represented thousands of port workers in fourteen unions around the bay. A regional strike of fifteen thousand workers in support of San Francisco teamsters stopped most shipping for more than two months and resulted in the deaths of five workers and injuries to hundreds. This marked the beginning of twenty years of labor ascendancy, a time when "San Francisco became known as the nation's strongest union town."[15] Labor historian Ira Cross called San Francisco "the only closed-shop city in the United States," in which one had to belong to a union in order to work.[16] A measure of the power of labor in that era was the election of Union Labor Party candidates as mayor: Eugene Schmitz in 1901, 1903, and 1905; and P. H. McCarthy in 1909.

The power of labor did not end employer-labor strife, however. Streetcar workers went on strike in 1902 and 1907, affecting the largest group of daily users of the port—those who came to and went from the Ferry Building on streetcars. The 1907 strike of the Carmen's Union against United Railroads, which called for higher wages and an eight-hour day, lasted almost a year and left twenty-five people killed and two thousand injured. The union was defeated, but the unpopular actions of United Railroads set the stage for the municipal takeover of the private streetcar lines.[17]

Employers' efforts to fight back began in 1916 with the establishment of the Merchants' and Manufacturers' Association, which, with the Chamber of Commerce, sought to end the closed shop. A series of events, precipitated by a long-shoremen's strike for higher wages, ended with a bomb that killed ten people at the corner of Market and Spear streets during a Preparedness Day parade. Sponsored by the Chamber of Commerce as a show of support for military buildup, the parade was boycotted by labor groups. Two union activists, Tom Mooney and Warren Billings, were convicted of murder, but

evidence later surfaced showing that prosecution witnesses had lied, fueling decades of recriminations over this issue.[18]

After a respite during World War I, during which the position of the unions was eroded, in 1919 the Riggers' and Stevedores' Union struck unsuccessfully against the Waterfront Employers' Union. The outcome marked another major shift in the balance of power, with the end of the Riggers' and Stevedores' Union and the start of an era of open-shop employment. The catalyst for this change was the creation of the Longshoremen's Association, an employer-backed union formed by "walking bosses"—gang bosses who supported the interests of the stevedoring companies for which they worked and of the shipping companies. The Blue Book Union, as it was called, "was undemocratic, corrupt, and exploitive—a labor racket, serving largely to enrich its officers. . . . From 1919 to 1933, San Francisco longshoremen had no true union representation and almost no control over their own

working conditions."[19]

In the aftermath of the 1919 strike, employers gained strength. Beginning about 1924, work on the piers began to speed up with the introduction of new cargo-handling machinery and systems. For example, in the mid-1920s, power trucks began to replace hand trucks. The early 1930s saw the introduction of motorized jitneys running on gas or electricity that could pull trains of four-wheeled hand trucks and electric low-lift and high-lift trucks designed to carry skids piled with cargo. In addition, mechanized stacking and piling equipment was in use by that time. Shipping companies owned most of the cargo-handling equipment, but in the 1918–1920 biennium the port had acquired elevators, stackers, an electric tractor, trailers, and generators for rental.[20]

As the work got faster, companies demanded more of labor; smaller gangs worked longer shifts—up to thirty-six hours. The onset of the Great Depression, with its decline in commerce and increase in unemployment, further heightened hardships for waterfront workers.

Aided by the National Industrial Recovery Act of 1933, San Francisco longshoremen challenged the Blue Book Union by the establishment of a new local chapter of the International Longshoremen's Association (ILA). A strike against the Matson Navigation Company in October 1933 was won by the ILA and destroyed the Blue Book Union. Emboldened by this victory, the ILA, under the leadership of Harry Bridges, led a strike in May 1934 of Pacific Coast maritime workers calling for a union hiring hall, a coast-wide contract, and a six-hour day with fair pay. Joining the ILA were the Sailors' Union of the Pacific; the Marine Cooks and Stewards; the Marine Firemen; the Marine Engineers; the Masters, Mates, and Pilots; the Marine Workers' Industrial Union; and the Teamsters. Strikebreakers were hired, and armed police fought the strikers up and down the coast. Undermining a traditional pool of strikebreakers, the ILA recruited African American members.

Violent confrontations involving strikers, strike breakers, and armed police resulted in hundreds of injuries and the deaths of two strikers in San Pedro, one in Seattle, and two in San Francisco. After the San Francisco killings, one of a longshoreman, on July 5, 1934—Bloody Thursday—the National Guard occupied the port of San Francisco from one end of the Embarcadero to the other, halting the violence. Four days later, a silent funeral march by thousands along Market Street was a powerfully moving event that gained the respect of the leader of the opposition, the Industrial Association.

A week later, building on these events, one hundred thousand workers in San Francisco, Oakland, and elsewhere in Alameda County staged a general strike that all but shut down the port, factories, stores, restaurants, and streetcars. It lasted from July 16 to 19, 1934, ending with an agreement to send the strike issues to arbitration by the National Longshoremen's Board, appointed by President Franklin D. Roosevelt. The Pacific Coast Maritime Strike—known as the Big Strike—finally ended on July 31, 1934. In October, the National Longshoremen's Board announced its decisions, agreeing to almost all of the unions' demands.

The Big Strike did more than restore labor to a position of strength at the port; it also changed the nature of the relationship between unions and employers. Labor historian Bruce Nelson described it as "one of the great battles in the history of the American working class . . . an eighty-three-day drama [that] transformed labor relations in the Pacific Coast maritime industry and ushered in an era of militant unionism."[21]

One of the leaders of the employers' opposition, Thomas Plant, described the nature of the change from the employers' point of view.

The old union had said to us, "We believe our interests are common with yours; we will cooperate with you in every way; we will produce more work and will try in every way to make your business profitable so you can pay us better wages." . . . The new union was to say to us, "We believe in the class struggle, that there is nothing common between our interests and yours, therefore, we will hamper you at every turn, and will do everything we can to destroy your interests, believing that by doing so we can advance our own."[22]

The workers in and around the port were classified by job and location: warehousemen moved goods in warehouses, teamsters drove wagons or trucks, longshoremen moved materials on the piers, and seamen were responsible for cargo on ships. In this scene, immediately after the 1934 Big Strike, warehousemen and teamsters are loading (or unloading) a truck at a warehouse.

Between 1934 and 1937 there were hundreds of strikes and other union actions focused on issues such as the speedup of work and the weight of sling loads. These issues were resolved in favor of labor after a three-month strike in the winter of 1936–1937. Another labor victory in 1940 provided for on-the-spot arbitration of disputes over issues of health and safety.

Labor-employer relations were generally stable during World War II, but one significant development in cargo handling from the late 1930s was widely adopted—the forklift and pallet system. This was an improvement over the lift-truck and skid system from the standpoint of efficiency because it reduced the number of steps—and the number of laborers—needed not only for moving cargo from ship to transit shed and vice versa but also for stacking cargo.

After World War II, amenities began to be provided for workers on the piers. They illuminate the enormous lack of amenities up until that time, although they required only minor expense. Partitioned spaces in the transit sheds furnished with tables and chairs provided indoor areas for workers eating lunch. Plumbing for toilets and hand washing was provided, replacing outhouselike facilities.

A key feature in the progression from slings to lift trucks to the forklift and pallet system was the trend toward standardized units of

packaging cargo. In the mid-1950s, this trend was accelerated with the introduction of containers—standardized steel boxes that represented a final shift from the traditional handling of break-bulk cargo to the handling of unitized cargo. Containerized cargo requires far less handling and far fewer workers. At the time this appeared to be another step in the development of cargo handling, but not a revolution that would replace virtually all other systems.

In 1961, the International Longshore and Warehouse Union (ILWU) and the Pacific Maritime Association, an organization of shipping companies, came to an agreement that allowed new cargo-handling technologies, such as containers, to be adopted while protecting union members in various ways. When this agreement expired in 1971, the revolutionary implications of container technology had only just become apparent in San Francisco. Issues around containerization were at the center of an ILWU strike in 1971 that lasted four-and-a-half months.

In this protracted story of relations between employers and workers at the port of San Francisco, the two groups were typically

The efficient and proper loading of break-bulk cargo on a ship had implications for the profits of the voyage and the safety of the ship. This cross section shows the right way to do it, considered both a science and an art.

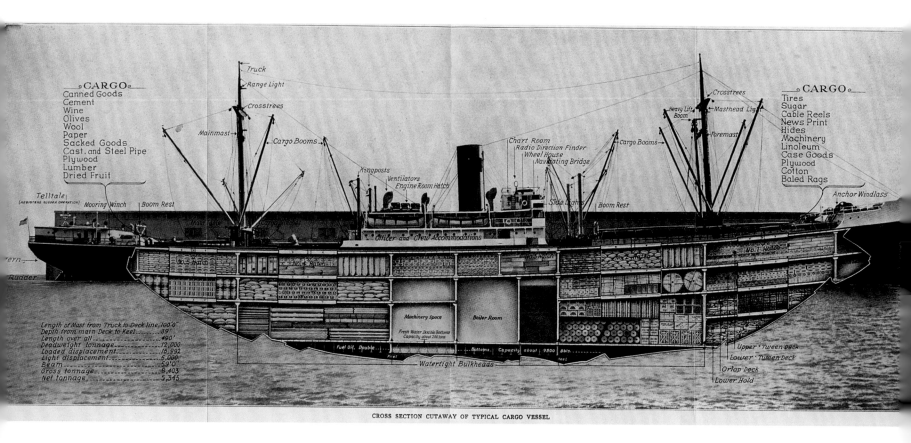

CROSS SECTION CUTAWAY OF TYPICAL CARGO VESSEL

antagonists. This was not always the case, however. In the 1918–1920 biennium, the BSHC was the agent for cooperative effort in the establishment of an advisory committee "to render assistance . . . from time to time." The commissioners invited "twenty men engaged in various activities connected with the shipping world, importers and exporters, ship owners and operators, representatives of railroad companies, stevedores, warehousemen, draymen, and the Chamber of Commerce." The committee met as a whole under the chairmanship of Robert Dollar and in subcommittees concerned with foreign commerce, ships and shipping, transportation, harbor extension, wharves and equipment, and warehouse and drayage.[23] The committee continued to serve through June 1922. There is no evidence that any such effort was made at any other time.

PRIVATE EMPLOYERS: SHIPPING COMPANIES AND OTHERS

In addition to the hundreds of people employed by the BSHC, many more worked for private companies involved in shipping, stevedoring, drayage, and other businesses. Many of these employers rented space from the BSHC on the bulkhead wharf, on the piers, and in the seawall lots. The port's policy was not to lease its facilities but to rent them month-to-month, thereby retaining more control over public assets. In practice, however, some companies remained in the same locations for years and were strongly identified with particular piers, buildings, or stretches of the waterfront. According to Edward Morphy's authorized history of the port,

"Steamship companies operating regularly out of San Francisco and having sufficient business to warrant such arrangement may have special piers assigned to their use on a monthly rental basis."[24]

The principal tenants on the waterfront were the major transportation and shipping companies. The predecessor of the current Ferry Building, the Ferry House of 1875, was occupied by the Central Pacific Railroad and its successor, the Southern Pacific, which were major ferry operators. The building was prominently painted with the initials "C.P.R.R." for the Central Pacific Railroad and with the destinations of its ferries. Railroad employees such as baggage handlers, ticket takers, and those who helped the ferries land also worked in the new Ferry Building; however, the railroad was no longer the principal tenant and the building itself did not advertise private companies.

On each side of the Ferry Building were extensions for baggage, automobile ferries, and freight. Next to these were buildings and piers for private freight carriers: Wells Fargo Express and American Railway Express. The U.S. Post Office, a public freight carrier, occupied a succession of buildings near the Ferry Building.

On the bulkhead wharf around the Ferry Building were a variety of small buildings and large structures for various purposes associated with the operations of the port on land and water. By 1893, the chief wharfinger's office was located in a two-story building that resembled an Italianate style house northwest of the Ferry Building. Other wharfingers were stationed in smaller and less ornate buildings up and down

A strong labor tradition in San Francisco, offset by intervals of weakness, reached its climax in 1934 with the Big Strike, an eighty-three-day strike that included a three-day General Strike joined by nonmaritime labor. San Francisco longshoremen led the victory by Pacific Coast Maritime Unions.

Among several influential figures in the labor victories of the 1930s and 1940s, the best known was Harry Bridges, shown here in front of a banner in 1936.

the bulkhead wharf. After 1900, the Draymen's Association—an organization of owners of horse-drawn wagons that were driven by hired teamsters—occupied a simple one-story building north of the chief wharfinger. It seems likely that this building served as the place where teamsters were hired or wagons were assigned to jobs.

In the few years after the 1906 earthquake, facilities were built south of the Ferry Building for service vessels. Located on the bulkhead wharf just below the Wells Fargo & Company Express offices at Pier 14 was the Launch Offices building for small working boats.

Flanking this operational core of the port, the next piers to the north and south were occupied by shipping companies that served inland destinations on the bay and rivers. The busiest of these were Piers 1, 3, and 5, from which the

The near universal adoption of containers about 1970 permanently changed the way cargo was handled. Break-bulk shipping was almost completely superseded, and the types of facilities that had been built for break-bulk shipping became obsolete. While the full impact of this development was sudden, it had taken place in many small steps, as indicated by this 1945 view of large uniform containers used by the Army.

California Transportation Company provided service to Sacramento and Stockton. Other companies on both sides of the Ferry Building offered passenger and freight service to Crockett, Vallejo, Benicia, Port Costa, Martinez, Antioch, Rio Vista, Stockton, and elsewhere.

The next group of piers generally served Pacific Coast cities. While some piers came to be identified with specific steamship companies, there were so many coastwise companies and so many that came and went or merged with others that sharing of piers and frequent turnover were typical. For example, Pier 17, one of the oldest piers on the waterfront, usually had at least two tenants at any one time. Between 1913 and 1962, at least eighteen different companies

operated from Pier 17. Some served inland ports and others served world ports, but most served coastal ports for either passengers or freight, much of it lumber. Several tenants remained for only one year. The longest tenants were the Los Angeles-San Francisco Navigation Company, which provided the last passenger service to Los Angeles, from 1927 to 1938; and the Alameda Transportation Company, which served inland ports from 1936 to 1949.[25]

The piers located farthest from the Ferry Building were generally rented to the shipping companies that operated the longest routes, those to the Gulf of Mexico, the East Coast of the United States, South America, Europe, Hawaii, the Philippines, and Asia. Companies that primarily served Hawaii and other destinations across the Pacific occupied a cluster of piers south of the Ferry Building. The American-Hawaiian Steamship Company and Williams, Dimond & Company were long based at Pier 24. The American-Hawaiian Steamship Company provided the oldest regular service to Hawaii, initially for the sugar trade, but also had regular routes on the Pacific Coast and to New York. Roger Lapham, the president of the company, moved its headquarters to San Francisco from New York in 1925; he would be mayor of San Francisco from 1944 to 1948. Williams, Dimond & Company, begun in 1862, was a founder of the American Hawaiian Steamship Company and was eventually taken over by it in 1942. Williams, Dimond & Company had its own ships but also functioned as an agent for other lines, many of which used the company's piers, including the Fred Olsen Line, Furness Withy & Company, Holland American Line, and Maersk. The principal cargoes of the company were sugar, copra, vanilla, whale oil, and hides.

The largest tenant of Pier 26, the American-Hawaiian Steamship Company, was also a principal tenant at Pier 28, which it shared with Matson Navigation Company. The waterfront headquarters for Matson was at Pier 30–32 from 1927 to 1962. For many decades, Matson was one of the largest tenants of the port, occupying up to four piers.

Pier 36, originally built as the rail freight terminal for the Western Pacific Railroad, was long occupied by Toyo Kisen Kaisha, a Japanese steamship company founded in 1896. In 1918, to support its use of the pier, the company leased the triangular seawall lot north of Pier 36, bound by Fremont, Brannan, and the Embarcadero. Although piers could only be rented by the month, seawall lots could be leased for long periods.

The last piers above China Basin were rented to the Pacific Mail Steamship Company and W. R. Grace & Company, each of which also leased nearby seawall lots. The Dollar Steamship Lines, with its well-publicized "Round the World Service," succeeded these companies on Piers 42 and 44. South of Channel Street, the port's tenants were railroads and handlers of commodities rather than shipping companies. North of the Ferry Building, the China Mail Steamship Company rented Piers 29 and 31 for a few years until it was forced out of business after World War I by larger competitors, including Matson and Dollar. China Mail Steamship Company was an American company with investors in the United States and China. Most of its business was with Chinese merchants in the two countries. From 1935 to 1960, the largest tenant at both piers was the Luckenbach Steamship Company, which operated between San Francisco and New York through the Panama Canal.

In addition to the piers, the seawall lots were an important resource for the port that could be rented and leased to a variety of tenants. However, first their purpose as set forth in the 1863 act that created the BSHC had to be redefined. The *Biennial Report* of 1888 described the problem:

> Under the existing laws these lots are set apart and dedicated to public use as open spaces, to be used in connection with the seawall and for the same purposes, and it is made the duty of the Board to put them in condition for such use. It is difficult to maintain these lots as open spaces. Teams and people cross them in every direction, and they are made a dumping ground for the refuse matter of the city. The sand from those filled in is blown on the seawall roadway, and this vast amount of valuable property thus becomes of no practical benefit to the people of the State. The Board sees no good reason why they should remain as open spaces. It believes that it should have the power to inclose [sic] them and to grant their use during the pleasure of the Board for the purpose of facilitating the commerce of the port.[26]

This change was necessary before construction of the Belt Railroad, for which the seawall lots were essential as rail yards. In addition, shipping companies, fuel companies, industries, lumber companies, and others would occupy the seawall lots over time.

Matson Navigation Company executives in 1933, the year before the Big Strike, dressed for work in downtown offices.

ENGINEERING

The history of the port of San Francisco is part of a worldwide story that is thousands of years old. Ports built by the Cretans at Pharos in Egypt by 1600 B.C., by the Greeks near Athens by 458 B.C., by Alexander the Great at Alexandria around 332 B.C., and by the Romans in many locations around the Mediterranean Sea and beyond before the fifth century A.D. were, in many cases, far more substantial and elaborate than those built since the industrial revolution: "Most of the ancient harbors were built upon a scale of solidity and architectural grandeur seldom or never attempted in modern times."[1] Among the most famous examples is the port of Alexandria with its levees, piers, and giant lighthouse on the island of Pharos.

Beginning in 1909, all piers were built of concrete, but the decision to erect transit sheds of modern fireproof materials—steel and concrete—or heavy timber was a function of anticipated use and the availability of funds. Pier 34, shown here under construction in 1910, was built of bolted heavy timber at the same time that Piers 36, 38, and 40 were built of concrete.

The impressiveness of these early ports notwithstanding, the physical character of the port of San Francisco north of China Basin has more in common with two-thousand-year-old ports— and with ports built between antiquity and the twentieth century—than it does with ports developed since about 1970. The fundamental requirement of both ancient ports and the port of San Francisco in the late nineteenth and early twentieth centuries was to provide a berth for a seagoing vessel in order to load and unload passengers and cargo. This was accomplished by the labor of numerous workers and with the assistance of cargo-handling machinery of varying levels of sophistication and complexity.

Until about 1960, ships always tied up at the same kinds of places—manmade platforms built alongside or projecting into navigable water. In the United States, these platforms are generally called wharves when they are parallel to the shoreline and piers when they project out from the shoreline into the water, although piers can also be called wharves. Many ancient piers were curved, but some were straight. Records from the ancient port of Eleusis near Athens document a "mole or jetty [pier], straight in plan, . . . probably intended for the discharge and loading of

vessels laid alongside it."[2]

Piers and other port structures in antiquity were built according to methods that were still used in San Francisco in the twentieth century. Like the builders of the San Francisco seawall, the Greeks erected harbor walls and piers in the simple but effective manner of throwing rubble into the water "until the mound reached water level, where it was leveled off and the masonry blocks were built up above."[3] Like many structures on the San Francisco waterfront, Roman structures were built on wooden piles that were either positioned along the shore or driven into navigable water away from shore. The Romans probably built "wooden quays and jetties"— i.e., wharves and piers—in Britain.[4] These were similar to the wood wharves and piers of nineteenth-century ports in the United States. According to a historian of the port of New York, "Until the mid-nineteenth century, many maritime building methods had not changed significantly since antiquity. Techniques first described by the Roman architect and engineer Marcus Vitruvius in the first century B.C.E. were still employed for constructing seawalls."[5]

For many centuries, the universal means of loading and unloading ships involved heavy physical labor by large numbers of workers. In ancient times, workers were usually slaves. In the late nineteenth and early twentieth centuries, workers were gangs of longshoremen. In order for workers to handle the cargo, it was generally broken down into units that one person could maneuver. In ancient times, amphorae (distinctive ceramic jugs with handles and pointed bottoms) were common containers for liquid cargoes such as olive oil and wine; marine archeologists have found many of them. In the nineteenth and twentieth centuries, sacks, barrels, crates, and bales were common types of packages. In contrast with bulk cargo—for example, grain or coal dumped into large bins, or oil poured into tanks—cargo carried in these small packages is called break-bulk cargo.

Even in ancient times, waterfront work had the benefit of machinery. Until the beginning of the industrial revolution in the eighteenth century, waterfront technology was simple and did not change much, consisting of pulleys, basic cranes, screw-pumps, and slings. This equipment was essential for constructing port structures, loading and unloading ships, and building and repairing ships.

At every era in the history of ports, there was a direct and inseparable connection between the design of port facilities, the availability of cargo-handling technology, the size of ships, and the character and practices of labor. At all times, a pier had to be at least as long as the ships that it served and wide enough to accommodate both the means of moving cargo and the cargo itself, as well as large numbers of workers. One known example of a Roman merchant ship was 120 feet long. Because slaves performed most of the waterfront work during Greek and Roman times, labor was cheap, and there was little incentive to use or improve cargo-handling technology. Pier sheds to cover the cargo were not built or were not common in antiquity, but the Romans built shelters between piers, called *cellae*, to protect ships at berth.

After the fall of the Roman Empire in the fifth century A.D., regular shipping in Europe disappeared except in Scandinavia, and there was virtually no development of ports for centuries. According to J. P. M. Pannell's historical study of civil engineering, "By the twelfth and thirteenth centuries, trade in Europe was again

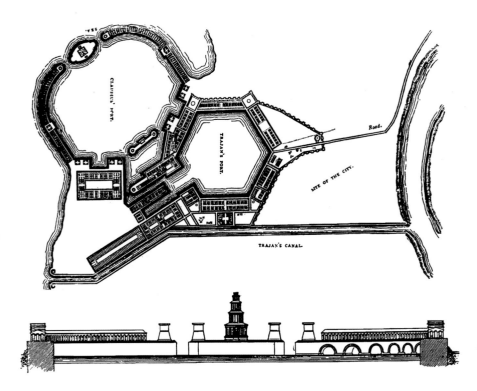

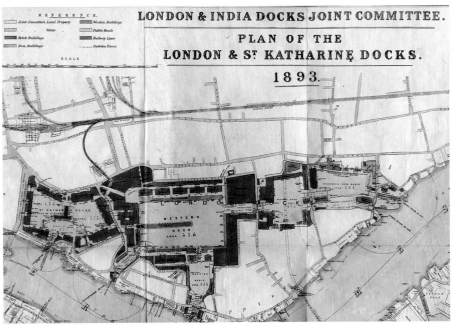

flourishing; quays and jetties were coming into use for convenience in loading and unloading ships" in Britain and around the Mediterranean and Baltic regions.[6] Venice became the center of trade routes that stretched to China. Port operations were sophisticated: "Shipping regulations of this period show that an elaborate system of inspections, loading rules, and construction regulations were effectively enforced."[7] Medieval

Above: San Francisco and most other ports of the nineteenth and twentieth centuries followed the relatively inexpensive model of port design that entailed seawalls, wharves, and piers. In northern Europe, where the tides are unusually high, far more elaborate and expensive ports were built that used locks, gates, and pumps to contain water in basins at low tide, such as the London and St. Katharine Docks planned in 1893.

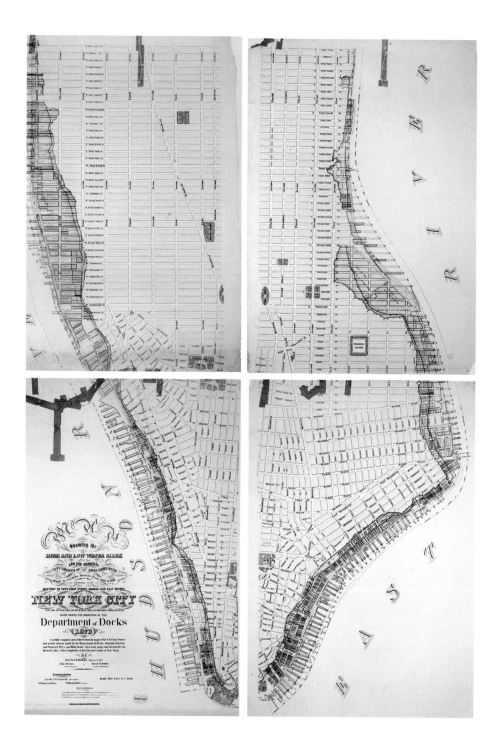

The design of the port of San Francisco followed a type common in the United States and best represented by New York, with its seawall, landfill behind the seawall, and rows of finger piers. New York's Department of Docks was created in 1870, seven years after the BSHC; its master plan of 1871 predated San Francisco's of 1877.

port technology was probably similar to that of the Roman Empire.

Beginning in the fifteenth century, changes began to take place that affected the development of ports over the next five hundred years. As Pannell explains, "The Renaissance and its almost inevitable consequence, the Industrial Revolution, brought about a great development of ports, and this became extremely rapid in the eighteenth century."[8] The most important

changes were the increasing size of ships and the longer distances that they traveled—across oceans and out of sight of land for long periods.

In the seventeenth and eighteenth centuries, the use of larger ships led to a need for deeper harbors in northern Europe, where tides were much higher than in the Mediterranean. This, in turn, gave rise to the development of new types of port facilities that provided berths of sufficiently deep water by means of locks, gates, dredged basins, and pumps, as well as wharves, piers, levees, and shoreline walls. Complexes of these facilities, called docks, captured deep water at high tide for the loading, unloading, or repair of ships. Docks were extremely expensive and required innovative structural and mechanical technologies, as well as centralized planning and control by the city or state. Le Havre, London, Liverpool, Hamburg, and Antwerp were among the ports developed early and extensively with docks.

In the same period, long-distance travel resulted in the establishment of new ports around the world—in cities such as Rio de Janeiro, Cape Town, Bombay, and New York. San Francisco's rapid emergence as a port in the mid-nineteenth century was part of this same development. The city presented certain advantages: "At this time, two main factors determined the commercial success of a port: one, the physical shape of the harbor and its suitability for shipping and the other, the capacity of its immediate hinterland for the production and absorption of goods carried by sea. It is mainly by changes in these factors that ports have risen or fallen in importance."[9]

In the nineteenth century, as United States ports were growing, the primary factors in the development of ports included the continuing increase in the size of ships in order to service commerce more efficiently; "the application of steam-power to cranes, pile-drivers, dredgers, and other plant; . . . improvements in materials, including concrete; . . . and a growing reliance on scientific and technological research to solve a variety of port problems."[10]

UNITED STATES PORTS

In the years following the American Revolution, the principal ports of Boston, New York, Philadelphia, Baltimore, and Charleston built

Bulkhead Wall as built at E.116th St. Section.

New York's seawall, built from 1874 to 1916, was comparable to San Francisco's, built from 1878 to 1915. Both consisted of a stone and concrete wall with earth fill behind it.

new wharves and piers to serve expanded trade and growing populations. In each of these cities, the waterfront was built up with rows of wood piers projecting from the shoreline, designed to accommodate a vessel on each side. Warehouses were built along the shore facing the waterfront. The shoreline itself was provided with a man-made edge—a wall, wharf, or a combination of the two   so that the water was deep enough for ships to come right to the waterfront. Private interests undertook many of these developments independently, creating irregular and uncoordinated waterfronts.

The basic features of ports in the United States were established very early. In the 1630s, the Dutch built "small platforms and seawalls" at the tip of Manhattan, and in the 1650s, they erected an expanded seawall using pile-driving

Unlike San Francisco's seawall, New York's riverwall was faced in cut granite blocks. Its vertical face obviated the need for a bulkhead wharf; ships could come right to the wall, which served as the edge of a wharf along the shore. The granite face had a more finished appearance and was more expensive than San Francisco's rubble stone wall.

Left: Among the distinctions of the port of San Francisco was its greater vulnerability than most to shipworms or marine borers, creatures that could cripple a wooden pier in less than five years. Research and experimentation led to the adoption of wooden piles treated with creosote but did not eliminate the need for constant replacement of wooden piles.

Below: Damage from ship collisions was a chronic concern of the port. Engineers experimented with ways to minimize the cost of inevitable collisions, and maintenance workers continually repaired damage. Cheap wooden fenders absorbed much of the impact, rather than the expensive ship hulls or the unforgiving concrete piers.

Above: The deterioration of wooden piles was one of the most vexing problems for port engineers, chronically draining funds and inhibiting development. Experiments with alternatives included wooden piles encased in concrete that the port made in forms, shown here in 1910.

Right: After 1910, the most common and long-lasting piles were square in section. Made by the port, they were used for piers and were driven through the seawall to support the bulkhead wharf.

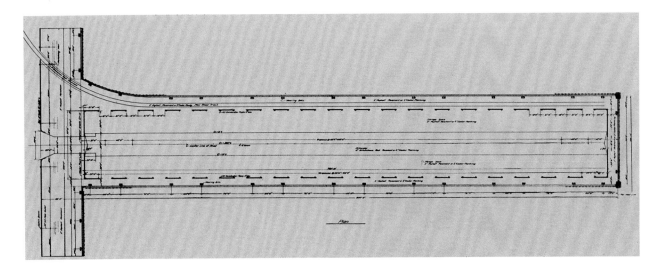

hammers. Behind each seawall they dumped fill, creating new land along the waterfront. By the 1670s, they had floating derricks for offshore dredging, which both maintained navigable water and provided fill for the area behind the seawall. The seawall itself created a waterfront that was useable for shipping. From the seawall "the first pier of substance," measuring twenty by one hundred feet, was completed in 1659. In 1727, a municipal ordinance established a limit for the length of piers to two hundred feet from shore. "By 1800, most of the southern tip of Manhattan had been ringed with bulkhead [seawall] and landfill" and "by the early nineteenth century" Brooklyn's waterfront had been similarly developed.[11]

Among United States ports, the port of New York provides a particularly useful point of comparison for San Francisco. In the 1850s, during the first decade of port development in San Francisco, New York passed Boston as the busiest port in the United States. Of those who traveled to California by sea during the nineteenth century, the majority came from New York (and most of the rest were from the similar ports of Boston and Philadelphia). Those who came from New York had a direct experience of the development of its port.

In 1853, there were 112 piers in lower Manhattan, some of them six hundred feet long. In 1855, the state established harbor lines for bulkheads and piers. By 1870, uncoordinated growth of the port of New York resulted in deplorable conditions. The *New York Times* described "mean, rotten and dilapidated wooden wharves" and "rotten structures, the abode of rats and the hiding place of thieves."[12]

As the Board of State Harbor Commissioners (BSHC) assumed control of the port of San Francisco in 1863, the Department of Docks took over the port of New York in 1870. In both cases the ports were placed under strong, centralized public administration in response to a variety of problems, including the effects of uncoordinated development, the demand for a stable shoreline and navigable water, and the need to rebuild piers to accommodate increasingly large vessels.

At a time when the BSHC was floundering, in 1871, New York's Department of Docks completed "a master plan for the waterfront" under the direction of George B. McClellan, the Civil War general and future candidate for president. The "main component" of the plan was "the construction of a monumental and continuous masonry bulkhead"—"a masonry riverwall to encircle the island with wood piers at given intervals"—and a wide street along the waterfront. The official plan did not include a rail line along the waterfront, which had been proposed during the planning process. In favoring a system of piers extending from a bulkhead, McClellan rejected specifically the far more expensive system of docks used in London, Liverpool, and elsewhere in northern Europe. The plan that was adopted provided "every facility for the cheap and rapid handling of vessels and their cargoes." This bulkhead-and-pier plan represented the continuation of a tradition in all major United States ports since the seventeenth century.[13]

The alignment of New York's planned

This 1911 plan of Pier 17 shows a concrete pier with a wooden transit shed built to the waterfront line. Its northern apron is wider than that on the south to accommodate a rail spur, which curved onto the pier from the north.

bulkhead—the riverwall—was a continuous curve. In contrast, the first San Francisco seawall, begun in 1867, was laid out in a zigzag alignment—a poor design that caused silting—

This interior view of the Pier 29 transit shed in 1918 shows a typical heavy timber frame, baffles to inhibit wind and fire, and natural lighting provided by side windows and roof monitors.

which had resulted from political considerations rather than from an engineering rationale. T. J. Arnold's 1873 proposal for a new seawall in San Francisco was similar to McClellan's New York riverwall in its gently curving plan. While conditions for these two walls were similar—intermittently shallow bedrock and deep mud—their basic designs were different (with variations according to location). San Francisco's seawall was a simple rubble stone wall with piles driven through it to support a bulkhead wharf. New York's riverwall was a modern version of the best-built walls of antiquity, with a rubble stone base supporting a masonry wall of precast concrete blocks. Unlike San Francisco's rubble wall, the masonry blocks of New York's riverwall created a vertical face that obviated the need for a bulkhead wharf.[14]

The two walls were erected about the same time and both underwent design modifications in the process. Construction began on New York's riverwall in 1874; it was built in segments and completed in 1916. San Francisco's seawall was also built in sections, from 1878 to 1915. The construction of both walls depended on steam-powered pile drivers and dredges.

As the bulkhead walls were completed, both ports built, rebuilt, and maintained piers. Except for two concrete and steel piers in New York (one of which, Pier A, survives), most nineteenth-century piers in both cities were made of wood. Engineers in both cities struggled with solutions to the accelerated deterioration of wooden piles from marine borers. The most effective solution was the use of creosote on the wooden piles, which substantially extended their lives. In the 1890s, new efforts were made in New York to build in permanent materials, followed by similar efforts in San Francisco. The first large development of modern piers in permanent materials was the Chelsea Piers in New York, built between 1902 and 1910. In 1901 and 1907, San Francisco attempted to build concrete piers, although these deteriorated rapidly due to problems with the quality of the cement used. Beginning in 1908, San Francisco built a series of permanent piers in reinforced concrete. Having experienced the earthquake and fire of 1906, San Francisco was one of the first cities in the United States, along with Los Angeles, to see the widespread use of this material. Therefore, the use of reinforced concrete at the port of San Francisco was related not only to developments in port construction in the United States but also to the port's context in a city where engineers, architects, manufacturers, and contractors were familiar with this newly appreciated material.

With the bulkheads in place in both cities and methods of permanent pier construction available and in use, port engineers in New York and San Francisco became increasingly concerned with adapting to changes in technology. Before any other port in the country, San Francisco had begun building a public waterfront railroad in 1890. Photographs of both ports taken about 1910 to 1915 show large machines loading coal and doing other heavy work on the waterfront. One of the principal adaptations made in both ports was the accommodation of ever-larger ships. In 1910, a proposal was made for "larger 'terminals' for railroad and marine use" in New York. Nothing came of it, however, until the

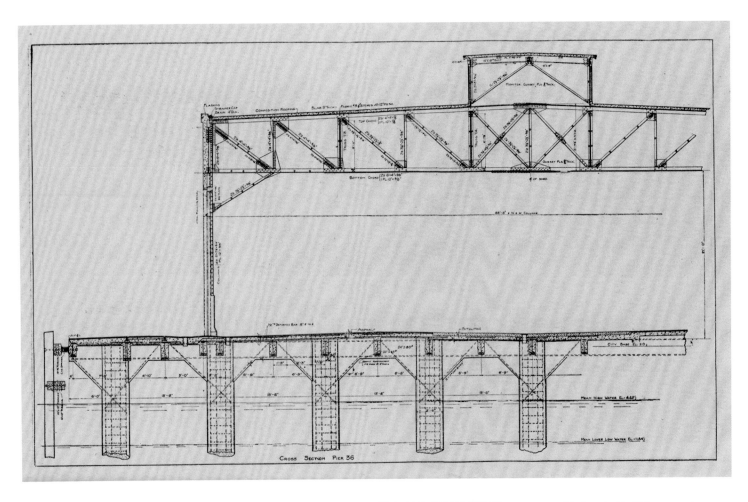

CROSS SECTION PIER 36

Interior of steel shed on new pier No. 36.

Above: Pier 36, shown in this 1909 cross section, was one of the first built of modern industrial materials, with its massive reinforced-concrete-pile foundation, reinforced-concrete deck, poured-concrete walls, and steel truss roof that spans the interior without columns.

Left: The responsibility of the BSHC's engineers was primarily for the durability and usefulness of their structures in the service of an efficient port. They also took pride in the elegance and beauty of structures like Pier 36.

Until the construction of Pier 45 began in 1926, all of San Francisco's piers were built on piles, allowing water to flow underneath and thereby helping to control the buildup of silt along the waterfront. In contrast, as the outermost pier most exposed to incoming tidal currents, Pier 45 was built of landfill to serve as a breakwater.

The port's engineers experimented continually with improvements in pier designs. As a result, few piers are identical. The walls of Pier 15 were built in 1931 of precast-concrete panels.

1920s, when large new piers and terminal complexes were established outside of Manhattan in Brooklyn, Queens, and Staten Island.[15] In San Francisco, large, mechanized developments were built on the previously undeveloped shoreline south of China Basin, away from downtown congestion. In addition, San Francisco built Piers 45, 48, and 50, which were twice as wide as those of the previous generation and could accommodate two rows of transit sheds.

Referring to the period ending in 1931, when the Department of Docks was closed and its duties were spread out among other city departments, the author of a recent historical study of the port of New York stated, "The New York City Department of Docks actively supervised the greatest public works projects of the period, employing over a thousand workers, and enlisted the most advanced engineering technologies to create the vast built fabric of Manhattan's river-walls and piers."[16] Although San Francisco's port is proportionally much smaller than New York's, a similar statement might be made about it.

With the great increase in the use of trucks for transport and motor vehicles generally, both ports made accommodations to the new situation. In the 1930s, New York built the Miller Highway (known as the West Side Highway), an elevated freeway above the wide shoreline street along the Hudson River from Canal Street to 79th Street, "to ease congestion." The highway separated waterfront traffic from other traffic bypassing the port. The Embarcadero Freeway in San Francisco, built in the 1950s, performed the same function until it was damaged in the Loma Prieta earthquake in 1989. The Miller Highway was closed in 1973 after a deteriorated section collapsed.[17]

Both ports flourished in World War II and declined after the war. The port of New York recovered under the unified administration of the Port Authority of New York and New Jersey, which moved port operations to Brooklyn and New Jersey and built larger facilities with up-to-date cargo-handling systems and transportation accommodations. The business of the port of San Francisco largely moved to the entirely separate port of Oakland. The same process of moving from old, congested areas to peripheral areas with more space occurred at major ports throughout the United States. While this process was under way for some time, it accelerated rapidly in the late 1960s and early 1970s when container technology was suddenly adopted everywhere.

Among all American ports, New York was most like San Francisco. San Francisco consistently compared itself to New York and aspired to become the New York of the Pacific. Conditions and facilities in the two places were similar. And the plan and appearance of the two ports were comparable, too, both having long, gently curving waterfronts on continuous bulkheads with rows of parallel piers near downtown business districts. By the 1980s, there was virtually nothing visible left of the New York port and its hundreds of piers. The riverwall is largely intact, although much of it has been buried in fill, such as at Battery Park City. Pier A of 1884 and the Municipal Ferry Piers of 1906–1909 remain at the tip of Manhattan. The South Street Seaport is a neighborhood of onshore historic buildings that faced the waterfront, whose piers and other maritime structures have all been lost.

Among all United States ports, San Francisco's is the only one that retains a substantial amount of historic fabric and the feeling of its era. Despite the loss of many of its piers and changes in its setting, San Francisco alone retains, in addition to its seawall and bulkhead wharf, rows of piers and a diversity of other structures—car-ferry slips, restaurants for workers, pile-driving rigs, the Ferry Building—that convey the scale and significance of the ports of the early twentieth century.

ENGINEERING OF STRUCTURES

The port of San Francisco was developed in phases, along with sections of the seawall, beginning in 1878. After 1878, the BSHC built, maintained, and rebuilt many wooden piers up and down the waterfront. Assaulted by marine borers, many piers were severely deteriorated in five to ten years. According to Paris Kilburn, an active president of the BSHC, "By reason of the great destructiveness of marine pests, this port has been one of the most expensive to keep in repair of any of the harbors of the world."[18] Quickly deteriorating piers were expensive and not worthy of adornment or other nonessential investment. Largely for this reason, few piers were initially outfitted with transit sheds, which

A view of a reinforced-concrete pier from below, showing piles and the underside of a deck.

would have to be replaced when their substructures collapsed. Altogether, according to an early harbor commissioner, "The designing of harbors constitutes confessedly one of the most difficult branches of civil engineering."[19]

On the open decks of the earliest wood piers, teamsters hauled cargo with horse-drawn wagons. Gangs of longshoremen loaded cargo on and off ships that were tied up on both sides of long, narrow piers. The hard physical work of the longshoremen was made easier by the use of derricks, animal power, and steam donkeys—portable machines that could lift heavy loads. The concerns of merchants led to increased construction of transit sheds, which sheltered cargo from the weather and provided security against theft. However, the presence of transit sheds on piers brought new problems in cargo handling. The movement of goods in and out of doors, to and from a confined space, led to congestion. In order to minimize congestion, it was important to tie up a ship in relation to the doors of a transit shed. The construction of transit sheds may also have been associated with the development of the first sections of the Belt Railroad north of Market Street, beginning in 1890. Although not yet extended onto the piers, the railroad both relieved some of the physical labor on the waterfront and sped up the pace of work.

The construction of more transit sheds at the

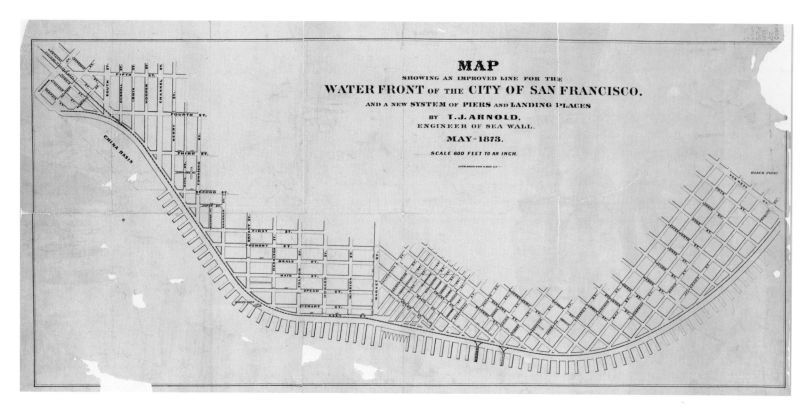

MAP
SHOWING AN IMPROVED LINE FOR THE
WATER FRONT OF THE CITY OF SAN FRANCISCO.
AND A NEW SYSTEM OF PIERS AND LANDING PLACES
BY I. J. ARNOLD,
ENGINEER OF SEA WALL.
MAY - 1873.
SCALE 600 FEET TO AN INCH.

This simple plan of 1873, adopted in 1878, represents one of the most significant and lasting developments in San Francisco's history, establishing the shoreline and, in the process, creating a vast amount of the most valuable land in the city. The drawing shows all the key elements of the port as it was built: the seawall, the bulkhead wharf, finger piers, the Embarcadero, the seawall lots, and the Belt Railroad.

end of the nineteenth century—by 1900, perhaps half of the piers had them—was also related to growing confidence in structural solutions to the problems of marine borers. In 1895, Pier 7 was built with steel-cylinder piles. From that time until 1908, a variety of methods were attempted to arrive at longer-lasting structures, including the use of wooden piles treated with various chemicals such as creosote, composite piles of wood encased in concrete, and unreinforced-concrete piles for at least seven piers. (These failed within ten years due to poor quality concrete.[20]) The solution to this problem was part of a general modernization that involved physical structures and cargo handling as inextricable issues.

As in other aspects of San Francisco's history, the earthquake of 1906 was a watershed event at the port, with important implications for both engineering and cargo handling. According to a report of the U.S. Geological Survey, "Most of the structures built on piles along the bay suffered considerable damage, especially the frame sheds on the wharves." A former chief engineer at the port, Marsden Manson, commented: "The facilities upon our waterfront were utterly inadequate before the catastrophe. They are more so now." Even a few years into the modernization effort,

the president of the BSHC said that the problem "is to begin the construction of a harbor, almost at the beginning."[21]

Reconstruction of the piers in permanent materials beginning in 1908, extension of the Belt Railroad across Market Street in 1913, and completion of the seawall by 1915 produced vastly improved port facilities that were associated with significant changes in cargo handling as well. The heightened business-oriented climate was summarized by the BSHC in 1908: "The rapidity with which a vessel loads and discharges her cargo is one of the factors which determine the profit of the voyage for the ship owner . . . especially . . . per diem. . . . Its advantage to the dock owner is also considerable, as a greater number of vessels can be accommodated within in a given time. . . . Efficiency of the labor employed in stevedoring and the convenient arrangement of the dock determine the rapidity with which cargo may be handled."[22]

Reflecting back on an earlier era, the BSHC commented in 1910, "A great deal of carrying was done in sailing vessels of comparatively small tonnage. These vessels did not have any set schedules for sailing and discharged or received their cargoes in a leisurely way. This sort of procedure did not require piers which

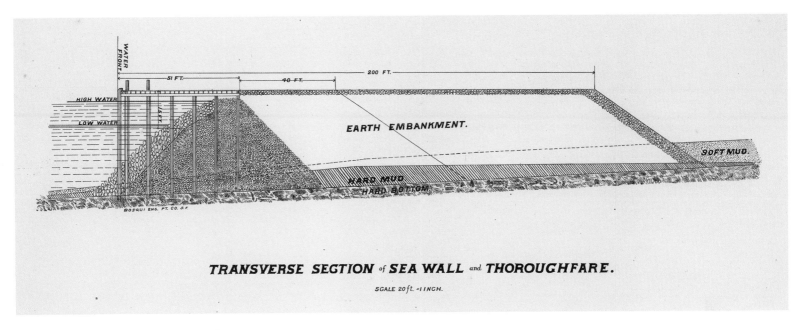

TRANSVERSE SECTION of SEA WALL and THOROUGHFARE.

SCALE 20 ft. = 1 INCH.

would accommodate a huge amount of freight, as it could be hauled away almost as fast as it was discharged."[23] By the time the BSHC issued its 1910 report, the modernization of the port was already having an impact: "The carriers are principally large steam vessels, carrying from 6 to 12 thousand tons of cargo. They run on a fixed schedule and are so expensive that they must lie at the wharf the least possible length of time. Consequently every possible means of hastening the discharge and taking on of cargo is employed. The result is that an enormous amount of freight is piled upon the piers, and they become congested."[24]

Also in 1910, assistant state engineer Ralph Barker recommended wider piers (from an average of one hundred feet to about two hundred feet) with central rail spurs between pairs of sheds and ten-foot aprons. "This will afford floor space sufficient to accommodate a large vessel on each side of the dock. The tracks will be in a position that will not interfere with the loading and discharging and will afford good facilities for the handling of general cargoes, which must be sorted before going into cars." (Nothing of this scale was built until Piers 45, 48, and 50 in the late 1920s.) Barker also recommended building other piers with rail spurs on the aprons, "so that

vessels can place their cargo directly into cars or vice versa when the character of the cargo is such that this is feasible."[25] This would be done by 1914. He recommended increasing the spaces between the piers to about 220 feet: "The space between piers also must be widened to accommodate the modern type of vessel. Vessels of this type must be handled with rapidity, consequently, while the cargo is being discharged and loaded, fuel must be taken on. This is done by having alongside the vessel coal or oil barges."[26]

The modernization of the port was accompanied by ongoing reconsideration of plans and policies and by constant modification of standards. Despite the superficial similarity of piers on the waterfront, they are different in many respects. In 1914, after having previously announced a plan to build all future piers in concrete, "the question of the proper class of construction to be employed was thoroughly discussed" and the conclusion was that "the use of creosoted piling in certain cases would be preferable to the exclusive use of concrete." Soil conditions along the waterfront south of Market Street were a factor. But another important consideration was that "constant changes in vessels and freight handling methods" meant that piers might have to be rebuilt much sooner than the

Until 1909, San Francisco's seawall, under construction in sections, was built largely to this design, which consisted of a rubble stone seawall and landfill behind it that supported the Embarcadero. Because the seawall had sloping sides, a ship could not come close enough to unload without the bulkhead wharf, which was built out over the toe of the seawall to deep water.

Above left: As seen in this view of the construction of Section 11 of the seawall in 1911, near the foot of Beale Street, a trench was dredged and a framework was built over it, from which railcars dropped rock for the base of the seawall. Then, a concrete wall was built on the rock base.

Above right: This 1909 view of the construction of Section 9 of the seawall, in its new alignment beyond the existing shoreline, shows pile-driving rigs building the bulkhead wharf. The future area of landfill for the Embarcadero and the seawall lots, still filled with water, are seen on the left.

Right: Pier 30–32, built in 1914 as a pair of piers attached along the bulk-head wharf, served a large tenant, the American Hawaiian Steamship Company. This circa 1950 view from the east end was made before a wharf was built over the water between the piers to accommodate trucks.

lifespan of concrete.[27] In other words, the structural character of the piers was directly related to cargo-handling methods. For example, in 1915, considering the depth and character of the mud and the currents in the proposed location for seven new piers on the northern waterfront, the port "decided to build the three most exposed piers . . . of concrete, to act as breakwaters and to deflect the current eastward away from the shore. For this reason piers 29, 35, and 39 have been designed as reinforced concrete piers, piers 29 and 39 as concrete cylinder piers, resting on wooden piles below the mud line, and pier 35 as a pile pier."[28]

Consulting engineers associated with the Chamber of Commerce proposed standards for transit sheds in 1914:

> The style and kind of sheds that have been constructed on the different piers along the water front have ranged from the cheapest board and batten structures, with wooden frames, to the reinforced concrete type of building, and there seems to be a diversified opinion among shipping men as to the proper style of shed to construct. Taking into consideration the many changes that are going on constantly in the manner and methods of handling cargoes from ship to wharf and from wharf to ship, we believe a type of moderate cost should be adopted, and would recommend that buildings supported by either steel or wooden trusses, preferably the latter, be erected, so designed as to make the members as large as possible; the roof to be constructed either of tar and gravel, corrugated iron or other similar roofing material; that the sides from the eaves to the head of the doors and the ends to be constructed of corrugated iron; that rolling metal doors be provided along the entire length of either side. It is also recommended that in case wooden trusses are used that they be planked on either side with redwood timber to act as fire breaks. Of course, it is expected that buildings of this kind would be given the proper attention, be painted sufficiently and minor running repairs kept up. Such buildings would not in any sense be fire proof, but each pier should be protected with proper fire fighting apparatus, such as hose, fire extinguishers, etc.
>
> With very small repairs sheds of this character would last a long time, and should it be found desirable at any time to make alterations due to changed conditions, they could be easily made.[29]

The standards proposed for these buildings placed the highest priority on their adaptability to ever-changing sizes and types of ships and to the means of handling cargo. The provision of rolling metal doors along the entire sides rendered irrelevant the relationship of a ship's cargo and the transit-shed doors.

At the same time, the BSHC provided a standard for railcar doors (twenty feet across and twenty-two feet high) and for the placement of rail spurs on the piers. "All new piers are provided with at least one track and where width permits with two, one surface and one depressed, the latter being generally placed on the northerly side." By this time, center tracks were found to contribute to congestion.[30]

This 1922 view of the construction of Section 4 of the bulkhead wharf, looking north from Pier 23, demonstrates the relationship of the bulkhead wharf to the piers. The bulkhead wharf was built over the seawall and extended to the wall's outer toe, while the piers and their transit sheds were built entirely beyond the outer edge of the wharf. Sometimes bulkhead buildings were erected at the wharf ends of the piers.

BUILDINGS AND STRUCTURES

The building blocks of the port are seawalls, bulkhead wharves, and piers.

Seawall

The seawall—a linear embankment of stone, concrete, and wood—defines the waterfront at the port of San Francisco. The need for a seawall in San Francisco was first recognized in 1851.[31] A seawall was seen as a way to provide a fixed shoreline and to protect buildings and property values along the waterfront. As the early port was developed haphazardly by private interests under weak city control, it became increasingly clear not only that a seawall was needed but that neither the city nor private interests were

PIER 31
JUNE 7, 1917.

1742-31-PH

In this view from Pier 31, the bulkhead wharf is visible along the shoreline. Concrete piles at its outer edge rise from the toe of the seawall to the wharf deck.

capable of getting the job done. The takeover of the waterfront by the state of California and the creation of the BSHC in 1863 were largely driven by the need for a seawall.

The first action of the BSHC after acquiring the waterfront and settling title issues was to address the seawall question. Two local engineers, William J. Lewis and G. F. Allardt, proposed a plan for the seawall to be built following the waterfront line shown on the Eddy Red Line map of 1851. This was a zigzag line defined by the extension of the city's grid over shallow tidelands along the existing shore. Lewis was hired as the superintendent and constructing engineer for the seawall and presented the

plan in the *First Annual Report of the Engineer of Sea Wall on the Water Front of San Francisco* of 1866.[32] The first two sections of the seawall were completed in 1869 and the third section was started that same year—these were the only sections of the first seawall to be built. The seawall was an embankment of piled rocks with naturally sloping sides, sixty feet wide at its base (in a trench) and thirteen feet across the top.[33] It was built without the specified facing of large slabs on the waterside or a masonry wall beginning at the mean low-tide line. Sand and dirt were dumped behind the seawall, transforming the water lots into solid ground whose streets were publicly owned and whose blocks were

419-43

modification of the line of the water front . . . and the enactment of such laws as would enable the Board to construct the wharves in such a manner, and upon such lines, that they would restrict the currents of the bay as little as possible."[35] The report included a map with a proposed waterfront line similar to that which was built and survives today.

In 1875, a federal advisory commission was appointed "for the purpose of determining proper harbor lines and considering any matter affecting harbor interests,"[36] notably the issue of a new line for the seawall. The commission, consisting of Rear Admiral John Rodgers, U.S. Navy; Colonel George H. Mendel, U.S. Army Corps of Engineers; and Professor George Davidson, U.S. Coastal Survey, issued its report in March 1877. In the meantime, in February 1876, the state legislature required that the governor, the mayor of San Francisco, and the BSHC determine a new waterfront line with input from consulting engineers and the engineer of the BSHC.

Following the recommendations of the advisory commission and T. J. Arnold, a new waterfront line was established as presented in the *Report of the Board of State Harbor Commissioners on the New Water Front Line of San Francisco to the Legislature of the State of California* in December 1877. This gently curving line was designed to allow for economical construction and to facilitate the uninterrupted flow of tidal currents, which would scour the surface of the harbor and minimize silting.

The line was placed so that the fill behind the seawall would be wide enough to allow "a thoroughfare two hundred feet in width along the whole city front."[37] In addition to this thoroughfare, the fill between the new seawall and the old seawall would provide a substantial amount of new land—called seawall lots—that would be owned by the BSHC.

The new seawall would run from Jones Street on the north side of the city to China Basin on the east, a distance of about four miles. Its funding was projected to come from the annual revenues of the port and would only be available in amounts sufficient to build sections of one thousand feet or less at a time. To accomplish this, the seawall was divided into twenty-one sections. The first contract was let on September 13, 1878, followed by contracts with outside

privately owned. As before, piers were built as extensions of streets and projected in a variety of angles to the waterfront.

In 1870, Thomas J. Arnold was placed in charge of the seawall and given the title "Engineer of Sea Wall."[34] In 1873, Arnold reported that construction on the seawall had stopped due to a lack of money. He stated that the seawall was a well-designed and well-built structure with one flaw—the zigzag alignment appeared to be causing problems. The irregular waterfront line created pockets where mud and silt accumulated, and the different angles of the variously sized piers contributed to the problem. "The only remedy," according to Arnold, was "a

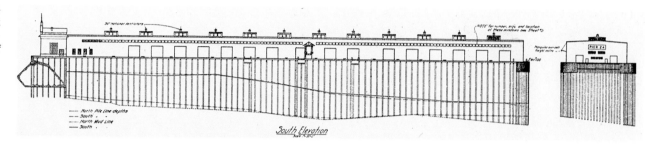

This 1915 section drawing of Pier 24 shows the relationships of the transit shed and pier to the bulkhead building, which sits on the bulkhead wharf above the seawall.

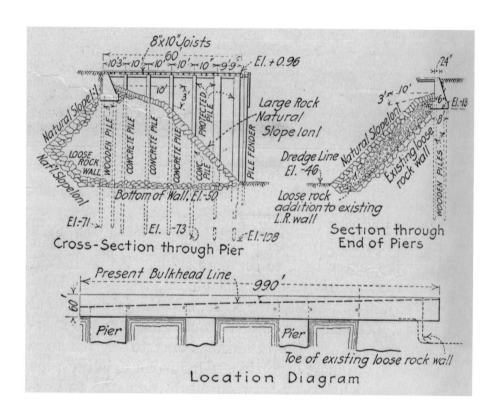

The original 1878 design of the seawall called for an all-rock structure with naturally sloping sides that was formed by dumping rock from above. Beginning in 1909, a series of design modifications incorporated reinforced concrete at the top of a somewhat shorter rock wall. This drawing shows a 1914 version of the rock and concrete seawall.

firms for the construction of each of the other sections. After starting on the north, the order of building the sections was determined by both commercial considerations and difficulties associated with soil conditions south of Market Street. Also, the Southern Pacific Railroad may have influenced the delay on the seawall north of China Basin because the construction of that section eliminated the company's direct private access to the water.

Lauren E. Crane, "expert on the construction of the seawall," illustrated the design of the seawall in 1882.[38] This design appears to have been followed in the construction of the first twelve sections of the seawall from 1878 to 1905 (in chronological order, sections A, 1, 2, 3, 4, 5, 6, 7, 8b, B, 8a, 13). This seawall consists of a pile of rocks, called a rock embankment, rising

from a trench that was originally dug twenty feet deep and one hundred feet wide. At mean high water, the embankment rises almost forty feet above its base. The natural slopes of the embankment on either side rise to a flat top about ten feet wide. The outer toe of the sloping bay side of the embankment is located close to the waterfront line as defined by the U.S. Army Corps of Engineers. Wooden piles driven through the rock embankment from the toe to the inside edge of the flat top originally supported a wood wharf called a bulkhead wharf, generally ranging from twenty-seven to sixty feet wide. This created a useable surface that extended over the sloping seawall to the edge of the waterfront line.

By 1882, five sections were complete or under way. By 1894, eleven sections were complete. By 1906, one more section was finished. While the seawall appears to be a gentle curve, in fact, it was built in straight segments.

Inland of the rock pile lies earthen fill, described by Crane as an "earth embankment." In the earliest contracts, this embankment was built so that the bulkhead wharf and the earth embankment together provided a flat surface for the proposed thoroughfare, which was at the level defined as the City Base. Between the earth embankment and the 1851 waterfront line were the seawall lots—mud flats of varying widths that were subsequently filled.

In 1909, the voters approved a bond issue of nine million dollars to hasten completion of the seawall, among other projects. The remaining sections of the original projected seawall were completed in May 1915.[39] These sections (8, 9, 10, 11, and 12), south of the Ferry Building, were built to revised specifications by H. J. Brunnier in the BSHC's engineering department. An article in the *San Francisco Call* in 1910 described them as "a type of seawall construction entirely different from any heretofore constructed in this harbor,"[40] and the *San Francisco Examiner* later noted they were "especially strong."[41] While in some respects the general character of this portion of the seawall was similar to that of earlier sections, the structural supports for the bulkhead wharf, the materials, and the process of construction were different. In these sections, the trench was first partially filled with rock. Then, concrete piles were driven through the rock fill and more rock was added around the piles to a point thirty feet below City Base. From that point, a reinforced-concrete wall was built along the crest of the pile, and more rocks were filled around the wall. The wall and the caps of the concrete piles then formed a surface for a frame of steel beams to support the bulkhead wharf.[42] Sections 9a and 9b, the last to be built, were raised higher in 1917 and again in 1931–1932 after settling damaged the seawall, the wharves and piers, and the buildings on them.[43]

Between 1908 and 1910, under a special agreement, the Santa Fe Railway extended the seawall three thousand feet south of China Basin to El Dorado Street.[44] The seawall was further lengthened south of El Dorado Street to the Central Basin, Islais Creek, and Hunters Point, mostly in the 1920s. By 1929, it was expanded one block west of Taylor Street to Jones Street, on the northern waterfront, to accommodate the construction of Pier 45.

Bulkhead Wharf

The bulkhead wharf was built along the top of the seawall in order to connect piers to the seawall and the Embarcadero and to provide berthing space for ships at the very outer edge of the seawall, which corresponded with the legally designated waterfront line. Because ships could not have come any closer to shore than the toe of the seawall, without the bulkhead wharf they would have remained as much as sixty feet away from the top of the seawall. There would have been no way to load or unload ships along the seawall without the bulkhead wharf.

The design, dimensions, and materials of the bulkhead wharf are closely associated with the history of the seawall. The bulkhead wharf was built, repaired, and rebuilt in the same twenty-one sections as the seawall until about 1912. From 1878 to 1909, the bulkhead wharf was constructed of wood; wooden piles were driven

through the rock embankment of the seawall to support a wooden deck. In 1909, a program was established to replace wooden sections of the bulkhead wharf with reinforced-concrete and steel structures. According to the engineer in charge, the new concrete bulkhead wharves had the advantages of being "absolutely fireproof and they afford no opportunity for vermin to exist."[45]

The bulkhead wharf was not just a walkway; it was designed for the berthing of ships, as evidenced by mooring bitts or bollards on most if its sections. Photographs show piers lined with cargo ships that are tied up by lines to the bulkhead wharf. In addition, smaller ships—launches, lighters, barges, tugs, and others—were tied up at the bulkhead wharf. Trucks loaded with cargo also used the wharf, and cargo was piled on the wharf.

The wharf also supports buildings, notably the bulkhead buildings at the Embarcadero ends of most piers that housed offices, ticket agencies, and waiting rooms. Sanborn maps show many small one- and two-story wood-frame buildings on the old wooden bulkhead wharf. These were generally located between the piers, leaving the wharf at the head of the pier unobstructed to allow space for teams of horses to pull loads on and off the piers.

While for many decades there were some small buildings on the bulkhead wharf at the heads of the piers, none had a bulkhead building in the sense that it later came to be understood: a building at the inshore end of the pier that usually extended up and down the wharf beyond the sides of the pier. The first new concrete wharves were also built without bulkhead buildings. The 1913–1915 Sanborn maps show a development pattern along most of the bulkhead wharf that was little changed. About that time, however, a new pattern emerged, which entailed large bulkhead buildings at the heads of piers, often extending up and down the wharf, and fewer small buildings on the wharf. The new pattern coincided with the rebuilding of the bulkhead wharves.

Freestanding structures for restaurants and for the offices of the chief wharfinger and assistant wharfingers, shipping companies, and stevedoring companies have all been built on the bulkhead wharf. Among these, only a few restaurants survive. Today, in addition to

major structures like the Ferry Building, the Agriculture Building, and the bulkhead buildings, there are several freestanding wharf structures that fit the traditional pattern—the Franciscan Restaurant near Pier 43½, the Pier 29 Annex (Belt Railroad Office Building), the Pier 23 Restaurant, the Pier 28½ Restaurant, and Java House (near Pier 40).

Piers

General Character of Piers

Piers are generally perpendicular to the seawall and extend from the seawall into the bay to distances of eight hundred feet or more. Most piers consist of three component elements. One is the pier *substructure*, a deck on piles that is strong enough to support rail spurs and loaded vehicles. Another is the *transit shed,* an enclosed space that rests upon and covers most of the pier deck. The transit shed is a short-term warehouse for goods either recently arrived in port or about to be shipped out. The third part is the *bulkhead building*, which is an enclosed structure located in front of the transit shed, near the Embarcadero. It houses offices and passenger facilities.

Pier Substructures

The substructures of piers consist of concrete or wooden piles that have been sunk into the bay mud; concrete, wooden, or steel caps that span these piles; and a concrete or wooden deck that rests upon these caps. The portion of the substructure under the transit shed is nearly always made of reinforced concrete; that is, a concrete deck lain over concrete caps that rest upon concrete piles.

The apron of the pier substructure—the portion that runs along the outside of the transit shed on each side—generally measures twenty feet in width. It is made of either concrete or wood and is supported by a substructure of the same material. Although wooden aprons are short lived and need to be replaced periodically, they can absorb the shock of contact with docking ships. On the waterside of the pier aprons are fenders, wooden piles that carry no load but serve to protect the structure of the pier against impact. Rail spurs were laid along the long sides of pier aprons. As a general rule, the rail spurs were flush with the pier deck on one apron and depressed to a level three or four feet below the deck on the other apron. A depressed rail spur formed a loading dock so that goods could be transferred easily from a railcar into the transit shed, or vice versa. Rail spurs of the Belt Railroad joined with the main tracks on the Embarcadero by passing through or running along the side of the bulkhead building.

Transit Sheds   Transit sheds are buildings constructed upon the decks of pier substructures. They serve as temporary warehouses for the storage of goods. They are usually, but not always, located behind an ornamental bulkhead building at the front of the pier. Their interiors are generally raw and unfinished, and the contrast with the more finished public face of the bulkhead buildings is an expression of their role as a workplace.

Structurally, there is great variety among the transit sheds of the waterfront. The majority of them have steel frames and walls of reinforced concrete. Some older transit sheds have concrete walls that were poured in place. The more recently built sheds, from the late 1920s and the 1930s, have walls of prefabricated concrete panels that were lifted onto their frames by cranes.

Transit-shed roofs are supported by steel or wooden trusses with columns of steel I-beams and wooden posts. The roof of a transit shed generally has an extremely shallow pitch and is equipped with a monitor to provide light and air.

The transit sheds open onto their aprons by large, metal roll-up or sliding wood doors. These cargo doors permit the movement of goods between the deck apron and the interior of the transit shed.

Bulkhead Buildings   Bulkhead buildings and transit sheds have different architectural treatments, uses, and often materials, and they were usually designed and built separately. Generally, the bulkhead building was built from one to three years after the transit shed was completed, although the two may have been designed simultaneously. In one case, at Pier 38, the bulkhead building was erected more than two decades later. Bulkhead buildings are framed in wood and clad in stucco. They have elaborate decorated fronts with architectural details of galvanized iron and a central flagpole. Piers 17 and 36 have no bulkhead buildings and have very plain fronts. Piers 26, 28, 45, and 48 have elaborate architectural fronts that are structurally integral to their transit sheds. These piers have no separate bulkhead buildings, although they also incorporate offices at the inshore end of the pier.

Bulkhead Connectors   Bulkhead connectors are buildings on the wharf between the piers, built to accommodate trucks.

This view north in 1917 from the bulkhead wharf at Piers 31 and 33, then under construction, shows rows of concrete piles and a pile-driving rig.

ARCHITECTURE AND PLANNING

During the nineteenth-century development of the port, little if any attention was paid to the appearance of the port's buildings, with the notable exception of the Ferry Building. The long waterfront north and south of the Ferry Building was a working area like a railroad yard or a large industrial plant. There was no public interest in improving the appearance of an area that was frequented primarily by port workers, and the impressions of ship passengers were apparently not a concern. The designers and builders of the port's facilities had one overriding task—to build practical structures as cheaply as possible. In this endeavor, the port had to contend with the frequently changing requirements of shipping and cargo handling and with the short life expectancy of wooden structures in water. Even if someone had proposed architecturally embellished buildings, it would have been impractical to build them because waterfront structures had to be replaced so often.

Even in the abbreviated form in which it was built, lacking its end pavilions, the Ferry Building was a magnificent and astonishing presence on a previously forlorn and forbidding industrial waterfront. Among other things, the Ferry Building was an announcement to the public that they were invited and that the waterfront belonged to them. It was a powerful and persuasive symbol of the ambitions of the port.

:VNION·DEPOT·AND·FERRY-HOVSE:
:SAN·FRANCISCO·: CALIFORNIA:
:A·PAGE·BROWN·ARCHITECT·S·F:

This 1893 rendering of the Ferry House from the office of the architect A. Page Brown for the Board of State Harbor Commissioners (BSHC) included projecting end pavilions that resembled triumphal arches. At the time it was planned and built, it was the only structure that showed the contribution of an architect amid a waterfront dominated by unadorned wooden sheds, many of them in a continual state of deterioration and collapse.

The earliest efforts to improve the appearance of waterfront buildings were perfunctory gestures at the foot of Market Street—the only area regularly encountered by the general public. The original Ferry House, which stood from 1875 to 1896, was a long wooden shed with a central tower, three symmetrically placed shallow gables, and an orderly arcade across the front that screened a chaotic interior.

In contrast to the plain industrial sheds elsewhere on the waterfront, the Ferry House displayed a restrained use of chamfered, turned, and jigsawn elements and the planned placement of painted signs in the frieze of each bay. Other modestly decorated buildings were located on port property nearby. Near the northwest corner of the Ferry House was a two-story wooden structure (perhaps for the chief wharfinger, as it stood in the vicinity of two later chief wharfinger offices) whose exterior was similar in a general way to Italianate style dwellings built by carpenters all over San Francisco. The branch receiving hospital, at the opposite end of the Ferry House, was a small one-story structure with decorative window and door frames typical of the period. Because of the extremely heavy traffic—pedestrians, cable cars, streetcars, horse cars, and omnibuses—passing back and forth in front of the ferry terminal, private property owners

facing the waterfront at the foot of Market Street and in the few blocks on each side sought to draw attention to their businesses. The primary means of getting attention was by installing large signs, sometimes on roofs and sometimes almost obscuring entire buildings.

THE FERRY BUILDING: A STYLISH ANOMALY ON THE WATERFRONT

In the late 1880s, the Board of State Harbor Commissioners (BSHC) decided to replace the 1875 Ferry House with a larger and more efficiently planned structure. The new building would serve as San Francisco's principal transportation terminal: the transcontinental railroad ended there via passenger ferry from Oakland, many cross-bay ferry boats brought thousands of workers there each day, and the city's several street and cable-car lines all terminated at the foot of Market Street, on the city side of the site. Recognizing not only the building's essential functions but also its great symbolic importance, the commissioners hired a well-respected architect, A. Page Brown, to begin designing it in 1892.

Brown had come to San Francisco in 1889 from New York, where he had worked for McKim, Mead, and White, the best-known architectural firm in the United States at that time.

Like that firm, Brown hired promising young architects, many of whom went on to successful careers elsewhere. Among his employees were Willis Polk, who had previously worked with Charles B. Atwood at the firm of D. H. Burnham & Company in Chicago, and A. C. Schweinfurth, who had previously worked with Brown in New York. Richard Longstreth, the author of a study of these architects, wrote of the new Ferry Building:

> Schweinfurth, who had charge of the design, patterned the facade's main block after Charles Atwood's railroad station at the Chicago Fair [the World's Columbian Exposition of 1893], then the academic movement's only precedent for a building of this type in the country. Above, he placed a tower that combines aspects of those on the Piazza San Marco in Venice and the Giralda at Seville . . . here rendered in a severe, almost Neo-Classical manner. The tower served as a beacon identifying the complex from across the Bay and from the further reaches on Market street.[1]

The long wings of the building recall McKim, Mead, and White's Boston Public Library (1888–1895), with its round-arched openings. Construction began on the Ferry Building in 1896. It was partially occupied in 1898 and completed in 1903.

When it was completed, the Ferry Building was an anomaly on the waterfront. While it might have suggested possibilities for embellishing other port buildings, little architectural attention was given to them for many years. The only other ornamented building on the waterfront in that era was the Romanesque Revival style Post Office, just southwest of the Ferry Building, built in 1900–1901. When planning began for a new Post Office a little more than ten years later, the former building was described as "an eyesore and an impediment to traffic."[2]

WILLIS POLK'S PROPOSAL FOR A PERISTYLE AND ARCH AT THE FOOT OF MARKET STREET

Before the Ferry Building was completed, a proposal was made by Willis Polk to improve its setting at the foot of Market Street. Polk may already have influenced the design of the Ferry Building in his 1891 drawings of buildings with campaniles for a proposed world's fair of 1900 in San Francisco.[3] According to Longstreth, the new Ferry Building's effect "was greatly diminished

by the dense pierside traffic and nearby shabby structures. Polk's proposal sought to organize this congestion and subordinate it to an ensemble commensurate with the ferry building's key functional and urbanistic role."[4] Polk proposed a semicircular peristyle that curved westward from the ends of the Ferry Building to a triumphal arch at Market Street. Flanking Market Street, outside of the peristyle, were two-story arcaded commercial buildings that provided an orderly edge to the previously chaotic space in front of the Ferry Building. According to Longstreth, "At that time, the design was more ambitious in scope than any other permanent scheme proposed as a civic ornament in the country."[5]

What Polk and the supporters of his scheme failed to recognize were the functional needs of the port, which made the proposal impractical. While the Belt Railroad did not yet cross Market Street at the time the proposal was first made, in 1897, it was already planned. If the peristyle were built, the railroad would never connect the north and south sections of the waterfront and the operation of the port would be inhibited. Repeatedly publicized until 1910, Polk's proposal was shelved after a decision was made to build the Belt Railroad across Market Street in 1910–1911. The fate of Polk's proposal perfectly represents the priorities of the BSHC and

Before the Ferry Building, the waterfront was a visually chaotic jumble of inharmonious buildings and eye-catching signs. This photograph probably dates from the mid-1890s, when the Chicago Clothing Co., whose large sign is shown on the left, was at 34–40 Kearny Street.

demonstrates its attention to the real needs of the working port.

THE BURNHAM PLAN

Among the supporters of Polk's proposal were Daniel H. Burnham and Edward H. Bennett, whose 1905 plan for San Francisco—commonly called the Burnham Plan—mentioned it briefly.[6] With respect to the waterfront as a whole, Burnham and Bennett's principal interests were in enlarging the port for economic reasons; providing recreational facilities along the bay; and connecting the waterfront to different parts of the city, such as working-class residential areas, by new streets:

The Ferry House, built in 1875, was the predecessor of the Ferry Building. Although it was designed and built by the BSHC on port land and served as the focal point of public activity on the waterfront, it was emblazoned with signs suggesting it was a depot of the Central Pacific Railroad.

> The freight depots, docks and wharves group naturally on the water-front. They should be planned for indefinite expansion and connected with a complete system of warehouses—served on the one hand by railroad tracks or canals and on the other by broad roadways. The warehouse system should be so schemed as to distribute the raw material directly to the manufacturing quarter, and other products as directly as possible to the wholesale trade districts. These in their turn must distribute easily to the retail quarter. The retail quarter follows, in general, in its growth, the residential districts which it serves, limited by the steeper grades of the contours. Thus the whole working city is governed in its location and growth by the two conditions of a maritime city—the water-front and the available level ground.

> San Francisco possesses about ten miles of water-front. As compared with other large cities this is very little, and there is no doubt that it will be inadequate to the needs of the future. Although there is nothing to check its expansion down the eastern bay shore to the county line and beyond, its value decreases as it becomes more remote from the center of the city. It is therefore thought necessary to develop as much as possible that part of the water-front extending from the ferries to Hunter's Point. A system of docks, inclosed [sic] by the sea wall, as shown on the plan, would triple or even quadruple the extent of wharfage. The increased quantities of cargo would be stored in a system of extensive warehouses, thus concentrating shipping as much as possible.[7]

Referring to the so-called Outer Boulevard, a proposed new road that would encircle the city, Burnham suggested:

> It is necessary to connect it with that section of the city lying near it, inhabited by people of moderate means. When the main arteries from this section intersect it, there should be piers for public recreation, a yacht and boat harbor and vast bathing places, both inclosed [sic], and open air. People will seek the Outer Boulevard, and will find refreshment and benefit from the water frontage. The design of the roadway arranges for this without interfering with its use for shipping.[8]

In addition, Burnham and Bennett made the first suggestion for improving the appearance of the waterfront as a whole. Describing the section of their proposed Outer Boulevard north of the Ferry Building, they wrote:

> Taking the foot of Market as a starting point, the Outer Boulevard runs north along East Street, traversing the docks and passing around the base of Telegraph Hill. The direction of this part follows the line of the water-front; where it passes close to the wharves it cannot take the same level as the street, but must be elevated. It is therefore proposed to carry it over the warehouses, its roadway forming their roofs. This will give the city an extensive line of fireproof storage property and will enhance the value of the neighboring realty. This elevated part of the boulevard may be beautifully treated. There should be enough space to allow a foot or two of earth for planting. It will then be an ideal place for a ride or a walk, the passer-by looking down on the shipping below, and when he tires of watching the activities and listening to the voices of the men engaged in the work of the port, he may note the changing aspects of the sea and study the effects of sunshine and shadow on islands and mountains seen through the masts of the ships. This treatment will lend delightful variety to a drive on the boulevard, and will add a special charm to the life of the city.[9]

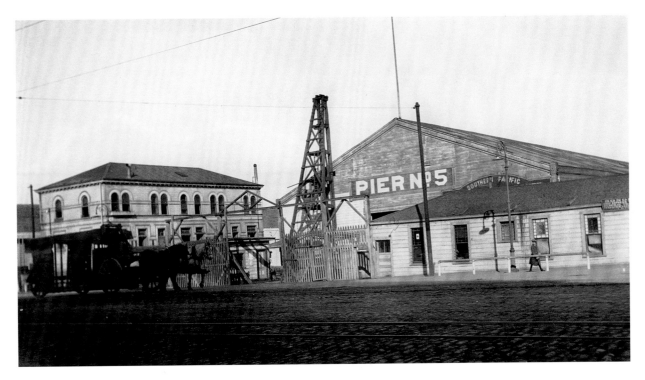

Until the piers were rebuilt in modern materials and provided with stylish facades, which occurred in increments from 1908 to 1938, large, plain transit sheds stood on the piers and an uncoordinated mix of wooden buildings lined the bulkhead wharf. In this 1919 view of Pier 5, a pile-driving rig on the bulkhead wharf is engaged in the endless task of replacing wooden piles.

East Street S.F

The BSHC designed and built the Ferry Post Office of 1901 with Romanesque Revival style details. Although the building had architectural pretensions, it was soon disliked for both its obstructive location forward of the Ferry Building and its appearance, considered out of date in a city attracted to the City Beautiful Movement. The rear of the building housed a planing mill and blacksmith shop for the port's maintenance department.

Elsewhere, Burnham and Bennett made general recommendations for the "adornment of streets and related matters by means of the design of curbs, sidewalks, lamp posts, and letter boxes; regulations regarding building heights, commercial signs and cornice heights; and the use of commemorative monuments, fountains, etc."[10] There is no record that these ideas, although specific to the port, were ever discussed by the BSHC, which would have been responsible for executing them. The Burnham plan was presented to the mayor and Board of Supervisors of San Francisco; the BSHC was a state agency. From the BSHC's point of view, the recommendations would have been expensive to realize, and they were irrelevant to the operation of the port.

OTHER PROPOSALS

While Polk's proposal was going nowhere, concern for improving the area in front of the Ferry Building took other forms. In November 1908, the Outdoor Art League advocated "improving the appearance of East Street opposite the ferry depot, where above a row of wooden shacks, there rises a skyline of noisily colored advertising signs"—outside the jurisdiction of the port.[11]

Ultimately, attention was paid to the appearance of the waterfront as a whole because of broader concerns about the city, of which the waterfront was a part. Writing in the *San Francisco Chronicle* in 1914, C. A. Horne observed that the waterfront had three facades: the outer ends of the piers, the facades of the piers along the Embarcadero, and the "most unpleasing conglomeration of shacks and billboards" on the opposite side of the Embarcadero. He was not hopeful that things could be much improved on the private buildings facing the port, except in the space in front of the Ferry Building—"The Front Door of San Francisco"— which ought to be beautified to symbolize San Francisco's role in America's Manifest Destiny.[12]

Horne also described a plan, which the BSHC was considering, to use the bulkhead wharf for a mile on each side of the Ferry Building "for a continuous structure through which the entrances to the wharves would be arched at regular intervals, and the second story of which might be utilized for an uninterrupted esplanade and passenger electric line."[13] The plan was not adopted.

Looking forward to the Panama-Pacific International Exposition (PPIE) in 1915, Horatio

Stoll, a journalist, wrote in *Architect and Engineer*: "We want to be able to show the millions of people who will visit San Francisco in 1915, when the Panama-Pacific Exposition is in full swing, that we have a sense of civic pride."[14] Stoll addressed ideas of beautification familiar from the Burnham plan and commented on several parts of the city, including the foot of Market Street: "It is true our Ferry Building is striking and unique, but whatever good impression is made from the water side is lost the moment the visitor passes through the building and looks out upon East Street. The semi-circle of temporary wooden buildings, topped with hideous signs, gives the city an air of crude provincialism and makes the stranger smile."[15] While Stoll reiterated old concerns, he did so in the context of advocating a general beautification of the public buildings and places of the city, including the waterfront.

In 1912, San Francisco's Commonwealth Club, which like the Chamber of Commerce routinely studied areas of public concern such as the port, addressed the appearance of the waterfront. The group noted as precedents that a new plan for New York's port included a park and that along the riverfronts of Antwerp and Vienna "artistic development [was] greatly promoted."[16] In speaking to the Commonwealth Club, the president of the BSHC, J. J. Dwyer, stated, "In reference to the port's current plans, we are trying to make this new construction ornamental as well as useful to

the city."[17] Dwyer modified a Burnham proposal, suggesting a rooftop promenade and outlook. He reiterated this idea in 1915: "Plans are being perfected to provide walks on the roofs of several of the docks."[18]

BEAUTIFICATION OF PIER FRONTS

In a 1917 construction handbook, *Wharves and Piers*, Carleton Greene wrote about transit sheds: "The facades of such buildings as well as the outshore ends of the pier sheds call for architectural ornamentation and embellishment to fit the aesthetic requirements of the structure and the locality."[19] He illustrated this idea with drawings and photographs of the sheds at the Chelsea Piers in New York, the 33rd Street Pier in Brooklyn, Commonwealth Pier 5 in Boston, and Piers 30–32 in San Francisco. For two of these, he showed both inshore and outer ends, the latter being much more simply and sparingly ornamented.[20]

Indeed, the first of San Francisco's piers with ornamental fronts were designed in 1912 while Dwyer was president of the BSHC and Augustus V. Saph was assistant state engineer. In the *Biennial Report* of 1910–1912, Saph wrote, regarding Piers 26, 28, and 30–32: "A modified Mission Style has been adopted for the front. This will serve to make the waterfront more attractive and will, it is thought, meet with general approval."[21] Two years later, with reference to a planned series of new piers,

The Burnham Plan of 1905 presented a grand City Beautiful vision of San Francisco as a whole while devoting substantial attention to the port. The plan proposed boulevards that would link the port to working-class neighborhoods, opportunities for recreation and views, and a substantial expansion of the port to the south, including docks like those in London. His idea for an elevated roadway along the waterfront was eventually realized, in a fashion, by the Embarcadero Freeway.

Saph's successor, Jerome Newman, wrote, "To add to the attractiveness of the front, the old ugly type of shed front was abandoned and the pier fronts south of Market Street are to be built in modified Mission style, those north of Market Street being designed on the lines of the Chelsea piers in New York."[22] This was the crucial moment that affected the appearance of almost all the piers that were subsequently built and that survive today.

TYPICAL SECTION OF ISLAIS CREEK PARK

Above: The Burnham Plan included a park with a free-flowing stream to the bay along Islais Creek and a roadway that crossed the creek on a bridge. The models for this park were Stony Brook Park in Boston and Rock Creek Park in Washington, D.C.

Opposite: For years after the failure of Polk's peristyle and arch proposal, the view that faced people leaving the Ferry Building was little changed, as seen here in 1913.

This moment came for two reasons: a change in attitude represented by the City Beautiful Movement and innovations in building technology that made it economically reasonable to invest money in architectural appearances. The lifespan of most piers up to this time was limited by the rapid deterioration of wooden structures exposed to seawater, salt air, and especially destructive marine creatures commonly called shipworms. As long as piers had to be frequently replaced, it made no sense to spend extra money on their appearance. However, with better technology—notably the Holmes patent of 1901 for concrete-jacketed piles and especially the satisfactory use of reinforced concrete in 1908—the longevity of piers increased substantially. Reinforced-concrete piers were described as "permanent." With a shift to long-lasting

construction, the cost of beautifying pier fronts could be justified. In relation to the cost of an expensive reinforced-concrete pier that would last many decades, the one-time investment in an ornamental facade did not seem an unreasonable expense.

CITY BEAUTIFUL MOVEMENT

The effort to beautify the piers and the BSHC's particular style choices can be understood in relation to broader historical and architectural developments of the time. The desire to improve the appearance of the piers was an aspect of the City Beautiful Movement. This widespread movement is generally considered to have begun with the World's Columbian Exposition—the Chicago World's Fair—of 1893, the same event that had provided models for the design of the Ferry Building. The fair was a temporary exposition of grand public buildings and heroic statuary located around landscaped courtyards and pools. The leading figure of the City Beautiful Movement, Daniel H. Burnham, was one of the designers of the World's Columbian Exposition and the author of several city plans—including those for San Francisco in 1905 and Chicago in 1909—that attempted to transfer some of the lessons of the fair to permanent urban settings. In these plans he proposed the general improvement of American cities through the selected actions of public authorities, such as the creation of ornamental streets, the establishment of cornice heights and height limits, the placement of monuments and fountains, and the design and construction of monumental public buildings, alone and in ensembles.

City Beautiful ideas were unusually popular in San Francisco, where they were realized more than in most American cities, a function of San Francisco's large number of Beaux-Arts–trained architects and the imperial aspirations of the city's leaders. Just before the earthquake and fire of 1906, the Board of Supervisors adopted the Burnham plan as the city's policy. While the earthquake changed the conditions under which the plan had been written, nevertheless many aspects of the plan were carried out over the next thirty years or more. Among these, in more or less modified form, were the park on top of Telegraph Hill, Aquatic Park, Park Presidio, the Great Highway, O'Shaughnessy Boulevard

WEST SIDE OF EMBARCADERO   JUNE 3, 1913

through Glen Canyon, and the Civic Center. As built, the Civic Center was in a different location and followed a completely different design from Burnham's plan. Nonetheless, it was the ultimate expression of the City Beautiful Movement in San Francisco.

While it was not part of Burnham's plan, the Panama-Pacific International Exposition represented similar ideas about planning and architecture. Like the Columbian Exposition, it consisted of an arrangement of monumental public buildings around courtyards and pools. The exposition was a celebration of San Francisco's rapid and impressive reconstruction after the 1906 earthquake and fire. In a more

practical sense, it was also a marketing effort, asserting that San Francisco was the best suited of the Pacific Coast ports to benefit from trade through the newly opened Panama Canal. The reinvigorated city was ready to follow the United States' military victory in the Philippines with a commercial conquest of trade routes across the Pacific Ocean. In practical terms, the port would be the primary agent of the great prosperity that would soon come to San Francisco.

The City Beautiful Movement also influenced the location and design of many other projects in San Francisco, including the decorated fronts of the Stockton Street tunnel, which connected the downtown hotel district to the exposition; the placement and design of numerous hillside walkways and balustrades throughout the city; the monumental designs of many downtown buildings, as well as of substations of the Pacific Gas & Electric Company; and not least of all, the architectural treatment of the inshore and outer ends of the piers along the Embarcadero. Burnham did not propose the decorated pier ends, but they were in the spirit of his suggestions for the waterfront and were similar to other City Beautiful–era projects in San Francisco.

The City Beautiful Movement was generally promoted by architects who had studied at the Ecole des Beaux-Arts in Paris, the leading architectural school in the world at that time, or at any of a number of schools or ateliers in the United States that were influenced by the Ecole. Although the buildings of the City Beautiful Movement were typically designed in monumental classical styles, sometimes referred to as Beaux-Arts classicism, neither the City Beautiful Movement nor the Ecole had an essential connection to any particular architectural style. More important were the principles associated with the Ecole's curriculum and the goals of improving and beautifying the city as a whole. The Ecole taught a method of design that followed principles of hierarchy, symmetry, axiality, and unity.

The City Beautiful Movement was related to the politics of reform, usually represented by members of the Progressive or Republican parties. Reform efforts were directed against corrupt machine politics that were typically associated with labor interests and immigrant groups. In California, much of the reform effort was directed at the Southern Pacific Railroad's control of politicians and political parties. In San Francisco, the reformers' greatest victory was the successful prosecution for graft of political boss Abraham Ruef and Mayor Eugene Schmitz. Reformers promised to apply good business practices to government as well as standards of honesty, openness, and fairness. Among the major City Beautiful efforts in the United States that were adopted as emblems of governmental reform were the McMillan Plan of 1901–1902 for Washington, D.C., and the San Francisco Civic Center.

The architectural imagery of the City Beautiful Movement was also associated with the United States' new status as an imperial nation following the annexation of Hawaii and the conquest of the Philippines. In San Francisco, this imagery expressed the "self-professed imperial destiny" of the city's commercial and political leaders.[23] Because the port provided the principal means for achieving the city's imperial destiny, it was natural that its piers would reflect these aspirations in their City Beautiful architecture.

MISSION REVIVAL STYLE AND VARIATIONS

In the absence of any record of discussion among the commissioners and others, one can only surmise the reasons why the "modified Mission style" was chosen for the pier ends south of the Ferry Building. In a very general sense, designs for buildings in California that drew on the Spanish missions and more generally on Mediterranean vernacular architecture were part of an effort to develop an architecture that reflected California's history and character. Like the many Southern Pacific and Santa Fe railroad stations, buildings in the Mission Revival style sought both to establish a distinctive identity for California and to market the state to outsiders as a special place that had its own honorable and romantic history.

At the time the decision on architectural style was made, the Belt Railroad did not yet link the areas to the south and north of the Ferry Building. In the nineteenth century, the southern area had been served only by the Southern Pacific. In fact, that area was sometimes referred to as Southern Pacific territory. Whether it was intentional or not, the use of architectural imagery identified with the Southern Pacific in an area that it had long served exclusively may have reinforced the connection between the southern part of the port and the railroad.

Although the Mission Revival style is not normally associated with the City Beautiful Movement, which saw its greatest impact in cities of the East and Midwest, its use at the port

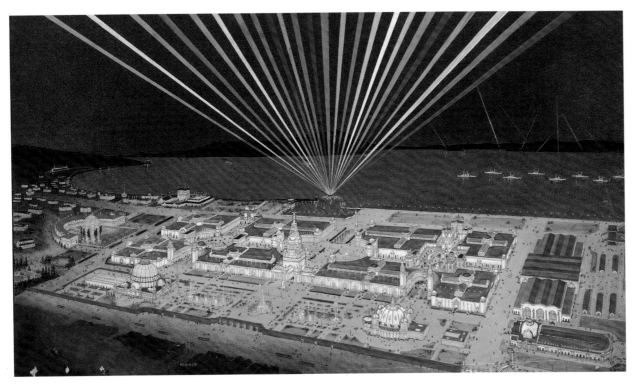

Business interests led the effort to organize an international exposition whose very name—the Panama-Pacific International Exposition—was an advertisement that encouraged ships coming through the newly opened Panama Canal to stop in San Francisco.

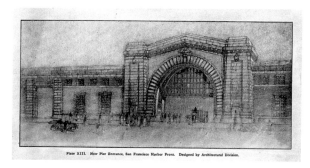

on a grand public scale reflected the goals and principles of the movement. In fact, the same can be said for many early-twentieth-century civic ensembles in California that adopted the Mission or Mediterranean style, including those in Ojai, Riverside, Palos Verdes Estates, and Santa Barbara. From 1912 to 1916, the bulkhead buildings of Piers 16–18–20, 22, 24, 26, 28, and 30–32 were all built in the Mission Revival style. Beginning in 1915, Pier 22½, Piers 38 and 40, and Piers 42, 44, and 46A were designed in a style more Mediterranean than Mission, but they were compatible in their stucco walls and red-tile roofs with the Mission Revival style pier fronts.

NEOCLASSICAL STYLE

Like the decision to use a "modified" Mission Revival style in the southern section of the port, the choice of the Neoclassical style for the piers north of the Ferry Building is similarly undocumented in BSHC records. It is evident that the Chelsea Piers in New York—the most modern facilities in the largest port in the United States—served as a model. As New York dominated trade on the Atlantic, San Francisco aspired to dominate trade on the Pacific. New York's port was facing the same issues as San Francisco's at the same time. At both ports, the length and width of piers, the construction of transit sheds and rail spurs on the piers, and the use of materials that were considered both

permanent and fire resistant were all means
of better serving increasingly larger ships and
providing for more efficient cargo handling. The
architectural decoration of the fronts of the piers
that met these other needs called attention to the
investments that had been made, the aspirations
of the port managers, and the capabilities of the
port. It also reflected a new concern for the port's
public image in the spirit of the City Beautiful
Movement.

The Chelsea Piers, proposed in 1907 and
completed in 1912, consisted of nine piers and
their bulkhead connectors along thirteen blocks
of the Hudson River waterfront below West
23rd Street. Warren and Wetmore, the architects
of Grand Central Station, designed them with

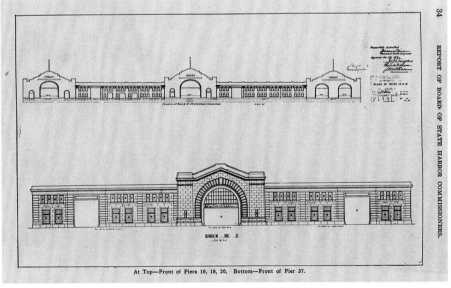

At Top—Front of Piers 16, 18, 20. Bottom—Front of Pier 37.

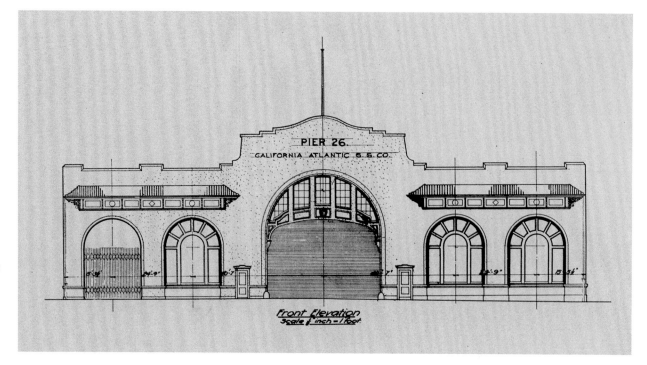

Pier 16 was designed in the Mission Revival Style and completed in 1915.

lavish, oversized details and rich sculptural elements. The ensemble provided a unified streetscape of identical pier fronts alternating with bulkhead connectors. San Francisco did not copy the Chelsea Piers directly but took the general idea as inspiration. New York's gabled pier fronts with wide arched openings and two-story bulkhead connectors provided the basic model, but the proportions and fenestration of their San Francisco counterparts were different to accommodate somewhat different functional requirements.

Whereas the Chelsea Piers were unified and regular because they were built as one project, San Francisco's pier fronts varied considerably in small ways. The pier fronts in San Francisco

took more than twice as long to build as those in New York and were carried out under a series of changing administrations. While the Chelsea Piers were the work of one of the leading architectural firms in New York, whose design partner had studied at the Ecole des Beaux-Arts, San Francisco's pier fronts were designed primarily by junior-level engineers. Only a few of San Francisco's pier fronts were realized with the participation of an architect. Piers 31, 3, and 24 were designed by A. A. Pyle, an unlicensed draftsman, in 1915–1918; and Pier 5 was designed in 1920 by Arthur D. Janssen, who did not receive his architectural license until several years later.

GOTHIC REVIVAL STYLE

Toward the end of the period when the decorated piers were constructed, Pier 45 at the north and Piers 48 and 50 at the south were designed with Gothic-inspired ornamentation on their facades. Somewhat removed from the main group of piers, Pier 45 was separated from Pier 41 by a car-ferry slip at Pier 43 and was adjacent to Fisherman's Wharf, a different type of neighborhood than that of the other piers. Piers 48 and 50 were separated from the piers to their north by China Basin. In addition to their locations and the style of their facades, these piers were distinctive for other reasons. They were the first piers wide enough to accommodate two parallel transit sheds. Pier 45 was longer than any of the other piers; it was built at an angle so that its length would fit within the official Pier Head Line. Catering to a new generation of larger ships and bigger business, these piers were intended to be the most modern and efficient on the waterfront.

The Gothic Revival was a common style for commercial buildings in the 1920s; one example, the thirty-one-story Russ Building of 1927, was the tallest building in San Francisco at the time. While the port did not explain why it used this style for Piers 45, 48, and 50, the differences in size and layout between these piers and others must account for the choice. The style helped distinguish them from the other piers and at the same time provided a unified image for a new type of larger pier.

OTHER STYLES

Two other styles are represented in the district, neither of which appears to have been selected with special consideration of its architectural relationship to other waterfront buildings. The building now called Pier 29 Annex, a small office building, was located originally near the north end of the Ferry Building and later moved to its present site. At the time it was built in 1909, the stylistic designations for the areas north and south of the Ferry Building had not yet been made. However, with its stucco walls and decorative tile detail, it would have been compatible with the Mission Revival style buildings later erected south of the Ferry Building. Its vertical band of windows under overhanging eaves shows the influence of Prairie School models.

The Ferry Station Post Office of 1914–1915, later known as the Agriculture Building, was conceived in the manner of many U.S. post offices around the country. Under a series of supervising architects of the U.S. Treasury—James Knox Taylor (1897–1912), Oscar Wenderoth (1913–1914), and James A. Wetmore (1915–1933)—a large number of post offices were built as two- or three-story rectangular structures with hip roofs and materials, colors, and details that suggested a small Italian Renaissance palazzo. Although the Ferry Station Post Office was designed by A. A. Pyle under

chief engineer Jerome Newman of the BSHC, its design followed the established pattern of post offices overseen by architects for the federal government. Thus, the designers of this post office chose an architectural image that associated it with buildings of its type rather than with other port buildings.

RESPONSE TO THE BEAUTIFIED PIERS

When the first of the decorated pier fronts were completed, *The Architect and Engineer* wrote admiringly: "Some wonderful changes have been effected along the San Francisco water front, and the dilapidated, unsightly buildings which once distorted the bay and street frontages are, happily, gradually giving way to substantial structures, carrying more than a mere suggestion of architectural beauty."[24] The article was illustrated with photographs and drawings of the new "modified" Mission Revival style buildings south of the Ferry Building: Piers 16–18–20, 26, 28, and 30–32. The article also included drawings of two buildings with classical and Renaissance imagery, an unspecified "New Pier Entrance," and a "building for the Wells Fargo Express Company" south of the Ferry Building.

The published drawing of the "New Pier Entrance" is similar in design to that of several pier fronts later built north of the Ferry Building. In the richness of detail, it is more like the Chelsea Piers than any of San Francisco's piers as they were built. The rendering is by a skilled architectural draftsman and is more like a presentation drawing prepared by an architectural firm for a prospective client than the as-built drawings on file at the port. All of the drawings published in *Architect and Engineer* were

The grandeur of the City Beautiful Movement, more commonly associated with the Neoclassical style north of the Ferry Building, was also expressed in the similar repetition of pier fronts to the south, though rendered with Mission and Mediterranean architectural imagery. The choice of this style was part of a wider effort to create a romanticized identity for California and to market that identity for a variety of purposes.

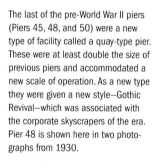

attributed to the "Architectural Division, State Department of Engineering," under the direction of the state architect, George B. McDougall. In a few instances, the office of the state architect prepared proposals for the pier fronts and other structures that were later modified by the staff of the BSHC. From 1908 to 1931, the state engineer appointed both the state architect and the assistant state engineer for the BSHC. In 1918, Irving Morrow explained the relationship in that period:

> The Board maintains its own drafting department in San Francisco, subsidiary to the State Department of Engineering, with Mr. A. A. Pyle as Architectural Designer. Most of the work erected by the Board is designed in this office; although the drawings for a few buildings have come from the Office of the State Architect at Sacramento, and certain others have been executed by the Board's drafting department from sketches furnished by the State Architect.[25]

Otherwise, the staff of the chief engineer of the BSHC designed all of the port's buildings.

Similarly, Morrow admired the individual buildings more than the ensembles, especially "some of the minor buildings, such as launch and barge offices, the Harbor Ferry Ticket office, etc.," and the Ferry Station Post Office most of all,

while criticizing the pier fronts as merely "facade design." In his analysis of the groups, he wrote:

> As a street of unusually ample width and continually changing alignment, bordered on the outer side of its curve by public structures of large size and generous scale, the Embarcadero offers at once peculiar problems of design and peculiar opportunities for effect. It is just this aspect of the street as a continuously diminishing perspective and continually changing alignment that seems to have escaped attention. Each pier front is what might be described as over-designed; by which we mean to indicate, not over-ornamented, but designed with excessive insistence upon its own entity, to the exclusion of a consideration of the ensemble of which it must form a part.[26]

This emphasis on individual designs was a function of the protracted period of construction, which was necessitated by a funding scheme that depended on annual revenues.

The influential critic B. J. S. Cahill considered the port's buildings to be well designed individually but disappointing as a group:

> They are strong, dignified buildings and though not carried out quite in the spirit of the original designs, they serve their ends by the substantiality of their aspect and sane economy in the material and detail

of their architectural composition. Although one might deplore the fact that in such a long succession of structures lining the Embarcadero, some more unifying type of design was not adopted that would tie this fine sweep of buildings into one splendid and extended composition.[27]

CONTINUATION OF THE ARCHITECTURAL PROGRAM

By mid-1914, the program for architectural decoration at the port of San Francisco was established. This program would be followed almost without exception through the late 1930s along the waterfront. By that time, the central section of the port was fully developed. The architectural program was not followed for the extension of Pier 36 in 1917 or for developments south of Pier 50. It is not clear why Pier 36 was not decorated like its neighbors. It may be simply that its construction was at a time when money was particularly scarce due to the shortages and demands caused by the war in Europe. The developments south of Pier 50 were farther from the center of the city and from general public view, in a large area referred to by the BSHC as the industrial lands. While they were important, modern facilities that were expensive to build, their architectural image would not have had the same public-relations benefit as that of the piers along the Embarcadero.

FROM ARCHITECTURE TO ADVERTISING AND PUBLIC RELATIONS

By the early 1920s, with the architectural program in place, the BSHC began to expand its efforts at business promotion and public relations beyond architecture. During the biennium of 1918–1920, the port created a new position for a "business solicitor" to advertise for new business.[28] By 1922, the port hired a commercial agent and advertising director. In that period, pamphlets were created, a motion picture was commissioned, a history of the port was prepared, and exhibits were displayed at the State Fair, the Fresno County Fair, and the California Industrial Exposition.[29] From this time forward, advertising and public relations would take an increasing share of the port's budget as the agency worked to maintain a positive image for itself.

In the aftermath of World War II, when the primary task of the engineering department was remodeling existing spaces, efforts to create new uses of port property—such as the proposal for Embarcadero City—went nowhere. Furthermore, the port landscape was degraded by the construction of the Embarcadero Freeway in 1954–1958.

The last design for the port in a prewar style was made after World War II, as part of an effort to reconfigure the little-used Ferry Building as an interurban terminal.

EPILOGUE: THE PORT SINCE 1969

Over many decades of change, the basic physical and operational character of the port of San Francisco remained the same. Since the time of the Gold Rush, the port had been developed largely with finger piers to handle break-bulk cargo and, to a lesser extent, with specialized facilities for bulk cargo. Cargo was hauled back and forth between the waterfront and inland warehouses and factories. Facilities for shipping companies, seamen, and other workers were also located inland. Even major changes—the increasing size of ships, the shift from wind power to steam power, the arrival of the railroads, the construction of the Belt Railroad, the opening of the bridges and the rise of trucking, the organization of labor, and the competition from other ports—did not by themselves alter the fundamental structure of the port and its relationship to the city. The port adapted to each of these changes with incremental improvements.

Pier 14, built in 2005, affords the public views of the waterfront.

Because the waterfront north of China Basin was fully developed, after World War II the port could expand only by moving south. The first large developments after the war were at Islais Creek and at Pier 50, which in 1950 was extended to an outcropping in the bay called Mission Rock, creating a hybrid known as Mission Rock Terminal. This 1959 photograph shows Pier 54 at the bottom, a Santa Fe car-ferry terminal just above it, and Mission Rock Terminal, with its triangular outer end, in the center.

In the late 1950s, a consultant to the port recommended moving shipping operations from the northern waterfront to new, larger facilities at the southern end and developing the northern waterfront with non-maritime uses that would produce income for the port. The first plan based on this idea was a 1959 proposal for Embarcadero City, which would have replaced the piers with housing, hotels, offices, retail, and commercial businesses.

Then, in a short period in the 1960s and 1970s, a variety of forces that had been building over time set in motion a major transformation of the port.[1] An irreversible decline in the fundamental business of the port—shipping—began after World War II. This was the product of many factors: competition from Oakland and other West Coast ports, higher labor costs, higher land values adjacent to port land that drove away port-related businesses, the suburbanization of warehousing and other industry in an era of flexible and cheap truck transportation, and, most of all, the decline of break-bulk cargo handling in the face of the rise of containerization.

These changes rendered the basic physical structures of the port obsolete. Rows of finger piers adjacent to a densely built-up city could not adequately serve container shipping, which involved larger ships that required larger wharves and much larger areas of open space for loading and unloading.

Frustration over the decline of the port and over efforts to reverse the situation was directed in large part toward its management by the state of California. This led to passage of the Burton Act in 1968, authorizing transfer of the port to the city of San Francisco. The actual date of final transfer on February 7, 1969, was only one of many events associated with the decline and reorientation of the port, but it can also be seen as representing other major changes. In particular, 1969 was roughly the midpoint of the short period when the revolutionary impact of containerization was widely recognized. In 1967, the port of Oakland surpassed that of San Francisco in the net income derived from its operations, largely because of its early commitment to container technology; two years later, Oakland surpassed San Francisco in the volume of cargo handled.[2] In 1971, Oakland was briefly the second largest port in the world, while San Francisco's shipping business sunk to a new low point.[3]

The transfer of the port to the city was a response to particular conditions of the time, but many of the issues were old ones that had been raised numerous times in the past—beginning in 1906, if not before, and again in almost every decade of the twentieth century. While various ideas to address the problems of the port had been proposed by 1969, no clear new direction had been adopted. Indeed, it would be twenty years after the city's takeover before definitive movement toward effective strategies would be made.

During the 1950s, there was a brief movement toward consolidating all Bay Area ports under a single state agency. In 1951, the San Francisco Bay Ports Commission on the Establishment of the Northern California Ports and Terminals Bureau was created by the legislature to promote and develop the bay as a single harbor. After issuing a couple of reports, the organization faded away. At a time when the port of San Francisco was losing business to other ports in the area, those other ports did not see an advantage in cooperation.

The core idea about how to redirect the port was first given concrete public expression in the 1959 report of Ebasco Services of New York, a consultant to the San Francisco Port Authority. Based on a comparison with trends at other ports, where new facilities were being built for larger ships with more open space, Ebasco recommended moving more shipping operations from the northern waterfront to the area south of the Bay Bridge and building new facilities there. On the northern waterfront, there was no room to expand on port property,

and adjacent land formerly used for support services was being redeveloped for residential and commercial projects such as the Golden Gateway Center and, later, the Embarcadero Center. Because new shipping facilities on the southern waterfront would still not provide adequate income to support the port, Ebasco proposed new commercial developments in the vacated port property on the northern waterfront. The port would use income from these developments for infrastructure improvements and other costs associated with shipping.[4]

In the absence of any formal plan for development of the port for several more years, these ideas, reiterated by others, provided an informal guide during the 1960s. In fact, the port had already begun moving in the proposed direction with the construction of a large grain elevator at Islais Creek in 1949 and the Mission Rock Terminal at Pier 50 in 1950.

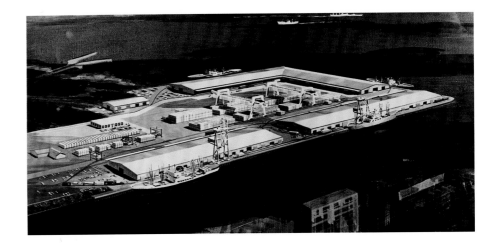

The first major manifestation of the new idea to develop the northern waterfront for nonmaritime purposes was the proposal by the Port Authority in 1959 for Embarcadero City—a complete redesign of the area from Fisherman's Wharf to the Ferry Building that would replace the finger piers with housing, hotels, offices, retail developments, and other commercial uses on new structures over the water. The geographer Jasper Rubin describes this as "a financial scheme reflected in a spatial pattern."[5] In other words, it was less a real proposal than an embodiment of the notion that commercial development on the northern waterfront could

The Army Street Terminal, which opened in 1967, represented an attempt to attract the break-bulk cargo business from the northern waterfront to a new, more spacious location.

If shipping and cargo handling were moving out of the neighborhood, then not only the piers and other port facilities but also the adjacent privately owned warehouses and port-related businesses would become obsolete. The International Market Center was a 1968 proposal by a private developer for the reuse of both port and private land on the northern waterfront as a multiblock complex with a hotel, exhibit halls, and showrooms for the wholesale trade.

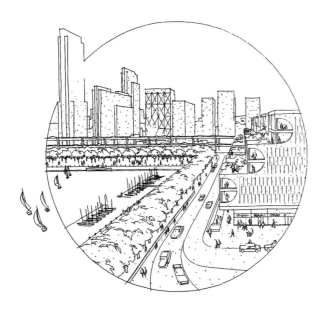

About the time of the transfer of the port from state to city jurisdiction in 1969, the port sponsored a proposal for Ferry Port Plaza, a complex of offices, a hotel, and shops built over the water in place of Piers 1–7.

support the shipping infrastructure on the southern waterfront. "Moreover," he claims, "the goal of such development was to produce a sort of triumphal architecture and design that would help San Francisco lay claim to a new place in the global urban hierarchy."[6] The proposal never advanced beyond its initial presentation.

A few proposals that conformed to the informal vision to move shipping south and develop the northern waterfront with non-maritime uses succeeded in being built. Pier 92 was developed for "Specialty Terminals" in the mid-1960s. The Specialty Oils Terminal opened in 1964 to ship tallow to Asia and to import coconut oil.

The Import Car Terminal opened in 1965 with a capacity for roll-on/roll-off loading, sometimes called Ro-Ro. Pier 92 also had a Cotton Terminal. In 1967, the Army Street Terminal opened at Pier 80 on the north side of Islais Creek. This was a large facility intended to draw scattered surviving break-bulk businesses from the northern waterfront to a single location that offered more room and better land-transportation connections. At the same time, however, Oakland was building container facilities that would handle far more business than even a large break-bulk terminal. Pier 80 was later modified to handle more containers.

In addition, office developments were built on port land, on seawall lots that were no longer needed as rail yards. The first two were in progress when the transfer took place and were completed afterward.

A by-product of the issues surrounding the port was an increase in public scrutiny of the port's direction and of any proposals that affected the area. This, together with new layers of government review, complicated proposals for any new actions. Although the port was still owned by the state of California, the city began to insist for the first time on the application of its own planning policies and zoning regulations. Prominent among these was a forty-foot height limit along the waterfront, enacted in 1964. At the state level, in 1965 the Bay Conservation and Development Corporation (BCDC) was created by the McAteer-Petris Act to control development along the shoreline of the bay. In 1969, BCDC completed its governing document, the Bay Plan.

The transfer agreement between the state and the city that took effect in February 1969 required that the city spend fifty million dollars on improvements in the first ten years and one hundred million dollars in twenty-five years. This requirement propelled the new Port Commission into new ventures that adhered to the existing notion to move shipping to the south and redevelop the northern waterfront for non-maritime uses that would generate income to support continued port operations.

Even before the official transfer date, in late 1968, developers proposed a multi-block project, the International Market Center, on a mix of private and port land along the Embarcadero from Union to North Point streets. This was a

MULTIPORT

This steady program of Port of San Francisco development is producing a versatile lineup of terminals. Pier 94 Intermodal Terminal is planned as the central facility.

four-million-square-foot project that combined elements of what had previously been proposed for the World Trade Center with facilities for the wholesale trade: a hotel, exhibit halls, and showrooms for home furnishings, international goods, and apparel. Except for rehabilitation of the Ice House, a cold-storage warehouse built in 1914, nothing of this project was realized before it went bankrupt in 1971.[7]

While the International Market Center was a private project—the port's role was principally to make some of its underused land available—the port proposed a second project before the transfer, Ferry Port Plaza, in January 1969. Designed by Skidmore, Owings & Merrill, Ferry Port Plaza would have replaced Piers 1 through 7 just north of the Ferry Building with a complex over the water that included a hotel, offices, and shops. Public opposition and non-conformance with BCDC policies defeated this project.[8]

Among all of the "grand plans" of this era, which Rubin calls "ill-considered schemes for development of incautious proportions,"[9] the most incautious would have replaced Piers 14 to 24, south of the Ferry Building, with a 550-foot-tall office tower for United States Steel and a ship passenger terminal. Also designed by Skidmore, Owings & Merrill, it was proposed in 1969 and defeated in 1971 by public opposition and its violation of BCDC and planning department policies, notably the height limit.[10]

The rationale for these proposals—that they would pay for port improvements on the southern waterfront—was one side of the coin. The other side was maintaining and increasing San Francisco's port business with real maritime projects. Following the transfer, the port, driven by its need to make major improvements, quickly proposed an eleven-million-dollar bond issue to build a large new shipping terminal at Pier 96 on the north side of India Basin. This was the first significant effort to respond to the new scale and technology of shipping. Rather than committing largely to container shipping, as Oakland and most other ports did, San Francisco sought to develop "a greater variety of specialized terminals than any other Pacific Coast port."[11]

The most ambitious of these plans was also the most highly publicized because of its great expense and rapid failure. It was the LASH Terminal at Pier 96, an unsuccessful method of adapting to changing methods of cargo handling. Shortly following the development of Pier 96, other shipping improvements were built on the southern waterfront, including new facilities for grain along Islais Creek. In 1975, Pier 94, abutting Pier 96 on the north, was opened on a large site as a container terminal with "advanced intermodal facilities . . . to create the most highly integrated land/sea terminal on the Pacific Coast," according to the port's publicity.[12]

In striking contrast to projects that were

Required by the transfer agreement to make major improvements in the 1970s, the port developed large facilities to accommodate new cargo-handling technologies. The 1972 LASH Terminal at Pier 96, shown in the upper left of this rendering, quickly proved to be a dead end. The container terminal at Pier 94, shown in the center, opened in 1975. Although they were called piers, both facilities were large areas of landfill with wharves along the water.

The remaking of port property north of China Basin for non-maritime uses was facilitated by the involvement of the Redevelopment Agency in building the South Beach Marina in 1986, South Beach Harbor Park in 1995–2005, and the stadium for the San Francisco Giants in 2000, a privately financed development approved by the voters. The area shown in this aerial view was previously occupied by Piers 42, 44, and 46A at the south end of the Embarcadero, by Pier 46b along China Basin, and by a tank farm on Seawall Lots 24 and 25.

As the need for railroads serving the port declined, the rail yards that dominated the large area north and south of Channel Street were closed. Together with the port's property along the waterfront, this area, known as Mission Bay, was the subject of numerous development proposals. The goal of this 1990 proposal was a mixed-use neighborhood that extended to former areas of the working port along the water.

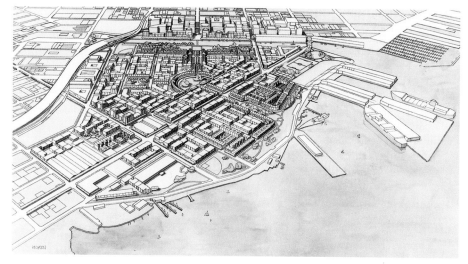

designed either to improve shipping facilities or to generate income to pay for the improvements, in 1973, a proposal was made for very different reasons. Called Embarcadero Gardens, this proposal was intended to provide public access and amenities along the waterfront. Designed by Richard Gryziec and funded by the National Endowment for the Arts, the plan called for an amusement park inspired by Tivoli Gardens in Copenhagen. It was to be built between Pier 7 at the north and Pier 24 at the south.

The failure of these several proposals to be realized on the northern waterfront was the result of a variety of new conditions. According to Rubin, "By the early 1970s a new context, at once complex and restrictive, confronted any proposal for development along the waterfront's northern stretches. The result for more than two decades was a stasis that few could

Pier 39, as it was rebuilt in 1978 with shops and restaurants, was the first project at the port to be built according to the idea that shipping would be replaced on the northern waterfront by profit-making non-maritime uses. Although criticized in sophisticated circles, it has proven to be a popular attraction and a financial success.

The first historic preservation project undertaken by the port was the conversion of the Belt Railroad Engine House in Seawall Lot 8 to an office complex that includes the engine house—with its concave wall of locomotive doorways, shown here—a small sandhouse along the Embarcadero, and a harmonious new building at the rear. It opened in 1985.

overcome. . . . The failure of both the Ferry Port Plaza and U.S. Steel projects signaled a dramatic shift in the balance of power for control of the waterfront."[13]

One notable exception was the development of Pier 39, as well as its parking garage on two seawall lots across the Embarcadero. The project was approved because it met the planning policies for the waterfront, including the height limit: it was a "water-oriented commercial recreation development of restaurants, entertainment and specialty shops."[14] These attributes were more important than its design—a shopping mall that evoked the New England waterfront in style. Although considered by many local residents to be solely for tourists and severely criticized by architects and critics, notably Allan Temko, who called it "a childish excrescence, which was stupidly allowed to deface the northern

waterfront,"[15] Pier 39 has been hugely popular and introduced a new type of income-producing development on port property.[16]

Other proposals solicited by the port for the northern waterfront failed. Among these were a series of proposals between 1972 and 1987 for Pier 45, including hotels, housing, retail, a convention center, and, because it lies next to Fisherman's Wharf, a "Fisheries Center."[17] In 1984–1985, I. M. Pei Partners designed a proposed renovation of the Ferry Building that would have included both restoration and expansion of the structure for a variety of new uses.[18] In 1985, the Pier Plaza project would have remodeled Piers 1½, 3, and 5 for offices, restaurants, and public access.

The era of unrealized projects ended with the adoption of a series of plans that had been written between 1979 and 1987 by the city's

Right: The Embarcadero Freeway, shown here during its construction in the late 1950s, was demolished in 1991–1992, having been damaged in the 1989 Loma Prieta earthquake. Its demolition removed a barrier to change and, just as importantly, awakened the public to possibilities for improving the waterfront environment.

Below: After 1998, the port began redesigning the Embarcadero—once a working artery for horse-drawn wagons, railcars, and trucks moving between piers and warehouses—to a passenger artery and scenic boulevard lined with ornamental palm trees.

Opposite top: Completed in 2003, the rehabilitation of the Ferry Building as a public space for restaurants, offices, and markets, together with the new Harry Bridges Plaza in front of the building, symbolize the transformation of the northern waterfront from a place of work to a place of consumption and leisure.

planning department, BCDC, and the port, along with substantial public involvement. The first projects in conformance with the spirit of these plans began with the creation of a redevelopment area on a mix of port and private land south of the Bay Bridge. The Rincon Point–South Beach Redevelopment Plan was produced in 1981, administered by the San Francisco Redevelopment Agency. Over many years, a great variety of developments would come out of this plan, including housing, parks, street beautification, a marina, and an office building. One of the principal results of the plan was to expand the area of the northern waterfront that was to be largely non-maritime in nature to the area between the Bay Bridge and China Basin.

Under this plan, the first project completed on port property—other projects were on private land—was South Beach Marina south of Pier 40. Completed in 1986, this marina for recreational boats replaced Piers 42, 44, and 46A. This was followed by two housing developments south of the Bay Bridge, by Delancey Street in 1990 and by Steamboat Point in 1992.

During the years from 1979 onward, a few other projects were realized. At a time most older port structures remained underused or vacant, one small but important exception was the Belt Railroad Engine House, which was converted to a small office building and opened in 1985.

Between 1995 and 2007, the Redevelopment Agency, working with the city and the port, also created numerous improvements along the waterfront between the Ferry Building and China Basin, including South Beach Park and Rincon Park, both on port land. These were realized by realigning and reconfiguring the Embarcadero.

The largest project within South Beach was the baseball stadium for the San Francisco Giants, a project approved by San Francisco voters in March 1996. Completed in 2000, the stadium was built on port land with private financing.

Another project on port property, the Watermark condominium, which was originally part of a larger plan to develop Pier 30–32 across the Embarcadero as a new cruise terminal for the port, was completed in 2006. The sale of

Obstacles to transformation of the northern waterfront were eased by completion of the port's Waterfront Land Use Plan in 1997. Pier 1 was the first rehabilitated pier on the waterfront in 2001, followed by Piers 1½, 3, and 5 (shown in the foreground) in 2006.

When the port abandoned plans to build Pier 98 as a container facility, already partially created by landfill, Heron's Head Park was established on the site. The park represents part of the port's response to the public desire for open space and access to the water, but it also represents the recognition that San Francisco's potential as a working port is limited.

An aerial view of the port of San Francisco in 1982, looking north from Pier 96.

the condos was intended to pay for the terminal project, which is now proposed for Pier 27.

The successful example of the development of port property for non-maritime projects in the South Beach–Rincon Point area was followed by the creation of redevelopment studies further south for both maritime and mixed-use projects. The Mission Bay North and Mission Bay South Redevelopment Plans were approved in 1998, and the India Basin Shoreline was established as a redevelopment study area in 2006.

A key event that heralded a new era in the transformation and development of the port was the 1989 Loma Prieta earthquake, which damaged the Embarcadero Freeway and led to its demolition in 1991. This not only removed a terrible blight on the waterfront; like the fall of the Berlin Wall, its absence suggested new possibilities.[19] These possibilities were most immediately addressed in the realm of transportation improvements that required the cooperation of city, state, and federal agencies, with the port.

Improving the setting for the rehabilitation of buildings, in 1997, Muni streetcars were extended from Market Street south along the Embarcadero and west to the Caltrain station at Fourth and Townsend streets. In 2000, the F-car line, which runs restored vintage trolleys from cities around the world, was extended from Market Street north along the Embarcadero to Fisherman's Wharf.

In 1998, work began on the Mid-Embarcadero Roadway Project between Broadway and the Bay Bridge. The project established Harry Bridges Plaza in front of the Ferry Building, Canary Island palm trees along the Embarcadero, railway tracks and stops, and a divided roadway around the plaza. The plaza included "Two 65-foot-tall light cannons . . . to shoot shafts of light 600 feet into the air for special evening occasions and to frame the historic gateway to the city up Market Street. There are benches and antique lampposts and a splash of greensward."[20]

These improvements—along with Herb Caen Way, an enhancement of the sidewalk along the waterfront that provides information about the history of the port on kiosks—more than anything transformed the environment of the waterfront. According to the port, these projects "singularly changed the character of the northern waterfront from an industrial service corridor to an outdoor living room for San Francisco."[21]

A second watershed event was a city ballot proposition in 1990 that effectively required the port to prepare a Waterfront Land Use Plan (WLUP). Achieved through extensive work with community groups, the WLUP was completed in 1997, opening the gates for reuse projects on the northern waterfront, for creation of the Port of San Francisco Embarcadero Historic District, and for use of the Secretary of the Interior's Standards in all rehabilitation projects.

The first building project of the new era following adoption of the WLUP was the renovation in 2001 of Pier 1 as office space for the port and private tenants. This was followed by the renovation of the Ferry Building for offices, interior market stalls, and restaurants. When Pier 1 was ready, the Port offices moved there from the Ferry Building, allowing work to begin. The work was completed in 2003. The next major project was the renovation in 2006 of Piers 1½, 3, and 5 for restaurants, offices, and walkways for public access to the waterfront.

A number of smaller projects involving public access have also been completed up and down the waterfront. From north to south, there have been improvements at Hyde Street Harbor, where the historic ships of the Maritime Museum are berthed; in 2007, a breakwater south of the Ferry Building was built by the port, with its surface treated as a public walkway; there is a boat launch at Pier 52, and another for non-motorized boats at Islais Landing on the south side of Islais Creek; and there is a restored salt marsh at Pier 94 and a restored wetland with a nature center at Heron's Head Park on the site of Pier 98.

Today, the port continues to develop and evolve with both maritime and non-maritime projects. Current planning efforts include a new cruise terminal at Pier 27, the relocation of the Exploratorium to Piers 15–17, the development of Seawall Lot 351 as part of a larger project called 8 Washington Street, the development of open space at the Brannan Street wharf between Pier 30–32 and Pier 38, a mixed-use development on Seawall Lot 337 across China Basin from the baseball stadium, master planning for Pier 70, Pier 90–94 Backlands for interim industrial uses, and planning for Gateway Sites on the southern waterfront.

While the changes at the San Francisco port since the 1950s, and especially since 1969, have resulted in the preservation of substantial maritime activity, most of that activity has moved out of the traditional shipping center to the area south of China Basin. And along much of the waterfront north of China Basin, as well as at many sites to the south, there has been a complete transformation, as Rubin says, "from production and industry to consumption and recreation."[22]

OFFICIAL MAP

PORT OF SAN FRANCISCO

Prepared for Board of State Harbor Commissioners, October, 1926.

Scale — 1 inch equals 1200 feet.

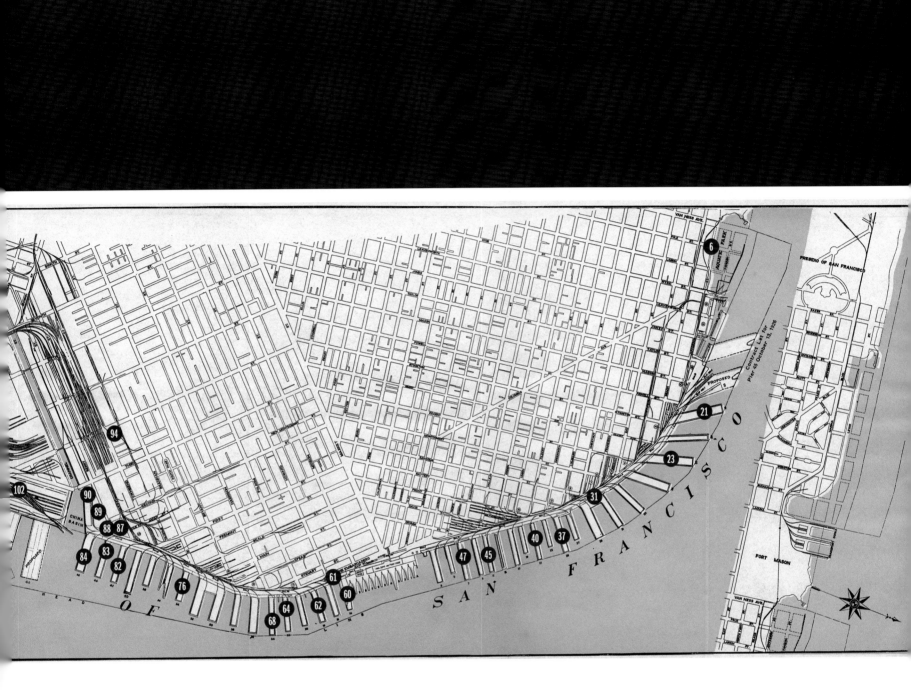

The sites and structures discussed in the following catalogue are organized from north to south. The entries are keyed to numbers on a 1926 map (above) or on sections detailed from a 2006 map (on the following spread). Most extant sites are shown on the 2006 map. Pink areas indicate city historic districts. The area shown in gray corresponds to the Port of San Francisco Embarcadero Historic District, listed on the National Register of Historic Places.

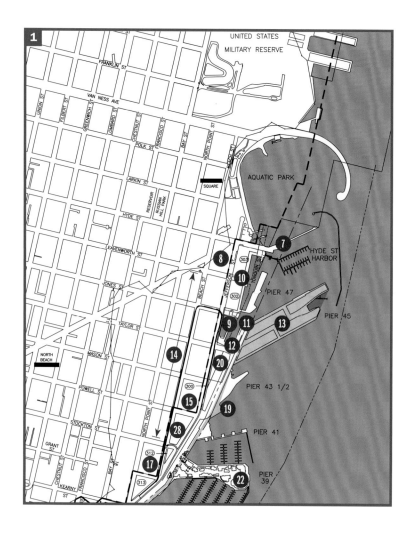

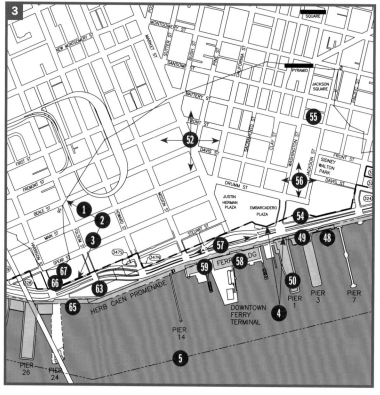

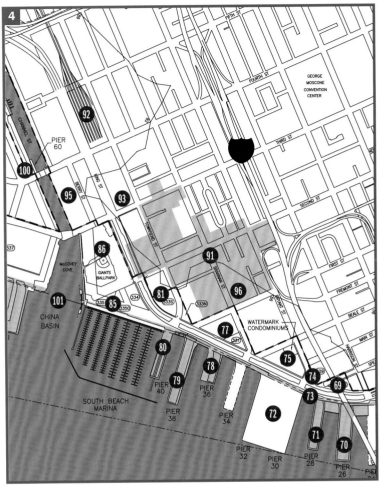

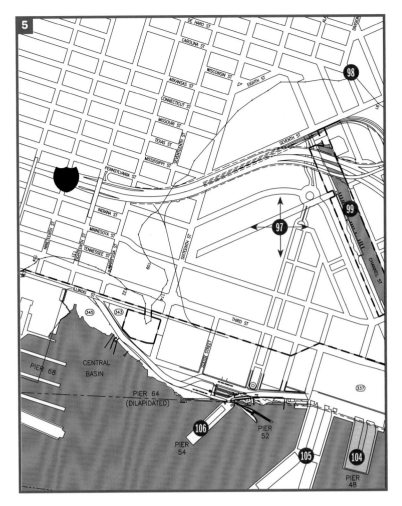

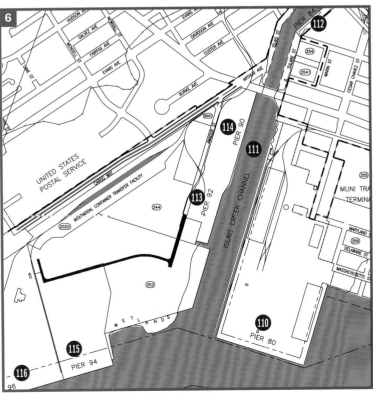

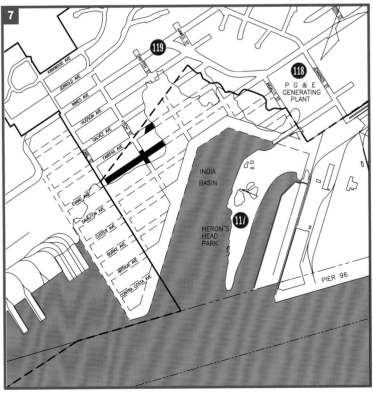

1. Shoreline

The term *shoreline* refers to the natural shoreline of the city at the time of the Gold Rush in 1848–1849.

2. Eddy Red Line (Jurisdiction Line)

In 1849, the city of San Francisco hired surveyor William M. Eddy to prepare an official map. The map showed all legally surveyed streets, whether in existence or not, including streets bounding blocks of water lots. The edge of the city, much of it in the water, was called the *jurisdiction line* because it marked the boundary between city and state jurisdiction.[1] A revised edition of this map, published in 1851, marked the jurisdiction line and the original shoreline in red and was called the Eddy Red Line Map.

Inside the jurisdiction line, water lots were sold to private parties and filled. Outside the jurisdiction line, the water of the bay was publicly owned and under the control of the state. In 1851, the state allowed piers to be built six hundred feet beyond the jurisdiction line into the waters of the bay. At that time, most piers were built over as-yet-unfilled water lots. In the area of the water lots, the city required that piers be built on alignment with the streets.

3. Waterfront or City Front

Waterfront and *city front* are two related terms that often describe the same thing—the edge of the city along the water—but viewed from different perspectives. Both were in use by 1850. The waterfront, or city front, moved over time, as water lots, tidelands, marshland, and seawall lots were filled.

The term *city front* describes the perspective of those approaching the city by water. In the mid-nineteenth century, almost everyone came to San Francisco by water, and daily life much more often included ferries, working boats, and other vessels. *Waterfront* describes the perspective of those on the land; from the land one went to the place where the land ended and the water began—the waterfront. As fewer people today experience the water on a regular basis, the term *waterfront* has survived. *City front* is now little used, except by a limited number of people; for example, the newsletter of the St. Francis Yacht Club is still called *City Front*.

Regardless of their origins, the terms appear to have been used interchangeably by people on land and water. However, *city front* sometimes referred to a zone back a few blocks from the water's edge, where there were many port-related businesses and institutions: saloons, hotels, and restaurants that served sailors, longshoremen, and other port workers; ship chandlers, sail makers, and shipwrights; union offices, missions, and medical and social services; and factories and warehouses. It was this area that was the source of the name City Front Federation, adopted by a group of labor organizations in 1901. Whereas waterfront workers worked on ships, piers, the Embarcadero, and the Belt Railroad, city-front workers worked either on the waterfront or in the adjacent part of the city. Used in this way, *city front* refers to specific neighborhoods north and south of Market Street, which were at the edge of the city before the seawall was built.

4. Water Front Line

When the BSHC was established in 1863, its jurisdiction began at the old jurisdiction line, or Eddy Red Line, which the commissioners called the Water Front Line. A few years later, in 1867–1870, the BSHC built sections of a seawall on this zigzag line. It also reaffirmed the 1851 regulation permitting piers to extend six hundred feet into the bay from this line. In 1868, the Water Front Line was extended south of Second Street to the County Line.

In 1876–1878, the BSHC created a new curving waterfront line in association with plans for the new seawall. Officially known as the Water Front Line, this was also called the Bulkhead Line—i.e., the line of the outer reach of the city's bulkhead or seawall, to which point the bay was dredged to a depth adequate for seagoing ships. When the BSHC was authorized to purchase and develop new port facilities at Islais Creek and India Basin in 1909, it also established an extension of the Water Front Line in those areas.

5. Pier Head Line

Until plans were developed for the new seawall in 1876–1878, piers could be built six hundred feet into state waters. With the new seawall, this rule took a new form when the state, in consultation with the Army Corps of Engineers, established the Pier Head Line, first defined as a line six hundred feet from the Water Front Line.

In 1890, the federal government first asserted its authority over this aspect of navigation in the bay when the Army Corps of Engineers adopted a Pier Head Line that was essentially the same as the state's line. In 1901, the state Pier Head Line was moved out to eight hundred feet from the Water Front Line in order to accommodate larger ships. The federal government followed suit in 1912.

Belt Railroad trestle to Fort Mason Tunnel between future site of Aquatic Park Casino (left) and Pumping Station No. 2 of the Auxiliary Water Supply System (right)

6. Fort Mason Tunnel and Aquatic Park

In 1914, this tunnel was cut through the bluff at Fort Mason in order to extend the Belt Railroad to the site of the Panama-Pacific International Exposition, then under construction. The purpose was not for passengers, but to facilitate the delivery of exhibits to the exposition from the port's piers. It also served Fort Mason and industrial sites along Jefferson Street. Built of reinforced concrete, the tunnel is fifteen hundred feet long, seventeen feet wide, and twenty-two feet high; it accommodates only one track. In 1917, after the close of the exposition, the rail line was extended further west to the Presidio. When it was first built, it crossed what later became the Aquatic Park Lagoon on an open trestle. In 1936, the trestle was enclosed by fill behind a new seawall for Aquatic Park. This fill covered the last remnant of the beach along the city's north shore, called North Beach, which extended from North Point to what is now Fort Mason.[2] The first proposal for Aquatic Park died, but the Works Progress Administration completed a new proposal, designed by William Mooser III, in 1939. Aquatic Park was built for the city of San Francisco and lies at the western border of the port.

7. Hyde Street Pier

In 1922, facilities were developed at the foot of Hyde Street for passenger ferries. These were modified to carry automobiles in 1931. Automobile service ended after the Golden Gate Bridge was completed in 1937. The Hyde Street Pier was converted for historic ships in 1963. Swimming and rowing clubs, first established in the nineteenth century, still survive adjacent to the pier.

8. California Fruit Canners Association North Point Cannery

The large cannery of the California Fruit Canners Association, later the Del Monte Cannery, was built in 1907 on the site of the pre-earthquake Selby Smelter. It was a principal seasonal employer of immigrant Italian women in North Beach. Its full-block complex included a four-story warehouse at the west end, a two-story cannery at the east end, and a loading area served by spurs of the Belt Railroad in between. The cannery was rebuilt as a complex of shops in 1966, and the warehouse was converted to a hotel in 2003.

9. Fisherman's Wharf

In 1900, Fisherman's Wharf was moved here from its previous location at the foot of Union Street (approximately the location of Pier 17 today). The Board of State Harbor Commissioners (BSHC) planned new wharves in that area, where the seawall had been completed and there was deep water for large ships. This new site for Fisherman's Wharf, located beyond the end of the seawall as it was originally planned, was shallow and not practical as a place for large ships. In addition to a wooden wharf, the port built a 785-foot stone breakwater in 1900 to protect the small fishing boats. These two structures created what came to be called the inner lagoon. After 1914, facilities at Fisherman's Wharf were expanded; by that year the bed for the Belt Railroad spur to Fort Mason was built along Jefferson Street, functioning as a seawall for the inshore edge of Fisherman's Lagoon. By that time, the main seawall was built to the foot of Jones Street, forming the outer boundary of the lagoon.

In 1917, the outer lagoon was enclosed by the construction of a breakwater, a stone levee built in the alignment of the main seawall to Hyde Street, from the termination of the original seawall at Jones Street. Leaving a gap for boats to pass through, another stone levee was built on the line of Hyde Street from Jefferson Street to the line of the seawall. Then, in 1918, an existing wharf on the line of the seawall from Jones to Leavenworth was substantially enlarged as a lumber wharf.

By 1920, a one-story wooden building with five stalls for fish markets was completed on Taylor Street, stretching north from Jefferson. A few years later, a second similar building with three stalls was erected between the first building and another, the Booth Packing House and Market building. The stalls in the three buildings were numbered from one to nine. As some of the stalls were converted to restaurants, they were given second-story additions. These restaurants adopted names that referred to the stalls where

Crab Fishermen's Protective Association

Taylor Street fish markets on the right, 1920

they originated—thus, Alioto's No. 8 and Fisherman's Grotto No. 9. Although built for local boats to sell their daily catch, from the beginning many of the market stalls sold "fish cocktails." By the 1930s, some also operated full restaurants as well.

In 1926, a two-story market for crab and salmon fishermen was built on Jefferson Street next to the end of the Taylor Street fish market. It is an unadorned wooden structure with stucco walls and a hip roof. This became

known as the Crab Fisherman's Protective Association after a tenant in the building, a group of independent crab fishermen struggling to survive against the companies of the Fish Trust.[3]

After years of neglect, the port commissioned a plan for Fisherman's Wharf in 1961.[4] Little came of this plan apart from the long-delayed construction of a new breakwater, completed in 1986.

10. Fish Alley

The construction in 1917 of the infrastructure forming the outer lagoon was the basis for extensive new development. In 1919 Seawall Lots C and D (now 302 and 303), between the outer lagoon (sometimes called Fisherman's Basin) from Jones to Hyde streets, were filled, a bulkhead wharf called J-10 was built on the seawall along Jefferson Street, and a long wooden fish-packing shed was built on the wharf, soon called Fish Alley. Also in 1919, a wharf called J-7 was built on the breakwater. A complex of wharves associated with J-7 has been called Pier 47 since about 1930. Fish-packing sheds were built on the wharves and the seawall lots were developed with fish-processing businesses, boat-repair shops, machine shops, and fuel-oil depots.

12. F. E. Booth Packing House

In 1918, a two-story reinforced-concrete building on concrete piles was built at the foot of Taylor Street at its intersection with the Embarcadero. It had a red-tile roof and Italian Renaissance details, notably a curving corner with a columned entry. Architectural drawings for the building were labeled "Fish Packing House and Market." From the beginning it was known for its lessee, the F. E. Booth Company. The *Oakland Tribune* described Frank Booth, the man responsible for the first cannery on Cannery Row in Monterey, as "founder of the sardine industry in California."[6] In addition, he owned at various times four salmon canneries along the Sacramento River and a fruit and vegetable cannery in Centerville (now part of Fremont). He was a pioneer in the processing and sale of unwanted fish parts for animal feed, fertilizer, and industrial oils. All of these products he shipped out from the ports of San Francisco and Oakland. The Booth building, substantially remodeled, became the Fisherman's Grotto No. 9 restaurant by 1935.

11. Barge Office

In 1917, the Barge Office of the United States Customs, Coast Guard, and Quarantine Service was constructed near the end of the main seawall, across the Embarcadero from the northwest corner of where Pier 45 would later be built. A two-story wood-frame building on concrete piles, the Barge Office was in the style of a Renaissance villa, with stucco walls, a red-tile roof, a symmetrical design, and an entrance arcade. The port later described the function of the building: "The Captain of the Port [Twelfth Coast Guard District] is charged with the safeguarding of vessels, harbors, ports, and waterfront facilities from destruction, loss or injury from sabotage, accidents or other causes. He must prevent the introduction through ports of persons, articles, or things inimical to national security including weapons of mass destruction."[5]

The Fishermen's and Seamen's Memorial Chapel, completed in 1982, now stands on the site of the Barge Office.

13. Pier 45 and the Marine Exchange
1929
Frank G. White, chief engineer
Substructure: H. Baldwin, designer;
Healy-Tibbitts Construction Co., contractor
Transit sheds: H. B. Fisher, designer; MacDonald & Kahn, contractor

Pier 45 is distinctive among piers north of China Basin, but it was planned at the same time as the similar Pier 48, located south of the channel, as part of a major expansion of port facilities that introduced a new type of pier. It was the largest pier of its time, measuring 1,428 feet on its longest side, which was possible within the 800-foot Pier Head Line because of its angled orientation.

Pier 45 is built on fill instead of piles. It is a quay-type pier with four transit sheds, two on each side, and space for rail spurs and truck access through the center, which originally led to a car-ferry hoisting tower and slip at the outer end. Gothic Revival detail was applied to the inshore ends. A lookout station at its outer end was operated by the Marine Department of the Chamber of Commerce. Under a variety of names and affiliations, the Marine Exchange—a ship-reporting service that included signals from Point Lobos on the Pacific Ocean side of the Golden Gate to Telegraph Hill to the Merchants Exchange downtown—played a key role at the port since its founding in 1849. A telegraph line was built along this route in 1853, the first year of telegraph operation in California. The Marine Exchange still exists; today, its historic role is best evoked in the maritime murals by William A. Coulter and Nils Hagerup that decorate the monumental room on the ground floor of the Merchants Exchange Building at 465 California Street.

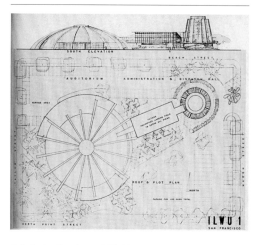

14. Auto Dock and Kirkland Yard—Longshoremen's Hiring Hall

From the mid-1930s to about 1950, the North Point Auto Dock terminated at Leavenworth Street between North Point and Beach streets. The BSHC built it on land leased from private owners. Operated by Southern Pacific, the dock was used for unloading automobiles from railcars. In 1938, the BSHC described this area as "one of the busiest spots" associated with the port.[7] During World War II, the five blocks between Stockton and Leavenworth streets, known as the Kirkland Yard, served as railroad storage.

The rail yard was gone by 1954 when the ILWU Local 10 bought the block bounded by North Point, Beach, Mason, and Taylor streets for its Longshoremen's Hiring Hall and Offices. Designed by Henry Hill, it opened in 1959.

15. Gas Holder

The large, cylindrical gas holder that stood on the southwest corner of Powell and Jefferson streets until after 1950 was the last remnant of a gas-manufacturing plant in this block, built in 1899 by the San Francisco Coke and Gas Company and later owned by the Pacific Gas and Electric Company. Production ended in 1930. Today the block is occupied by hotels and tourist-oriented businesses.

16. North Point, the Harbor Warehouses, and the North Point Sewage Treatment Plant

North Point was part of Telegraph Hill at the time of the Gold Rush, dropping into the bay so abruptly that it was impossible to travel by land around its waterside. As Telegraph Hill was quarried for ballast and landfill, North Point was reduced to a shelf of land, on which a road was opened along the water in 1855. On the 1851 Eddy Red Line map, North Point itself was just north of Bay Street between Kearny and Grant, and the rest of the block bounded by Kearny, Grant, Bay, and North Point streets was shown as tideland, surveyed for sale and ready for filling. This block was filled after Sections 1 and 2 of the seawall were completed in 1879 and 1880, respectively.

From 1906 to 1949, the entire block was occupied by the Harbor Warehouse Company, whose four brick buildings were prominent in many photographs of the north waterfront from the first half of the twentieth century. They were succeeded on the site by the North Point Sewage Treatment Plant in 1950.

In 1907, Hiram W. Johnson, the attorney

HARBOR WAREHOUSE CO.
KEARNY AND NORTH POINT STS. FRONTING ON NEW SEAWALL WHARF AND BELT RAILROAD

for the Harbor Warehouse Company, led the objections to Southern Pacific's effort to expand its dominance of rail facilities to the north waterfront. Johnson would be elected governor of California in 1910 on a promise of good government and ending the corrupt influence of Southern Pacific and others.

17. Otis Elevator Company Building

This is one of the few industrial buildings facing the port that was given a finished architectural appearance. Located at the southwest corner of Beach and Grant streets, it was designed by the company's architectural office in Yonkers, New York, and completed in 1924. The building housed manufacturing spaces and sales offices.

18. Northeast Waterfront Historic District

The Northeast Waterfront Historic District, a city landmark district, is located east of Telegraph Hill between Broadway and Union Street. It is a multi-block concentration of warehouses and industrial buildings associated with the history of the port. The district includes the Gibb Warehouses, which were built on the waterfront in the 1850s, before landfill moved the shoreline outward; a number of large brick warehouses—for glass, wine, and general merchandise—that survived the earthquake and fire of 1906; several cold-storage warehouses, built after the earthquake, for perishable goods such as meat and fruit; and manufacturing and storage buildings, from the 1910s and 1920s, for flour, paper, biscuits, and machine shops.

Scattered industrial buildings also survive to the northwest, outside the boundaries of the historic district. These include the National Paper Products Company Building at the southwest corner of Montgomery and Francisco streets. The eight-story reinforced concrete warehouse, designed and built by the engineers and contractors MacDonald & Kahn in 1916, is a conspicuous backdrop in many early-twentieth-century photographs of the port. Paper and printing were major industries in San Francisco at that time.

19. Car-Ferry Head House at Pier 43
1914
Jerome Newman, chief engineer
Charles Newton Young, designer; Healy-Tibbitts Construction Co., contractor

Built for the Belt Railroad, the Car-Ferry Head House was used for railcar-ferry traffic to and from the Northwestern Pacific terminal in Tiburon, the Santa Fe terminal in Richmond, and other cross-bay terminals. Following a fire, it was rehabilitated in 2002.

Altogether, this facility consisted of a car-ferry slip, where a barge could load or unload railcars via an adjustable ramp with a rail spur. The ramp was raised and lowered according to the tides by means of a hoisting mechanism located inside the Neoclassical style head house.

20. Seawall Lot B—Franciscan Restaurant

The port built the Franciscan Restaurant on Seawall Lot B in 1957. Designed by the architect Hewitt C. Wells, the restaurant represents an early expansion of the port's development of non-maritime, tourist-oriented business.

21–27. PIER 41 TO PIER 29

In the biennium of 1910–1912, plans were announced for seven new piers from Pier 41 to Pier 29, along with freight-ferry slips and unfinished sections of the seawall and bulkhead wharf. The piers were built in 1913–1917, the transit sheds soon after, and the bulkhead buildings over a longer period, all eventually with Neoclassical facades. Four of these piers were 200 feet wide to serve freighters and three were 140 feet wide for passenger ships. Several longer piers were angled In order to fit within the 800-foot Pier Head Line.

21. Pier 41 and Meigg's Wharf
(Old Fisherman's Wharf)

Pier 41 consisted of a substructure (1914), a transit shed (1919), and a Neoclassical style bulkhead building (1920), all of wood construction. It was demolished about 1976.

Henry Meiggs built a wharf here in 1852. Through the end of the nineteenth century, it was the focal point of shipping and entertainment on the north waterfront. By 1865 it was known as Fisherman's Wharf. In 1872, the fishermen moved to a location designated by the harbor commissioners at the foot of Clay and Commercial streets.

22. Pier 39

Pier 39, first built in 1914, consisted of a reinforced-concrete pier and a wooden transit shed. A Neoclassical style bulkhead building was added in 1932. The transit shed and bulkhead building were demolished about 1976 when construction began on the new Pier 39, which has shops and restaurants. Portions of the 1914 pier were incorporated into the new structure. Opened in 1978, it was the first major development to reflect the new realities of the port—that container shipping had largely replaced break-bulk shipping, that there was little use for the extensive break-bulk facilities north of China Basin, and that there was tremendous potential for non-maritime development along the waterfront.

The current Pier 39, designed by Walker & Moody, is part of a complex that includes a parking garage across the street and a park at the site of Pier 37. Its architectural imagery—that of vernacular wooden shacks on a pier—has no precedent on San Francisco's waterfront, except for one element, the Eagle Cafe, a relocated structure that was first occupied by McCormick Steamship Lines when it was built in Seawall Lot 1 (now 311), on the southeast corner of Powell and Jefferson streets, after 1913.

23. Pier 37

Pier 37, including its pier on wooden piles and its timber-frame transit shed and bulkhead building, was one of the first Neoclassical style structures at the port when it was built in 1914. In that year, the BSHC used a drawing of Pier 37 to announce the new style for piers north of the Ferry Building.[8] It was destroyed by fire in 1975. A surviving stub of Pier 37 and the adjacent bulkhead wharf were transformed into Sidney Rudy Waterfront Park in 1981 by the developers of Pier 39. Sidney Rudy was an attorney who facilitated the development of Pier 39.

24. Pier 35
1914–1916
Jerome Newman, chief engineer
Substructure and transit sheds: A. C. Griewank, designer; Healy-Tibbitts Construction Co., contractor
Bulkhead building: A. A. Pyle, designer; Healy-Tibbitts Construction Co., contractor

The design of Pier 35 represents one of many varied special attempts to build long-lasting facilities in the harsh environment of the waterfront. The substructure, measuring 200 by an average of 896 feet, included reinforced-concrete piles that were 106 feet long by twenty inches square, according to the chief engineer at the time: "These very long and heavy piles, weighing 23 tons each, . . . were believed to be the longest piles of this kind ever used." The wood siding on the transit shed was originally "covered with asbestos-protected metal . . . on account of its fire-resistant qualities." Along the sides of the shed, rolling steel doors provided fire protection as well as security.[9] The interior has three aisles; above the central aisle is a continuous roof monitor for light and air. The state architect contributed to the design of the timber-frame bulkhead building, which is Neoclassical in style.[10] The facade was restored in 2008.

In 1933, Pier 35 was extended seventy-eight feet further into the bay to accommodate the Grace Line's new, larger steamships for both cargo and passengers. Inside were a new passenger lobby, waiting rooms, and baggage facilities. The Grace Line served Latin American and Caribbean ports between New York and San Francisco and was an important presence in San Francisco since the Gold Rush.

View south along the Embarcadero, with Pier 33 on the left

25. Pier 33
1917–1919
Frank G. White, chief engineer
Substructure: G. A. Wood, designer; Healy-Tibbitts Construction Co., contractor
Transit shed and bulkhead building: Oliver W. Jones, designer, and A. A. Pyle, facade;
J. L. McLaughlin, contractor

Pier 33 consists of a reinforced-concrete pier measuring 150 by 800 feet, with a three-aisled timber-frame transit shed enclosed in concrete walls. Like Pier 31, it was built with "a series of separate monitors or penthouses on the center section of the roof, with windows on four sides. . . . The result is exceptionally well-lighted pier sheds."[11] The outer end is embellished with a restrained Neoclassical design that is compatible with the bulkhead building.

Piers 31 and 29

26. Pier 31
1917–1918
Frank G. White, chief engineer
Substructure: G. A. Wood and B. G. Hill, designers; Healy-Tibbitts Construction Co., contractor
Transit shed and bulkhead building: Oliver W. Jones, designer, and A. A. Pyle, facade; J. J. McHugh, contractor

Pier 31's substructure and transit shed are similar to those of Pier 33. It shares its Neoclassical style bulkhead building with Pier 29.

When it was completed, Pier 31 was occupied by the China Mail Steamship Company, organized in 1915 by Chinese-American business interests in San Francisco. The company was first based at Pier 29.

Piers 33, 31, and 29 on the Embarcadero

27. Pier 29
1915–1918
Jerome Newman, chief engineer (substructure)
Frank G. White, chief engineer (transit shed and bulkhead building)
Substructure: L. Alden, G. A. Wood, and A. C. Griewank, designers; Clinton Construction Co., contractor
Transit shed: Clinton Construction Co., contractor
Bulkhead building: A. A. Pyle, facade; J. J. McHugh, contractor

Pier 29 consists of a reinforced-concrete substructure measuring 161 by 800 feet, a steel-frame transit shed with reinforced-concrete walls, and a timber-frame stuccoed bulkhead building in the Neoclassical style. The transit shed is designed with three gabled aisles that are lit by square roof monitors over the central aisle. In 1965, Pier 29 was extended about 75 feet further into the bay and joined to a new Pier 27 to form a triangular quay-type pier. Like Pier 31, Pier 29 was first occupied by the China Mail Steamship Company.

28. Seawall Lots 1 and 2 (now 311 and 312)— Pier 39 Garage

Seawall Lots 1 and 2 were leased to the Santa Fe Railway as a single rail yard that crossed Stockton between Beach and the Embarcadero, a block that was owned by the port. Today these lots are occupied by a large parking garage built for Pier 39 and an approach to it.

29. Seawall Lot 3 (now 313)—Blue Shield Building

Seawall lot 3 was long leased to the Northwestern Pacific Railroad as a rail yard. In 1973, Embarcadero Triangle, an office building for Blue Shield designed by Gensler and Associates, was completed on this site.

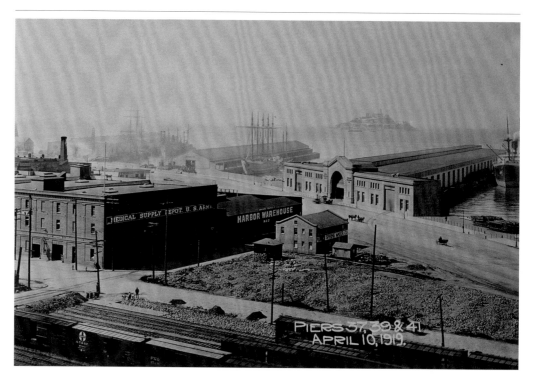

30. Seawall Lot 4 (now 314)

In the 1910s and 1920s, Seawall Lot 4 was leased in parts to two tenants, the Purity Spring Water Company and the National Packing Company, the latter of which used the space for cattle corrals. For many years it has been a parking lot, one of the principal uses of seawall lots since the 1950s. The BSHC proposed a six-story reinforced-concrete warehouse here in 1918 but never built it.

31. Bulkhead Wharf, Section 3 of the Seawall

After Section 3 of the seawall was completed between Lombard and Francisco streets in 1879–1881 with a wooden bulkhead wharf, a 1,870-foot-long grain shed was built on it and grain warehouses appeared on private land nearby, below Telegraph Hill. Part of the Globe Milling Company plant on Chestnut Street between Montgomery and Kearny is still standing. This was San Francisco's response to competition from Port Costa on the Carquinez Strait, which was a leading world grain port from the 1870s to 1900s. After 1906, the San Francisco port erected a large grain elevator at this location, which stood until construction began on a new concrete bulkhead wharf in 1915 and a new grain terminal at Islais Creek.

32. Seawall Lots 5, 6, and 7 (now 315, 316, and 317)—San Francisco Bay Office Park

Seawall Lots 5 and 6 were leased to the Santa Fe Railway, whose tracks crossed the port-owned block of Montgomery between Francisco and Bay streets. Seawall Lot 7 was leased for many years to the Western Pacific Railroad as a rail yard. These three lots were developed in 1974–1975 as the San Francisco Bay Office Park, including Houston's Restaurant, designed by Robinson & Mills.

33. Belt Railroad Office Building

This structure was built in 1909 as one of a pair of similar buildings on the bulkhead wharf north of the Ferry Building. They were erected under the supervision of Nathaniel Ellery, the state engineer, and were among the very few port structures not designed by the BSHC. These were also the last buildings (with the exception of minor sheds for wharfingers and simple, impermanent-looking restaurants) constructed on the bulkhead wharf before a new plan was adopted that consolidated all offices in bulkhead buildings at the inshore ends of piers.

Designed before the 1914 decision to apply the Neoclassical style to buildings north of the Ferry Building and a "modified" Mission Revival style to buildings south of it, this building is closer in style to Mission, with Craftsman and Prairie style features. It was originally located near the Washington Street Pier (near the later site of Pier 3) and occupied by the California Transportation Company. When plans were announced in 1918 for the new Belt Railroad Engine House on Seawall Lot 8, this structure was moved to a new site on the bulkhead wharf, across the Embarcadero from the Engine House, to serve as offices for the Belt Railroad. When the Belt Railroad ceased operation, it continued as an office building known as Pier 29 Annex.

On the left: Belt Railroad Engine House; on the right: Pier 27

34. Seawall Lot 8 (Now 318)—Belt Railroad Engine House and the Sounds of the Port

The Belt Railroad Engine House was built in Seawall Lot 8 in 1914, a year after the northern and southern zones of the rail line were first linked by tracks in front of the Ferry Building and the same year that the line was extended through a tunnel under Fort Mason to the site of the Panama-Pacific International Exposition. At its peak, the Engine House serviced eight locomotives. It closed in 1982 and was reopened in 1985 as an office building with a harmonious addition, designed by Daniel, Mann, Johnson & Mendenhall Architects.

The working port was a noisy place, and except for the occasional blasts of ships' horns, little was louder than the twenty-four-hour sounds of the Belt Railroad—the rumble of steam engines and later diesel engines, the squeaking of steel wheels and couplings as the cars turned on their rails, the grinding of the hoisting mechanisms at the car-ferry slips, the thud of cargo being loaded into steel or wooden cars, and steam or electric whistles. At most times in the port's active years there was a constant pounding of steam-powered pile drivers. Adding to the cacophony were the sounds of wind in sails, ropes snapping, foghorns and bells, men shouting, animal hooves and cries, and the starting and running of engines of ships, cars, trucks, steam donkeys, and cargo-handling equipment.

35. Seawall Lot 9 (now 319)—Old Roundhouse

Before the Engine House was built on Lot 8 in 1914, there was a small Belt Railroad roundhouse and machine shop on this lot for maintenance of the locomotives. It was replaced by a small wooden restaurant. Today, this lot and Lot 10 are part of the Levi-Strauss office complex gardens, the only pieces of that development not on private land.

Many piers between Pier 27 and the Ferry Building were built between the 1890s and 1908. Constructed of wood, they were all in poor condition by the 1920s and were "part of the program of elimination of obsolete piers and their replacement with modern structures."[12] The work proceeded as sections of the bulkhead wharf were rebuilt in reinforced concrete.

36. Pier 27

A wooden pier, known as the potato wharf, was built at this location in 1906. Its transit shed, which was designed before the BSHC decided on a plan for pier styles in 1914, had a Mission Revival style parapet at its outer end. In 1920, a Neoclassical style bulkhead building was added. The pier and transit shed were deteriorated by 1948 and subsequently demolished, leaving the bulkhead building standing until about 1965, when it was removed for the Pier 27 Terminal.

Pier 27 Terminal, also known as Pier 27–29, is a quay-type facility that was created out of the preexisting Pier 29 and a new Pier 27, designed in 1965–1967. Pier 27 was built at an angle from the bulkhead wharf to the outer end of Pier 29, making a triangular complex with a connecting wharf for trucks in the angle between the two piers. The last major attempt to salvage shipping on the northern waterfront, Pier 27–29 was built as part of a larger plan that also included the LASH Terminal for the Pacific Far East Lines at Pier 96 in 1972. In fact, Pier 27–29 survived as the last major cargo terminal on the northern waterfront, handling newsprint for the daily papers until 1997–1998.

From left to right: Piers 25, 23, 19, and 17 (opposite Sperry Flour warehouse and tower)

37. Pier 25

Pier 25 was a wooden structure built in 1909; it received a transit shed at an unknown date. In 1927, a new Neoclassical style bulkhead building was constructed, linking Piers 23 and 25.

This bulkhead building was altered three years later when Pier 23 and its portion of the bulkhead building were demolished. Pier 25 remained in use until it was demolished about 1965.

38. Pier 23 Restaurant

This simple wooden restaurant structure was built in 1937 by employees of the BSHC for $1,854.69. Following the labor victory in the 1934 Big Strike, restaurants catering to waterfront workers proliferated on port property.

39. Pier 23
1931–1932

Frank G. White, chief engineer

Substructure: H. B. Fisher, designer; Healy-Tibbitts Construction Co., contractor

Transit shed and bulkhead building: H. B. Fisher, designer; Barrett & Hilp, contractor

Following demolition of the old wooden Pier 23, a much bigger pier was built to accommodate a new generation of larger ships. The substructure of the new pier, measuring 150 by 800 feet, was constructed of reinforced concrete with wood pilings jacketed in concrete. The transit shed has a steel frame and precast concrete walls; above the center of its three interior aisles is a continuous roof monitor for light and air. The outer end has a Moderne style finish and the bulkhead building is Neoclassical.

40. Pier 21

Pier 21, an early-twentieth-century wooden pier and transit shed, was demolished about 1931 to make way for the new, enlarged Pier 23. Until 1935, when the port was at its maximum development, the section north of the Ferry Building had piers with almost every odd number from 1 to 45—lacking only Pier 13 and Pier 21.

From left to right: Piers 19 (before bulkhead building added), 17 (opposite Sperry Flour tower), and 15

41. Pier 19
1936–1938

Frank G. White, chief engineer

Substructure and transit shed: G. A. Wood, designer; Barrett & Hilp, contractor

Bulkhead building: H. B. Fisher, designer; Barrett & Hilp, contractor

Pier 19 was built almost exactly to the same plans and at the same time as Pier 9. The transit sheds and bulkhead buildings were also executed under the same contracts. The substructures of each pier, measuring 153 by 800 feet, are made of reinforced concrete on concrete-jacketed timber piles. The steel-frame transit sheds have walls of precast reinforced-concrete panels. Inside each shed are three aisles and a continuous roof monitor above the center aisle to provide light and air. While the bulkhead buildings of Piers 9 and 19 are Neoclassical in style, the outer ends are finished with Moderne style details. The Pacific Oriental Terminal Company occupied Pier 19 from 1939 to 1962. This photograph, taken July 28, 1934, predates the addition of the bulkhead buildings.

42. Pier 17
1912

A. V. Saph, assistant state engineer

Designer possibly Frank G. White; Healy-Tibbitts Construction Co., contractor

Pier 17 was one of a group of five piers proposed in 1911; the others were in a group south of the Ferry Building: Piers 26, 28, 30, and 32. Pier 17 is distinctive in several ways. With its lack of a bulkhead building and its unadorned transit shed separated from the Embarcadero by the width of the bulkhead wharf, it resembles the piers of the late nineteenth and early twentieth centuries rather than its contemporaries and later piers, with their ornamental bulkhead buildings. (It is also narrow like earlier piers, measuring 120 by 800 feet.) Pier 17 is also distinctive for the predominance of wood in its structure.

In 1955–1956, Pier 17 was joined to Pier 15, forming a single quay-type pier with a connecting wharf for trucks. The substructure includes "the first pre-stressed pilings used in U.S. pier construction."[13] Pier 17 was used primarily for coastwise shipping. Planning is under way to develop Piers 15–17 as the new location for the Exploratorium.

From 1880 to 1900, Fisherman's Wharf was located on piers at the foot of Union and Green streets, approximately the site of Piers 15 and 17 today. From 1872, when state law first required accommodations for fishermen, until 1880, fishermen had been located officially at the foot of Clay and Commercial streets.

44. Pier 13

Pier 13 was built as Pier 11 as early as the 1890s. It was demolished about 1915. Because of space limitations, no subsequent pier has been designated Pier 13.

43. Pier 15
1930–1931

Frank G. White, chief engineer

Substructure: designer unknown; Healy-Tibbitts Construction Co., contractor

Transit shed and bulkhead building: H. B. Fisher, designer; E. T. Lesure, contractor

Pier 15 was the first begun in "the program of replacement of the group of old and more or less obsolete piers now existing between the Ferry Building and Pier 29," announced in 1930.[14] The previous Pier 15, built in 1915, was a narrow wooden structure that supported coal bunkers; with the adoption of fuel oil, coal was much less in demand by 1930. The new substructure, measuring 160 by 800 feet, was constructed of reinforced concrete. The transit shed has a steel frame and walls of precast concrete; its interior has three aisles and a continuous roof monitor above the central aisle. The outer end is in the Moderne style, while the bulkhead building is Neoclassical. In 1955–1956, it was joined to Pier 17 (see above).

45. Pier 11

Pier 11 was built as early as the 1890s. By July 1918, it received a Neoclassical style bulkhead building, designed in collaboration with the state architect.[15] The entire structure was demolished about 1935 to make way for the new, larger Pier 9.

46. Pier 9—Bar Pilots
1936–1938
Frank G. White, chief engineer
Substructure and transit shed: G. A. Wood, designer; A. W. Kitchen, contractor
Bulkhead building: H. B. Fisher, designer; Barrett & Hilp, contractor

Pier 9 was built at the same time and to the same plans as Pier 19 (see above).

The San Francisco Bar Pilots are based at the end of Pier 9. Organized in 1835 by Captain William P. Richardson, they perform the essential function of guiding ships in and out of the bay, a difficult passage because of rough water, high winds, fog, strong currents, rocks, and bars. They were first regulated by the state in 1849.

47. Pier 7
1915–1916
Frank G. White, chief engineer

Pier 7 was built in 1902, and it received a transit shed at an unknown date. A Neoclassical bulkhead building was added in 1916. After a fire destroyed the pier in 1973, a portion of the bulkhead building was saved and remodeled for use as a restaurant—an early non-maritime use of a structure built as part of the working port. The San Francisco Bar Pilots were located on this pier for many years, moving to Pier 9 after Pier 7 burned. A new Pier 7 for fishing and public access was built south of here in 1990.

48. Pier 5
1922
Frank G. White, chief engineer
Bulkhead building: A. D. Janssen, designer; Hannah Brothers, contractor

Pier 5 has a complicated history beginning in 1895 when a wooden pier built at this site was designated as Pier 7. That structure, measuring 100 by 600 feet, was renamed Pier 5 in 1915. (Until that time, another structure called Pier 5 was located where Pier 3 is today.) In 1920–1922, a new bulkhead wharf and Neoclassical style bulkhead building were built at the inshore end of Pier 5. Although replacement of the pier and transit shed were planned as part of a modernization program begun in 1930, it was never done. Finally, the deteriorated pier was demolished in 1990–1992, leaving the bulkhead building by itself. Pier 5 had been used for coastwise and inland transportation. In 2007, San Francisco Waterfront Partners rehabilitated the Pier 5 bulkhead building, together with Pier 3.

49. Pier 3 (and 1½)
1917–1919
Frank G. White, chief engineer
Substructure: A. C. Griewank, S. E. Evans, and F. E. Ballou, designers
Transit shed and waiting rooms: A. C. Griewank and Bun Bearwald-Froberg, designers
Bulkhead building: A. A. Pyle, designer

Pier 3 is unique among San Francisco piers, consisting of two projections on parallel piers, one short and one long (the short pier at the complex has been called Pier 1½ since about 1939). It was designed to accommodate two aspects of the coastal and river business of two related tenants, the California Transportation Company and the California Navigation and Improvement Company, which had been in this vicinity since at least 1880. The main pier handled the freight business, including produce from Central Valley farms; and the short pier, which had a waiting room, handled passenger traffic to Sacramento, Stockton, and elsewhere, including luxurious over-night service between San Francisco and Sacramento on the Delta King and Delta Queen.[16] Next to the Ferry Building, Pier 3 was probably the busiest place on the waterfront. The twin-pier design ameliorated congestion between teams hauling produce from the waterfront to the Produce District across the Embarcadero and the constant stream of passengers.[17]

The reinforced-concrete substructure measured 138 by 706 feet for the main pier and 67 by 99 feet for the short pier. The original wooden transit shed on the main pier was largely removed in 1976. The waiting room on the short pier is of wood construction with a stucco exterior and plaster interior finishes. The Neoclassical style bulkhead building that fronts both piers has the finest interior materials and finishes among all the piers and bulkhead buildings, including oak paneling, decorative moldings, terrazzo, and marble floors.

In 2007, Piers 3 and 5 were rehabilitated for offices, restaurants, and public access. The project was designed by a team of architects, including Hannum Associates, Tom Eliot Fisch, and Page & Turnbull, for a development firm called San Francisco Waterfront Partners.

50. Pier 1
1929–1931
Frank G. White, chief engineer

Pier 1 was built with a reinforced-concrete substructure measuring 165 by 706 feet. The transit shed is a steel-frame structure with reinforced-concrete walls, and its interior was designed with three aisles and a continuous roof monitor. The Neoclassical style bulkhead building is a timber-frame structure with stucco walls. In 2001, it was rehabilitated for offices and public access by SMWM Architects for the AMB Property Corporation. The principal tenant is the Port of San Francisco, which moved from its longtime home in the Ferry Building when work began to transform that structure for new uses.

51. Clarke's Point

A rocky projection into the bay that marked the northern edge of Yerba Buena Cove at the time of the Gold Rush, Clarke's Point is now landlocked east of the intersection of Broadway and Battery Street. San Francisco's first wharves were built in this area.

52. Yerba Buena Cove

At the time of the Gold Rush, this shallow cove between Clarke's Point and Rincon Point was the destination of ships from around the world. The cove was surveyed and its water lots were sold from 1847 to 1852. In the 1850s, abandoned ships were used as warehouses until the lots were filled. Port-related businesses that first developed here—warehousing, commission merchants, produce markets, ship chandlers, marine insurers, and machine shops and other industry—still characterized the area until the 1950s.

53. Seawall Lots 10, 11, 12, 13, and 14 (now 320, 321, 322, 323, 324), and 15— ABC TV, Housing, and Offices

Until the 1890s, the seawall lots were restricted for use as open space or parks. Seawall Lots 11 and 12 were the first to be put to other uses, initially as a Southern Pacific yard and later as a Northwestern Pacific Railroad yard. The tracks crossed the port-owned blocks of Union, Green, and Vallejo streets, and extended a block further to Broadway. Today, Lot 10 is part of the Levi-Strauss complex, along with Lot 9. Lot 12 was developed in 1974 with a building for ABC television. Lots 11, 13, and 14 are parking lots. Lot 15 was transferred to the Redevelopment Agency for one block of the Golden Gateway Redevelopment Project, Phase 2 housing, designed by Fisher-Freidman and completed in 1982.

54. Seawall Lots 16 and 351—The Free Public Market

Seawall Lots 16 and 351 are now part of the Golden Gateway Tennis and Swim Club. Lot 351 was previously undeveloped. On Lot 16, a small triangular block bound by Pacific, Drumm, and the Embarcadero, a long-running effort to establish a Free Market at the port was realized in a very modest form. In 1895, the Free Market movement was begun by the Grangers and other agricultural groups, "a network of special interest groups that could bring pressure in high places."[18] Wide support resulted in state legislation, passed in 1897, requiring the port to provide contiguous piers and administration for a market for "all possible products arriving by boat, rail, or other conveyance, including fruit, vegetables, eggs, poultry, game, dairy products, and fish, and to permit the sale of such products therein by or for account of producers only."[19] The port evaded what it considered impractical requirements of the law, despite an amendment in 1903, claiming, "all wharves and bulkheads at which fruit, perishable products, etc. are now landed, shall constitute a Free Public Market."[20]

In 1905, numerous commission merchants were convicted of violating the law and lost their licenses to buy and sell perishable products on the piers. Also in that year, the port's attorney wrote, "The Board has been unable to follow the provisions of the free market act and establish the market provided for. Owing to the crowded condition of the water front there is no available site for the construction of a suitable building."[21]

Finally, in 1907, the BSHC asked permission from the city of San Francisco to build a temporary, non-fireproof building in a fireproof building zone to accommodate the Free Market. This building, a one-story wood-frame structure clad in iron, opened on Lot 16 in April 1908.

It is not known how long the market lasted after 1913. According to Lamberta Voget, a historian of the port, "The market proved a complete failure through lack of patronage on the part of producers."[22] In the 1930s, there was a gas station on this site.

View south along Battery Street, past paper and printing warehouses to the Customhouse, with the Shell Building in the distance

55. U.S. Customhouse

After several short-lived locations, in 1856 a U.S. Customhouse was established here, facing the water across Battery Street and presenting incoming ships with a familiar image of the authority of the federal government. As Yerba Buena Cove was filled, the waterfront moved eastward, leaving this location four blocks away when Section 7 of the seawall was completed in 1899. The 1856 customhouse was demolished in 1905, and a new customhouse was completed at the same location in 1911.

The Customs Service was a key institution at the port, especially until 1914. In the years before the income tax, tariffs collected by the Customs Service were the largest source of income for the federal government.

56. Produce (or Commission) District

At the time of the Gold Rush, specialized areas quickly developed close to the waterfront. Among the first was a district for perishable farm products. From the beginning this area was located north of Market Street and near the water, where goods could be brought from boats easily and quickly. Called the Produce District or Commission District, because it was run by commission merchants who bought produce from farmers and sold it to restaurants, hotels, institutions, and retailers, this area moved east with the filling of Yerba Buena Cove. By 1893, produce market buildings—one-story structures open to the street—were clustered in the area defined by Clay, Merchant, and Sansome streets.[23] The Produce District was rebuilt after the 1906 earthquake in the same general location but covered a larger area. In the mid-1950s, it was demolished for Golden Gateway Center and moved to a new Produce Market at Islais Creek. The new market was further from the congested waterfront but was much better served by trucks. A bay of the storefront from the Colombo Market Building still stands on the west edge of Walton Park.[24]

57. The Embarcadero

With the revised design of the seawall in 1876–1878, a wider "marginal" street was proposed parallel to the Water Front Line for the whole length of the seawall. This street would be two hundred feet wide, accommodating the Belt Railroad, wagon traffic (and later motor vehicles), and sidewalks for pedestrians. It was conceived as an active working area of the port, over which goods would be carried back and forth between piers and warehouses.

The great width of this street was a key element in a radical vision that created a huge amount of new land all under the control of one agency—the Board of State Harbor Commissioners. The new seawall had to be planned far enough out to make room for the roadway, which would occur entirely on newly filled ground. The Embarcadero and the seawall lots behind it were filled to the level of the City Base, established in 1853 at 6.7 feet above "the ordinary high water mark" of the bay.[25]

First called East Street, it was officially renamed the Embarcadero in 1909. The Spanish origin of the new street name reflected the same effort to recognize California's cultural identity as the plan to design pier fronts in the Mission Revival style, adopted in 1912.

The Embarcadero was built in sections, as the seawall was constructed and the seawall lots were filled, from about 1880 to 1915. Similarly, its surface was created and re-created over many years. Beginning in the 1880s, sections of the street were paved in basalt blocks to serve horse-drawn wagons. The Belt Railroad, also built in phases, was begun in 1890. After 1906, the street was paved in asphalt, first in strips alongside the basalt paving and later across its entire surface, to accommodate motor vehicles.

Built in the late 1950s, the Embarcadero Freeway, an elevated structure on concrete piers, overtook the Embarcadero, leaving parking lots, working yards, and a diminished street below. It was damaged in the 1989 Loma Prieta earthquake and demolished in 1991–1992.

The refurbishment of the Embarcadero began in 1998. In 2000, the port's Mid-Embarcadero Project was completed. The Embarcadero was realigned, bifurcated, and lined with palm and sycamore trees; a segment of the F-line streetcar was routed down the middle of the roadway; and Harry Bridges Plaza, containing two sixty-five-foot-high Millennium Lights, was established between the opposing lanes of traffic in front of the Ferry Building. The principal designer for the project was ROMA Design Group.

**58. Ferry Building: The Union Depot
and Ferry House
1896–1903**
Howard C. Holmes, chief engineer
A. Page Brown, architect
Edward R. Swain, supervising architect
Foundation: San Francisco Bridge Co.,
contractor
Building: multiple contractors

From the beginning, the conception for the Ferry Building (officially the Union Depot and Ferry House) was ambitious, bold, and impressive—particularly considering the ragtag character of the port at the time, the routine shortages of money for construction, and the chronic allegations of mismanagement and corruption on the part of the BSHC. The board's *Biennial Reports* of 1888 and 1890 outlined a building 800 feet long and 150 feet wide, "a commodious building of iron, wood, and glass."[26] But, after the state authorized a bond election to pay for the building, it was barely approved on November 8, 1892—by 866 votes out of 181,726 cast.

In 1894, after plans were approved and the massive foundations were under construction, the BSHC wrote of the unique challenge that those who built the Ferry Building faced: the design, they wrote, "will make the building compare favorably with the great structures of similar character which have been erected during the last few years about New York harbor and other ports in this country and Europe. There are very few terminal points, however, which can be compared with the problems of the San Francisco waterfront."[27] The building was conceived as "the gateway to San Francisco," but unlike the rail stations that served as gateways in other great cities, it was a ferry station located on the edge of the city. There was no clear precedent for solving the practical or aesthetic problems of designing

this building. Its success was a great achievement of architecture, engineering, construction, and administration—in any context.

Construction began March 20, 1896, and was completed in two phases. The immense, horizontal ferry terminal was opened to its tenants and the public on July 13, 1898, but work on the tower and various interiors continued until 1903.

As built, the terminal was 696 feet long, but it was designed to measure 840 feet; extensions at each end with projecting fronts similar to that at the center were never executed. The BSHC declared, "The tower is intended not only to mark the foot of Market Street and be the first object of interest to those coming over the bay, but it will serve as a beacon and clock tower which can be seen for many miles in every direction."[28] The tower is seen at a slight angle from Market Street because the entire building is aligned with the seawall, which is part of its foundations, rather than with the street grid.

The monumental design was justified by the image it would present of San Francisco

and its people: "Through its magnificent corridors, arcades, and waiting rooms will pass the tourist from abroad, with whom first impressions are the most lasting, and from the splendor surrounding the entrance leading him within the portals of the 'City by the Golden Gate,' will he judge the enterprise and progressiveness of our people, and will, therefore, inspire him to investigate the resources of our great commonwealth."[29] The design approach displayed a mix of pride and public relations.

At its peak in the 1930s, fifty million people per year passed through the Ferry Building.[30] After the Bay Bridge was completed in 1937, however, ferry service stopped, leaving the terminal without a reason for being. Having survived various demolition proposals in the 1950s, it was rehabilitated in 2003 as a market hall and office building with revived ferry service. The renovation was designed by a team of architects led by SMWM, including Page & Turnbull for restoration issues and Baldauf Catton Von Eckartsberg for retail spaces, for a group of developers led by Wilson Meany Sullivan.

59. United States Post Office (Agriculture Building)
1914–1915
Jerome Newman, assistant state engineer/ chief engineer

Substructure: Healy-Tibbitts Construction Co., contractor

Building: A. A. Pyle, designer; Teichert & Ambrose, contractor

The first U.S. Post Office at the port, called Station D, was located in the Old Ferry House in 1884. When the new Ferry Building opened in 1898, Station D moved to a space on two floors that was designed specifically for it. At the time, the port described the work of what was technically a branch post office: "The district covered by Station 'D' embraces all that portion of the city east of Montgomery Street, which includes the great wholesale business section of San Francisco. In addition to this, all the incoming and outgoing mail of the city is directly handled at this station, so the volume of business transacted thereat makes it really more like a general post office than a branch station."[31] After only two years, however, when the Santa Fe Railway began operations at the port, the rail company was assigned to the main post-office space in the Ferry Building. In 1900–1901, a new Romanesque Revival style structure, called the Ferry Post Office, was built just south of the Ferry Building. It was designed under the supervision of Howard C. Holmes, chief engineer of the port, rather than under the supervising architect of the United States Treasury, as were most post offices at the time. The port leased the building to the post office.

In 1914, the BSHC reported: "The old wooden building so long occupied by the United States Government as a ferry post office, and most unfortunately located out in the main thoroughfare, the Embarcadero, at the southern corner of the Ferry Building, will soon cease to be an eyesore and an impediment to traffic."[32] A new concrete and steel post office was built on a wharf just east of the previous structure: "The building will become the main distributing post office in the business district of the city, thus saving hours of time to the merchants, who have complained bitterly of the long delays incident to the present distributing point of the mail, far uptown."[33]

Like many post offices of its day, the building was designed in the style of the Italian Renaissance. Its designer, A. A. Pyle, was moved from the State Department of Engineering to the BSHC during this project. The architect and critic Irving F. Morrow commented, "The Ferry Station of the Post Office really stands above in a class by itself. . . . it remains distinctively creditable and one of the best pieces of public architecture for which the State is responsible."[34]

In 1925, the U.S. Post Office moved across the Embarcadero to a large new building, the Ferry Annex Post Office, between Washington and Merchant streets, and in 1940 it moved to Rincon Annex. The former post office was rented as office space to various commercial tenants until it was assigned to the California Department of Agriculture in 1933, at which time it was remodeled inside and became known as the Agriculture Building.

60. Pier 14—Wells Fargo & Company Express Building

The first pier south of the Ferry Building was Pier 14, a wooden structure with a bulkhead building and transit shed built in 1914–1915 for Wells Fargo & Company Express. The bulkhead building was one of the first built after the port announced its plan to apply the "modified" Mission Revival style to structures south of the Ferry Building, which were to be designed in collaboration with the state architect.[35] However, rather than recall the architecture of the California missions, its design is based on Renaissance and Baroque precedents, with engaged pilasters, decorative moldings and details, and a red-tile roof that resemble features of the Wells Fargo & Company Building of 1902, still standing a few blocks away at the northeast corner of Mission and Second streets. Two of its three ground-floor bays accommodated deliveries by horse-drawn wagons and motor vehicles. In 1917, a U.S. Naval Training Station Building was erected near the end of the pier, an early example of military presence at the port, just before World War I. The buildings were removed after a fire in 1959, and the pier was demolished after 1975. A new Pier 14, providing public access, was built on top of a breakwater in 2005.

61. Launch Offices

The Launch Offices building—for companies providing small working boats for hire to pilots, ships' agents, customs officials, repairmen, and crew members—was built in 1916 on the bulkhead wharf between Piers 14 and 16. It was a long, narrow, one-story structure with two-story towers at each end. Its prominence was commensurate with the important daily role of launches in the working of the port. The building had smooth stucco walls, red-tile roofs, and decorative details inspired by Renaissance architecture. By the 1920s, Crowley Launch and Tugboat Company and Henry C. Peterson occupied this building. It was demolished in the 1960s.

From left to right: Launch Offices, Pier 16

62. Piers 16–18–20

The 1913 design for the continuous bulkhead building that linked Piers 16–18–20 was used by the port to illustrate its intention to use the "modified" Mission Revival style for buildings south of the Ferry Building.[36] With its parapets at the inshore ends of each pier, the architecture looked more like that of the Alamo than of any building in California. The complex was demolished or destroyed in stages between 1959 and 1983; Pier 20 was destroyed by fire in 1972.

63. Seawall Lot 17 (Now 327)—Rincon Park

Rincon Park occupies two acres along the waterfront, including Seawall Lot 17 (now 327) and other lots acquired by the port when the Embarcadero Freeway was built in the 1950s. Seawall Lot 17 was never developed for port uses. The park was a Redevelopment Agency project developed by the Gap and Wilson Meany Sullivan as part of a package with the Gap Headquarters, built in 2001 at Folsom Street and the Embarcadero. It was designed by the Olin Partnership and the Office of Cheryl Barton and completed in 2003. *Cupid's Span*, a fifty-foot-high sculpture by Claes Oldenburg and Coosje van Bruggen, gives visibility to the park from great distances. The playful landscape, the artwork, and the two restaurants at the south end of the park create an atmosphere of leisure that is the antithesis of the hard-working environment of the port and of the labor battles that took place in this area in 1934, where Piers 16 through 24 met the seawall.

64. Pier 22

Pier 22, built in 1915–1916, had a "modified" Mission Revival style facade. It was demolished in the late 1970s.

65. Pier 22½

Fire Station 35, built for the city Fire Department, was built at Pier 22½ in 1915 and has functioned continuously as a fire station since that time. The first permanent home of the San Francisco fireboats, which were introduced after the earthquake and fire of 1906 as part of the plan for an auxiliary water supply, it is a two-story structure with a garage on the Embarcadero for "a motor-drive fire engine."[37] Fireboats dock behind it. There are sleeping and living rooms for firefighters upstairs. It is built in the zone designated for buildings in the "modified" Mission Revival style, but its style is loosely derived from that of a Renaissance villa. A seismic rehabilitation was completed in 2010.

66. Coffee and the Smells of the Port

The longtime place of the coffee business at the port of San Francisco was summarized in a 1955 company newsletter article that proclaimed, "Coffee: Queen of S.F. Imports": "Next to banking, insurance and printing coffee is San Francisco's biggest industry. A half dozen major coffee companies and scores of smaller businesses are located within short distances of the Embarcadero, where mountains of green coffee arrive almost daily from Central and South America and other countries."[38] Coffee was first brought to San Francisco during the Gold Rush, when it was picked up on ships stopping in South and Central American ports. Along with New York and New Orleans, San Francisco became a leading global producer and marketer of roasted coffee, in part due to the invention of vacuum-packed coffee by Hills Brothers in 1900. In the mid-twentieth century, coffee was "the most valuable single import arriving here from foreign countries."[39]

The old coffee-roasting companies are gone, but the architecturally distinguished buildings of two of the biggest—Hills Brothers and Folgers—are still standing near the waterfront. Located at the foot of Harrison Street and facing the Embarcadero, Hills Brothers was a conspicuous symbol of the importance of coffee to San Francisco. Completed in 1924, the building was designed by George W. Kelham, who was better known for his corporate and civic architecture such as the Russ and Shell buildings and the San Francisco Public Library. In 1986 it was remodeled and enlarged as an office building. The Folgers Coffee Company building at the southwest corner of Howard and Spear streets was designed by Henry Schulze, a prominent leader in the profession, and completed in 1905.

Roasting coffee was one of the many distinct smells of the waterfront, along with saltwater and the decay of marine life, steam, sweat, vegetable oils, fuel oil, solvents, lubricants, gasoline, and diesel exhaust—and, in the early days, coal, sewage, horses, manure, and hay.

67. Rincon Point

Rincon Point was a prominent projection of land into the bay that marked the southern end of Yerba Buena Cove at the time of the Gold Rush. In the 1850s, there was a Chinese fishing village here. A landmark of the early city front, the U.S. Marine Hospital for sick and disabled seamen was built on Rincon Point, at the northwest corner of Harrison and Spear streets, in 1852.[40] At the time, Rincon Point was a U.S. government reserve. An enormous building for its day, the hospital was a four-story brick structure for five hundred patients. After 1876, it was occupied by the Sailors' Home. Because of its size and location it was a conspicuous feature in many photos of San Francisco until its demolition in 1919. A few blocks to the south, on a bluff above South Beach on the north side of Bryant Street between First and Second, was another large brick structure, St. Mary's Hospital, built in 1861. It was destroyed in 1906.[41]

From left to right: Piers 20, 22, 22 1/2, and 24

68. Pier 24

Pier 24 was a wooden structure built in 1915. The facade of its bulkhead building was almost identical to that of Pier 22. The transit shed and bulkhead building were demolished in 1997 after a fire, followed by the last remnants of the substructure in 2004. Pier 24 Annex, built in 1928 on the connecting wharf between Piers 24 and 26, was rehabilitated in 2006.

69. Seawall Lot 18 (Now 328)—The Bay Bridge

Seawall Lot 18 was one of the last lots to be filled, in 1914—a few years after completion of Section 9 of the seawall in 1910. In the mid-1930s, Pier W-1 of the San Francisco-Oakland Bay Bridge was built on this site.

70–72. PIERS 26, 28, 30, 32

These four piers were designed as a group in the "modified" Mission Revival style.[42] The principal tenants of these piers, including Matson Navigation Company and American-Hawaiian Steamship Company, were engaged in coastwise and Hawaiian trade.

70. Pier 26
1912–1913

A. V. Saph, assistant state engineer, design phase

Jerome Newman, assistant state engineer, construction phase

Charles Newton Young, designer; Grant Smith & Co., contractors

In the diverse mix of design and construction types among the piers, Pier 26 is unique. Its substructure is reinforced concrete, and the transit shed has steel columns and heavy timber trusses. There is no building on the bulkhead wharf; its decorated facade, although it resembles the fronts of the bulkhead buildings on most of the piers, is simply the west end of the transit shed. While the design of this facade suggests a central aisle on the interior, a feature of most piers, instead a central row of columns forms two interior aisles, each of which originally had a traveling crane to move cargo within the shed. On each side of Pier 26 are long, narrow buildings on connecting wharves that are designed to accommodate trucks; they were built in 1928 (north) and 1930 (south).

71. Pier 28
1912–1913

A. V. Saph, assistant state engineer, design phase

Jerome Newman, assistant state engineer, construction phase

Charles Newton Young, designer; San Francisco Bridge Co., contractor

Pier 28, like Pier 26, does not have a separate bulkhead building, and the decorated front of the structure is the west end of the transit shed. Constructed almost entirely of fire-resistant materials, it has a reinforced-concrete substructure and a steel-frame transit shed with concrete walls, roof, and monitor. The interior has three aisles.

72. Pier 30–32

All that remains of Pier 30–32 after a fire in 1984 is the reinforced-concrete substructure. Pier 30–32 was built in 1912–1913 as the first pair of piers in San Francisco conceived as a single development. It was also the first with "up-to-date freight handling devices consisting of traveling cranes, telphers, and shiptowers."[43] A distinctive bulkhead building with two towers linked its parallel piers. To accommodate ever-larger ships, the two piers were lengthened in 1926; in 1952 they were joined by a connecting wharf to provide for trucks.

73. Waterfront Restaurants

Cheap restaurants were fixtures on the waterfront for much of its history. They were housed in the large bulkhead buildings at the inshore ends of the piers and in small, freestanding wooden buildings on the bulkhead wharf. Workers on indefinite shifts that ended at all hours of the day and night depended on them. They had short breaks and could not go far to eat—a 1942 schedule allowed twenty minutes for lunch in an eight-hour day and two lunch breaks in a fourteen-hour day.[44] Similarly, these restaurants served the interests of the shipping companies and merchants who depended on the labor force. After the 1934 strike, they acquired a new purpose and more of them were built. Whereas previously workers had to be at the hiring shape-up at seven o'clock A.M., once the shape-up was eliminated it became customary to gather for breakfast on the waterfront, a practice that lasted until the rise of container shipping in the late 1960s.[45]

The surviving examples, typically simple wooden buildings, are among the last waterfront restaurants built by the BSHC on port property. The Bayview was operating at Pier 28½ by 1935 and has since been known as the Boondocks and the Hi Dive. Its bar dates from the period of the city's ownership. Red's Java House, at Pier 30, also from the mid-1930s, miraculously escaped destruction in the 1984 fire at Pier 30–32. The Java House at Pier 40 was in operation by 1937.

74. Seawall Lot 19 (now 329)

One of the last seawall lots to be filled, in 1914, Seawall Lot 19 was leased upon completion to the Santa Fe Railway as a rail yard that extended across Bryant Street to a privately owned block. Today the lot is largely in the right-of-way of the realigned foot of Bryant Street.

75. Seawall Lot 20 (now 330)—The Watermark

One of the last three seawall lots filled, in 1914, Seawall Lot 20 was leased as a rail yard to Western Pacific Railroad. The Watermark tower, a twenty-two-story condominium, was built on the site in 2006. Designed by three architectural firms—Moore, Ruble, Yudell; Kwan Henmi; and Fisher-Friedman—it was part of a larger plan to develop Pier 30–32 as a new terminal for cruise ships.

77. Seawall Lots 21 and 22 (now 331 and 332)—Delancey Street

Seawall Lot 21 was leased in 1918 to Toyo Kisen Kaisha, a Japanese steamship line. By 1948 there was a stevedore's equipment warehouse on the site. Lot 22 was a Western Pacific Railroad yard for many years. Both lots, as well as a portion of Fremont Street owned by the port, were redeveloped in 1990 for Delancey Street, "a residential self-help organization for substance abusers, ex-convicts, homeless and others who have hit bottom."[46] Designed by Backen, Arrigoni & Ross, it includes 177 low-income apartments and a restaurant.

View south along the Embarcadero, with Pier 34 on the left and the Pacific Mail Steamship Company Warehouse and a restaurant on the right

76. Pier 34

Pier 34 was planned in 1909 at the same time as Piers 36, 38, and 40 but was built of inferior materials, having a wooden deck and transit shed on concrete-jacketed wooden piles. It never had a bulkhead building or a decorated front and was similar in appearance to Pier 17. It was demolished in 2001.

78–80. PIERS 36, 38, 40
1908–1909
Ralph Barker, assistant state engineer
H. J. Brunnier, designer

Following the approval of two million dollars in bonds in November 1904, the development of Piers 36, 38, and 40, utilizing fireproof and permanent construction, inaugurated what the BSHC considered the modern era in San Francisco's waterfront facilities. Previous piers were supported on wooden piles or had experimental reinforced-concrete designs that failed within a few years. Designed by the prominent engineer H. J. Brunnier at the beginning of his long career, Piers 36, 38, and 40 were all built on reinforced-concrete substructures and had steel and concrete transit sheds. None were originally given bulkhead buildings.

Several striking photographs reproduced in the 1910 *Biennial Report* in a large, foldout format indicate the pride that the port took in these structures. The severe simplicity of Pier 36, in particular—with its column-free space of reinforced concrete and steel, its proportion of windows to wall surfaces, the quality of natural light on its interior, and its clarity of structure—was a powerful statement of the progress represented by modern engineering at the time, and it presented an image that in retrospect, at least, has a strong aesthetic appeal.

78. Pier 36

Pier 36 was a unique facility, with a wide pier that supported both a transit shed and a deck for four rail spurs that led to a hoisting tower for railcar ferries at the outer end. The transit shed is a steel-frame structure with poured-concrete walls and roof. Lit by a band of clerestory windows and a roof monitor, the eighty-three-foot-wide interior space is spanned by steel trusses, eliminating the need for interior columns.

Pier 36 originally included wooden fenders and a wooden transit shed at its outer end. In 1917, the transit shed at the inshore end was extended across the bulkhead wharf to the Embarcadero. The original rear wooden transit shed was removed after 1962.

Pier 36 was originally built for the Western Pacific Railroad but was soon used by other railroads as well. Starting about 1918, Toyo Kisen Kaisha, a Japanese steamship company, and Western Pacific were secret partners here in the silk trade at a time when San Francisco was the second largest sik port.[47] Pier 36 is proposed for demolition as part of the Brannan Street Wharf project, a park dominated by a large lawn.

79. Pier 38

The second modern pier at the port, Pier 38 has a reinforced-concrete substructure, a transit shed with a steel frame and roof trusses, and concrete walls. The interior has three aisles, the center of which originally had a rail spur. When problems with the interior rail became evident, the port adopted a universal plan for spurs on the aprons alongside the outer walls of the transit sheds. The construction of Piers 38 and 40, which were similar, made it "impossible for rats to get in or out of them when the doors are closed."[48]

In the 1920s, pipelines from Pier 38 to tanks in Seawall Lot 24 (below King Street) were used for vegetable oils. In 1932, the pier was extended by 241 feet to accommodate the larger ships of the McCormick Steamship Company, which had routes along the Pacific Coast, to the East Coast, and to the West Indies. In 1936, Piers 38 and 40 were linked at the front by a steel-frame bulkhead building that blended Mission and Mediterranean stylistic features. Pier 38 currently provides services for maritime recreational boating.

80. Pier 40

Pier 40 was the first modern pier at the port. It was built with a reinforced-concrete substructure and a steel-frame transit shed with a poured-concrete roof and walls. Like Pier 38, Pier 40 originally included a central interior rail spur that was removed after a few years. It was extended in 1925 to accommodate the larger ships of the McCormick Steamship Company. In 1936, a new bulkhead building spanned Piers 38 and 40. The Pier 40 section of this building and parts of the transit shed were removed in the late 1970s. Although subsequently shortened and altered, Pier 40 today looks much as it did when it was completed in 1909, except for a new facade built in 2008.

View toward the Embarcadero from Townsend and Japan (now Colin P. Kelly) streets, with Seawall Lot 23 on the right

81. Seawall Lot 23 (Now 333)— Steamboat Point

In 1909, Seawall Lot 23 was leased to the Southern Pacific Railroad as a rail yard for twenty-five years. In the 1940s, it was a truck yard and station. In 1992, Steamboat Point, a low-income housing development with 108 units, was built on the site. Designed by Backen, Arrigoni & Ross for Bridge Housing, the development was named for a geographical feature called Steamboat Point in the mid-nineteenth century. Long obscured by fill, Steamboat Point once stretched more or less from Second to Fourth Street along Townsend, between Rincon Point and Mission Bay. It played an important role in the early history of the port as a place where steamships were built.

82–84. PIERS 42, 44, 46A

Piers 42, 44, and 46 (later called 46A) were built at different times but were unified in 1916–1918 by a similar Mediterranean style treatment of their bulkhead buildings. All were demolished in the 1970s–1980s. In 1986, the Redevelopment Agency built the South Beach Marina in the bay where these piers had been.

82. Pier 42

Pier 42 was a wooden structure built in 1906 and rebuilt in 1918. It was long occupied by Dollar Steamship Lines.

83. Pier 44

Pier 44 was a wooden structure built in 1904 and rebuilt in 1917.

84. Pier 46A

Pier 46A, a wooden structure, was built in 1914 and destroyed by fire shortly thereafter. Following much discussion about whether to replace it in fireproof materials, it was rebuilt in wood in 1917–1918.

85. South Beach Harbor Park

South Beach Harbor Park was built by the Redevelopment Agency in two phases from 1995 to 2005. Consisting of five acres immediately south of Pier 40, it occupies the bulkhead wharf and portions of the Embarcadero where the street was terminated at King Street because of construction of the ballpark.

The park contains the South Beach Yacht Club and a sixty-foot-high steel sculpture, *Sea Change*, by Mark di Suvero. It is named for South Beach, which had lain generally between Steamboat Point and Rincon Point at the time of the Gold Rush.

86. Baseball Stadium

The baseball stadium for the San Francisco Giants was designed by HOK Sport and was built in 2000 on the site of several port properties, including three seawall lots and Pier 46B; one privately owned block; and portions of Berry Street, Second Street, and the Embarcadero.

87. Seawall Lot 24 (now 334)

Beginning in 1909, the east end of Seawall Lot 24 was leased for twenty-five years to the Southern Pacific Railroad whose affiliate, the Pacific Mail Steamship Company, had a warehouse and repair shop here by 1913. The west end was leased to the Associated Oil Company. In the 1940s, vegetable-oil tanks, owned by W. R. Grace & Company, occupied most of the block.

88. Seawall Lot 25 (now 335)

In 1913 there was a gravel bunker on Seawall Lot 25. In 1917, the lot was leased for twenty years to W. R. Grace & Company for vegetable-oil tanks, which still stood in the 1940s.

89. Seawall Lot 26 (now 336)

Seawall Lot 26 was filled after the China Basin seawall was finished in the early 1920s. Nothing was ever built on this site.

90. Pier 46B—Refrigerated Products Terminal

Pier 46B, along the north side of China Basin in the area closest to the bay, was proposed as the site of China Basin Terminal in 1922. The terminal was to be a six-story reinforced-concrete building measuring 816 by 123 feet. The BSHC called it "the greatest project undertaken for many years. . . . Too great emphasis can not be laid upon the importance of this project, which will be unequalled by any port in the United States, or in the world."[49] In fact, only the first two floors were built, reflecting the deflated vision of San Francisco's future when the great promise of the Panama Canal was not realized. This building opened as the Refrigerated Products Terminal in 1925. In 1930, the second floor was expensively modified as a cold-storage plant, called the State Refrigeration Terminal, "for the handling of export shipments of perishable farm products, particularly fresh fruit."[50] In the 1960s, it was modified again to serve as a newsprint terminal.

View from the Embarcadero across Seawall Lot 23

91. South End Historic District

The South End Historic District, a city landmark district, spreads inland to the north and west from what was the southern waterfront at the foot of First and Second streets until the completion of the seawall in 1915 moved the waterfront further east. The district first developed in the late 1860s and 1870s with warehouses adjacent to the railroad that were used by wholesale businesses for the long-term storage of goods transported to and from the piers. These facilities were distinct from the early warehouses in the Northeast Waterfront Historic District, which stored perishable goods for immediate, local consumption. The district includes the 1867 Oriental Warehouse of the Pacific Mail Steamship Company and the 1903 Southern Pacific Warehouse, the two representing the dominant landowners on the waterfront. It also includes several warehouses built from the 1870s to 1906 on the first Southern Pacific rail spurs, as well as a newer generation of reinforced-concrete warehouses and industrial buildings along Second Street, which were served by a major expansion of Southern Pacific's network of spurs in the 1910s.

View south along Third Street, from right to left: Southern Pacific Passenger Depot, China Basin Building, and Third Street Bridge

92. Rail Yards

When the Southern Pacific rail yards were established in 1869, they terminated at Ritch Street, a short distance west of Third, and connected to a spur continuing down King Street to the car-ferry slip on the waterfront.

93. Passenger Depot

The Southern Pacific Passenger Depot was located on the south side of Townsend Street just east of Fourth from 1869 to 1913. A new Mission Revival style station was built at the southwest corner of Third and Townsend streets in 1914. It was demolished in 1947.

94. General Office

From the 1870s to 1906, the Southern Pacific headquarters was in a three-story brick building at the northeast corner of Fourth and Brannan streets, across the street from the rail yard and the passenger depot.

95. China Basin Building

The China Basin Building, a large warehouse designed by Bliss & Faville for the Southern Pacific Railroad, was completed in 1922.

96. Pacific Mail Steamship Company and the Oriental Warehouse

The Pacific Mail Steamship Company was established in New York in 1848. With a government contract to carry the mail between New York and San Francisco, and subsequently between San Francisco, China, and other Pacific ports, the company built some of the first substantial facilities on the San Francisco waterfront. First located at the Broadway wharf and then at the foot of Folsom Street, in the mid-1860s, before the railroad was built, the company moved to the foot of First Street. In the 1870s it was the second largest employer in the city. The ownership and management of Pacific Mail Steamship and the Central Pacific-Southern Pacific railroad were linked in various ways over many years, beginning with rate-fixing agreements in 1870 and culminating in Southern Pacific's ownership of Pacific Mail between 1900 and 1915. Thus, their waterfront facilities were developed in relation to each other, notably with the Southern Pacific spur serving the Pacific Mail Steamship Company complex in the block bounded by Townsend, Japan (now Colin P Kelly), Brannan, and First streets.

The complex included a coal yard, ship repair shops, the wooden Occidental Warehouse at the edge of the water for the storage of flour and grain, and the brick Oriental Warehouse, a bonded facility used for storing valuables such as opium and silk and for warehousing Chinese immigrants. A short pier served the Occidental Warehouse. A long pier with a transit shed—called a "Freight House and Dock" and known as the mail dock—projected into the bay more or less in a continuous line with First Street.

The Oriental Warehouse was built in 1867, the year that Pacific Mail began service across the Pacific Ocean. In 1999, condominiums were built inside the perimeter walls after the interior burned in a fire.

The grounds of the Pacific Mail Steamship Company, with repair shops on the lower left, the three-gabled Occidental Warehouse in the center, and the brick Oriental Warehouse and the long Freight House and Dock at the rear

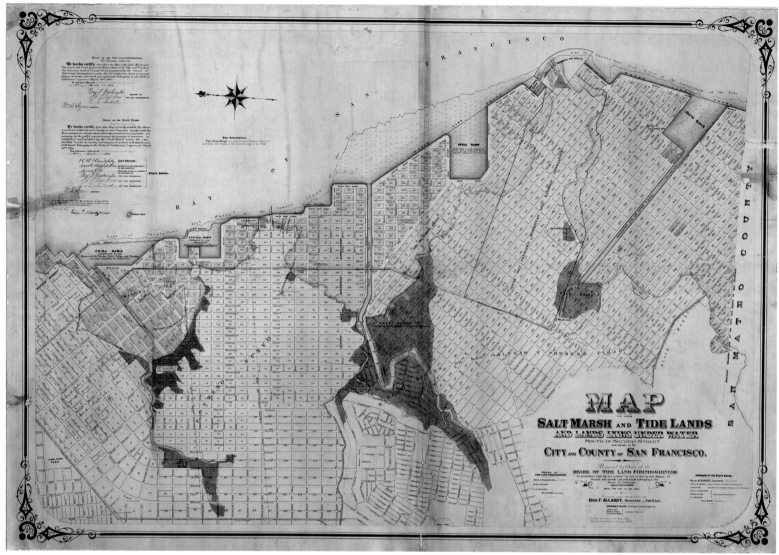

Bodies of water, from left to right: Mission Bay, Islais Creek and India Basin, and South Basin

97. Mission Bay

Like Yerba Buena Cove to the north, where the business and manufacturing center of the city first developed as it was filled with land, Mission Bay was filled under the pressure of urban development, although somewhat later. Located roughly between Steamboat Point and the foot of Sixteenth Street, Mission Bay was the outlet for Mission Creek, named for its proximity and usefulness to Mission Dolores and its agricultural enterprises. Much of the north half of Mission Bay was surveyed and sold as water lots from 1847 to 1852, followed by some filling, particularly north of Channel Street. However, the conditions for the wholesale filling of Mission Bay were not established until the creation by the state of the Board of Tide Land Commissioners in 1868. The Tide Land Commissioners surveyed the rest of the bay and auctioned lots from 1869 to the early 1870s. It was widely expected that the tidelands would be filled and developed for industry. From a shallow body of water, Mission Bay was an industrial and railroad district for more than one hundred years. Today the area is being redeveloped as a city neighborhood with housing and a new research campus for the University of California, San Francisco.

98. Mission Creek

Mission Creek entered the bay in the vicinity of King and Division streets. While measures were taken to survey and sell the tidelands of Mission Bay for development, state laws enacted in 1851 and 1867–1868 sought to protect or control Mission Creek and its flow of water. The latter law reserved a canal or waterway that would convey the water of Mission Creek to the bay, regardless of the filling of tidelands on each side.

99. Channel Street

The law of 1867–1868 referred to the reserved waterway through the tidelands as a channel 60 feet wide from Mission Creek to Seventh Street and 107 feet wide from Seventh Street to its outlet in the bay. From Seventh Street to the bay were to be wharves ten feet wide on both sides of the channel.

In fact, the official 1851 Eddy map of the city already showed "Channel Street" in its future location; it was depicted as a channel but ambiguously called a street. An 1873 map labeled it "Channel Street or Open Canal"—the issue not yet settled. However, the channel later known as Channel Street did not take shape until the years 1878–1887, when lots on both sides were filled and utilized as lumberyards and related industries that were served by ships at the wharves along the channel. The 1887 Sanborn map labeled the waterway Mission Creek Channel.

The dispute over whether this was a street or a channel surfaced periodically. A public meeting in 1871 reaffirmed the public interest in Mission Creek as a navigable stream, according to the state law of 1867–1868. Sometime between 1887 and 1901, the dispute was glossed over by retaining the waterway as a channel but continuing to call it "Channel Street." In 1901, the channel was dredged to 140 feet wide within the state-controlled 200-foot-wide corridor as far as Seventh Street; the narrower channel between the mouth of Mission Creek and Seventh Street had been covered and lost to view.

100. Pier 60   Banana Terminal

In 1928, a Banana Terminal was established at Pier 60 on the south side of Channel Street. Cranes at this terminal moved bananas from the refrigerated holds of ships to refrigerated railcars.

101. China Basin

With the establishment of the Pacific Mail Steamship Company at First and Townsend streets and the prevalence in the area of shipping business dealing with China, the nearby water of Mission Bay was referred to as China Basin as early as the 1860s. As the tidelands were filled and Mission Bay disappeared, the shrinking area of water that remained was commonly known as China Basin. From 1901 to 1914, the seawalls on both sides of the basin were built; at that time, the widened area of water at the mouth of Channel Street and east of the Third Street Bridge was called China Basin. Since the ballpark was completed in 2000 on the north side of China Basin, the basin has been known to baseball fans as Willy McCovey Cove, named for the Giants' first baseman from 1959 to 1973.

102. Santa Fe Railway Yards and Terminal

Beginning in 1901 under an agreement with the BSHC, the Santa Fe Railway began filling a large portion of Mission Bay east of Third Street, from Channel Street on the north to El Dorado Street on the south. The railroad built a seawall generally along the waterfront line and filled behind it; the company then purchased the new lots south of Fourth Street and leased the area north of Fourth Street from the BSHC under what was called the China Basin Lease, with the commissioners retaining a corridor along the waterfront. The area of the China Basin Lease was designated Seawall Lot 27 (now 337). The entire area was treated as a single rail yard. In 1902, a Santa Fe car-ferry terminal stood at the foot of Fourth Street, and later another occupied the northeast corner of the fill. Seawall Lot 337 is now the subject of development proposals.

103. Southern Pacific Mission Bay Yards

In 1867, a long bridge was built across Mission Bay to get workers to industrial jobs at Potrero Point. East of the bridge, Southern Pacific built its Mission Bay rail yards on the tidelands that the company first received in a grant from the state and then filled. These yards included a roundhouse between Sixteenth and Mariposa streets.

104–107. PIER 48 TO PIER 54

Following the completion of the large area south of China Basin for the Santa Fe Railway and the Santa Fe's construction of its own pier, the port developed a plan for new piers on the waterfront of that newly filled area. In 1924, the port proposed three new quay-type piers between China Basin and the foot of Fourth Street that would be substantially larger than anything yet built in San Francisco. Pier 52 was never built. In 2010, the port is implementing a shoreline improvement project, increasing public access to the waterfront in this area.

104. Pier 48
1928–1930
Frank G. White, chief engineer
Substructure: Oliver W. Jones, designer; Healy-Tibbitts Construction Co., contractor
Transit sheds: H. B. Fisher and B. P. Hudspeth, designers; L. M. King, contractor

In 1926, plans were announced for Piers 48 and 45, the latter a similar quay-type pier at the far north end of the port. Pier 48 has a pair of parallel transit sheds along the sides, leaving room for rail and truck access through the center. The substructure is built on reinforced-concrete piles. The transit sheds are steel-frame structures with precast concrete walls and Gothic Revival ornamental detail on the facades. Each transit shed was designed with three aisles. There are no separate bulkhead buildings. In 1938, a building was added to connect the ends of the transit sheds.

105. Pier 50 and Mission Rock Terminal
1925–1926
Frank G. White, chief engineer
Substructure: Clinton Construction Co., contractor
Transit sheds: David Nordstrom, contractor

Pier 50 was the first quay-type pier in San Francisco and ultimately the biggest of its generation. As built in its first phase, it was 600 feet long by 386 feet wide and had a transit shed on each side. The substructure is reinforced concrete. The sheds are timber frame and have walls of precast reinforced-concrete slabs. The facades of the transit sheds—there were no separate bulkhead buildings—were finished with Gothic Revival ornamental details. Construction of the outer section of this pier was delayed for more than twenty years because of legal complications over Mission Rock.

After Pier 50 was extended in 1950 to cover Mission Rock—an outcropping in the bay—and the area around it, the expanded structure was known as Mission Rock Terminal. The triangular extension more than doubled the pier's size, exceeding fourteen acres. This section had steel-frame transit sheds on its sides.

Mission Rock has a complicated history of ownership and use.[51] In the nineteenth century, facilities on Mission Rock were used to transship grain from the interior of California to oceangoing ships. At the end of the century, the Alaska Packers Association kept long wooden warehouses on Mission Rock. Later, strike breakers and "bay pirates" squatted there. In 1899, the U.S. government tried to take the area from its owner, the Mission Rock Company, as a Naval reserve. The issue went to court and was not settled until 1944, when it was awarded to the Navy. The Navy sold it to the BSHC shortly thereafter. The original long-term tenant of Mission Rock Terminal was American President Lines. Pier 50 remains in maritime and industrial use, including the port's maintenance facility in shed D.

106. Pier 54
1909–1910
Ralph Barker, assistant state engineer
Substructure: Thompson Bridge Co., contractor

Pier 54 was built for the Santa Fe Railway and is adjacent to the railroad's main yards. It is a reinforced-concrete structure that originally had a wooden transit shed. Its unusual width—it was the widest of its day—is the result of a scandal. According to the reformed BSHC of 1910–1912, the incompetent previous board—under the corrupting influence of the Southern Pacific Railroad—failed to blast out a ledge of rock along the north side of the pier before construction began. Because blasting after the fact would have destroyed the new structure, the new board decided to widen the pier over the rock. The original transit shed has been replaced.

From left to right: Wharves and dry dock of Union Iron Works (Pier 70), Central Basin, Pier 54 (angled), Santa Fe Railroad car-ferry slip, Mission Rock Terminal, Pier 48, and Channel Street–China Basin

107. Central Basin

Located between two promontories of Point San Quentin, later called Potrero Point, Central Basin has largely served as a basin for shipbuilding activities at what is now called Pier 70. When wharves were proposed along the periphery of Central Basin in 1908, the Union Iron Works objected to the potential interference with its shipbuilding operations. Nevertheless, in 1928–1930, four acres were filled between Seventeenth and Mariposa streets, east of Illinois, from which Pier 64 was later built. Pier 64 was demolished after 1973. After Southern Pacific lost its car-ferry slip north of China Basin to construction of the seawall, the company operated a new slip on Central Basin between El Dorado and Sixteenth streets until after World War II.

108. Potrero Point: The Private Waterfront

On the entire waterfront of San Francisco between Aquatic Park and the San Mateo County line, only two spots—Potrero Point and Hunters Point (see no. 120)—were situated well enough that private parties were able to develop them with lasting waterfront facilities. Both sites projected into relatively deep water, making these developments possible. Where the natural conditions were lacking, it took a public agency—the BSHC—to acquire the property and raise the money to build what was necessary to create adequate port facilities. Everywhere else, a useable waterfront in public ownership was created by seawalls, landfill, and dredging.

The densest concentration of heavy industry in San Francisco—or in any place west of Chicago and St. Louis—developed at Potrero Point beginning after the Civil War, in anticipation of the transcontinental railroad. Tubbs Cordage Works, Pacific Rolling Mills, the San Francisco Gas and Electric Company, the California Sugar Refinery Company, the Union Iron Works, and the Arctic Oil Works were all established in this area between 1856 and 1884. Later the California Barrel Works, the American Can Company, and others appeared. To accommodate the expansion and changing needs of these industries, seawalls, landfill, and dredging were employed.

These companies represented several of the key industries at the port. Tubbs Cordage Works, with its narrow, fourteen-hundred-foot-long rope-manufacturing building, called a ropewalk, made rope used on ships, in cargo handling, and for many other purposes. The sugar industry, linking San Francisco with Hawaii and with the development of land for sugar-beet farming in California, dominated shipping on Piers 26 to 30–32 from the 1910s to 1960s. Barrels, one of the units of break-bulk cargo handling, were made here. As fish processing and the commercial canning of fruits and vegetables increased, the manufacturing of cans for food products became a significant industry. Whale oil was another important type of cargo in San Francisco, beginning in the 1850s. From 1885 to 1905, San Francisco was "the principal whaling port in the world," home to a fleet of whaling ships and the producer of oil for lighting and lubrication. The Arctic Oil Works was established here in 1885 "to refine, transport, and trade in whale oil."[52] Finally, the Union Iron Works was a major shipbuilder from 1884 to 1945.

In 1982, the sites of the core Potrero Point industries were acquired by the Port of San Francisco and designated Pier 70.

109–119. ISLAIS CREEK AND INDIA BASIN

The stretch of the waterfront between Potrero Point and Hunters Point, now marked by a bewildering—because it is generally closed to the public—mix of landfill and facilities for shipping, railroads, and industry, was acquired by the port in a single effort and was initially the subject of a grandiose plan for expanding the port. The ultimate failure of this plan reflects the collapse of San Francisco's hopes that the opening of the Panama Canal in 1914 would bring the city vastly increased business and greater prosperity.

The two adjacent stretches of tidelands on this waterfront—Islais Creek basin on the north and India Basin on the south—were purchased following the approval of bonds for the purpose in 1909 and 1913. The actual purchase of sixty-three blocks was delayed by technical difficulties and legal challenges until 1918. In 1918, the BSHC published plans and a bird's-eye artist's perspective showing the entire area built up with warehouses on filled ground behind a new seawall, large piers along the waterfront, extensive rail facilities, and a dredged channel on Islais Creek.[53] In 1925, money was finally available to begin work on large projects, and the area was developed piecemeal over the next fifty years.

Long before permanent development, animals were slaughtered along Islais Creek Basin at Butchertown. In 1869, the tidelands were sold at auction. India Basin had been an early site of Chinese fishing camps.

View south along Third Street near Army Street (now Cesar Chavez Street)

109. Western Pacific Yards
By 1931, the large area between Twenty-Fifth and Army streets was filled for the Western Pacific's rail yards, which were adjacent to its car-ferry terminal at the foot of Twenty-Fifth Street.

110. Pier 80—Army Street Terminal
Bonds approved in 1958 were used to fill the area between Twenty-Fifth Street and the north side of Islais Creek Channel. Completed in 1967 and 1970, Pier 80, known as the Army Street Terminal, was a large quay-type terminal on landfill with transit sheds on the perimeter and a large space for rail and trucks at the center. The project was an attempt to provide more up-to-date facilities for break-bulk shipping than existed north of China Basin.

111. Islais Creek Channel
Islais Creek Channel was maintained through surrounding landfill both to provide for the flow of water from Islais Creek and for protected wharfage. In 1926, a seawall was built along the south side of the channel.

112. Pier 84—Islais Creek Copra Terminal

Copra, the sun-dried meat of coconuts, was long brought to San Francisco from Tahiti and other South Pacific islands in sacks on sailing ships. With the Spanish-American War, the Philippines became the principal supplier of copra in 1901—especially to San Francisco, the leading copra port in the United States. Following a 1946 plan, the Islais Creek Copra Terminal was established at Pier 84 on the north side of Islais Creek, west of Third Street, to consolidate the bulk handling of copra and its transfer to warehouses by truck. In 1949, a blower system was installed that moved the copra in flexible pipes from the holds of ships to scales and then to warehouses. From the warehouses it went to an adjoining mill, where its oil was extracted for food, soap making, and other industries, and its waste was processed into pellets for animal feed. The animal feed was then loaded into sacks and hoisted into ships by means of a large crane. This crane is still standing, a monument to waterfront labor from the 1940s until 1977, when the copra operation closed.[54]

113. Pier 90—Cotton Warehouse

A cotton warehouse was built at Pier 90 in the mid-1960s to facilitate the export of California cotton. A steel and reinforced-concrete structure, it protected cotton bales from the weather.

114. Pier 92—Grain Terminal, Liquid Commodities, and Automobiles

In 1918, as soon as the area was purchased, the BSHC built a wharf on the south side of Islais Creek Channel and established the State Islais Creek Oil Plant for the processing of vegetable oils from coconuts, cottonseed, peanuts, and soybeans. In 1920, it was converted to a grain terminal that included an elevator and mill; these replaced the port's recently demolished grain operation on Section 3 of the bulkhead wharf, between Vallejo and Union streets. After World War II, grain was handled increasingly in bulk rather than in sacks. To accommodate this change, a modern reinforced-concrete plant replaced the Islais Creek facilities in 1949. The new plant included a workhouse, rail and truck loading facilities, and a tall elevator with storage bins for five hundred thousand bushels, creating a skyline on the southern waterfront. The principal grain at the time it opened was barley. In 1971, a new elevator doubled the size of this facility.

Next to Pier 92, the Specialty Oils (or Liquid Commodities) Terminal opened in 1965. It had large storage tanks and pipelines for transferring liquids: "Ships depart from Pier 92 with full cargoes of refined tallow for delivery in the Far East and return with cargoes of coconut oil produced by refineries in the Philippines."[55]

Behind the Liquid Commodities Terminal was a vast Automobile Terminal for imported cars. Today, there is a restored salt marsh on the site.

From bottom to top: Heron's Head Park, Piers 96 and 94, Islais Creek, and Army Street Terminal

115. Pier 94

Pier 94, contiguous with Pier 96, was a container terminal known as the Consolidation Freight Station. It opened in 1975.

116. Pier 96

Pier 96, known as the LASH terminal (for "lighter aboard ship"), was, according to the port, "the first home in the world of the revolutionary LASH shipping concept. . . . The totally new LASH concept uses water to move, not only container filled ships, but the containers themselves." The system involved huge, specially designed ships, the largest and fastest in the world: "The ships' outstanding feature will be a massive gantry crane which runs the length of the ship for loading and discharging the 500-ton lighters." Very large ships would anchor offshore in deep water and lighters on special barges would convey containers between the ships and shore. The LASH terminal opened in 1972 with the expectation that Pacific Far East Lines, one of the port's biggest tenants, would successfully make use of the new technology. However, the widespread adoption of a simpler container system instead of LASH and the failure of Pacific Far East Lines left the port with a large, expensive, unused facility.

117. Pier 98—Heron's Head Park

Heron's Head Park occupies twenty-four acres that began as fill for a shipping terminal called Pier 98 in the early 1970s. It opened in 1999.

118. Power Plant

The Great Western Power Company opened an electricity-generating plant on private land in 1929. Subsequently sold to PG&E, the plant closed in 2007.

119. 900 Innes—Shipwright's Cottage

This tiny cottage, built in 1875, is the last remnant of a longtime community of wooden-boat builders.

120. Hunters Point

Along with Potrero Point (see no. 108), Hunters Point was one of only two areas of the waterfront that was developed by private parties. Shipbuilding began on private land at Hunters Point in the 1860s. The shipyard expanded in 1903 and was bought by Bethlehem Steel in 1908. In 1940, the U.S. Navy purchased it. The Hunters Point Naval Shipyard closed in 1995.

APPENDIX
THE CHIEF ENGINEER AND THE ENGINEERING DEPARTMENT

Except for the Ferry Building, all the buildings and structures of the Board of State Harbor Commissioners (BSHC) were designed by the chief engineer and his staff in the board's own engineering department. In a few cases between 1908 and 1918, the engineering department collaborated with the office of the state architect. There is no evidence in the *Biennial Reports* or in the drawings that architects or other consultants were ever hired to design or supervise construction of the buildings and structures at the port—with the exception of the Ferry Building. The principal historian of the port through 1930 commented in regard to all the jobs at the BSHC: "Perhaps the most difficult and constructive has been the office of the Chief Engineer."[1] The chief engineer was responsible for overseeing the design, construction, and maintenance of the port's facilities—principally the seawall and the wharves and piers—and for hiring and managing a staff. Since 1908, when the earliest of those wharves and piers that still survive were first built, the staff has included at least fifteen engineers and two architects in positions of responsibility for design and supervision of construction. Most of these individuals were involved in work on several structures. While it seems likely that they specialized in particular aspects of the work—piers, for example, involved the piers themselves, transit sheds, and bulkhead buildings—the presence of multiple signatures on drawings makes it difficult to know who were the principal designers and who reviewed the drawings. Because little is known about most of those who actually did the work—whose job titles were "assistant engineer" and "draughtsman"—the role of the engineering department is best understood through the office of the chief engineer.

THE FIRST ENGINEER: WILLIAM J. LEWIS

For the first few years after the BSHC was established in 1863, it was concerned with legal and financial matters. Because there was no work for engineers to do, none were on the staff. Following a competition for the design of the first seawall in 1866, one of the members of the winning team, William J. Lewis, was appointed superintendent and constructing engineer for the seawall. He was paid not out of general funds but out of a separate seawall account, as if the engineer's function were temporary. Before joining the BSHC, Lewis was chief engineer for construction of the Western Pacific Railroad between Sacramento and San Francisco, and for the San Francisco and San Jose Railroad. In addition, a consulting civil engineer, Thaddeus R. Brooks, was hired to survey the soil conditions along the waterfront.

THE ENGINEER OF THE SEAWALL: T. J. ARNOLD

On May 17, 1870, T. J. Arnold succeeded Lewis and was given the title "Engineer of Sea Wall," responsible for overseeing construction. Arnold's observations led him in 1871 to the conclusion that the alignment of Lewis's seawall was flawed because it caused silting. By 1873 he had designed a new seawall, but in doing so he presented a proposal for the waterfront that went far beyond a technological solution to silting. Arnold's concept—consisting of the new alignment of the seawall, the bulkhead wharf, the two-hundred-foot-wide Embarcadero, the Belt Railroad, and numerous seawall lots between the Embarcadero and the existing waterfront of the city—would provide not only a lasting technological solution to existing problems but also a new vision of the port and of the responsibilities of the BSHC. Before Arnold's plan, the commissioners had been only concerned with the edge of the city and with wharves and piers that projected into the water. The ambitious plan created a vast amount of new, extremely valuable land that would serve as space for movement and facilities that did not exist previously. This space enabled the port to operate and grow in ways that would have been impossible otherwise. Until new acquisitions in the late twentieth century, the entire port was built on land created by Arnold's plan and by its extension, after 1900, to the area south of China Basin and to Islais Creek and India Basin.

Arnold's career as a civil engineer began in 1854. In 1872 he was city engineer for Oakland. He died sometime between 1876 and 1881.

THE FIRST CHIEF ENGINEER: MARSDEN MANSON

According to the *Biennial Report* of 1875–1877, there was no longer an "Engineer of Sea Wall" but a chief engineer and an assistant to the chief engineer. The new title reflected the broadening responsibilities of the BSHC for engineering work, notably the design, maintenance, and repair of wharves and piers in addition to the seawall. By the biennium of 1882–1884, Marsden Manson served as chief engineer.[2] Manson was a well-regarded civil engineer who subsequently served as San Francisco city engineer from 1908 to 1912, in which role he helped design the Hetch Hetchy water system. During his tenure, Manson oversaw construction of several sections of the seawall. In addition to Manson, in 1881 and 1882 several other engineers were hired as consultants to advise on matters pertaining to the seawall.

HOWARD C. HOLMES: THE FERRY BUILDING AND A PATENTED PILE DESIGN

In 1892, Manson was succeeded by Howard C. Holmes. Holmes represented the BSHC during the construction of the Ferry Building. He built the seawall under the Ferry Building and appears to have designed the notable foundations of the building as well. Holmes was the first of the chief engineers who was reported to have made professional visits to the facilities of other ports. In the biennium of 1896–1898, he visited the ports of New York, Boston, and Philadelphia "for the purpose of investigating their methods of . . . wharf and dock building generally, the methods of ferry slip construction, the question of timber and pile preservation, and of seawall and harbor embankment construction."[3] Holmes and his assistant, Carl Uhlig, patented a design

for concrete-jacketed timber piles that proved highly successful. Holmes resigned from his position in 1901 in order to pursue business opportunities associated with this patent. A lawsuit against the BSHC over rights to the patent was settled in Holmes's favor during the biennium 1904–1906.

LOTT D. NORTON: A REVISED SEAWALL DESIGN

In 1901, Holmes was succeeded as chief engineer by Lott D. Norton. Norton was one of at least three chief engineers with strong connections to the Southern Pacific Railroad Company. Apart from a brief period of study at Hesperian College in Woodland, Norton's entire education and experience in engineering was as a railroad employee. In 1878, "he joined a surveying party engaged in the construction of rail lines for the Old Central Pacific. . . . He remained with the Central Pacific three years and then joined the Southern Pacific as assistant engineer in charge of railroad line construction."[4] After working thirty years for Southern Pacific, he served as chief engineer for the BSHC from 1901 to 1907, "when he returned to railroad surveying."[5] During Norton's tenure, the commissioners adopted a new design for the seawall and built San Francisco's first reinforced-concrete piers. The concrete was of poor quality, and the piers deteriorated as quickly as wooden piers.

REORGANIZATION: THE ASSISTANT STATE ENGINEER REPLACES THE CHIEF ENGINEER

On January 1, 1908, the power to appoint the chief engineer was taken out of the control of the BSHC and moved to the newly established State Department of Engineering. The governor appointed the head of the department, the state engineer. The state engineer, in turn, appointed two assistant state engineers, one of whom occupied the position of the chief engineer of the BSHC. The effect of this reorganization was to place the chief engineer—now called the assistant state engineer—closer to the governor. The law that created this reorganization was signed by the recently elected governor, James N. Gillette—"the railroad's candidate"[6]—in March 1907. Together with the Southern Pacific–controlled legislature, this created new possibilities for patronage.

RALPH BARKER: PERMANENT REINFORCED-CONCRETE STRUCTURES AND A PROFESSIONAL STAFF

Ralph Barker, who succeeded Norton on June 1, 1907, became the first assistant state engineer under the new arrangement on June 1, 1908. Barker studied at the University of California but did not graduate (class of 1903). He served until May 1911 when he was fired. The headline in the *San Francisco Call* read: "Inefficiency, Not Graft, In Assistant Engineer's Office, Is Verdict." While he was "exonerated of all suspicion of graft," according to the newspaper account, his "inefficiency" in failing "to take proper soundings in the vicinity of Pier 54" ultimately cost the BSHC eighteen thousand dollars. Barker's staff failed to identify a substantial hazard—a rock outcropping—"that should have been removed before the pier was built."[7]

Notwithstanding the circumstances under which Barker departed, substantial advances were made during his tenure. He oversaw the design and construction of the first professionally built reinforced-concrete piers (Piers 40, 36, and 38) and stronger seawall sections, and he initiated a program for reconstruction of the bulkhead wharf.

In 1909, Henry J. Brunnier joined the staff.[8] Brunnier was a 1904 engineering graduate of Iowa State College. According to two biographical sketches, Brunnier, in his position as draftsman, "designed the first concrete piers and seawalls for the San Francisco Harbor Commission."[9] The plans for the first piers of an improved design (Piers 38 and 40) were complete and construction was under way before Brunnier was hired. However, Brunnier's signature appears on the 1909 plans for the steel and concrete portions of Pier 36, including the substructure, the hoisting tower, and the inshore section of the transit shed. The redesigned seawall with a reinforced-concrete wall, whose construction lasted from December 1909 to March 1910, was built while Brunnier was at the BSHC and appears to have been designed by him.

After leaving the BSHC, Brunnier established a long and successful private practice in which he became one of the most prominent engineers in California. Among the different aspects of his work, he designed harbor and port structures throughout California and in Hawaii, concrete ships during World War I, and the structural frames of many of the tallest and best-known buildings in San Francisco, including the Russ Building, the Shell Building, and the Hunter-Dulin Building. He was involved in designing bridges, including the Bay Bridge and a Humboldt County bridge with "the largest concrete girder span in the world."[10]

NATHANIEL ELLERY, STATE ENGINEER

Nathaniel Ellery of Eureka, the first state engineer, was appointed by Governor Gillette to a four-year term in 1907. Under the reorganized engineering staff of the BSHC, the assistant state engineer for the port was appointed by and worked for the state engineer, who also signed the engineering drawings for port structures. Apart from his signature of approval, there is no evidence that the state engineer played an active role at the port, except in the case of one building—a small office building on the bulkhead wharf. This building, designed by Nathaniel Ellery in 1909, was moved in 1919 from the foot of Washington Street "to the bulkhead wharf between Piers 27 and 29" for use by the Belt Railroad.[11] It is now known as Pier 29 Annex.

CARL UHLIG: INTERIM ASSISTANT STATE ENGINEER

After Ralph Barker was fired, Carl Uhlig,[12] his assistant, served in his place on an interim basis. Uhlig had been Howard Holmes's partner in the development of the patented design for concrete-jacketed piles that led to Holmes's resignation. Uhlig was a German immigrant who "assisted in building, tearing away and reconstructing the San Francisco water front improvements for forty-two years." At the time of his death in 1919, he was "the oldest active engineer known on the Pacific Coast. Different political parties have come and gone at Sacramento and there have been scores of changes in the personnel of the Harbor Commissions, but Uhlig remained in his position. When the new officials reported for work and appointed a new Chief Engineer, it was always Uhlig who could tell of the details of the work. . . . Uhlig was as necessary to the Harbor Board as the Ferry building, and was more dependable than the big clock."[13]

AUGUSTUS V. SAPH: PURGING THE SOUTHERN PACIFIC, EXPANDING THE STAFF, AND BUILDING PERMANENTLY

Barker's permanent replacement, the first appointed during the administration of the Progressive reform governor Hiram W. Johnson, was Augustus V. Saph. Saph served only from May 1911 to August 1912, when he was fired.

During Saph's tenure, the role of the engineering department and its chief engineer was undergoing redefinition. Saph was hired at a legally limited salary of three thousand dollars per year, considered "ridiculously low."[14] Efforts to raise the salary were associated with efforts to professionalize the workforce throughout the BSHC staff. Civil-service rules were proposed. Many employees considered beholden to Southern Pacific were fired. The staff of the engineering department was increased substantially: "More assistants, draughtsmen and inspectors were demanded to prepare the plans and specifications and supervise the work of building the many new and additional piers, wharves, seawall, and other constructions. . . . More mechanics and laborers of various classes were employed to keep up and maintain the old and decaying piers. . . . The force of electricians has been increased from five to nine, due to large additions to the system."[15]

Among the changes, the number of engineering draftsmen increased from two in 1909 to twenty by June 30, 1912. Among the draftsmen Saph hired were Frank G. White, later the chief engineer; Alfred W. Nordwell; Oliver W. Jones; A. C. Griewank; and Charles Newton Young. Nordwell, a 1907 structural engineering graduate of the University of California, remained with the BSHC until 1951. Jones was also a 1907 structural engineering graduate of the University of California. He worked for the BSHC until at least 1923 and practiced as an engineer until the early 1950s. Griewank, who studied at the University of California Extension, left for a private engineering and real estate practice in which he developed industrial structures with architectural distinction. Before joining the BSHC, Young worked for the Bay City Water Company and the Associated Oil Company. He remained with the BSHC until 1922.

Although he served for only a short time, Saph oversaw the design and construction of Pier 17 and the design and part of the construction of Piers 26, 28, and 30–32. All of these were fireproof, concrete piers. Piers 26, 28, and 30–32 were the first in San Francisco with decorated fronts.

Despite the anti-patronage reputation of the Progressives, the *San Francisco Call* accused the BSHC, which the newspaper called the Johnson board (for Governor Johnson), of reorganizing the engineering staff and firing Saph in order to create patronage positions.[16]

JEROME NEWMAN: RESTORATION OF THE CHIEF ENGINEER, EXPANSION OF THE PORT, AND THE FIRST ARCHITECT

While the *Call* was critical of Saph's firing, it acknowledged the professional qualifications of his successor, Jerome Newman. Newman was an 1883 graduate of the University of California. He came to the BSHC from Southern Pacific, where he was "first assistant under Chief Engineer Hood."[17] Whatever Newman's qualifications, the fact that he came from a job with the Southern Pacific contradicted the assertions of the commissioners that they had rid themselves of connections to the railroad.

The position continued to change under Newman. He was hired at a salary of three thousand dollars per year but received a substantial increase to five thousand per year. In 1915, his title was changed back to chief engineer, although he was still appointed by the state engineer.

A *San Francisco Chronicle* article in January 1916 summarized his accomplishments in three years on the job. He "designed and superintended the building of fifteen new piers, four passenger ferry slips and two car ferry slips. Under his direction the ferry post office, belt railroad engine house, Ferry Building extension, the connection of the Belt Railroad at the foot of Market Street and the extension to the United States Transport docks via the Fort Mason tunnel have also been completed. Extensive repairs have been made to piers which had deteriorated. . . . The chief engineer's responsibilities are large and varied."[18]

Among the new staff members hired during Newman's tenure was Alfred A. Pyle. Pyle was the first of only two employees of the engineering staff who was also an architect. In 1911, before joining the BSHC, he was a draftsman for Willis Polk and Company, one of the leading architectural firms in San Francisco. In 1920, he left the commission to work for San Francisco architect B. J. Joseph. Before his death in 1936, Pyle, like many architects during the Depression era, found work outside the architectural field—as a salesman. Pyle designed the 1915 Post Office (later the Agriculture Building), Pier 22½ (the firehouse), and the bulkhead buildings at Piers 29, 31, and 3.

In June 1916, Newman was fired for failing to show up when a pier caught fire.

FRANK G. WHITE: CHIEF ENGINEER FROM 1916 TO 1948

In July 1916, Frank G. White, an assistant to Jerome Newman, was appointed chief engineer. White "graduated from the University of Iowa in 1889 with a B.S. in Civil Engineering. He was engaged in railroad and municipal engineering for a time in Iowa and Illinois, and then attended the College of Engineering at Columbia University. There was a period of nine years of municipal engineering in Salt Lake City and San Francisco before he joined the staff of the Harbor Commissioners in 1911."[19] After the relatively short terms of most of his predecessors, White served as chief engineer for thirty-two years, retiring in 1948. During his tenure, the structure of the job continued to change. In 1921, the State Department of Engineering whose chief, the state engineer, appointed the chief engineer of the BSHC, became the Department of Public Works. In 1931, the connection with the Department of Public Works was ended. Thereafter the BSHC appointed the chief engineer directly.

White's tenure was marked by steady progress in the development of well-built port facilities and by an absence of scandal in his office. He was active in professional organizations, notably the Pacific Coast Association of Port Authorities and the American Association of Port Authorities, whose annual meetings allowed the opportunity to observe many other ports. In August 1917, he made a seven-week trip to "the principal ports of the United States and Canada . . . the most important ports on the Pacific and Atlantic coasts as well as on the

Great Lakes and the Gulf of Mexico." In February 1918, he traveled to "Seattle to investigate and report concerning the importation and handling of Oriental vegetable oils."[20] In the biennium of 1920–1922 he went to "Baltimore, Philadelphia, New York, Boston, and New Orleans in order to inspect and study the recent harbor development,"[21] and in the period from 1928 to 1934 he visited the ports of Chicago, Toronto, Montreal, New York, Vancouver, and Seattle. He was president of the association when it met in San Francisco in 1936.

In 1936, when White had been with the BSHC for twenty-five years and chief engineer for twenty years, he summarized his accomplishments:

> The construction of 26 piers of which 17 are of reinforced concrete; the construction of the State Terminal building and the installation therein of the refrigeration terminal; the reclamation of 25 acres of submerged land at Islais Creek and the construction of the grain terminal and lumber wharves; the completion of the seawall from Jones Street to Channel Street by the construction of the section between Mission and Harrison Streets; the construction of more than two-thirds of the reinforced concrete bulkhead wharf which now extends from Powell Street to Third and Channel Streets; the construction of the Belt Railroad along the Embarcadero from Spear Street to Broadway to connect the two isolated sections and the extension through the Ft. Mason tunnel to the U.S. Army transport docks and the Presidio; the construction of two car ferry slips and five automobile and passenger ferry slips; the construction of the Embarcadero subway, the Ferry Building viaduct, the Belt Railroad roundhouse and shops, and the south annex to the Ferry Building.[22]

He continued to serve as chief engineer until his retirement in 1948, although he oversaw the construction of only a few major structures after 1936. When he died in 1967, the *San Francisco Chronicle* reported, "He had much to do with modernizing and developing the Port of San Francisco."[23]

Among the staff hired by White were Harry E. Squire, later chief engineer; Harold B. Fisher; and Arthur D. Janssen. Fisher attended the University of California from 1908 to 1911 but did not graduate. According to his obituary, after serving in World War I he "held numerous engineering assignments until he joined the California Highway Department. He worked as a surveyor on the first highway project in the state, the San Juan Grade, and later worked with the State Harbor Commission where he designed and inspected many of the facilities of San Francisco Harbor. At the time of his retirement in 1957, he was Associate Harbor Engineer, and held a license as a civil engineer."[24] Janssen, designer of the 1920 bulkhead building for Pier 5, was only the second BSHC employee until the 1950s known to have been an architect. Nothing is known about his training. He was granted an architectural license from the state of California in 1928—at least two years after he had left the BSHC. At that time he was listed in the Oakland city directory as a draftsman for the prominent Oakland architect C. W. McCall. He remained listed as an architect in Oakland until 1938. The two staff members hired by White—along with Griewank, Jones, Pyle, Nordwell, and Wood, who were all hired by White's predecessor, Jerome Newman—designed and built the majority of wharves and piers still standing along the waterfront in 2010.

HARRY E. SQUIRE

White was succeeded as chief engineer of the BSHC by his long-time assistant, Harry E. Squire. Squire was a 1906 engineering graduate of the University of California. Before he was hired by White in 1917, he worked on the Mare Island dry dock, on harbor facilities at Puget Sound, and for the San Francisco Bridge Company. During his years at the San Francisco Bridge Company, from 1914 to 1917, the company was engaged in several construction projects for the BSHC, including Piers 15 and 41, slips adjacent to the Ferry Building, the foundation for an extension to the Ferry Building, Pier 18 with its shed and bulkhead building, and repair of Pier 21. Squire was White's assistant from 1917 to 1949, which was an extended period of active development at the port. However, little was built at the port during his tenure as chief engineer from 1949 until his retirement in 1952.

SIDNEY S. GORMAN

Squire's successor, Sidney S. Gorman, was chief engineer for the remainder of the 1950s. Gorman earned a degree in civil engineering from the University of California in 1920. "He was engaged in private practice of several years, following which he was employed by the state of California on the construction of the San Francisco-Oakland Bay Bridge, and later as Chief Construction Engineer, Golden Gate International Exposition, Treasure Island. He then became principal construction engineer for the Signal Oil Company, Los Angeles, and from 1941 to 1943 was assistant chief engineer for the Bethlehem Steel Co. in the construction of a Navy shipyard and Maritime Commission shipyard."[25] Gorman was principal civilian engineer for the Public Works Department at the San Francisco Naval Shipyard, Hunters Point, when he was hired by the BSHC in 1949. Descriptions of the engineering department during Gorman's years stressed its great variety of work. Responsible for "a city within a city," the department had many tasks, including maintenance, construction, dredging, "work usually done by the Department of Public Works, the P.G. & E. and the Water Department."[26] In this period, an architectural and design section of the engineering department included architects, civil engineers, and structural engineers.[27]

NOTES

Note to the reader: The biennial reports of the Board of State Harbor Commissioners were an important primary source in the research for this book. The abbreviation *BSHC* is used here to denote authorship for all references listed in the bibliography under "California. Board of State Harbor Commissioners for the State of California."

THE PORT LANDSCAPE AND THE CITY

1. The identity and location of industries mentioned here and in following paragraphs are shown on Sanborn maps.

2. Paul A. Lord Jr., *South End Historic District Case Report* (San Francisco: Landmarks Preservation Advisory Board, 1990), 22–25.

3. "Work Is Rushed on Big Building," *San Francisco Chronicle*, August 21, 1920.

4. "Eight-Story Concrete Building Is Planned," *San Francisco Chronicle*, January 27, 1907, 62.

5. René De La Pedraja, *A Historical Dictionary of the U.S. Merchant Marine and Shipping Industry: Since the Introduction of Steam* (Westport, Conn.: Greenwood Press, 1994), 177–178.

6. Irving F. Morrow, "The Robert Dollar Building," *Architect and Engineer* (April 1921): 57.

7. Mortimer Todd, *The Argonaut*, November 17, 1923, 23.

8. Susan P. Sherwood and Catherine Powell, *The San Francisco Labor Landmarks Guidebook* (San Francisco: Labor Archives and Research Center, San Francisco State University, 2007), 1–2.

COMMERCE

1. James E. Vance Jr., *Geography and Urban Evolution in the San Francisco Bay Area* (Berkeley: University of California Institute of Governmental Studies, 1964).

2. Ibid., 9, 10.

3. Ibid., 20.

4. James P. Delgado, *Gold Rush Port* (Berkeley: University of California Press, 2009), 60.

5. Vance, *Geography and Urban Evolution*, 26.

6. Robert W. Cherny and William Issel, *San Francisco: Presidio, Port and Pacific Metropolis* (San Francisco: Boyd & Fraser, 1981), 11.

7. Edward Morphy, *The Port of San Francisco* (Sacramento: Board of State Harbor Commissioners, 1923), 29.

8. Ibid., 29.

9. California State Senate, *Final Report of the Senate Fact-Finding Committee on San Francisco Bay Ports* (Sacramento: California State Senate, 1951), 105.

10. U.S. Board of Engineers for Rivers and Harbors and the U.S. Shipping Board, *The Ports of San Francisco, Oakland, Berkeley, Richmond, Upper San Francisco Bay, Santa Cruz and Monterey, California. Port Series No. 12* (Washington, D.C.: U.S. Government Printing Office, 1933), 141.

11. Cherny and Issel, *San Francisco*, 20.

12. Ibid., 24.

13. U.S. Board of Engineers for Rivers and Harbors and the U.S. Shipping Board, *Ports of San Francisco* (1933), 141.

14. Vance, *Geography and Urban Evolution*, 39.

15. Joint Committee from the Chamber of Commerce and the San Francisco Produce Exchange, *Report . . . on Sea Wall and Warehousing* (San Francisco: C. A. Murdock & Company, 1886), 4.

16. Cherny and Issel, *San Francisco*, 35.

17. Gerald Nash, "Government Enterprise in the West: The San Francisco Harbor, 1863–1963," in *The American West: A Reorientation* (Laramie: University of Wyoming Publications, 1966), vol. 32, 87–88.

18. Walter J. Bartnett, *The Harbors of California: Some Suggestions as to Their Improvement and Administration* (San Francisco: Dettner-Travers Press, 1906), 3.

19. Marsden Manson, *Report of Marsden Manson to the Mayor and Committee on Reconstruction: On Those Portions of the Burnham Plan Which Meet Our Commercial Necessities* (San Francisco: Committee on Reconstruction, 1906); Nash, "Government Enterprise in the West," 88; Luther Wagoner and W. H. Heuer, *San Francisco Harbor, Its Commerce and Docks with a Complete Plan for Development* ([San Francisco]: Federated Harbor Improvement Associations, 1908).

20. BSHC, *Biennial Report of the Board of State Harbor Commissioners for the Fiscal Years Commencing July 1, 1908 and Ending June 30, 1910* (Sacramento: Superintendent of State Printing, 1910), 12.

21. Ibid., 16.

22. BSHC, *Biennial Report of the Board of State Harbor Commissioners for the Fiscal Years Commencing July 1, 1912 and Ending June 30, 1914* (Sacramento: California State Printing Office, 1914), 15.

23. H. M. Chittenden and A. O. Powell, "Ports of the Pacific," *Proceedings of the American Society of Civil Engineers: Papers and Discussions* 38, no. 7 (November 20, 1912): 1094.

24. "The Future of San Francisco Harbor," *Overland Monthly* 15, no. 5 (November 1875): 401.

25. Werner Hegemann, *Report on a City Plan for the Municipalities of Oakland and Berkeley* ([Oakland]: The Municipal Governments of Oakland and Berkeley, the Supervisors of Alameda County, the Chamber of Commerce and Commercial

Club of Oakland, the Civic Art Commission of the City of Berkeley, the City Club of Berkeley, 1915), 19–20.

26. Chittenden and Powell, "Ports of the Pacific," 1097.

27. BSHC, *Biennial Report of the Board of State Harbor Commissioners for the Fiscal Years Commencing July 1, 1914 and Ending June 30, 1916* (Sacramento: California State Printing Office, 1916), 13.

28. BSHC, *Biennial Report of the Board of State Harbor Commissioners for the Fiscal Years Commencing July 1, 1916 and Ending June 30, 1918* (Sacramento: California State Printing Office, 1919), 21.

29. Mel Scott, *The San Francisco Bay Area: A Metropolis in Perspective* (Berkeley: University of California Press, 1959), 159.

30. BSHC, *Biennial Report of the Board of State Harbor Commissioners for the Fiscal Years Commencing July 1, 1918 and Ending June 30, 1920* (Sacramento: California State Printing Office, 1921), 63.

31. BSHC, *Biennial Report of the Board of State Harbor Commissioners for the Fiscal Years Commencing July 1, 1920 and Ending June 30, 1922* (Sacramento: California State Printing Office, 1923), 13.

32. U.S. Board of Engineers for Rivers and Harbors and the U.S. Shipping Board, *Ports of San Francisco* (1927), 163.

33. BSHC, *Biennial Report of the Board of State Harbor Commissioners for the Fiscal Years Commencing July 1, 1922 and Ending June 30, 1924* (Sacramento: California State Printing Office, 1924), 51.

34. BSHC, *Biennial Report of the Board of State Harbor Commissioners for the Fiscal Years Commencing July 1, 1924 and Ending June 30, 1926* (Sacramento: California State Printing Office, 1926), 10.

35. Ibid., 63.

36. Ibid., 9.

37. California State Senate, *Final Report*, 105.

38. Nash, "Government Enterprise in the West," 88–89.

39. Henry F. Grady and Robert M. Carr, *The Port of San Francisco: A Study of Traffic Competition, 1921–1933* (Berkeley: University of California Press, 1934), 3–4.

40. BSHC, *Biennial Report of the Board of State Harbor Commissioners for the Fiscal Years Commencing July 1, 1930 and Ending June 30, 1932* (Sacramento: California State Printing Office, [1932]), 11, 33.

41. BSHC, *Biennial Report of the Board of State Harbor Commissioners for the Fiscal Years Commencing July 1, 1932 and Ending June 30, 1934* (Sacramento: California State Printing Office, [1934]), 9.

42. U.S. Board of Engineers for Rivers and Harbors and the U.S. Shipping Board, *Ports of San Francisco* (1939), 20–21.

43. BSHC, *Biennial Report of the Board of State Harbor Commissioners for the Fiscal Years Commencing July 1, 1936 and Ending June 30, 1938* (Sacramento: California State Printing Office, [1938]), 28–29.

44. Ibid., 37.

45. Ibid.

46. BSHC, *Biennial Report* (1934), 23.

47. BSHC, *Biennial Report* (1938), 36–37.

48. BSHC, *Biennial Report of the Board of State Harbor Commissioners for the Fiscal Years Commencing July 1, 1938 and Ending June 30, 1940* (Sacramento: California State Printing Office, 1941), 33.

49. Ibid., 9.

50. BSHC, *Biennial Report* (1938), 43.

51. Nash, "Government Enterprise in the West," 90–91. Apparently because of security concerns, publication of biennial reports and other public statistical summaries was suspended during the war.

52. "Marine News: U.S. Defense Needs Port Space in SF," *San Francisco Chronicle*, December 7, 1940, 5H.

53. BSHC, Minutes, vol. 38 (December 6, 1940), 719, Port of San Francisco.

54. David E. Snow and Erwin N. Thompson, *San Francisco Port of Embarkation Headquarters, Ft. Mason: Historic Structure Report* (Denver: Pacific Northwest/Western Team Branch of Historical Preservation, National Park Service, n.d.), 14.

55. Ibid., 7.

56. Ibid., 46.

57. "Marine News," *San Francisco Chronicle*, 5H.

58. James W. Hamilton and William J. Bolce Jr., *Gateway to Victory: The Wartime Story of the San Francisco Army Port of Embarkation* (Stanford: Stanford University Press, 1964), 66.

59. Bernice Freeman, "State Grants Three Million to S.F. Port," *San Francisco Chronicle*, March 11, 1945, 4.

60. Jack Foisie, "The Second Busiest Harbor," *San Francisco Chronicle*, September 17, 1945, 7.

61. Ibid.

62. Ibid.

63. Freeman, "State Grants Three Million to S.F. Port," 4.

64. U.S. Board of Engineers for Rivers and Harbors and the Maritime Administration, *The Ports of San Francisco and Redwood City, California. Port Series No. 30* (Washington, D.C.: U.S. Government Printing Office, 1952), 110.

65. Jack Foisie, "S.F.'s Oldest Pier (27) Being Torn Down 'Before Wind Topples It,'" *San Francisco Chronicle*, January 3, 1949, 13.

66. U.S. Board of Engineers for Rivers and Harbors and the Maritime Administration, *Ports of San Francisco* (1952), 110.

67. Ibid.

68. BSHC, *Good News for World Travelers* (San Francisco: Board of State Harbor Commissioners, 1948).

69. Richard Terry, *San Francisco Chronicle Index: 1950–1980* (Sacramento: California State Library, California Section; Bellevue, Wash.: Commercial Microfilm Service [1986]), microfiche. The index lists "San Francisco Port Reestablishes Itself as Leading Port on the Pacific Coast" June 28, 1956, 22; and "1959 Was Worst Year Since 1903," January 15, 1960, 34.

70. California, Secretary of State, *California Blue Book* (Sacramento: State Printing Office, 1961), 438.

71. Arthur D. Little, Inc., *The Port of San Francisco: An In-Depth Study of Its Impact on the City, Its Economic Future, the Potential of Its Northern Waterfront* (San Francisco: San Francisco Port Authority, 1966), 6.

72. Woodruff Minor, *Pacific Gateway: An Illustrated History of the Port of Oakland* (Oakland: Port of Oakland, 2000), 50.

THE BOARD OF STATE HARBOR COMMISSIONERS

1. James Henry Deering, *The Political Code of the State of California: Adopted March 12, 1872. With Amendments up to and Including Those of the Forty-first Session of the Legislature, 1915* (San Francisco: Bancroft-Whitney, 1916), chap. 2505, article 8, 616.

2. Joseph Jeremiah Hagwood Jr., *Engineers at the Golden Gate* (San Francisco: U.S. Army Corps of Engineers, San Francisco District, [1982]), 51.

3. BSHC, *Biennial Report* (1941), 14.

4. Morphy, *Port of San Francisco*, 1.

5. Ibid., 11.

6. Nash, "Government Enterprise in the West," 79.

7. Lamberta Margarette Voget, "The Waterfront of San Francisco, 1863–1930: A History of Its Administration by the State of California" (PhD diss., University of California, 1943), 172.

8. William A. Bullough, *The Blind Boss and His City* (Berkeley: University of California Press, 1979), 117–119.

9. W. V. Stafford, "Improvements That Have Been Made, and Where the Money Came From," *San Francisco Call*, February 20, 1910, 26–27.

10. U.S. Army Corps of Engineers, *Annual Report of the Chief of Engineers* for 1890, Appendix QQ (Washington, D.C.: U.S. Government Printing Office, 1890), 2890–2892.

11. U.S. Army Corps of Engineers, *Annual Report of the Chief of Engineers* for 1901, Appendix UU (Washington, D.C.: U.S. Government Printing Office, 1901), 3460–3462; U.S. Army Corps of Engineers, *Annual Report of the Chief of Engineers* for 1903, Appendix VV (Washington, D.C.: U.S. Government Printing Office, 1903), 2202–2203.

12. Morphy, *Port of San Francisco*, 28.

13. California Legislature, *The Statutes of California Passed at the Fourteenth Session of the Legislature, 1863* (Sacramento: State Printer), chap. 106, 406–413.

14. Voget, "Waterfront of San Francisco," 185–186.

15. Morphy, *Port of San Francisco*, 44.

16. "The Harbor Commissioners' New Quarters," *San Francisco Chronicle*, January 7, 1875, 2.

17. California, Secretary of State, *California Blue Book* (1899), 20.

18. Voget, "Waterfront of San Francisco," 77.

19. BSHC, *Biennial Report of the Board of State Harbor Commissioners for the Fiscal Years Commencing July 1, 1910 and Ending June 30, 1912* (Sacramento: California State Printing Office, 1913), 13.

20. James J. Rawls and Walton Bean, *California, An Interpretive History*, 7th ed. (San Francisco: McGraw-Hill, 1998), 175.

21. BSHC, *Biennial Report* (1913), 15.

22. "News Gathered Along the Docks," *San Francisco Chronicle*, January 23, 1897, 12.

23. BSHC, *Biennial Report* (1913), 17.

24. Ibid.

25. California, Secretary of State, *California Blue Book* (1907), 84–88.

26. California, Secretary of State, *California Blue Book* (1913), 39–42.

27. Phil Francis, "Comment and Opinion," *San Francisco Call*, July 22, 1912, 4.

28. BSHC, *Biennial Report* (1913), 28.

29. Russell Sturgis et al., *Sturgis' Illustrated Dictionary of Architecture and Building* (1901–1902; reprint, New York: Dover Publications, 1989), vol. 2, 750.

30. Voget, "Waterfront of San Francisco," 187.

31. "Woman Serves Harbor Board," *San Francisco Chronicle*, December 5, 1918, 3.

32. BSHC, *Biennial Report of the Board of State Harbor Commissioners for the Fiscal Years Commencing July 1, 1926 and Ending June 30, 1928* (Sacramento: California State Printing Office, 1928), 46.

33. Morphy, *Port of San Francisco*, 32.

34. W. V. Stafford, "The State Wharves of San Francisco: A Lucrative Public Property," *Overland Monthly* 56, no. 4 (October 1910): 344.

35. Morphy, *Port of San Francisco*, 49–50.

36. Voget, "Waterfront of San Francisco," 65.

37. Ibid., 216.

38. California, Secretary of State, *California Blue Book* (1899), 23–24.

39. California, Secretary of State, *California Blue Book* (1928), 145.

40. BSHC, *Biennial Report* (1919), 25.

41. BSHC, *Biennial Report* (1921), 20–21.

42. Morphy, *Port of San Francisco*, 51.

43. BSHC, *Biennial Report of the Board of State Harbor Commissioners for the Fiscal Years Commencing July 1, 1924 and Ending June 30, 1926* (Sacramento: California State Printing Office, 1926), 17.

44. BSHC, *Biennial Report* (1921), 13, 53.

45. BSHC, *Biennial Report* (1926), 58.

46. "San Francisco Harbor Improvement Program," *Engineering News Record* 105 (December 25, 1930): 1026.

47. BSHC, *Biennial Report* (1923), 25; Nash, "Government Enterprise in the West," 89; Voget, "Waterfront of San Francisco," 217ff.

48. BSHC, *Biennial Report* (1932), 11, 13.

49. BSHC, *Biennial Report* (1938), 51; BSHC, *Biennial Report* (1941), 61.

50. Nash, "Government Enterprise in the West," 91.

SHIPS, RAILS, AND TRUCKS

1. BSHC, *Biennial Report* (1921), 18.

2. BSHC, *Biennial Report* (1913), 103–131.

3. Ibid., 95–98.

4. BSHC, *Biennial Report* (1926), 10.

5. J. H. McCallum, "The Port of San Francisco: A History of the Development of Commerce and an Analysis of the Growth of Port Facilities on San Francisco's Waterfront," *Pacific Marine Review* 20, no. 3 (March 1923): 133.

6. BSHC, *Biennial Report* (1913), 13.

7. Hegemann, *Report on a City Plan*, 53.

8. BSHC, *Biennial Report* (1938), 7.

9. Morphy, *Port of San Francisco*, 33.

10. Ibid.

11. Nash, "Government Enterprise in the West," 85.

12. BSHC, *Biennial Report* (1910), 54.

13. Ibid.

14. BSHC, *Biennial Report* (1914), 18.

15. BSHC, *Biennial Report* (1916), 17.

16. Ibid., 6, 17, 18.

17. BSHC, *Biennial Report* (1914), 52.

18. BSHC, *Biennial Report* (1916), 21.

19. BSHC, *Biennial Report* (1919), 43.

20. BSHC, *Biennial Report* (1921), 21.

21. BSHC, *Biennial Report* (1924), 17.

22. BSHC, *Biennial Report* (1932), 15.

23. U.S. Board of Engineers for Rivers and Harbors and the Maritime Administration, *The Ports of San Francisco* (1952), 50.

24. BSHC, *Biennial Report* (1934), 27.

25. BSHC, *Biennial Report* (1938), 27.

26. Ibid., 33.

27. Ibid., 29.

28. BSHC, *Biennial Report* (1941), 61.

29. BSHC, *Biennial Report* (1938), 33.

30. Ibid., 13.

31. "Know Your Port," *Portside News* 1, no. 2 (May 1957): 7.

32. BSHC, *Biennial Report* (1941), 17, 23.

TENANTS AND WORKERS

1. Bill Pickelhaupt, *Shanghaied in San Francisco* (San Francisco: Flyblister Press, 1996), 74.

2. "Harbor Commissioners Sued," *San Francisco Chronicle*, November 21, 1893, 6.

3. "Local News Notes," *San Francisco Chronicle*, May 20, 1892, 12.

4. BSHC, *Biennial Report of the Board of State Harbor Commissioners for the Two Fiscal Years Commencing July 1, 1900 and Ending June 30, 1902* (Sacramento: State Printer, 1903), 89.

5. This description is largely based on Marjorie Dobkin's section on labor in Michael R. Corbett, Marjorie Dobkin, and William Kostura, "Port of San Francisco Embarcadero Historic District: National Register of Historic Places Registration Form" (Washington, D.C.: U.S. National Park Service, U.S. Department of the Interior, 2006), 136–150.

6. Otto Hagel and Louis Goldblatt, *Men and Machines* (San Francisco: ILWU and Pacific Maritime Association, 1963), 14.

7. BSHC, *Biennial Report* (1921), 27–29.

8. Roy S. MacElwee and Thomas R. Taylor, *Wharf Management: Stevedoring and Storage* (New York: D. Appleton and Co., 1921), 51–53.

9. BSHC, *Biennial Report* (1921), 18–19.

10. MacElwee and Taylor, *Wharf Management*, 53.

11. Boris Stern, *Cargo Handling and Longshore Labor Conditions*, Bulletin 550 of the Bureau of Labor Statistics, U.S. Department of Labor (Washington, D.C.: U.S. Government Printing Office, 1932), 71–72.

12. David F. Selvin, *A Terrible Anger: The 1934 Waterfront and General Strikes in San Francisco* (Detroit: Wayne State University Press, 1996), 8–11.

13. Ira Brown Cross, *A History of the Labor Movement in California* (Berkeley: University of California Press, 1935), 145, 178, 183, 198, 203, 325, 332.

14. Selvin, *Terrible Anger*, 20.

15. Ibid., 23.

16. Cross, *History of the Labor Movement*, 37.

17. Sherwood and Powell, *San Francisco Labor Landmarks Guidebook*, 44.

18. Ibid., 76–77.

19. Dobkin, in Corbett, Dobkin, and Kostura, "Port of San Francisco Embarcadero Historic District," sect. 8, 68.

20. BSHC, *Biennial Report* (1921), 27–29.

21. Bruce Nelson, *Workers on the Waterfront: Seamen, Longshoremen and Unionism in the 1930s* (Urbana and Chicago: University of Illinois Press, 1988), 127; cited by Dobkin, in Corbett, Dobkin, and Kostura, "Port of San Francisco Embarcadero Historic District," 93.

22. Thomas G. Plant, quoted in Selvin, *Terrible Anger*, 240.

23. BSHC, *Biennial Report* (1921), 20–21.

24. Morphy, *Port of San Francisco*, 51.

25. Marjorie Dobkin, "Pier 15 and Pier 17, San Francisco, California: Draft Labor History Report" (San Francisco: The Exploratorium, September 2009).

26. BSHC, *Biennial Report of the Board of State Harbor Commissioners for the Two Fiscal Years Commencing July 1, 1886 and Ending June 30, 1888* (Sacramento: State Printer, 1888), 5.

ENGINEERING

1. F. M. Du-Plat-Taylor, *The Design, Construction, and Maintenance of Docks, Wharves, and Piers* (London: Ernest Benn Ltd., 1928), 1.

2. Ibid., 11.

3. Ibid., 12.

4. J. P. M. Pannell, *An Illustrated History of Civil Engineering* (London: Thames and Hudson, 1964), 134, 136.

5. Kevin Bone, "Horizontal City: Architecture and Construction in the Port

of New York," in *The New York Waterfront: Evolution and Building Culture of the Port and Harbor,* edited by Kevin Bone (New York: Monacelli Press, 1997), 87.

6. Pannell, *Illustrated History of Civil Engineering,* 136.

7. Leslie A. Bryan, *Principles of Water Transportation* (New York: The Ronald Press Co., 1939), 8.

8. Pannell, *Illustrated History of Civil Engineering,* 140–141.

9. Ibid., 139.

10. Charles Singer, E. J. Holmyard, A. R. Hall, and Trevor I. Williams, eds., *A History of Technology: The Late Nineteenth Century, 1850 to 1900,* vol. 5 (New York and London: Oxford University Press, 1958), 539.

11. Donald Squires and Kevin Bone, "The Beautiful Lake: The Promise of the Natural Systems," in *New York Waterfront,* 27.

12. Quoted in Mary Beth Betts, "Masterplanning: Municipal Support of Maritime Transport and Commerce, 1870–1930s," in Bone, *New York Waterfront,* 39–40, 43.

13. Ibid., 35, 44–46, 56, 65–66.

14. Bone, "Horizontal City," 108.

15. Betts, "Masterplanning," 77.

16. Ibid., 40.

17. Michael Z. Wise, Wilber Woods, and Eugenia Bone, "Evolving Purposes: The Case of the Hudson River Waterfront," in Bone, *New York Waterfront,* 210.

18. Paris Kilburn, *The State's Harbor: Another View of the Question* (San Francisco: Board of State Harbor Commissioners, 1900), 1.

19. Thomas Stevenson, "Harbors and Docks," *Encyclopaedia Britannica,* 9th ed., American reprint (Philadelphia: J. M. Stoddard & Company, 1880), vol. 11, 406.

20. C. E. Grunsky, "The Behavior of Concrete in Structures on the San Francisco Water Front," *Architect and Engineer* 29, no. 1 (May 1912): 69.

21. U.S. Department of the Interior, Geological Survey, *The San Francisco Earthquake and Fire of April 18, 1906, and Their Effect on Structures and Structural Materials* (Washington, D.C.: U.S. Government Printing Office, 1907), 28; Manson, *Report of Marsden Manson,* 6; and Commonwealth Club of California, "Control of San Francisco Harbor," *Transactions of the Commonwealth Club of California* 7 (March 1912): 36.

22. BSHC, *Biennial Report of the Board of State Harbor Commissioners for the Two Fiscal Years Commencing July 1, 1906 and Ending June 30, 1908* (Sacramento: State Printer, 1908), 16.

23. BSHC, *Biennial Report* (1910), 36.

24. Ibid., 36.

25. Ibid., 36, 38.

26. Ibid., 38.

27. BSHC, *Biennial Report* (1914), 32–33.

28. "Recent Work of the California State Engineering Department," *Architect and Engineer* 43, no. 1 (October 1915): 71.

29. BSHC, *Biennial Report* (1914), 63.

30. Ibid., 19, 33.

31. BSHC, *Report of the Board of State Harbor Commissioners on the New Water Front Line of San Francisco to the Legislature of the State of California, 1877–1878* (Sacramento: Superintendent State Printing, 1877), 9.

32. This was a subsection of BSHC, *Report of the State Harbor Commissioners for 1866 and 1867* (Sacramento: State Printer, 1867). The plan and specifications for construction of the seawall were also published in the *Biennial Report* of 1867.

33. The top of the seawall was built to the height of the City Base, 6.7 feet above high water. Gerald Robert Dow, "Bay Fill in San Francisco: A History of Change" (Master's thesis, California State University, San Francisco, 1973), 47.

34. BSHC, *Biennial Report of the Board of State Harbor Commissioners for the Two Fiscal Years Ending June 30, 1871* (Sacramento: State Printer, 1871).

35. BSHC, *Biennial Report of the Board of State Harbor Commissioners for the Two Fiscal Years Ending June 30, 1873* (Sacramento: State Printer, 1873), 13.

36. BSHC, *Biennial Report of the Board of State Harbor Commissioners for the Two Fiscal Years Ending June 30, 1875* (Sacramento: State Printer, 1875), 27.

37. BSHC, *Report of the Board* (1877), 5.

38. Lauren E. Crane, *Report of Lauren E. Crane, Expert, On the Construction of the Sea-Wall, San Francisco, Addressed to Governor George C. Perkins for the Board of State Harbor Commissioners* (Sacramento: Superintendent State Printing, 1882).

39. "San Francisco Seawall Built at Last," *San Francisco Examiner,* May 7, 1915, 3.

40. Stafford, "Improvements That Have Been Made," 26–27.

41. "San Francisco Seawall Built at Last," *San Francisco Examiner,* 3.

42. Jerome Newman, "The Improvement of San Francisco's Water Front," *Engineering News* 73, no. 7 (February 18, 1915): 326.

43. Studies showed that soil conditions ranged from hard surfaces to deep soft mud, situations that called for different design solutions. Among these was the use of creosoted wooden piles in place of concrete in some situations. BSHC, *Biennial Report* (1914), 32. The seawall under the Agriculture Building (the U.S. Post Office at that time) settled unevenly, damaging the building. The building was jacked up and the seawall was raised in the mid-1920s. BSHC, *Biennial Report* (1926), 56–57; BSHC, *Biennial Report* (1932), 21.

44. BSHC, *Biennial Report* (1910), 28. Partly during the same period and partly afterward, the seawall was extended at both ends.

45. Ibid., 23, 34.

ARCHITECTURE AND PLANNING
1. Richard Longstreth, *On the Edge of the World: Four Architects in San Francisco at the Turn of the Century* (New York: Architectural History Foundation; Cambridge, Mass.: MIT Press, 1983), 241.

2. BSHC, *Biennial Report* (1914), 17.

3. Longstreth, *On the Edge of the World*, 224–225. Gray A. Brechin suggested the same in "San Francisco: The City Beautiful," in *Visionary San Francisco*, ed. Paolo Polledri (San Francisco: San Francisco Museum of Modern Art; Munich: Prestel Verlag, 1990), 47.

4. Longstreth, *On the Edge of the World*, 241.

5. Ibid., 242.

6. Daniel H. Burnham assisted by Edward H. Bennett, *Report on a Plan for San Francisco*, Presented to the Mayor and Board of Supervisors by the Association for the Improvement and Adornment of San Francisco (San Francisco: Sunset Press, 1905), 211.

7. Ibid., 42; map of future development following page 184.

8. Ibid., 42.

9. Ibid., 53.

10. Ibid., 179–180.

11. "New Concrete Pier Contract Is Let," *San Francisco Call*, November 20, 1908, 10.

12. C. A. Horne, "Beauty and the Harbor Front: Why Not Beautify the Water Gate to Receive Manifest Destiny?" *San Francisco Chronicle*, January 18, 1914), 3.

13. Ibid.

14. Horatio F. Stoll, "Beautifying San Francisco for 1915," *Architect and Engineer* 20, no. 2 (March 1910): 45.

15. Ibid., 52.

16. Commonwealth Club of California, "Control of San Francisco Harbor," 27, 28.

17. Ibid., 39.

18. "Beautification of Bay Shore Discussed," *San Francisco Examiner*, February 5, 1915, 17.

19. Carleton Greene, *Wharves and Piers: Their Design, Construction, and Equipment* (New York: McGraw-Hill Book Co., 1917), 161.

20. Ibid., 159–161.

21. BSHC, *Biennial Report* (1913), 46.

22. BSHC, *Biennial Report* (1914), 45.

23. Brechin, "San Francisco: The City Beautiful," 40.

24. "Recent Work of the California State Engineering Department," *Architect and Engineer*, 65.

25. Irving F. Morrow, "San Francisco Harbor," *Architect* 16, no. 5 (November 1918): 230. Morrow cites Chief Engineer Frank G. White as the source of this information.

26. Ibid., 231.

27. B. J. S. Cahill, "Recent Work from the Office of the California State Architect," *Architect and Engineer* 54, no. 3 (September 1918): 71.

28. BSHC, *Biennial Report* (1921), 13.

29. BSHC, *Biennial Report* (1923), 23, 25. The film is missing from the collection of the California State Archives.

EPILOGUE: THE PORT SINCE 1969

1. This epilogue provides a very brief picture of a complicated and important period in the development of the port, bridging the detailed history of the earlier years of the port presented in the previous chapters and the present day. A thorough history of much of this period is presented in Jasper Rubin, *A Negotiated Landscape: The Transformation of San Francisco's Waterfront Since 1950* (Chicago: Center for American Places at Columbia College and University of Chicago Press, forthcoming). My understanding of the port's problems and the complicated process of addressing them comes largely from this book. Many of the developments mentioned here are presented in greater detail in the section titled "Catalogue."

2. Bill Bancroft and Bill Eaton, "S.F. Port Dilemma: Years of Decline; A Sudden Crisis," *Oakland Tribune*, September 29, 1974, 3C.

3. Minor, *Pacific Gateway*, 50.

4. Ebasco Services Incorporated, *Port of San Francisco: Facilities Improvement Survey for the San Francisco Port Authority, Summary Report* (New York: Ebasco Services Incorporated, 1966).

5. Rubin, *Negotiated Landscape*, 162.

6. Ibid., 162–163.

7. Much of this was later realized at Showplace Square under the leadership of Henry Adams, who was the lead designer of International Market Center. Sally B. Woodbridge, "Visions of Renewal and Growth: 1945 to the Present," in *Visionary San Francisco*, ed. Paolo Polledri (San Francisco: San Francisco Museum of Modern Art; Munich: Prestel Verlag, 1990), 132–134.

8. Ibid., 134–135.

9. Rubin, *Negotiated Landscape*, 154.

10. Woodbridge, "Visions of Renewal and Growth," 134–135.

11. San Francisco Port Commission, *Port of San Francisco Ocean Shipping Handbook* (San Francisco: San Francisco Port Commission, 1970), 17.

12. San Francisco Port Commission, *Multiport* (San Francisco: San Francisco Port Commission, 1971).

13. Rubin, *Negotiated Landscape*, 324.

14. "Pier 39: San Francisco's Premier Bay Attraction" (2010), http://pier39.com.

15. Allan Temko, *No Way to Build a Ballpark and Other Irreverent Essays on Architecture* (San Francisco: Chronicle Books, 1993), 175.

16. Rubin, *Negotiated Landscape*, 331–336.

17. Ibid., 339–347.

18. Woodbridge, "Visions of Renewal and Growth," 135–136.

19. Personal communication from Diane Oshima, Assistant Deputy Director, Waterfront Planning, Port of San Francisco, August 16, 2010.

20. Edward Epstein, "Ceremony Opens an Era of Optimism for S.F. Embarcadero," *San Francisco Chronicle*, June 17, 2000, A-14.

21. Port of San Francisco, "Information Presentation on a Ten-Year Review of the Waterfront Land Use Plan," staff

memorandum to the Port Commission, December 3, 2008, 15; cited in Rubin, *Negotiated Landscape*, 415.

22. Rubin, *Negotiated Landscape*, 3.

CATALOGUE

1. Voget, "Waterfront of San Francisco," 61.

2. Dow, "Bay Fill in San Francisco," 62.

3. Alessandro Baccari Jr., *San Francisco's Fisherman's Wharf* (San Francisco: Arcadia Publishing, 2006), 112, 114.

4. John S. Bolles and Ernest Born, *A Plan for Fisherman's Wharf: Comprising the Fisherman's Wharf-Aquatic Park Area* (San Francisco: San Francisco Port Authority, 1961).

5. "Where We Are," *Portside News* 4, no. 2 (February 1961): 4.

6. *Oakland Tribune*, "Large Plant Employs Many," *Oakland Tribune Yearbook* (1937).

7. BSHC, *Biennial Report* (1938), 64.

8. BSHC, *Biennial Report* (1914), 34.

9. BSHC, *Biennial Report* (1916), 35–36.

10. Morrow, "San Francisco Harbor," pl. 61.

11. BSHC, *Biennial Report* (1921), 40.

12. BSHC, *Biennial Report* (1932), 17.

13. San Francisco Port Authority, *Port of San Francisco Ocean Shipping Handbook* (San Francisco: San Francisco Port Authority, 1956), 7.

14. BSHC, *Biennial Report of the Board of State Harbor Commissioners for the Fiscal Years Commencing July 1, 1928 and Ending June 30, 1930* (Sacramento: California State Printing Office, 1931), 18.

15. Morrow, "San Francisco Harbor," pl. 61.

16. Stan Garvey, *King and Queen of the River: The Legendary Paddle Wheel Steamboats Delta King and Delta Queen* (Menlo Park: River Heritage Press, 1995).

17. J. Gordon Turnbull, "Central Embarcadero Piers Historic District: Piers 1, 1½, 3, and 5: National Register of Historic Places Registration Form" (Washington, D.C.: National Park Service, Department of

the Interior, 2002), sect. 8, 17–21.

18. Voget, "Waterfront of San Francisco," 106.

19. BSHC, *Biennial Report of the Board of State Harbor Commissioners for the Two Fiscal Years Commencing July 1, 1896 and Ending June 30, 1898* (Sacramento: State Printer, 1899), 8–9.

20. Ibid., 9.

21. BSHC, *Biennial Report of the Board of State Harbor Commissioners for the Two Fiscal Years Commencing July 1, 1902 and Ending June 30, 1904* (Sacramento: State Printer, 1905), 51.

22. Voget, "Waterfront of San Francisco," 107.

23. Sanborn Map Company, *Insurance Maps of San Francisco*, vol. 1 (New York: Sanborn Map Company, 1893), 7.

24. The 1949 Jules Dassin movie *Thieves Highway* is a film noir treatment of truckers, corrupt commission merchants, workers, and hangers-on that is largely set on Washington Street in the Produce District and also includes scenes on the waterfront and around the Belt Railroad.

25. Marsden Manson, "City Grades," in *Municipal Reports* (San Francisco: Board of Supervisors, 1909).

26. BSHC, *Biennial Report of the Board of State Harbor Commissioners for the Two Fiscal Years Commencing July 1, 1886 and Ending June 30, 1888* (Sacramento: State Printer, 1888), 10.

27. BSHC, *Biennial Report of the Board of State Harbor Commissioners for the Two Fiscal Years Commencing July 1, 1892 and Ending June 30, 1894* (Sacramento: State Printer, 1894), 26.

28. Ibid., 25.

29. BSHC, *Biennial Report* (1899), 10.

30. BSHC, *Biennial Report* (1934), 17.

31. BSHC, *Biennial Report of the Board of State Harbor Commissioners for the Two Fiscal Years Commencing July 1, 1898 and Ending June 30, 1900* (Sacramento: State Printer, 1900), 8.

32. BSHC, *Biennial Report* (1914), 17.

33. Ibid., 17.

34. Morrow, "San Francisco Harbor," 231.

35. Ibid., pl. 65.

36. BSHC, *Biennial Report* (1914), 34.

37. BSHC, *Biennial Report* (1916), 41.

38. "Coffee: Queen of S.F. Imports," *P.G. and E. Progress* 32, no. 8 (July 1955): 1–2.

39. William A. Geary, "The History of the Coffee Trade at the Port of San Francisco," *Port of San Francisco, California U.S.A.: Quarterly Report of the Board of State Harbor Commissioners* (3rd–4th quarter 1949): 8.

40. Frank Soulé, John H. Gihon, and James Nisbet, *The Annals of San Francisco* (1855; reprint, Berkeley: Berkeley Hills Books, 1999), 443–444.

41. Albert Shumate, *Rincon Hill and South Park: San Francisco's Early Fashionable Neighborhood* (Sausalito: Windgate Press, 1988), 27–28.

42. BSHC, *Biennial Report* (1913), 146.

43. Ibid., 43–46.

44. BSHC, *Schedule of Rates of Pay and Working Conditions* (Sacramento: State Printing Office, 1942).

45. Herb Mills, "The Social Consequences of Industrial Modernization," in *Case Studies on the Labor Process*, ed. Andrew Zimbalist (New York: Monthly Review Press, 1979), 130.

46. "Delancey Street Foundation" (2007), http://delanceystreetfoundation.org.

47. Marjorie Dobkin, "Pier 36, San Francisco, California: Draft Labor History and Workplace Report" (San Francisco: URS Corporation and the Port of San Francisco, 2010), 23.

48. BSHC, *Biennial Report* (1910), 36.

49. BSHC, *Biennial Report* (1923), 15.

50. BSHC, *Biennial Report* (1932), 19.

51. Dow, "Bay Fill in San Francisco," 137.

52. John Haskell Kemble, *San Francisco*

Bay: A Pictorial Maritime History (Cambridge, Md.: Cornell Maritime Press, 1957), 107.

53. Frank G. White, "The India Basin-Islais Creek Harbor Project," *Architect* 16, no. 5 (November 1918): 232–234.

54. Sherwood and Powell, *San Francisco Labor Landmarks Guidebook*, 34.

55. San Francisco Port Authority, *Port of San Francisco Ocean Shipping Handbook* (1968), 18.

APPENDIX: THE CHIEF ENGINEER AND THE ENGINEERING DEPARTMENT

1. Voget, "Waterfront of San Francisco," 178.

2. Marsden Manson's papers are at the Bancroft Library at the University of California, Berkeley.

3. BSHC, *Biennial Report* (1899), 53.

4. Denis McCarthy, "Snappy Shots: Lott Day Norton, Retired Engineer," *San Francisco Examiner*, January 27, 1926.

5. Ibid.

6. Rawls and Bean, *California*, 255.

7. "Barker Suspended by Harbor Board," *San Francisco Call*, May 12, 1911, 20.

8. "Henry J. Brunnier," *Architect and Engineer* 102, no. 1 (October 1930): 24. A profile of Brunnier emphasizing his contributions to the Rotary Club appears in Theresa Whitener, *A Tradition of Fellowship and Service: The Rotary Club of San Francisco at 100* (San Francisco: The Rotary Club of San Francisco, 2008), 82–93.

9. Bailey Millard, *History of the San Francisco Bay Region,* vol. 2 (Chicago: American Historical Society, 1924), 179; "Henry J. Brunnier," 24.

10. Millard, *History of the San Francisco Bay Region*, 180.

11. BSHC, *Biennial Report* (1921), 41.

12. Carl Uhlig's papers are at the State Archives in the collection of the Board of State Harbor Commissioners.

13. "Veteran Engineer, Carl Uhlig, Dies at His Home Here," *San Francisco Chronicle*, March 6, 1919, 3.

14. BSHC, *Biennial Report* (1913), 17.

15. Ibid., 27.

16. "Patronage Ax Cuts Saph Out of State Job," *San Francisco Call*, August 4, 1912, 39.

17. "S.P. Engineer Appointed in Saph's Place," *San Francisco Call*, August 9, 1912, 5.

18. "Harbor Engineer Is Important Official: Jerome Newman Makes Big Record as Chief of State Department," *San Francisco Chronicle*, January 12, 1916, 39.

19. BSHC, *Port of San Francisco, California U.S.A.* (second quarter 1948): n.p.

20. BSHC, *Biennial Report* (1919), 49–50.

21. BSHC, *Biennial Report* (1923), 41.

22. BSHC, *Biennial Report* (1938), 57.

23. "Frank G. White," *San Francisco Chronicle*, February 7, 1967, 57.

24. "H.B. Fisher, Pioneer Citizen, Dies," *Alameda Times Star*, November 18, 1966, 1.

25. BSHC, *Port of San Francisco, California U.S.A.* (fourth quarter 1948): n.p.

26. Ray F. Quan, "Engineering Department Duties Cover 'City Within City,'" *Portside News* 1, no. 2 (May 1957): 4.

27. Ray F. Quan, "Engineering Dept. Has Big Variety of Talent," *Portside News* 1, no. 4 (July 1957): 6.

BIBLIOGRAPHY

Alameda Times Star. "H. B. Fisher, Pioneer Citizen, Dies." November 18, 1966, 1.

American Association of Port Authorities. Committee on Standardization and Special Research. *A Port Dictionary of Technical Terms.* New Orleans: American Association of Port Authorities, 1940.

Architect and Engineer.

"Henry J. Brunnier." 102, no. 1 (October 1930): 24.

"Recent Work of the California State Engineering Department." 43, no. 1 (October 1915): 65–76.

"San Francisco's Experience with Concrete Wharf Supports." 49, no. 1 (April 1917): 81–83.

Architectural Resources Group. "Historical Resources Report: Piers 27, 29, 31." San Francisco: Port of San Francisco, 1999.

Arnold, T. J. *Map Showing an Improved Line for the Waterfront of the City of San Francisco; And a New System of Piers and Landing Places.* San Francisco: Britton and Rey, 1873.

_____. *Report to the Board of State Harbor Commissioners on the Preservation of Timber.* San Francisco: Joseph Winterburn & Company, 1873.

Baccari, Alessandro, Jr. *San Francisco's Fisherman's Wharf.* San Francisco: Arcadia Publishing, 2006.

Bancroft, Bill, and Bill Eaton. "Did Oakland Guess Right on Its Port?" *Oakland Tribune.* September 30, 1974, F3.

_____. "S.F. Port Dilemma: Years of Decline; a Sudden Crisis." *Oakland Tribune.* September 29, 1974, 3C.

Bancroft, Hubert Howe. *Why a World Centre of Industry at San Francisco Bay: The First Port of the Pacific; Its Present and Its Future. An Exposition in Politics and Economics.* New York: The Bancroft Company, 1916.

Bartnett, Walter J. *The Harbors of California: Some Suggestions as to Their Improvement and Administration.* San Francisco: Dettner-Travers Press, Inc., 1906.

Blanding, William, George S. Evans, and W. A. Phillips. *Report of the Board of State Harbor Commissioners on the Sea Wall and Means for Its Construction.* San Francisco: Joseph Winterburn & Company, 1881.

Bolles, John S., and Ernest Born. *A Plan for Fisherman's Wharf: Comprising the Fisherman's Wharf-Aquatic Park Area.* San Francisco: San Francisco Port Authority, 1961.

Bone, Kevin, ed. *The New York Waterfront: Evolution and Building Culture of the Port and Harbor.* New York: Monacelli Press, 1997.

Bonnett, Wayne. *A Pacific Legacy: A Century of Maritime Photography, 1850–1950.* San Francisco: Chronicle Books, 1991.

_____. *San Francisco: Gateway to the Pacific.* Sausalito: Windgate Press, 2010.

_____. *Victorian San Francisco: The 1895 Illustrated Directory.* Sausalito: Windgate Press, 1996.

Brechin, Gray A. "San Francisco: The City Beautiful." In *Visionary San Francisco.* Edited by Paolo Polledri. San Francisco: San Francisco Museum of Modern Art; Munich: Prestel Verlag, 1990.

Bryan, Leslie A. *Principles of Water Transportation.* New York: The Ronald Press Company, 1939.

Bullough, William A. *The Blind Boss and His City: Christopher Augustine Buckley and Nineteenth-Century San Francisco.* Berkeley: University of California Press, 1979.

Burnham, Daniel H., assisted by Edward H. Bennett. *Report on a Plan for San Francisco.* Presented to the Mayor and Board of Supervisors by the Association for the Improvement and Adornment of San Francisco. San Francisco: Sunset Press, 1905.

Benedict, Burton, et al. *The Anthropology of World's Fairs: San Francisco's Panama Pacific International Exposition of 1915.* London and Berkeley: The Lowie Museum of Anthropology in association with Scolar Press, 1983.

Cahill, B. J. S. "Recent Work from the Office of the California State Architect." *Architect and Engineer* 54, no. 3 (September 1918): 43–72ff.

California. Board of State Harbor Commissioners for San Francisco Harbor. *Biennial Reports* (title varies). 39 vols. Sacramento: State Printing Office, 1865–1941.

_____. *Biennial Report of the Board of State Harbor Commissioners for the Two Years Ending November 3, 1869.* Sacramento: State Printer, 1869.

_____. *First and Second Annual Reports of the Board of State Harbor Commissioners, for the Years 1864 and 1865.* Sacramento: State Printer, [1865].

_____. *Gateway of the Pacific.* San Francisco: n.p., 1923.

_____. *Good News for World Travelers: Foreign Trade Zone No. 3, Port of San Francisco at Your Service from June 1948.* San Francisco: Board of State Harbor Commissioners, 1948.

_____. *Minutes, 1910–1915, 1939–1943.* Port of San Francisco.

_____. *The Port of San Francisco: A Special Report of the Board of State Harbor Commissioners.* San Francisco: California State Printing Office, First Quarter 1948.

_____. *Port of San Francisco, California U.S.A.: Quarterly Report of the Board of State Harbor Commissioners.* 6 vols. San Francisco: California State Printing Office, 1949.

_____. *Report of the Board of State Harbor Commissioners for the Year Commencing July 1, 1879 and Ending June 30, 1880.* San Francisco: Joseph Winterburn & Company, 1880.

_____. *Report of the Board of State Harbor Commissioners on the New Water Front Line of San Francisco, to the Legislature of the State of California, 1877–1878.* Sacramento: Superintendent State Printing, 1877.

_____. *Report of the State Harbor Commissioners for the Years 1866 and 1867.* Sacramento: State Printer, 1867.

_____. *Schedule of Rates of Pay and Working Conditions Covering Locomotive Engineers, Firemen and Hostlers Represented by the Brotherhood of Locomotive Firemen and Enginemen and the Yard Engine Foremen and Helpers Represented by the Brotherhood of Railroad Trainmen Employed by the State Belt Railroad.* Sacramento: State Printing Office, 1942.

California. Joint Committee on Harbors. *Report and Recommendations of the Joint Committee on Harbors Appointed by the Legislature of the State of California.* Sacramento: Superintendent State Printing, 1908.

California Legislature. *An Act to Create a State Board of Harbor Commissioners for the Port of San Francisco (as Amended) Approved February 28, 1876.* Sacramento: State Printing Office, 1876.

_____. *The Statutes of California Passed at the Fourteenth Session of the Legislature, 1863.* Chapter 106. Sacramento: State Printer, 1863, 406–413.

California. Secretary of State. *California Blue Book.* Sacramento: State Printing Office, 1899, 1907, 1913, 1928, 1932, 1954, 1961.

California State Senate. *Final Report of the Senate Fact-Finding Committee on San Francisco Bay Ports.* Sacramento: California State Senate, 1951.

Cameron, Robert. *Above San Francisco, Volume II: A New Collection of Nostalgic and Contemporary Aerial Photographs of the Bay Area.* San Francisco: Cameron and Company, 1975.

Camp, William Martin. *San Francisco Port of Gold.* Garden City: Doubleday & Company, Inc., 1947.

Chellis, Robert D. *Pile Foundations.* 2nd ed. New York: McGraw-Hill Book Company, Inc., 1961.

Cherny, Robert W. "San Francisco Longshoremen, 1849–1860." In *Dockworkers: International Explorations in Comparative Labor History, 1790–1970.* 2 vols. Aldershot, Hampshire, UK: Ashgate Publishing, 2000. Vol. 1, 102–140.

_____, and William Issel. *San Francisco: Presidio, Port, and Pacific Metropolis.* Golden State Series. San Francisco: Boyd & Fraser, 1981.

Chevalier, Auguste. *The Chevalier Commercial, Pictorial, and Tourist Map of San Francisco from the Latest U.S. Government and Official Surveys.* San Francisco: Auguste Chevalier, 1911.

Chittenden, H. M., and A. O. Powell. "Ports of the Pacific." *Proceedings of the American Society of Civil Engineers: Papers and Discussions* 38, no. 7 (November 20, 1912): 1093–1158.

Cohen, Andrew Neal. *Gateway to the Inland Coast: The Story of the Carquinez Strait.* [Crockett]: Carquinez Strait Preservation Trust; Sacramento: California State Lands Commission, 1996.

Colson, Charles. *Notes on Docks and Dock Construction.* New ed. Longmans' Civil Engineering Series. London, New York, and Bombay: Longmans, Green, and Company, 1906.

Commonwealth Club of California. "Control of San Francisco Harbor." *Transactions of the Commonwealth Club of California* 7, no. 1 (March 1912): 1–68.

_____. "The Port of San Francisco." *Transactions of the Commonwealth Club of California* 2, no. 1 (January 1906): 1–64.

Corbett, Michael R. "A Brief History of Creosoted Wood Piles in San Francisco Bay." Oakland: San Francisco Estuary Institute, 2008.

_____, Marjorie Dobkin, and William Kostura. "Port of San Francisco Embarcadero Historic District: National Register of Historic Places Registration Form." Washington, D.C.: National Park Service, U.S. Department of the Interior, 2006.

Courland, Robert. *The Old North Waterfront: The History and Rebirth of a San Francisco Neighborhood.* San Francisco: Ron Kaufman Companies, 2004.

Crane, Lauren E. *Report of Lauren E. Crane, Expert, On the Construction of the Sea-Wall, San Francisco, Addressed to Governor George C. Perkins for the Board of State Harbor Commissioners.* Sacramento: State Superintendent of Printing, 1882.

Cross, Ira Brown. *A History of the Labor Movement in California.* Berkeley: University of California Press, 1935.

Cunningham, Brysson. *A Treatise on the Principles and Practice of Dock Engineering.* London: Charles Griffin & Company; Philadelphia: J. B. Lippincott Company, 1904.

_____. *A Treatise on the Principles and Practice of Dock Engineering.* 3rd ed. London: Charles Griffin & Company, 1922.

Daggett, Stuart. *Chapters on the History of the Southern Pacific.* Reprints of Economic Classics. New York: Augustus M. Kelley, 1966.

De La Pedraja, René. *A Historical Dictionary of the U.S. Merchant Marine and Shipping Industry: Since the Introduction of Steam.* Westport, Conn.: Greenwood Press, 1994.

Deering, James Henry. *The Political Code of the State of California: Adopted March 12, 1872. With Amendments up to and Including Those of the Forty-first Session of the Legislature, 1915.* San Francisco: Bancroft-Whitney, 1916.

"Delancey Street Foundation." 2007. www.delanceystreetfoundation.org.

Delehanty, Randolph. *San Francisco: The Ultimate Guide.* San Francisco: Chronicle Books, 1995.

Delgado, James P. *Gold Rush Port: The Maritime Archeology of San Francisco's Waterfront.* Berkeley: University of California Press, 2009.

Dobkin, Marjorie. "Pier 15 and Pier 17, San Francisco, California: Draft Labor History Report." San Francisco: The Exploratorium, September 2009.

_____. "Pier 36, San Francisco, California: Draft Labor History and Workplace Report." San Francisco: URS Corporation and the Port of San Francisco, 2010.

Dow, Gerald Robert. "Bay Fill in San Francisco: A History of Change." Master's thesis, California State University, San Francisco, 1973.

Du-Plat-Taylor, F. M. *The Design, Construction, and Maintenance of Docks, Wharves, and Piers.* London: Ernest Benn Limited, 1928.

Ebasco Services Incorporated. *Port of San Francisco: Facilities Improvement Survey for the San Francisco Port Authority, Summary Report.* New York: Ebasco Services Incorporated, 1959.

Engineering News. "New Ferry House at San Francisco, Cal." 38, no. 5 (July 29, 1897): 66–67.

Engineering News Record. "San Francisco Harbor Improvement Program." 105 (December 25, 1930): 1026.

Epstein, Edward. "Ceremony Opens an Era of Optimisim for S.F. Embarcadero." *San Francisco Chronicle.* June 17, 2000, A-14.

Foisie, Jack. "S.F.'s Oldest Pier (27) Being Torn Down 'Before a Wind Topples It.'" *San Francisco Chronicle.* January 3, 1949, 13.

———. "The Second Busiest Harbor. 23 Million Tons of War Cargo Shipped from S.F. During 45-Month Period." *San Francisco Chronicle.* September 17, 1945, 7.

Ford, A. G. *Handling and Stowage of Cargo.* 2nd ed. Prepared for the United States Maritime Service. Scranton, Pa.: International Textbook Company, 1942.

Francis, Phil. "Comment and Opinion." *San Francisco Call.* July 22, 1912, 4.

Freeman, Bernice. "State Grants Three Million to S.F. Port." *San Francisco Chronicle.* March 11, 1945, 4.

Garvey, Stan. *King and Queen of the River: The Legendary Paddle Wheel Steamboats Delta King and Delta Queen.* Menlo Park: River Heritage Press, 1995.

Gieger, C. W. "San Francisco as a Fuel Oil Port." *Scientific American* 122 (February 21, 1920): 183–200.

Glover, E. S. *The Illustrated Directory.* San Francisco: Illustrated Directory Company, 1895. David Rumsey Collection.

Grady, Henry F., and Robert M. Carr. *The Port of San Francisco: A Study of Traffic Competition, 1921–1933.* Berkeley: University of California Press, 1934.

Greene, Carleton. *Wharves and Piers: Their Design, Construction, and Equipment.* New York: McGraw-Hill Book Company, 1917.

Grunsky, C. E. "The Behavior of Concrete in Structures on the San Francisco Water Front." *Architect and Engineer* 29, no. 1 (May 1912): 69–71.

Hagel, Otto, and Louis Goldblatt. *Men and Machines.* San Francisco: ILWU and Pacific Maritime Association, 1963.

Hagwood, Joseph Jeremiah, Jr. *Engineers at the Golden Gate: A History of the San Francisco District, U.S. Army Corps of Engineers, 1866–1980.* San Francisco: U.S. Army Corps of Engineers, San Francisco District, [1982].

Hall, William Hammond, Calvin Brown, and Frank Soule Jr. *Report of the Board of Engineers Appointed to Examine into the Matter of the Measurement of Materials Used in the Construction of the Sea-Wall and Embankment at San Francisco.* Sacramento: State Office, Superintendent of Printing, 1882.

Hamilton, F. W. "Foiling the 'Woodpeckers of the Sea.'" *Architect and Engineer* 65, no. 1 (April 1921): 110–112.

Hamilton, James W., and William J. Bolce Jr. *Gateway to Victory: The Wartime Story of the San Francisco Army Port of Embarkation.* Stanford: Stanford University Press, 1964.

Hansen, Gladys. *San Francisco Almanac: Everything You Want to Know about the City.* San Francisco: Chronicle Books, 1975.

Harlan, George H. *San Francisco Bay Ferry Boats.* Berkeley: Howell-North Books, 1967.

———, and Clement Fisher Jr. *Of Walking Beams and Paddle Wheels: A Chronicle of San Francisco Bay Ferry Boats.* San Francisco: Bay Books, 1951.

Harris, David, and Eric Sandweiss. *Eadweard Muybridge and the Photographic Panorama of San Francisco, 1850–1880.* Montreal: Canadian Center for Architecture, 1993.

Harris, Frederic R. "Harbor and River Works." *American Civil Engineers Handbook, Section 19.* 5th rev. ed. New York: John Wiley & Sons, 1930.

Hegemann, Werner. *Report on a City Plan for the Municipalities of Oakland and Berkeley.* [Oakland]: The Municipal Governments of Oakland and Berkeley, the Supervisors of Alameda County, the Chamber of Commerce and Commercial Club of Oakland, the Civic Art Commission of the City of Berkeley, the City Club of Berkeley, 1915.

Horne, C. A. "Beauty and the Harbor Front: Why Not Beautify the Water Gate to Receive Manifest Destiny?" *San Francisco Chronicle,* January 18, 1914, 3.

Horton, C. C. "Concrete as a Preservative of Wooden Piles Exposed to Seawater." *Architect and Engineer* 21, no. 1 (May 1910): 65–67.

Huntington, Harriet E. *California Harbors.* Garden City, N.Y.: Doubleday & Company, 1964.

Issel, William, and Robert W. Cherny. *San Francisco 1865–1932: Politics, Power and Urban Development.* Berkeley: University of California Press, 1985.

Joint Committee from the Chamber of Commerce and the San Francisco Produce Exchange. *Report . . . on Sea Wall and Warehousing.* San Francisco: C. A. Murdock & Company, 1886.

Kemble, John Haskell. *San Francisco Bay: A Pictorial Maritime History.* Cambridge, Md.: Cornell Maritime Press, 1957.

Kilburn, Paris. *The State's Harbor: Another View of the Question.* San Francisco: Board of State Harbor Commissioners, 1900.

Kinnard, Lawrence. *History of the Greater San Francisco Bay Region.* 3 vols. New York: Lewis Historical Publishing Company, 1966.

Kofoid, Charles A. "The Hardy Teredo." *Architect and Engineer* 81, no. 1 (April 1925): 105–108.

Langley's San Francisco Directory. San Francisco: Francis Valentine & Co., 1884.

Little, Arthur D., Inc. *The Port of San Francisco: An In-Depth Study of Its Impact on the City, Its Economic Future, the Potential of Its Northern Waterfront.* San Francisco: San Francisco Port Authority (C-67233), 1966.

Livingston and Blayney. *What to Do About the Waterfront.* San Francisco: Citizens Waterfront Committee, 1971.

Longstreth, Richard. *On the Edge of the World: Four Architects in San Francisco at the Turn of the Century.* New York: Architectural History Foundation; Cambridge, Mass.: MIT Press, 1983.

Lord, Paul A., Jr. "South End Historic District Case Report." San Francisco: Landmarks Preservation Advisory Board, 1990.

MacElwee, Roy S. *Port Development.* New York: McGraw-Hill, 1926.

———. *Ports and Terminal Facilities.* New York: McGraw-Hill, 1926.

———, and Thomas R. Taylor. *Wharf Management: Stevedoring and Storage.* New York: D. Appleton and Company, 1921.

Manson, Marsden. "City Grades." In *Municipal Reports.* San Francisco: Board of Supervisors, 1909.

———. *Report of Marsden Manson to the Mayor and Committee on Reconstruction: On Those Portions of the Burnham Plans Which Meet Our Commercial Necessities: And an Estimate of the Cost of the Same: Fire Avenues and Thoroughfares, Lowering Russian Hill, Auxiliary Fire System, Water Front Improvements.* San Francisco: Committee on Reconstruction, 1906.

McCallum, John H. "The Port of San Francisco: A History of the Development of Commerce and an Analysis of the Growth of Port Facilities on San Francisco's Waterfront." *Pacific Marine Review* 20, no. 3 (March 1923): 131–134.

———. "San Francisco Has Abundant Industrial Sites, Areas Served by Rail and Water Lines." *San Francisco Chronicle.* June 12, 1922, D2.

McCarthy, Denis. "Snappy Shots: Lott Day Norton, Retired Engineer." *San Francisco Examiner.* January 27, 1926.

McGloin, John B. *San Francisco: The Story of a City.* San Rafael, Calif.: Presidio Press, 1978.

McWilliams, Brian T. "The Working Waterfront." *National Maritime Museum Association Sea Letter,* no. 58 (Summer 2000): 20–23.

Merchant, William Gladstone. *San Francisco World Trade Center.* Prospectus. San Francisco: San Francisco World Trade Center Authority, n.d.

Merriman, Thaddeus, ed. *American Civil Engineers Handbook.* 5th ed. New York: John Wiley & Sons, 1930.

Millard, Bailey. *History of the San Francisco Bay Region.* 2 vols. Chicago: American Historical Society, 1924.

Mills, Herb. "The Social Consequences of Industrial Modernization." In *Case Studies on the Labor Process.* Edited by Andrew Zimbalist. New York: Monthly Review Press, 1979.

Minor, Woodruff. *Pacific Gateway: An Illustrated History of the Port of Oakland.* Oakland: Port of Oakland, 2000.

Morphy, Edward. *The Port of San Francisco.* Sacramento: Board of State Harbor Commissioners, 1923.

Morrow, Irving F. "The Robert Dollar Building." *Architect and Engineer* 65, no. 1 (April 1921): 57–77.

———. "San Francisco Harbor." *Architect* 16, no. 5 (November 1918): 229–231.

Myrick, David F. *Southern Pacific Water Lines: Marine, Bay, and River Operations of the Southern Pacific System.* Pasadena: Southern Pacific Historical and Technical Society, 2007.

Nash, Gerald. "Government Enterprise in the West: The San Francisco Harbor, 1863–1963." In *The American West: A Reorientation.* Laramie: University of Wyoming Publications, 1966. Vol. 32, 77–93, 159–160.

Nelson, Bruce. *Workers on the Waterfront: Seamen, Longshoremen and Unionism in the 1930s.* Urbana and Chicago: University of Illinois Press, 1988.

Newman, Jerome. "The Improvement of San Francisco's Water Front." *Engineering News* 73, no. 7 (February 18, 1915): 326–328.

Nolte, Carl. "The Changing San Francisco Waterfront." *National Maritime Museum Association Sea Letter,* no. 58 (Summer 2000): 4–7.

Northern California Writers' Project, Works Progress Administration. "Port of the Argonauts." Compilations of research in numbered and unnumbered volumes and manuscripts, 1941–1947. State Archives, Sacramento. Board of State Harbor Commissioners Collection (3A F3413, B3403).

Oakland Tribune. "Large Plant Employs Many." *Oakland Tribune Yearbook.* 1937.

Official Historical Atlas Map of Alameda County, California. Oakland: Thompson & West, 1878.

Olmsted, Nancy. *The Ferry Building: Witness to a Century of Change.* San Francisco: Port of San Francisco; Berkeley: Heyday Books, 1998.

———. *Vanished Waters: A History of San Francisco's Mission Bay.* San Francisco: Mission Creek Conservancy, 1986.

Olmsted, Roger R., Nancy L. Olmsted, and Allen Pastron. "San Francisco Waterfront: Report on Historical Cultural Resources for the North Shore and Channel Outfalls Consolidation Projects." San Francisco: San Francisco Wastewater Management Program, 1977.

Overland Monthly. "The Future of San Francisco Harbor." 15, no. 5 (November 1875): 401–407.

P.G. and E. Progress. "Coffee: Queen of S.F. Imports." 32, no. 8 (July 1955): 1–2.

Pacific Marine Review. "Squire Chief of State Harbor Board." (March 1949): 84.

Pannell, J. P. M. *An Illustrated History of Civil Engineering.* London: Thames and Hudson, 1964.

Pastron, Allen G., and Jack Prichett, eds. "Behind the Seawall: Historical Archeology Along the San Francisco Waterfront." Prepared by Archeo-Tec. San Francisco: San Francisco Clean Water Program, 1981.

Pickelhaupt, Bill. *San Francisco's Aquatic Park.* Images of America Series. San Francisco: Arcadia Publishing, 2005.

_____. *Shanghaied in San Francisco.* San Francisco: Flyblister Press, 1996.

"Pier 39: San Francisco's Premier Bay Attraction." 2010. www.pier39.com.

Plant, Thomas G. *The Pacific Coast Longshoremen's Strike of 1934. Statement of Thomas G. Plant, President of the Waterfront Employers Union of San Francisco to the National Longshoremen's Board, July 11, 1934.* San Francisco: Waterfront Employers Union of San Francisco, 1934.

Port of San Francisco. "Information Presentation on a Ten-Year Review of the Waterfront Land Use Plan." Staff memorandum to the Port Commission. December 3, 2008.

Praetzellis, Mary, and Adrian Praetzellis, eds. "Tar Flat, Rincon Hill, and the Shore of Mission Bay: Archeological Research Design and Treatment Plan for SF-480 Terminal Separation Rebuild." 2nd ed. Prepared by Anthropological Studies Center, Sonoma State University Academic Foundation, Inc. Oakland: Caltrans District 4, June 1995.

Portside News.

"Know Your Port." 1, no. 2 (May 1957): 7.

"PFEL to Shift to Remodeled Piers 29-31-33." 5, no. 1 (January–February 1962): 2.

"Where We Are." 4, no. 2 (February 1961): 4.

Quan, Ray F. "Engineering Department Duties Cover 'City Within City.'" *Portside News* 1, no. 2 (May 1957): 4.

_____. "Engineering Dept. Has Big Variety of Talent." *Portside News* 1, no. 4 (July 1957): 6.

_____. "Engineering Dept.'s Design Section Leads Busy Life: From $50 Million to Just $26." *Portside News* 1, no. 3 (June 1957): 6.

Quin, Mike. *The Big Strike.* Olema, Calif.: Olema Publishing Company, 1949.

Quirin, E. J., and Peter Davidson Gunn Hamilton. "Docks." *Encyclopaedia Britannica.* Chicago: Encyclopaedia Britannica, 1957. Vol. 7, 466–487.

Rawls, James J., and Walton Bean. *California: An Interpretive History.* 7th ed. San Francisco: McGraw-Hill, 1998.

Reinhardt, Richard. "On the Waterfront: The Great Wall of Magnin." In *The Ultimate Highrise: San Francisco's Mad Rush Toward the Sky.* San Francisco: San Francisco Bay Guardian Books, 1971.

Riesenberg, Felix, Jr. *Golden Gate: The Story of San Francisco Harbor.* New York: Alfred A. Knopf, 1940.

Rubin, Jasper. *A Negotiated Landscape: The Transformation of San Francisco's Waterfront Since 1950.* Chicago: Center for American Places at Columbia College and University of Chicago Press, forthcoming.

Sanborn Map Company. *Insurance Maps of San Francisco.* New York: Sanborn Map Company, 1899. Digital Sanborn Maps, 1867–1970, from Library of Congress collection, available at San Francisco Public Library.

_____. *Insurance Maps of San Francisco.* New York: Sanborn Map Company, 1913. Vol. 2. Digital Sanborn Maps, 1867–1970, from Library of Congress collection, available at San Francisco Public Library.

_____. *Insurance Maps of San Francisco.* New York: Sanborn Map Company, 1914. Vol. 6. Digital Sanborn Maps, 1867–1970, from Library of Congress collection, available at San Francisco Public Library.

_____. *Insurance Maps of San Francisco.* New York: Sanborn Map Company, 1913, updated to 1949. Digital Sanborn Maps, 1867–1970, from Library of Congress collection, available at San Francisco Public Library.

_____. *Insurance Maps of San Francisco.* New York: Sanborn Map Company, 1913, updated to 1952. San Francisco Architectural Heritage.

_____. *Insurance Maps of San Francisco.* New York: Sanborn Map Company, 1913, updated to 1986. San Francisco Public Library.

San Francisco. Board of Supervisors. *San Francisco Municipal Reports for the Fiscal Year 1888–89, Ending June 30, 1889.* Appendix page 121 in "Street Grades." San Francisco: W. M. Hinton and Company, 1889.

San Francisco Call.

"Barker Suspended by Harbor Board. Inefficiency, Not Graft, in Assistant Engineer's Office, Is Verdict." May 12, 1911, 20.

"New Concrete Pier Contract Is Let." November 20, 1908, 10.

"Patronage Ax Cuts Saph Out of State Job. Assistant Engineer Resigns Because Governor Johnson Needs the Place." August 4, 1912, 39.

"S.P. Engineer Appointed in Saph's Place. Political Activity of Board in Creating Jobs Greatly Discounted Able Man's Work." August 9, 1912, 5.

San Francisco Chamber of Commerce. *Facts About the Port of San Francisco: A Brief Handbook Containing Information of General Interest to the Shipper and Businessman Together with Maps, Views and Statistical Information Relative to San Francisco's Foreign Trade.* San Francisco: Schwabacher-Frey, 1921.

_____. *The Golden Gate, San Francisco: Through These Protecting Headlands $473,793,940 Worth of Foreign Commerce Passed in During 1919.* San Francisco: San Francisco Chamber of Commerce, 1920.

_____. *San Francisco: The Financial, Commercial and Industrial Metropolis of the Pacific Coast.* San Francisco: H. S. Crocker Co., 1915.

San Francisco Chronicle.

"Eight-Story Concrete Building Is Planned." January 27, 1907, 62.

"Ferry Building Union Depot for Ocean Liners Seen." December 7, 1938, 1.

"Frank G. White." February 7, 1967, 57.

"Galen A. Wood." Death Notice. September 22, 1967.

"Harbor Board to Build More Wooden Piers. Disregards All Advice and Lessons Taught by Past Experience." December 20, 1917, 4.

"Harbor Commissioners Sued." November 21, 1893, 6.

"The Harbor Commissioners' New Quarters." January 7, 1875, 2.

"Harbor Engineer Is Important Official: Jerome Newman Makes Big Record as Chief of State Department." January 12, 1916, 39.

"Local News Notes." May 20, 1892, 12.

"Marine News: U.S. Defense Needs Port Space in S.F." December 7, 1940, 5H.

"Mendacity of the Harbor Board is Shown. Officials Seek to Blame the Business Men for Proposed Wooden Pier Program. Latter Deny the Charges. Commerce Chamber Officials Say They Never Favored Temporary Wharves." December 22, 1913, 16.

"News Gathered Along the Docks." January 23, 1897, 12.

["Pier 7 Destroyed by Fire"]. March 22, 1973. San Francisco Bar Pilots Scrapbook, Pier 9.

"Pyle." Death Notice of Alfred A. Pyle. May 31, 1936.

"Veteran Engineer, Carl Uhlig, Dies at His Home Here: For 42 Years He Aided in Developing San Francisco Water Front." March 6, 1919, 3.

"Woman Serves Harbor Board: Hilda Gohrman's Selection as Secretary Ratified by Governor Stephens." December 5, 1918, 3.

"Work Is Rushed on Big Building." August 21, 1920, 8.

San Francisco Examiner.

"Beautification of Bay Shore Discussed." February 5, 1915, 17.

"Chief Harbor Engineer Is Forced Out. Jerome Newman's Resignation Demanded by Board." June 28, 1916, 5.

"Frank G. White Made S.F. Harbor Engineer." July 8, 1916, 7.

"San Francisco Seawall Built at Last. After Almost 20 Years, Task of Constructing Permanent Piers on Water Front Is Ended." May 7, 1915, 3.

San Francisco Port Authority. *Port of San Francisco Ocean Shipping Handbook.* San Francisco: San Francisco Port Authority, 1956–1968.

San Francisco Port Commission. *Multiport.* Brochure. San Francisco: San Francisco Port Commission, 1971.

_____. *Port of San Francisco Ocean Shipping Handbook.* San Francisco: San Francisco Port Commission, 1970.

Schwartz, Stephen. *Brotherhood of the Sea: A History of the Sailor's Union of the Pacific, 1885–1985.* New Brunswick, N.J.: Transaction Books, Rutgers University, and Sailor's Union of the Pacific, AFL-CIO, 1986.

Scott, Mel. *The San Francisco Bay Area: A Metropolis in Perspective.* Berkeley: University of California Press, 1959.

Selvin, David F. *A Terrible Anger: The 1934 Waterfront and General Strikes in San Francisco.* Detroit: Wayne State University Press, 1996.

Sherwood, Susan P., and Catherine Powell. *The San Francisco Labor Landmarks Guidebook: A Register of Sites and Walking Tours.* 1st ed. San Francisco: Labor Archives and Research Center, San Francisco State University, 2007.

Shumate, Albert. *Rincon Hill and South Park: San Francisco's Early Fashionable Neighborhood.* Sausalito: Windgate Press, 1988.

Singer, Charles, E. J. Holmyard, A. R. Hall, and Trevor I. Williams, eds. *A History of Technology: The Late Nineteenth Century, 1850 to 1900.* Vol. 5. New York: Oxford University Press, 1958.

Snow, David E., and Erwin N. Thompson. "San Francisco Port of Embarkation Headquarters, Fort Mason: Historic Structure Report." U.S. Army Historical and Architectural Data Sections. Denver: Pacific Northwest/Western Team Branch of Historical Preservation, National Park Service, U.S. Department of the Interior, n.d.

Soeten, Harlan. "A Seaman Remembers the San Francisco Waterfront, Circa 1930." *National Maritime Museum Association Sea Letter,* no. 58 (Summer 2000): 14–19.

_____. "A Seaman's History of the San Francisco Waterfront in the 1930s." *Steamboat Bill* 45, no. 4 (Winter 1988): 257–269.

Soulé, Frank, John H. Gihon, and James Nisbet. *The Annals of San Francisco.* 1855. Reprint, Berkeley: Berkeley Hills Books, 1999.

Squire, Harry E. "Concrete Pile Construction on the San Francisco Water Front." *Architect and Engineer* 51, no. 1 (October 1917): 69–74.

Stafford, W. V. "Improvements That Have Been Made, and Where the Money Came From." *San Francisco Call.* February 20, 1910, 26, 27.

_____. "The State Wharves of San Francisco: A Lucrative Public Property." *Overland Monthly* 56, no. 4 (October 1910): 341–352.

Stern, Boris. *Cargo Handling and Longshore Labor Conditions.* Bulletin 550 of the Bureau of Labor Statistics, U.S. Department of Labor. Washington, D.C.: U.S. Government Printing Office, 1932.

Stern, Robert A. M., Gregory Gilmartin, and John Montague Massengale. *New York 1900: Metropolitan Architecture and Urbanism, 1890–1915.* New York: Rizzoli, 1983.

Stevenson, Thomas. "Harbors and Docks." *Encyclopaedia Britannica.* 9th ed. (American reprint). Philadelphia: J. M. Stoddart & Company, 1880. Vol. 11, 406–422.

Stoll, Horatio F. "Beautifying San Francisco for 1915." *Architect and Engineer* 20, no. 2 (March 1910): 45–52.

Sturgis, Russell, et al. *Sturgis' Illustrated Dictionary of Architecture and Building.* Unabridged reprint of the 1901–1902 edition. 3 vols. New York: Dover Publications, 1989.

Temko, Allan. *No Way to Build a Ballpark and Other Irreverent Essays on Architecture.* San Francisco: Chronicle Books, 1993.

Terry, Richard. *San Francisco Chronicle Index: 1950–1980*. Sacramento: California State Library, California Section; Bellevue, Wash.: Commercial Microfilm Service, [1986]. Microfiche.

Thiemann, Harry J. "The Big Picture: Parking Along San Francisco's Sprawling Waterfront." *Portside News* 2, no. 5 (May 1958): 6–8.

Todd, Mortimer. *The Argonaut*. November 17, 1923, 23.

Turnbull, J. Gordon. "Central Embarcadero Piers Historic District: Piers 1, 1½, 3, and 5: National Register of Historic Places Registration Form." Washington, D.C.: National Park Service, U.S. Department of the Interior, 2002.

U.S. Army Corps of Engineers. *Annual Report of the Chief of Engineers for 1890*. Appendix QQ. Washington, D.C.: U.S. Government Printing Office, 1890.

_____. *Annual Report of the Chief of Engineers for 1901*. Appendix UU. Washington, D.C.: U.S. Government Printing Office, 1901.

_____. *Annual Report of the Chief of Engineers for 1903*. Appendix VV. Washington, D.C.: U.S. Government Printing Office, 1903.

_____. *Annual Report of the Chief of Engineers, U.S. Army*. Report on the Improvement of Rivers and Harbors in California, 1874–1957.

U.S. Board of Engineers for Rivers and Harbors and the Maritime Administration. *The Ports of San Francisco and Redwood City, California, Port Series No. 30*. Washington, D.C.: U.S. Government Printing Office, 1952, 1962.

U.S. Board of Engineers for Rivers and Harbors and the U.S. Shipping Board. *The Ports of San Francisco, Oakland, Berkeley, Richmond, Upper San Francisco Bay, Santa Cruz and Monterey, California, Port Series No. 12*. Washington, D.C.: U.S. Government Printing Office, 1927, 1933, 1939.

U.S. Department of the Interior. Geological Survey. *The San Francisco Earthquake and Fire of April 18, 1906, and Their Effect on Structures and Structural Materials*. Bulletin No. 324, Series R, Structural Materials, 1. Washington, D.C.: U.S. Government Printing Office, 1907.

Vance, James E., Jr. *Geography and Urban Evolution in the San Francisco Bay Area*. Berkeley: University of California Institute of Governmental Studies, 1964.

Vanderslice, Allison, Nancy Goldenberg, Marjorie Dobkin, Chris Meyer, and Karen McNeil. "Port of San Francisco Union Iron Works/Bethlehem Steel Historic District—Pier 70 National Register of Historic Places Registration Form." San Francisco: Carey & Company for the Port of San Francisco, draft June 2008.

Vernon-Harcourt, Leveson Francis. "Dock." *Encyclopaedia Britannica*. 11th ed. New York: Encyclopaedia Britannica Company, 1910. Vol. 8, 353–364.

Voget, Lamberta Margarette. "The Waterfront of San Francisco: 1863–1930: A History of Its Administration by the State of California." PhD diss., University of California, 1943.

Wagoner, Luther, and W. H. Heuer. *San Francisco Harbor, Its Commerce and Docks With a Complete Plan for Development. Report of the Engineers*. [San Francisco]: Federated Harbor Improvement Associations, 1908.

White, Frank G. "The Embarcadero Subway, San Francisco." *Architect and Engineer* 76, no. 1 (January 1924): 94–98.

_____. "The India Basin—Islais Creek Harbor Project." *Architect* 16, no. 5 (November 1918): 232–234, plates.

Whitener, Theresa. *A Tradition of Fellowship and Service: The Rotary Club of San Francisco at 100*. San Francisco: The Rotary Club of San Francisco, 2008.

Wollenberg, Charles. *Golden Gate Metropolis: Perspectives on Bay Area History*. Berkeley: University of California Institute of Governmental Studies, 1985.

Woodbridge, Sally B. *San Francisco in Maps and Views*. New York: Rizzoli, 2006.

_____. "Visions of Renewal and Growth: 1945 to the Present." In *Visionary San Francisco*. Edited by Paolo Polledri. San Francisco: San Francisco Museum of Modern Art; Munich: Prestel Verlag, 1990.

INDEX

Page numbers in *italics* refer to illustrations.
Numbers in **boldface** refer to Pier number or
Seawall Lot number, accordingly.

A. B. McCreery Building, 83, *83*

ABC television offices, 195, *195*

Agriculture Building, 78, 159, 224, 230n43; architectural style, 82–83, 199, *199*

Alameda Transportation Company, 120

Alaska Commercial Building, *46, 47,* 49–50

Albion Hall, 53

Alden, L., 187, *187*

Alexandria (Egypt), port of, 123

Allardt, G. F., 138

American-Hawaiian Steamship Company, 120, *136,* 203

American Society of Civil Engineers, 61

Appraiser's Warehouse, 78

Aquatic Park, 179, *179*

architects and designers: L. Alden, 187, *187*; Backen, Arrigoni & Ross, 205, 207; C. Barton, 200; Bearwald-Froberg, Bun, 194, *194*; E. Bennett, 148; Bliss & Faville, 51, 210, *210*; J. Bolles, 75; E. Born, 75; A. P. Brown, 146–47, 198, *198*; H. J. Brunnier, 206, *206*; D. Burnham, 148, 150 (*see also* Burnham Plan); Daniel, Mann, Johnson & Mendenhall, 189; V. DeMars, *105*; B. von Eckartsberg, 198; S. E. Evans, 194, *194*; T. Fisch, 194; Fisher-Freidman, 195; H. B. Fisher, 191, *191, 192, 192,* 193, *193,* 214, *214*; Gensler and Associates, 188; A. C. Griewank, 186, *186,* 187, *187,* 194, *194,* 223, 225; R. Gryziec, 168; Hannum Associates, 194; H. Hill, 182; HOK Sport, 208; B. P. Hudspeth, 214, *214*; I. M. Pei Partners, 169; A. Janssen, 158, 193, *193,* 224, 225; O. Jones, 187, *187,* 214, *214,* 223, 225; B. J. Joseph, 224; G. Kelham, 201, *201*; Kwan Henmi, 205, *205*; C. McCall, 51; G. McDougall, 160; McKim, Mead, and White, 51, 146–47; W. Merchant, 74; J. R. Miller, *71*; Moore, Ruble, Yudell, 205, *205*; W. Mooser III, 179; Olin Partnership, 200; T. Osmundson, *105*; Page & Turnbull, 194, 198; T. L. Pflueger, *71*; W. Polk, 147–148, *150*; A. Pyle, 158, 159, 160, 186, *186,* 187, *187,* 194, 199, *199,* 223–24, 224, 225; Robinson & Mills, 188; ROMA Design Group, 197; H. Schulze, 201; A. C. Schweinfurth, 147; Skidmore, Owings & Merrill, 167; SMWM Architects, 194, 198; E. Swann, 198, *198*; Walker & Moody, 185; Warren and Wetmore, *156,* 157–58; H. Wells, 184; Willis Polk and Company, 224; G. A. Wood, 187, *187,* 191, *191,* 193, *193,* 225; C. Young, 184, *184,* 203, *203,* 223

architectural styles: Baroque, 199, *199*; Beaux-Arts, 152, 154; Craftsman and Prairie, 159, 189, *189*; Gothic Revival, 158–59, *160,* 182, 214; Italian Renaissance, *48,* 82, 181, *181,* 199, *199,* 200, *200*; Italian-villa inspired, 201, *201*; Mediterranean, 156, *159,* 206, *206,* 207, *207*; Mission, 189, *189*; Mission Revival, and "modified" style, 151–52, 155–156, *157, 158,* 159, 189, 190, 197, 199, 200, *200,* 201, *201, 203,* 206, 210; Moderne, 191, *191,* 192, *192*; Neoclassical, 156–58, *157, 159,* 184, 185, 186, *186,* 187, *187,* 190, 191, *191,* 192, 193, 194, *194*; Romanesque Revival, 82–83, 147, 149, 199; Victorian, *14,* 15

Arctic Oil Works, *43,* 216

Army. *See* U.S. Army

Army-Navy YMCA, 53, *53*

Army Street Terminal, *165,* 166, 217, *217*

Arnold, T. J. ("Engineer of the Seawall"), 38, 96, 99, 130, 139, 220–21

Audiffred Building, 53, 114

Auto Dock and Kirkland Yard—Longshoremen's Hiring Hall, 182, *182*

Automobile Terminal, 218, *218*

automobile travel: impact on Embarcadero, *104,* 105; pier apron design changes, for, 102

Balfour, Guthrie & Company, 52

Ballou, F. E., 194, *194*

Banana Terminal, 213, *213*

Barbary Coast (Pacific Avenue), 53

Barge Office, 181, *181*

Barker, Ralph, 135, 206, *206,* 215, *215,* 221–22

Baroque style, 199, *199*

Bar Pilots, 193, *193*

Bartlett, Washington, 81

Bartnett, Walter, 60

Bay Bridge, 202, *202,* 222, 225; effect on Port traffic, 104, *104,* 198; opening (1936), *100,* 104; rail line, *104,* 105

Bay Plan (1969), 166

Bay Street, 188

BCDC (Bay Conservation and Development Corporation), 166, 167, 169

Bearwald-Froberg, Bun, 194, *194*

Beaux-Arts style, 152, 154

Belt Railroad, *98, 134,* 147; beginning of (1890), 38–39, 47, 99, 101; and BSHC, 81, *84,* 88, 99, 102; built on seawall lots, *84,* 121; capabilities of, *47, 97,* 101; construction phases, *84,* 101; decrease in activity (1930–1932), 66; engineers, 99, 223, 224; extensions, 39, 64, 70, *91,* 101, 102, 223; impact on port development, 47, 63; offices, *90,* 142, 189, *189*; private railheads served by, 41, *42*; roundhouse, 101, 189, 224 (*see also* Old Roundhouse); scope of facilities, 99, 101; spurs, 36, 37, 39, *42,* 48, 67, *68,* 88, *98,* 99, 101, 143, 180, 197; and transit shed access, *98,* 101, 133; work force, 84, 108–9

Belt Railroad Engine House, *169,* 170, 189, *189,* 223

Belt Railroad Office Building, 142, 189, *189*

Benicia, port of, 70, 120

Bennett, Edward H., 148, 150

Bethlehem Steel, 219

Big Strike of 1934, *52,* 53, *116,* 117, *117, 119,* 190, 204

Bliss & Faville, 51

Bloody Thursday (1934 strike), *116,* 117

Blue Book Union, 116, 117

Blue Shield Building, 188, *188*

Board of Engineers for Rivers and Harbors, 74

Board of State Harbor Commissioners. *See* BSHC (Board of State Harbor Commissioners)

Board of Tide Land Commissioners, 38, 212

Bolce, William J., Jr., 71

Bolles, John S., 75

Booth Packing House and Market building, 180, 181, *181*

Born, Ernest, 75

Boyd Estate Building, 49

Brannan Street Wharf, 173, 206

break-bulk cargo handling, 63, *106–7,* 109, *112–13, 118,* 125; Army Street Terminal, *165,* 166, 217, *217*; replaced by containerization, 164–65, 185

Bridges, Harry, 117, *119*

Brooks, Thaddeus R., 220

Brown, A. Page, 146–47, 198, *198*

Brunnier, H. J., 140, 206, *206,* 222

BSHC (Board of State Harbor Commissioners): Advisory Committee, 89, 119; and Belt Railroad, 38–39 (*see also* Belt Railroad); chief engineer, versus state engineer, 221; commissioners, 80–81, 83, *83,* 86, 91; competition from truck traffic, 104–5; construction projects (*see specific project*); creation of (1863), 37–38, 57, 80, 88–89; employees, 83, 85–86, 89, *89,* 90, 107, 220, 223; Engineering Department, 83, 85, 87, 89, 160, 220–25 (*see also specific names*); framework adopted by other ports, 89; functions of, 77, 88, *88, 89, 90, 91,* 95, *131,* 147–48; office locations, 83, *83* (*see also* Ferry Building); and politics, 81, 85, 88, 89; port beautification efforts, 152, *154,* 156, 159, 160, 161, 190; port control and jurisdiction, 35, 42, *76–77,* 138, 178; port modernization initiatives, 73–74, 134–35, 137, 206, *206*; presidents, 81, 85, 86, 87–88, 133, 151; replaced by San Francisco Port Commission, 91; revenue sources, 84–85, 88, 90, 94, 140; ties to Southern Pacific, 81, 85, 215, 221, 223; Traffic Department, 103, 105; Wharfingers Department, 86–87, *90,* 94, 110, 119–20, 141

bulkhead buildings, *66*; architectural styles, 156, *156,* 185, *185–94,* 199, *200, 202–5,* 206, 207; described, 141, 142, *143*; locations for, *137, 140,* 189, 206; rail access to, 101, 143; shipping company offices in, 95, 107

Bulkhead Line, 178; described, 36; establishment of (1876), 82. *See also* Water Front Line

bulkhead wharves, *110, 138–39*; construction of, *38, 135, 136,* 141, *143, 149*; described, 140; engineering of, 141–42, *143,* 224; freestanding, 141–42; in port design, *134, 135, 137, 140,* 141; Section 3, 188, *188*; Section 4, *137*; structures on, *140,* 141–42, *142*

Burnham, Daniel H., 148, 150. *See also* Burnham Plan of 1905

Burnham Plan of 1905, *104,* 148, 150, 151, *151,* 152, *152,* 154

Burton Act (1968), 164

Cahill, B. J. S., *66,* 160–61

California Chamber of Commerce, *61, 66,* 89, 137, 182

California Division of Ports, 89

California Fruit Canners Association North Point Cannery, 179, *179*

California Industrial Accident Board, 108

California Navigation and Improvement Company, 194

California state, 200; BSHC established by (1863), 57, 80; and port jurisdiction, 78, 80, 166

California state legislature, 39, 58, 165; and BSHC, 80, 81, 82, 88–89; and Free Public Market, 195, *195*; "harbor lines" adopted by, 82, 139

California Street, *46, 47,* 48, *48,* 50, 83, *83,* 182

California Transportation Company, 189, 194

canning industry, 179, *179,* 216

Car-Ferry Head House at Pier 43, 184, *184*

car-ferry terminals, 36, 41, *42,* 96, 98, *98,* 99, 101–2, 104, *164, 179,* 224; Car-Ferry Head House, 184, *184*;

Santa Fe Railway, 39, *98*, 101–2, *164*, 213

cargo handling: break-bulk process, 63, *106–7*, 109, *112–13, 118,* 164–65; changes in technologies, *109,* 109–10, 116, 118, 124–25, *167*; containerization, 118, *120,* 133, 164–65, *167*, 185; and port design, 125, 134–35, 137, *167*; and stevedores, 110; transit sheds used for, 133, 143. *See also* transshipments

Carquinez Strait, 58, 63, 188

Central Basin, 215, *215*

Central Pacific Railroad, 38, *41,* 96, 98, 113, *148,* 211; and BSHC, 81, 85; offices, 119. *See also* Southern Pacific Railroad

Channel Street, *40, 88,* 168, 213, *213*

Charles Hall Page & Associates, 15–16

Cherny, Robert W., 57

Chevalier Map of 1911, 64, *65*

Chicago, port of, 95

Chicago Clothing Co., *147*

Chicago World's Fair. *See* World's Columbian Exposition of 1893

China Basin, 67, 168, 213, *213*; car ferries, *98*, 102; lumberyards, *112*; non-maritime development, *168–69*; seawall construction, 140, 208; transshipments, *94*

China Basin Airport proposal (1928), 71

China Basin Building, *40*, 210, *210*

China Basin Terminal, 209

China Mail Steamship Company, 121, 187

Chittenden, H. M., 61

City Base: establishment of, 197; and seawall, 141, 230n33

City Beautiful Movement, 149, *151,* 152, *154,* 154–55, *156,* 157, 159, *159*; and architectural style, 155–56 (*see also* Mission Revival, and "modified" style)

city front, 36, *36, 52, 174–77*

Clarke's Point, 55, 195, *195*

Clinton Construction Co., 187, 214, *214*

coal bunkers, 63, *64, 72–73*

coffee trade, 48, 69, 201, *201*

Colnon, E. L., 85

Colombo Market Building, 196

Commission District. *See* Produce (or Commission) District

commodities trade, 41, 49, 63, 68, 74–75, 121

Commonwealth Club, 151

Consolidation Freight Station, 219

containerization, 118, *120,* 133, 164–65, *167,* 185; break-bulk replaced by, 164–65, 185

contractors: Barrett & Hilp, 191, *191,* 193, *193*; Clinton Construction Co., 187, 214, *214*; Grant Smith & Co., 203, *203*; Hannah Brothers, 193, *193*; Healy-Tibbitts Construction Co., 184, *184,* 186, *186,* 187, *187,* 191, *191,* 192, *192,* 199, *199,* 214, *214*; L. M. King, 214, *214*; A. W. Kitchen, 193, *193*; E. T. Lesure, 192, *192*; MacDonald & Kahn, 182, *182,* 184; J. J. McHugh, 187, *187*; J. L. McLaughlin, 187, *187*; D. Nordstrom, 214, *214*; San Francisco Bridge Co., 198, *198,* 203, *203*; Teichert & Ambrose, 199, *199*; Thompson Bridge Co., 215, *215*; Tibbitts Construction Co., 192

Cotton Terminal, 166

Cotton Warehouse, 218, *218*

Coulter, William A., 182

Cowell's Wharf, *42*

Crabmen's Protective Association, *75*

Craftsman and Prairie style, 189, *189*

Crane, Lauren E., 140

Crocker, Henry J., 81

Cross, Ira, 114

cruise ship terminals, 170, 173, 205

Customhouse, 78, 196, *196*

D. Ghirardelli Company, 23, 41

Davis Street Wharf, 98

day-labor system, 85

Delancey Street development, 170, 205

Del Monte Cannery, 179

DeMars, Vernon, *105*

Department of Public Works, 224, 225

Dollar, Robert, 119

Dollar buildings (California Street), *46, 47, 50, 51*

Dollar Steamship Lines, *46, 47,* 49, 50, 51, 121, 207

Draymen's Association, 120

Dwyer, J. J., 151

Eagle Cafe, 185

East Street, *64, 70,* 96, 99; name changed to Embarcadero, 96, 197

Ebasco Services of New York, 165

Eddy, William M., 178

Eddy Red Line Map of 1851 (Jurisdiction Line), *79, 82,* 138, *174–77,* 178, 183, 213

Ellery, Nathaniel, 189, 222

Embarcadero, *39, 43, 166,* 169, 188, 197, *197,* 200; Army-Navy YMCA, 53, *53*; automobile traffic, *101,* 102, *102,* 103, *103,* 104, 105, 169; beautification efforts, 154, 156, *156,* 160; Belt Railroad built on, 64, *84, 98, 99*; and Big Strike (1934), *116*; creation of, *76–77, 135, 136,* 197; described, 36, 62; elevated highway proposal, *104* (*see also* Embarcadero Freeway); historic preservation, 15–16, 169; naming of, *64,* 197; pedestrian traffic, 103; on Port map, *134*; redevelopment and refurbishment, 170, *170,* 197; South Beach Harbor Park, 208, *208*; traffic-types on, *99, 100, 101,* 103, 197; vegetable oil pipelines across, *72–73*; viaduct built across (1918–1919), 103

Embarcadero Center, *105*

Embarcadero City, 161, 164, *164,* 165

Embarcadero Freeway, *104,* 105, *105,* 132, *151,* 161, 170, *170,* 197, 200; demolition (1991), 18, 23, 173, 197

Embarcadero Gardens, 168

Embarcadero Historic District, 16

Embarcadero Post Office, 82

Embarcadero Triangle (office building), 188

engineers: G. F. Allardt, 138; T. J. Arnold, 38, 96, 99, 130, 139, 220–221; R. Barker, 135, 206, *206,* 215, *215,* 221–222; H. J. Brunnier, 140, 222; Charles Hall Page & Associates, 15–16; W. Eddy, 178; N. Ellery, 189, 222; H. B. Fisher, 224–25; S. Gorman, 225; A. C. Griewank, 186, *186,* 187, *187,* 194, *194,* 223, 225; W. Hegemann, 61; H. Holmes, 198, *198,* 199, 221, 222; Hood (BSHC chief engineer), 223; A. Janssen, 158, 193, *193,* 224, 225; O. Jones, 187, *187,* 214, *214,* 223, 225; W. Lewis, 138, 220; MacDonald & Kahn, 182, *182,* 184; M. Manson, 60, 134, 221; J. Newman, 152, 159, 184, *184,* 186,

186, 187, *187,* 199, *199,* 203, *203,* 223, 224, 225; A. Nordwell, 223, 225; L. Norton, 221; A. Pyle, 158, 159, 160, 186, *186,* 187, *187,* 194, 199, *199,* 223–224, 224, 225; A. Saph, 151, 192, *192,* 203, *203,* 223; H. Squire, 224, 225; C. Uhlig, 221, 222; F. White, 89, 182, 187, *187,* 191, *191,* 192, *192,* 193, *193,* 194, *194,* 214, *214,* 223, 224, 225; C. Young, 184, *184,* 203, *203,* 223

Eureka, port of, 89

Exploratorium, 173, 192

F. E. Booth Packing House, 181, *181*

Fairmont Hotel, *62*

Federated Harbor Users Association, 60

Fell Street, 53

ferries, 105, *112*; effect of Bay Bridge on, 104, 198. *See also* car-ferry terminals; Ferry Building; passenger ferries

Ferry Annex Post Office, 199

Ferry Building, *64, 89, 105,* 111, 149, 198, *198,* 225; annex, 199, 223, 224; architecture, *144–45, 146,* 146–47, 220; Belt Railroad extended past (1913), 39, *91*; BSHC offices in, *49,* 83; construction of, 81, 85, 198; decline in use of, 105; demolition proposed (1948), 75; described, *62, 94*; and longshoremen, 110, *115*; passenger traffic, *108*; proposed renovation (1984–1985), 169; rehabilitation (2003), 18, 23, *171,* 173, 198; site beautification efforts, 147–48, *150,* 150–51, *152,* 161 (*see also* Burnham Plan; Polk, Willis)

Ferry Building tower, *49, 64, 92–93,* 147, 198, *198*

Ferry House (1875), 93, 98, 119, 146, 148, *148*

Ferry Port Plaza, *166,* 167, 168

Ferry Post Office, 159, 160, 199, 223

finger piers, 18, *134,* 163, 164, 165; Port of New York, 22, *22,* 126

Fire Department, 78; Fire Station 35, 201, *201*

Fish Alley, 181, *181*

Fisher, H. B., 191, *191,* 192, *192,* 193, *193,* 214, *214,* 224–25

Fisher-Friedman, 205, *205*

Fisheries Center, proposed, 169

Fisherman's Wharf, 71, *75,* 78, 158, 180, *180*; redesign plans, 75, 165, 169, 173, 180, *180*. *See also* Old Fisherman's Wharf

Fishermen's and Seamen's Memorial Chapel, 181

Folgers Coffee Company, 201

Folsom Street, *70*

Fort Mason, 36, 39, 70, 102

Fort Mason Tunnel and Aquatic Park, 179, *179*

Fort McDowell, 70

Free Public Market, *100,* 195, *195*

Gas Holder, 183, *183*

Gateway Sites, 173

General Strike of 1934. *See* Big Strike of 1934

Ghirardelli Square, 23, 41

Giants. *See* San Francisco Giants stadium

Gibb Warehouses, 41, 184

Gillette, James N., 221, 222

Globe Milling Company, 188

Golden Gate Bridge, 104, 179

Golden Gate International Exposition, 225

Golden Gate Tennis and Swim Club, 173

Golden Gateway Center, *44, 105,* 196

Golden Gateway Redevelopment Project, 195

Golden Gateway Tennis and Swim Club, 173, 195

Gold Rush, *44,* 178, 183; and coffee imports, 201; impact on port, 41, 55, 56, 186, 195; specialized waterfront districts, 196

Gorman, Sidney S., 225

Gothic Revival style, 158–59, *160,* 182, *182,* 214

Grace Line (steamship line), 186

grain terminals, 58, 61, 63, *66,* 188, 218, *218*

Great Depression, 64, 66, 90, 117, 224

Great Western Power Company, 219, *219*

Greene, Carleton, 151

Green Street, *98*

Greenwich Street, *45*

Greenwich wharf, *59*

Griewank, A. C., 186, *186,* 187, *187,* 194, *194,* 223, 225

Groninger, Homer M., 72–73

Gryziec, Richard, 168

H. M. Newhall & Company, 50

Haas-Lilienthal House, *14,* 15

Hagel, Otto, 109

Hale, Marshall, 81

Hamilton, James W., 71

Hamilton Field, 70

Harbor Court Hotel, 53

Harbor Police Station, 78

Harbor Warehouse Company, 183, *183*

Harrison Street, 45, 47, *52, 53,* 201, *201,* 202, *202*

Harry Bridges Plaza, *171,* 173, 197

Healy-Tibbitts Construction Co., 184, *184,* 186, *186, 187, 187,* 191, *191,* 192, *192,* 199, *199,* 214, *214*

Hegemann, Werner, 61, 98

Herb Caen Way, 173

Heritage. *See* San Francisco Architectural Heritage

Heron's Head Park, *171,* 173, 219, *219*

Hill, Henry, 182

Hills Brothers coffee, 201, *201*

Hobart, Lewis, *104*

Holmes, Howard C., 198, *198,* 199, 221, 222

Horne, C. A., 150

Howard Street, 53, 201

Howard Street Wharf, *106–7*

Humboldt Bank tower, *62*

Humboldt Bay piers, 70

Hunter-Dulin Building, 222

Hunters Point, 36, 38, 68, 216, 219, *219*

Hyde Street Harbor, 173

Hyde Street Pier, 179, *179*

I. M. Pei Partners, 169

Ice House, 167

ILA (International Longshoremen's Association), 117

ILWU (International Longshore and Warehouse Union), 118, 182, *182*

Import Car Terminal, 166

India Basin, 167, 173, 178, 217, *217;* acquisition of, 85, 217

India Basin–Islais Creek Plan (1918), 62, *68,* 217, *217*

Industrial Revolution, 123, 125, 126

Innes Avenue—Shipwright's Cottage, 219, *219*

International Market Center, *166,* 166–67, 231n7

Islais Creek, 68, *152,* 165, 217, *217;* boat launch, 173; land reclamation, 224; modernization program (1946), 74; post-war development, *164;* Produce Market, 196; vegetable oil plant, 62, 63

Islais Creek Channel, 217, *217,* 218

Islais Creek Copra Terminal, 218, *218*

Issel, William, 57

Italian Renaissance style, 181, *181,* 199, *199,* 200, *200,* 201, *201*

J. Harold Dollar building, *46, 47*

Janssen, Arthur D., 158, 193, *193,* 224, 225

J-10 bulkhead wharf, 181

Johnson, Hiram W., 85 98, 183, 223

Jones, Oliver W., 187, *187,* 214, *214,* 223, 225

Jurisdiction Line. *See* Eddy Red Line Map of 1851 (Jurisdiction Line)

J-7 wharf, 181

Kelham, George W., 201, *201*

Key System rail line, 105

Kilburn, Paris, 133

Kirkland Yard, 182, *182*

Kostura, William, 16

labor force, 106–21; and cargo-handling process, *106–7,* 108–9; closed-shop versus open-shop, 114, 116; day-labor system, 85; described, 56, 107, *112,* 112–13, *117;* and discrimination, *112,* 113–14; employment statistics (mid-1960s), 75; industrial accidents, 102, 108–9, 114; oversight agencies, 78; parking built for, *102;* warehousemen, 112, *117,* 118; waterfront restaurants, for, 190, 204, *204;* and workers' rights, 108–10, 112, *112,* 113, 114, *115,* 116–18, 223 (*see also* unions). *See also* longshoremen; pile-drivers/rigs; sailors/seamen; stevedores; teamsters

labor strikes, 112–18; Big Strike of 1934, *52, 53, 116,* 117, *117, 119,* 190, 204; Bloody Thursday (1934 strike), *116,* 117; government intervention, 117; strikebreakers and "bay pirates," 117, 214

labor unions, *52,* 53, 113–19, 180, 193, *193;* and City Front Federation, 178; closed-shop versus open-shop, 116; and Trades Assembly, 114

La Follette Seamen's Act, 108

landfill. *see* Port of San Francisco, landfill extension of shoreline

Landmarks Preservation Ordinance, 15

Lapham, Roger, 120

LASH Terminal, 167, *167,* 190, 219, *219*

Launch Offices, 200, *200*

Levi-Strauss office complex, 189, 195

Lewis, William J., 138, 220

Liquid Commodities Terminal, 218, *218*

Loma Prieta earthquake of 1989, *170,* 173, 197

Long Beach, port of, 89

longshoremen, *115;* duties, *106–7, 109,* 109–10, 112, *112, 117,* 125, 133; shape-ups, 110, 112, *114;* worker rights, 108, 112, *115,* 116–17

Longshoremen's Association (employer-backed union), 116

Longshoremen's Hiring Hall, 182, *182*

longshoremen's strikes, *112,* 112–14, *114. See also* labor strikes

longshoremen's unions, *52,* 53, 116–19, *119,* 182, *182;* ILA, *119*

Longstreth, Richard, 147

Los Angeles, port of, 60, 63, 74, 89

Los Angeles-San Francisco Navigation Company, 120

Luckenbach Steamship Company, 121

MacDonald & Kahn, 182, *182,* 184

MacElwee, Roy, 109–10

Manson, Marsden, 60, 134, 221

Marine Building, *46,* 49

Marine Exchange, 182, *182*

Marine Firemen, 53

Marine Hospital, 78

Maritime Museum, 173

Market Street, *46,* 48, *59,* 94, *94,* 98, 117, 146, 173, 198; Polk's proposal for, 147–48, *150. See also* Ferry Building

Market Street Railway, 44, 51

Marvin Building, *46*

Matson Building, 51–52, *92–93*

Matson Navigation Company, *46,* 51, 73, 120, *121,* 203; strike against (1933), 117

McAteer-Petris Act, 166

McClellan, George B., 129

McCoppin, Frank, 81

McCormick Steamship Lines, 185, 206

McDougall, George B., 160

McKim, Mead, and White, 51, 146–47

McLaughlin, J. L., 187, *187*

Mediterranean style, 155, 156, 159, *159,* 206, 207, *207*

Meigg's Wharf (Old Fisherman's Wharf), 185, *185*

Merchant, William Gladstone, 74

Merchants' and Manufacturers' Association, 114

Merchants Exchange Building, *46,* 49, *62,* 182; Southern Pacific offices in, 51

Mid-Embarcadero Roadway Project, 173

Miller, J. R., *71*

Mills Building, 51

Mission Bay, *37,* 168–69, 212, *212,* 213

Mission Bay North and Mission Bay South redevelopment areas, 173

Mission Creek, 212, *212*

Mission Revival, and "modified" style, *157, 158,* 159, 189, 190, 197, 199, 200, *200,* 201, *201,* 203, *203,* 206, 210; adoption of, 151–52, 155–56, 197, 200, *200*

Mission Rock, *37, 164;* destruction of, 82, 222

Mission Rock Terminal, 74, *164,* 165, *172,* 173, 214, *214*

Mission Street, 42, 44, 51, 52, 57, 114

Mission style, 189, *189*

Moderne style, 191, *191,* 192, *192*

Montgomery Street, *46, 83, 83,* 184, 188

Mooney, Tom, 116

Moore, Ruble, Yudell, 205, *205*

Mooser, William, III, 179

Morphy, Edward, 80, 87, 88, 90, 119

Morrow, Irving F., 160, 199

Nash, Gerald, 64, 80, 90, 101

National Historic Preservation Act of 1966, 15

National Industrial Recovery Act of 1933, 117

National Longshoremen's Board, 117

National Maritime Union, 53

National Paper Products Company Building, 184

National Register of Historic Places, 16

Nelson, Bruce, 117

Neoclassical style, 156–58, *157, 159,* 184, 185, 186, *186,* 187, *187,* 190, 191, *191,* 192, 193, 194, *194*

Newhall Building, *46,* 50

Newman, Jerome, 152, 159, 184, *184,* 186, *186,* 187, *187,* 199, *199,* 203, *203,* 223, 224, 225

New Orleans, port of, 75

New York, port of, 75, 201; architecture, 151, 152; beautification and revitalization, 22, *22,* 151; Chelsea Piers, 22, 130, 151, 152, 156, *156,* 157, 158, 159; Department of Docks, *126,* 129, 132; dominant period, 50; finger piers, 22, *22, 126;* and port design, 124, *126,* 127, *127,* 129–30, 132; San Francisco port compared with, 61, 63, 64, 129–30, 132–33

Nordwell, Alfred W., 223, 225

Norris, Frank, 42

North Beach, 53, 179

Northeast Waterfront Historic District, 18, *18,* 23, 184, *184,* 209

North Point, *36, 59,* 183, *183*

North Point Auto Dock, 182, *182*

North Point Sewage Treatment Plant, 183, *183*

North Point Street, 53, 67

Northwestern Pacific Railroad, 36, 39, *42,* 184, 188, 195

Norton, Lott D., 221

Oakland, port of, 64, 70, 96, 98; administration of, 89; car ferries, 98, 101; as container port, 75, 91; improvements to, 74, 75; military facilities, 70, 75; as San Francisco competitor, 91, 95, 132, 164, 165, 166; transcontinental rail line, 99

Oakland Army Base, 70, 71

Occidental Warehouse, 211

O'Farrell, Jasper, 81

oil-bunkering facilities, 63, 66–67, *72–73,* 96

Old Ferry House, 199

Old Fisherman's Wharf, 185, *185,* 192

Old Roundhouse, 189, *189*

Oregon, port competition from, 58

Oriental Warehouse (Steamboat Point), 42, 209, 211, *211*

Orient Building (Pine Street), 50

Osmundson, Theodore, *105*

Otis Elevator Company Building, *103,* 184, *184*

Pacific Avenue, 53

Pacific Coast Steamship Company, *109*

Pacific Far East Lines, 190, 219

Pacific Gas & Electric Company, 154

Pacific Mail Steamship Company, *41,* 42, 98, 101, 113–14, 121, 208, 209, 211, *211,* 213

Pacific Maritime Association, 118

Pacific Oriental Terminal Company, 191

Panama Canal, *155;* effect of, on San Francisco port, 50, 58, 60–61, 62, *66, 68,* 209, 217; opening of (1914), 46, 50

Panama-Pacific International Exposition (1915), 39, 102, 150–51, 151, 154, *155,* 179

Pannell, J. P. M., 125, 126

Passenger Depot, 210, *210*

passenger ferries, 39, 56, *103,* 120, 146, 179, 223, 224

Pelton Water Wheel, 45, 47

Pflueger, T. L., *71*

PG&E, *66, 103,* 219, 225

Pier: **1,** 18, *89,* 120, *171,* 173, 194, *194;* **1½,** 18, 169, *171,* 173, 194, *194;* **3,** 18, 120, 158, 169, *171,* 173, 189, 193, 194, *194,* 224; **5,** 18, 120, *149,* 158, 169, *171,* 173, 193, *193,* 194; **7,** 70, *100,* 134, 193, *193;* **9,** 90, *109,* 191, 192, 193, *193;* **11,** *98, 99, 109,* 191, *191,* 192, *192;* **13,** 191, *191,* 192, *192;* **14,** 120, 199, *199,* 200; **15,** 61, 71, 74, *132,* 191, *191,* 192, *192,* 200, 225; **15–17,** *100,* 173, 192; **16,** *158,* 200; **16–18–20,** 156, 159, 200, *200;* **17,** 70, 74, 120, 129, 143, 191, *191,* 192, *192,* 205, 223; **18,** 225; **19,** 70, 90, 191, *191,* 193; **20,** 70; **21,** 191, *191,* 225; **22,** 71, 156, 201, *201,* 202; **22½,** 78, 156, 201, *201,* 224; **23,** *45, 137,* 190, *190,* 191, *191;* **24,** *64,* 70, *98,* 120, *140,* 156, 158, 200, 202, *202;* **25,** 70, 71, 190, *190;* **26,** 120, 143, 151, 156, *158,* 159, 192, 203, *203,* 216, 223; **27,** 71, 170, 173, 187, 190, *190,* 216, 222; **27–29** (Pier 27 Terminal), 190; **28,** 120, 143, 151, 156, 159, 192, 203, *203,* 216, 223; **28½,** 204; **29,** *43, 66,* 71, *90,* 121, *130, 137,* 187, *187,* 216, 222, 224; **30,** 74, 120, 192, 204; **30–32,** *136,* 151, 156, 159, 170, 173, 204, *204,* 205, 216, 223; **31,** *43,* 71, 120, 121, *138–39, 143,* 158, 187, *187,* 224; **32,** 74, 120, 192; **33,** 71, *143,* 187, *187;* **33½,** 78; **34,** 101, *122–23,* 205, *205;* **35,** *39,* 71, 90, 137, 186, *186;* **36,** 41, *95,* 101, 120–21, 123, *131,* 143, 161, 205, 206, *206,* 222; **37,** *39,* 70, 90, *103,* 185, 186, *186;* **38,** 101, 123, 143, 156, 173, 205, 206, *206,* 222; **39,** *39,* 70, *103,* 137, 169, *169,* 185, *185,* 186, 188, *188;* **40,** 39, *96,* 101, 123, *124,* 142, *142,* 156, 204, 205, 206, *206,* 208, 222; **41,** 70, *97, 103,* 158, 185, *185,* 225; **42,** *72–73,* 101, 121, 156, *168–69,* 170, 207, *207;* **43,** 158, 184, *184;* **43½,** 142; **44,** *72–73,* 101, 121, 156, *168–69,* 170, 207, *207;* **45,** 36, 67, 68, 70, *73,* 75, 100, 101, 132, *132,* 141, 143, 158, 159, *160,* 169, 181, 182, *182,* 214; **46A,** *72–73, 98,* 156, *168–69,* 170, 207, *207;* **46B,** *168–69,* 208, 209, *209;* **47,** 181; **48,** 36, 39, 71, 100, *132,* 143, 158, 159, *160,* 182, 214, *214;* **50,** 36, 71, 74, 82, 100, *132,* 158, 159, *160, 164,* 165, 214, *214;* **52,** 39, 102, 173; **54,** 39, 71, *164,* 215, *215,* 222; **56,** 71; **60,** 213, *213;* **64,** 215; **70,** 173, 215, 216 (*see also* Potrero Point); **80,** *165,* 166, 217, *217;* **84,** 67, 218, *218;* **90,** 70, 71, 218, *218;* **90–94,** 173; **92,** 71, 166, 218, *218;* **94,** 167, *167,* 173, 219, *219;* **96,** 167, *167,* 190, 219, *219;* **98,** *171,* 219, *219;* **W-1,** 202

Pier 29 Annex, 99, 142, 159, 189, 222

pier aprons, 102, 135, 142–43

pier fronts, beautification of, 151–61, *156–59*

Pier 39 Garage, 188, *188*

Pier Head Line, 82, 159, *174–77,* 178, 182, 185; described, 36, 82

Pier Plaza project (1985), 169

piers, *156–59;* beautification efforts, 151–61, 223; design evolution, 95, *95, 100,* 130, *132;* elements of, 142–43 (*see also specific element*); engineering of, 142–43; finger-style (*see* finger piers); first modern pier, 206, *206;* numbering system, *156, 158,* 191; placement, in port design, 124, *137;* private-company assignments, 119–21; quay-type, 74, *100,* 104, *160,* 182, *182,* 187, 192, 214, *214;* rehabilitation of, *171,* 191; reinforced-concrete, 64, 90, *95,* 130, *132,* 133, *133,* 134, 221, 222; substructures, 133, 142–43, 182, 185–87, 191–94, 199, 202–4, 206, 214, 215; timekeepers and wharfingers, 110, 119–20, 141; twin-pier design, 194, *194;* versus wharves, 124; widening of, 135

pile-drivers/rigs, *110, 111, 136, 143, 149*

piles, *110, 111, 128, 133,* 135, *138–39, 143,* 152; concrete-jacketed, 152; steel-cylinder, 134

Pioneer Woolen Mill, 41

Plant, Thomas, 117

Point Richmond, 39, 63, *98*

Point San Quentin (Potrero Point), 215, *215*

Polk, Willis, 147–48, *150*

Port Commission, creation of (1969), 166

Port Costa, 58, 120

port design: ancient times, 123–26, *125;* basic features, 124, 127, 129–30; U.S. versus Europe, *125,* 126–27, 129

Portland, port competition from, 58

Port of San Francisco: beautification efforts, 145–61; Belt Railroad (*see* Belt Railroad); boundaries, 35–36, 36, *59,* 82; as break-bulk port, 63, *106–7,* 109, *112–13, 118;* and "city front," 36; competing ports, 58–59, *71,* 74, 75; as container port, 118, *120;* control of, 35, 42, 78, 80, 138, 164–65, 166; early development of, *37,* 41, 78, 80, *80–81,* 81–83; earthquake repair (1906), 85, *86–87;* elements of, *134, 137*–43 (*see also specific* elements); engineering of, 123–43; Foreign Trade Zone, 67, *73,* 75; geographical advantage of, *61,* 119–20, 126; harbor lines, 82, *174–77,* 178; historic preservation initiatives, 16, *18,* 23, *169,* 173 (*see also* San Francisco Architectural Heritage); landfill extension of shoreline, 41, *56, 57,* 82, *135, 136;* lifecycle, 17; maps, 48, 64, *65, 79, 82, 134,* 141, *174–77,* 178, 213; modernization initiatives, 60, 64, *65,* 73–74, 85, 95, 134–35; most vigorous period, 58; non-maritime development proposals, 18–19, 20, *164,* 165–70, *166, 168–72,* 173; offices, 173, 194, *194* (*see also* Ferry Building); policing of, 78; port-related offices, 48–53; principal trade goods, 60–61, 63, 74; prostitution control (1917), 53; rehabilitation and revitalization efforts, 18–19, 20, 22–23; revenue sources, 84–85, 85, 88, 90, 94, 140 (*see also* BSHC, revenue sources); specialized terminals, 166, 167, *167,* 218, *218;* surveys, 15–16, *16,* 73, 78, *79,* 134, 139, 195, 212, 220; tonnage statistics, 57, 58, 60, 61, 62, 63, 64, 66, 74; vessel-types served by, 95–96; views, *23, 25-33,* 67, *69, 172;* waterfront height limit, 166, 167, 169; waterfront line, 139, 140; work force (*see* labor force)

ports, "specialized," 58; threat of, to Port of San Francisco, 58–59

Potrero Point, 38, 42, 213, 216, 219; Arctic Oil Works, 42, *43;* early development of, *37,* 38; known as Pier 70, 36 (*see also* Pier 70); private waterfront, 216, *216;* worker housing at, *40*

Prairie School style, 159

preservation, historic, 8–9, 15–16, *18,* 23, *169,* 173. *See also* San Francisco Architectural Heritage

Presidio, 70, 102, 179, 224

Produce (or Commission) District, *44*, 47, *54–55*, 56, 67, 196, *196*, 232n24

Public Works Administration (PWA), 90

Pyle, Alfred A., 158, 159, 160, 186, *186*, 187, *187*, 194, 199, *199*, 223–24, 224, 225

Quarantine Station, 78

quay-type piers, 74, *100*, 104, *160*, 182, *182*, 187, *190*, 192, 214, *214*, 217, *217*

railroads: and car-ferry connections, 96, 98, 101–2; establishment of, at port, 36, *41*, 98–99; industry stimulus from, 41–45, *42*, *43*, 47–48; private railroads, 36–39, *37–40*, 41 (*see also specific names*); regulation of, 78; "specialized ports" created for, 58; worker strikes, 114. *See also* Belt Railroad; transcontinental railroad

rail spurs, 36, 42, *42*, 44, 62, 135, 137, 142; on pier aprons, 142. *See also* Belt Railroad, spurs

Redevelopment Agency, 15, *168–69*, 170, 200, 207, 208

Redwood City, port of, 89, 95

Refrigerated Products Terminal, 209, *209*, 224

restaurants, 190, 204, *204*; Alioto's No. 8 (restaurant), 180; Fisherman's Grotto No. 9, 180; Franciscan Restaurant, 142, 184, *184*; Houston's Restaurant, 188; Pier 23 Restaurant, 142, 190, *190*; Pier 28½ Restaurant, 142; Red's Java House restaurant, 204

Richardson, William P., 193

Richmond, port of, 89, 95, 99, 101

Riggers' and Stevedores' Association, 113

Rincon Annex, 199

Rincon Hill, 51, *52*, *80–81*

Rincon Park, 200, *200*

Rincon Point, 53, *56*, *60*, *64*, 202, *202*

Rincon Point–South Beach Redevelopment Plan, 170, 173

Robinson & Mills, 188

ROMA Design Group, 197

Romanesque Revival style, 147, 149, 199

Roney, Frank, 114

Roosevelt, Franklin D., 117

"ropewalk" building, 216

"Ro-Ro" (roll-on/roll-off loading), 166

roundhouse, 38, 213; Old Roundhouse, 189, *189*. *See also* Belt Railroad, roundhouse

Rubin, Jasper, 165–66, 167, *168–69*, 173

Russ Building, 159, 222

Sacramento, port of, 89, 95, 120

Sailors' Home, 202

sailors/seamen, *51*, 78, 114; duties, 110, *112*, *117*; union halls, *52*, 53, 114, 117; working conditions, 108

Sailors Union of the Pacific, *52*, 53, 117

San Diego, port of, 60, 89

San Francisco, city of: aerial view, *23*; Burnham Plan (*see* Burnham Plan of 1905); and "City Base," 82; City Beautiful Movement, *151*, 152, *154*, 154–55; Downtown Plan, 16, *16*; earthquake and fire (1906), *45*, 47, 49–50, *54–55*, 60, *84*, 85, *86–87*, 132, 134, 154, 155, 184; political reform efforts, 154–55; port control, 80, 164–65, 166

San Francisco and Pacific Glass Works, *62*

San Francisco and San Jose Railroad, 220

San Francisco Architectural Heritage: founding of, 12, 15; headquarters (Haas-Lilienthal House), *14*, 15; preservation initiatives, *14*, 15–16, 23

San Francisco Bar Pilots, 193, *193*

San Francisco Bay: agricultural landings, *63*; dredging of, 82; early explorers, 17, *17*; and port building, 80

San Francisco Bay Office Park, 188, *188*

San Francisco Chamber of Commerce, 60, 114, 151

San Francisco Civic Center, 154, *154*, 155

San Francisco earthquake and fire of 1906, *45*, 47, 49–50, *54–55*, 60, *84*, 85, *86–87*, 132, 134, 154, 155, 184

San Francisco Giants stadium, *168–69*, 170, 208, *208*, 213; pre-ballpark view, *72–73*

San Francisco-Oakland Bay Bridge. *See* Bay Bridge

San Francisco Planning and Research (SPUR), 16, 18

San Francisco Port Authority, 165

San Francisco Port Commission, 91

San Francisco Port of Embarkation, 69–73, 70

San Francisco Waterfront Partners, 193, 194

San Francisco World Trade Center Authority, 75

San Jose, port of, 89

San Jose Railroad, 96

Sansome Street, 48, 49, 52, *59*, 99, 196

Santa Fe Building, *50*, 51

Santa Fe car ferry, *98*, 213

Santa Fe Railway, 36, 155, 184, 213, 214; beginning of port service, 39, 48; car ferry, 39, *42*, *98*, 101, 102, 213; land acquisition, 39; Main Street wharf, 98–99; offices, 199 (*see also* Santa Fe Building); Pier 54 built for, 215, *215*; railroad spurs, 39, 47–48, 62; seawall extension, 141; seawall lots leased to, 188, 204; Yards and Terminal, 213, *213*

Saph, Augustus V., 151, 192, *192*, 203, *203*, 223

Sausalito, port of, 102

Schmitz, Eugene, 81, 114, 155

Schulze, Henry, 201

Schweinfurth, A. C., 147

Scott, Mel, 62

Seamen's Institute, 53

Seamen's Protective Union, 114

Seattle, port of, 58, 62–63, 74

seawall, *41*; advisory commission on, 139; and alignment, *38*, 130, 139; completion of, 64, 88; construction method, 130, *135*, *136*, *137*, 138, 140, *140*, 141; construction period, 36, 57, 81, *82*, 84, 130; engineering of, *135*, 137–41, *138–39*, *140*, 220–21, 224, 230n43; extensions, 38, 141; first seawall, 138, *140*; funding for, 84–85, 139, 140; on Port map, *134*; realignment of, 220; second seawall, 81, 139–40; Section 3, 188; Section 7, 196; Section 9, *76–77*, *136*, 202; Section 11, *136*; Section 13A, 38; sectioning of, 139–40; and T. J. Arnold ("Engineer of the Seawall"), 38, 96, 99, 130, 139, 220–221

Seawall Lot: **1 (now 311)**, 185, 188, *188*; **2 (now 312)**, 188, *188*; **3 (now 313)**, 188, *188*; **4**, *62*; **4 (now 314)**, 188, *188*; **5**, *39*; **5 (now 315)**, 188, *188*; **6 (now 316)**, 188, *188*; **7**, *43*; **7 (now 317)**, 188, *188*; **8**, *169*, 189; **8 (now 318)**, 189, *189*; **9 (now 319)**, 189, *189*; **10**, *88*, 189; **10 (now 320)**, 195, *195*; **11 (now 321)**, 195, *195*; **12**, *98*; **12 (now 322)**, 195, *195*; **13 (now 323)**, 195,

195; **14 (now 324)**, 195, *195*; **15**, 195, *195*; **16**, *100*, 195, *195*; **17 (now 327)**, 200, *200*; **18 (now 328)**, 202, *202*; **19 (now 329)**, 204, *204*; **20 (now 330)**, 205, *205*; **21 (now 331)**, 205, *205*; **22 (now 332)**, 205, *205*; **23 (now 333)**, 207, *207*; **24**, *168–69*, 206; **24 (now 334)**, 208, *208*; **25**, *168–69*; **25 (now 335)**, 208, *208*; **26 (now 336)**, 208, *208*; **27 (now 337)**, 213; **337**, 173; **351**, 173, 195, *195*; **B**, 184, *184*; **C (now 302)**, 181; **D (now 303)**, 181

seawall lots: Belt Railroad built on, *84*, 121; creation of, *76–77*, 139, 140; leased to private companies, 121; office developments built on, 166; on Port map, *134*; and railroad industries, 39, *41*, *43*; rail yards built on, 102, 121; replaced by parking lots, *102*, 105

seawalls, New York versus San Francisco, *127*, 130

Second Street, 38, *41*, 42, 44–45, 51, *51*, 52, 53, 98, 178, 199, *208*, *209*

Selvin, David, 113

Shell Building, 222

Ship Owners Association, 114

shipping companies: downtown locations of, 49–50; Panama Canal-induced building boom, 50–52. *See also* steamship companies; *specific name*

ships: classifications, 95–96; design evolution, 96; shift from wind-powered to steam-powered, 95, 96. *See also* ferries

ships, abandoned: used for warehouses and offices, *80*

Shipwright's Cottage, 219, *219*

Showplace Square, 44, 231n7

Sidney Rudy Waterfront Park, 186

Skidmore, Owings & Merrill, 167

SMWM Architects, 194, 198

South Basin, 36

South Beach Harbor Park, *168–69*, 170, 208, *208*

South Beach Marina, *168–69*, 207

South Beach-Rincon Point, 173. *See also* Rincon Point–South Beach Redevelopment Plant

South Beach Yacht Club, 208

South End Historic District, 209, *209*

Southern Pacific Building, *46*, 48, *48*, 49, 51, *92–93*

Southern Pacific Mission Bay Yards, 213, *213*

Southern Pacific Passenger Depot, 210, *210*

Southern Pacific Railroad, 42; auto docks and car-ferry slips, *42*, 62, 102, 182, *182*; Bay Bridge rail line, 105; and BSHC, 81, 85, 215, 221, 223; China Basin Building, 210, *210*; hospital for employees (Fell Street), 53; influence on Port, 39, *48*, 98, 155, 183, 215; land holdings, 38, *40*; landlocking of (1909), *41*; office locations, 51, *97*, 210, *210*; and Pacific Mail Steamship Company, 38, 98, 211; passenger depots, *40*, 210, *210*; purchase of Tichenor's Ways (1870), 38; rail spurs, 42, 44–45, *64*, 209, 210, 211; rail yards, 210, *210*; roundhouse, 213; and seawall construction, 140; seawall lots used by, 195, 207, *207*, 208

Southern Pacific Warehouse, 209

Specialty Oils Terminal, 166, 218, *218*

Sperry Flour, 50, *99*

Spreckels, Adolph B., 48, 49

Squire, Harry E., 224, 225

St. Clair building, *46*

Stafford, W. V., 81, 87–88

State Department of Engineering, 160, 221–24

State Islais Creek Oil Plant, 218

State Products Terminal Building, 67

State Shipside Refrigeration Terminal, 67

State Terminal building, 224

Steamboat Point, 42, 51, 207, *207*; housing development, 170; Oriental Warehouse, 42, 209, 211, *211*

steam donkeys, *106–7, 107–8,* 109, 133

steamship companies, *109,* 120–21, 185, 186; long-term pier rentals, by, 119–20. *See also* Pacific Mail Steamship Company

Stern, Boris, 110

Steuart Street, *51,* 53

stevedores, 110, *112,* 141, 205; labor organizations, 113, 114

Stockton, port of, 70, 89, 95, 120

Stockton Street tunnel, 154

Stoll, Horatio, 151

strikes. *See* labor strikes

substructures, pier: defined, 142. *See also* piers, substructures

sugar industry, 42, 48, 51–52, 120, 216, *216*

Sydney, port of, 20, *21*

Taylor, Thomas R., 109–10

teamsters, *106–7, 112, 117*; strike (1901), 114; unions, *52,* 53, 113, 117, 120

Telegraph Hill, *45, 47, 54–55,* 184

Temko, Allan, 169

Third Street Bridge, 39

Tibbitts Construction Co, 192

tidelands, 39, 56, 75, 78, 80, 98, 212, *212,* 213. *See also* Islais Creek-India Basin Plan (1918)

Tidelands Act (1868), 38

Townsend Street, 38, *40, 41,* 42, 51, *97,* 101, 173, *210,* 213

Toyo Kisen Kaisha (steamship company), 120–21, 205, 206

Trades Assembly, 114

transcontinental railroad, 216; completion of (1869), *37,* 37–38, 56, 57; effect on labor movement, 113; impact on Port of San Francisco, 56, 57–58

transit sheds, *96, 98,* 109, 110, *129, 149*; and architecture, 143, 149, 151–52; Belt Railroad access to, *98,* 101, 133; in break-bulk process, 109, 110, *112–13,* 118; BSHC maintenance of, *88*; construction methods, *124, 130,* 133–34, 137, 143; described, 142, 143; fireproof-construction of, *122–23*; first-generation, *64*; mail dock, *211*; military use of, 69; modernized, *96, 124*; parallel rows of, 132, 159; placement considerations, 133, *137, 140,* 142, 143; worker amenities provided, 118; and worker rights, 118

Transit Sheds at Pier: **1,** *194*; **3 (and 1½),** *194*; **5,** *193*; **7,** *193*; **9,** *193*; **14,** *199*; **15,** *192*; **17,** 192; **19,** *191*; **21,** *191*; **23,** *191*; **24,** *202*; **26,** *203*; **27,** *190*; **28,** *203*; **29,** *130, 187*; **31,** *187*; **33,** *187*; **34,** *205*; **35,** *186*; **36,** *206*; **37,** *186*; **38,** *206*; **39,** *185*; **40,** *206*; **41,** *185*; **45,** *182*; **48,** *214*; **50,** *214*; **54,** *215*; **80,** *217*

transshipments, 58, 75, 96, *96,* 214; Belt Railroad used for, 101; BSHC-imposed shipping tolls, 94; cargo-handling process, 103, 109; described, 56; and Foreign Trade Zone, 67

truck traffic: increases in, *100,* 105; quay-type piers built to accommodate, 104

Tubbs Cordage Works, 41

Uhlig, Carl, 221, 222

Union Depot and Ferry House. *See* Ferry Building

Union Ice Company, 42

Union Iron Works, 216

unions, employer, 114, 116

unions, labor. *See* labor unions

Union Shovel Works (later Union Iron Works), 56–57

Union Street, *88,* 180, 184

U.S. Army: Army-Navy YMCA, 53, *53*; beginning of port presence, *70*; containerized cargo used by, *120*; Fort Mason, 39, 70, 102, 179, *179,* 223, 224; offices, 71; piers assigned to, 68–69, 70, 71–72, 73

U.S. Army Air Corps, 70, 71

U.S. Army Corps of Engineers: functions of, 78, 82; Mission Rock destroyed by, 82; Oakland port improvements, 75; Pier Head Line established by, 36, 178; Pier Head Line extended by, 82; reports on port economy, 58, 62–63, 74; in seawall federal advisory commission, 139; waterfront line established by, 140

U.S. Army Transport service, 70

U.S. Coast Guard, 78, 181

U.S. Customs Service, 66, 78, 181, 196, *196*

U.S. Government: Port advisory commission (1875), 139; and World War II, 69

U.S. Marine Hospital, 53, 202

U.S. Navy, 68, 199, 214, 225; Army-Navy YMCA, 53, *53*; Ferry Building office, 71; housing for, 36; Hunters Point Naval Shipyard, 36, 219, *219*; port facilities assigned to, 67, 68, 71, 225; in seawall federal advisory commission, 139

U.S. Post Office, 119; Agriculture Building, 82–83, 199, *199,* 224; beginning of port tenancy (1884), 78; Embarcadero Post Office, 82; Ferry Post Office of 1901, 147, *149,* 199, 223; Ferry Station Post Office of 1914–15, 82, 159, 160; and Pacific Mail Steamship Company, 211, *211*

U.S. Post Office (Agriculture Building), 199, *199*

U.S. Railroad Administration, 110

U.S. Steel, 167, 168–69

U.S. War Department: Army Transportation Corps, 70

Vallejo, port of, 95, 102, 120

Vance, James E., Jr., 56, 57, 58

Vancouver, port of, 19, 20, *21,* 224

vegetable food products trade, 74

Vegetable Oil Station (Islais Creek), 62, 63

vegetable oil trade, 62, 63, *72–73,* 206, 208, 218, 224

Victorian style, *14*

Voget, Lamberta, 81, 85, 88–89, 195

W. R. Grace & Company, 50, 121, 208

Walker & Moody, 185

Walton Park, 196

warehouse district, 56; cold-storage district, in, 47

warehousemen, 112, *117,* 118

warehouses, 41–48; Harbor Warehouses, *39,* 183; pre-railroad port locations for, 41, *41, 42,* 47, *59*; served by Belt Railroad, 47; served by private rail spurs, 36, *41,* 42, *42,* 44–45, 47. *See also specific* name

warehouses, publicly-owned: BSHC plans for construction of, 61–62

Washington (state), port competition from, 58

Washington Street Pier, 189

Waterfront Land Use Plan (WLUP), 173, *173*

Water Front Line, *174–77,* 178; and Embarcadero, 197, *197*

Watermark condominium, 170, 205, *205*

Welch Building, *46,* 49

Wells, Hewitt C., 184, *184*

Wells Fargo & Company Express, 52–53, 119, 120, 199, *199*

Western Addition project, *14,* 15

Western Pacific Railroad, 36, 39, 41, *42,* 98, 120; and Belt Railroad, 39, *42*; and BSHC engineers, 220; car-ferry slips, 41, 101, 102; land acquisition, 38, 39; office locations, 51; Pier 36 built for, 206, *206*; rail spurs, *42,* 48; rail yards, 217, *217*; seawall lots leased to, *43,* 188, 205; taken over by Southern Pacific, 36; transcontinental line (Richmond), 99

wharfingers, 110, 119–20, 141, 146. *See also* BSHC, Wharfingers Department

wharves, bulkhead. *See* bulkhead wharves

wharves, versus piers, 124

White, Frank G., 89, 182, 187, *187,* 191, *191,* 192, *192,* 193, *193,* 194, *194,* 214, *214,* 223, 224, 225

wholesale districts, 96; location chosen for, 56

Williams, Dimond & Company, 120

Willy McCovey Cove, 213

Wilson Meany Sullivan, 198, 200

Wood, G. A., 187, *187,* 191, *191,* 193, *193,* 225

Workmen's Educational Association, 53

World's Columbian Exposition of 1893, 147, 152, 154

World Trade Center, *74,* 75, 166

World War I, 89, 102; effect of, on port economy, 61, 62, 64, *73*

World War II, 90, *115,* 118, 182; effect of, on port economy, 68–73, *73*; post-war port developments, *164*

Yerba Buena Cove, 41, *46,* 49, 195, *195,* 202; early development of, 78, 80, *80–81*; landfill expansion of, *57, 59, 60,* 196; pre-Gold Rush era, *56*; warehouses first established, 56. *See also* Rincon Point

YMCA. *See* Army-Navy YMCA

Young, Charles Newton, 184, *184,* 203, *203,* 223

Page numbers are given in **bold**, along with the abbreviations **t** (top), **m** (middle), **b** (bottom), **l** (left), and **r** (right). Full publication data for reprinted material appears in the bibliography. The abbreviation *BSHC* denotes authorship for all references listed in the bibliography under "California. Board of State Harbor Commissioners for the State of California."

Every effort has been made to obtain permissions from the rights holders of the images reproduced in this book. Any omission will be corrected in a reprint.

Airview Aerial Photography (www.airviewonline.com.au): **21t**

Courtesy Anne Rand Library and Archives, International Longshore and Warehouse Union: **43b**, **61** (reprinted from San Francisco Chamber of Commerce, *Facts About the Port of San Francisco*, 106–107), **74** (reprinted from William Gladstone Merchant, *San Francisco World Trade Center*, cover), **96**, **98m**, **112mb**, **114**, **119l+r**, **120**, **142**, **165**, **172**, **203r**, **214**, **218r**

Reprinted from *Architect and Engineer* 48, no. 2 (February 1917): 56: **50**

Courtesy Bancroft Library. University of California, Berkeley: **37**, **38l**, **43t**, **59b**, **62b**, **63** (reprinted from *Official Historical Atlas Map of Alameda County, California*, 199), **67**, **134** (reprinted from T. J. Arnold, *Map Showing an Improved Line for the Waterfront of the City of San Francisco*, unpag.) **135** (reprinted from Lauren E. Crane, *Report of Lauren E. Crane*, unpag.)

Photograph by Richard Barnes. Courtesy Page & Turnbull, Inc.: **171t**

Photograph by Shawn Bishop. Courtesy and © the City of Vancouver: **21b**

Board of State Harbor Commissioners for San Francisco Harbor (BSHC): **95** (reprinted from *Biennial Report* [1910], 14)

California Historical Society: **34–35** (*Aerial View of San Francisco*, ca. 1950s, silver gelatin print. San Francisco Chamber of Commerce Collection, FN-28885/CHS2010.313), **57l+r** (Martin Behrman, *San Francisco Waterfront at Yerba Buena Cove* [2 panels], 1851, silver gelatin prints. FN-26277/CHS2010.316, FN-23992/CHS2010.315), **60** (Martin Behrman, *General Sherman's House on Rincon Road, San Francisco, Cal.*, ca. 1856, silver gelatin print. George A. Berton Collection, FN-19615/CHS2010.318), **69** (W. Wesley Swadley, *Piers 9 & 11 and Rolph Navigation and Coal Co.*, ca. 1910–1920s, silver gelatin print. FN-36393/CHS2010.314), **112–113** (R. J. Waters & Co., *Shipping Warehouse, San Francisco Waterfront*, ca. 1920s, silver gelatin print. CHS2010.312), **164t** (Henri Van Wandelen, *American President Lines' Pier 50, Mission Rock Terminal*, San Francisco, ca. 1950s, silver gelatin print. CHS2010.284)

Courtesy of the California History Room, California State Library, Sacramento, California: **59t**, **79**, **86–87**

Courtesy California State Archives, Sacramento. Dept. of Finance, Harbor Commissioners: **39** (F3254:59[18]), **70t** (F3254:271[1–2]), **136b** (F3413:2463)

Courtesy California State Archives, Sacramento. Dept. of Public Works, Architecture: **90** (F3253.242d[17]), **156bl** (F3253:242d[misc]), **199t+b** (F3253:242d[10+13])

Collection of the California State Lands Commission: **212**

Courtesy California State Railroad Museum: **88l**, **98r**, **101**

Photograph by Charles W. Cushman, Courtesy Indiana University Archives: **75** (P01896), **105b** (P14844)

Courtesy Delancey Street Foundation: **205tr**

Photograph by Harre Demoro. Courtesy John Harder: **42t**

Reprinted from F. M. Du-Plat-Taylor, *The Design, Construction, and Maintenance of Docks, Wharves, and Piers*, 17: **124t**

Courtesy Environmental Design Archives, University of California, Berkeley: **150** ("Drawing of Proposed Ferry Building." Willis Polk Collection, 1934-1), **155** ("Night View of the PPIE." Fairs and Expositions Collection, 1999-2), **166t** ("International Trade Mart." William W. Wurster/WBE Collection, 1976-2)

Reprinted from A. G. Ford, *Handling and Storage of Cargo*, after 204: **118**

Courtesy Garzoli Gallery, San Rafael, California: **17b**

Photograph by Cliff Hamilton: **184br**

Reproduced by permission of The Huntington Library, San Marino, California: **56** (William Rich Hutton, *San Francisco—From the Hill Back*, 1847, drawing. HM43214 #81)

Photograph © Herb Lingl/aerialarchives.com: **168–169**, **215r**, **219tl**

Reprinted from Irving F. Morrow, "San Francisco Harbor," *Architect* 16, no. 5, (November 1918): plate 58: **159**

© Museum of London: **125b**

Reprinted from Jerome Newman, "The Improvement of San Francisco's Water Front," *Engineering News* 73, no. 7 (February 18, 1915): 327: **140b**

Collection of the New-York Historical Society: **126** (David T. Keiller and John Mecham, *Department of Docks, City of New York*, 1873, black ink with color wash on paper. 2N L6.2.19), **22l** (Thomas Airviews, *Lower Manhattan, July 10, 1948*, 1948, gelatin silver print. negative number 75896)

Courtesy NYC Municipal Archives: **127t+b**, **156tl**

Courtesy Page & Turnbull, Inc.: **16**, **18**

Courtesy Port of San Francisco: **25**, **26b**, **29b**, **32–33**, **45**, **66t**, **66b** (reprinted from BSHC, *Gateway of the Pacific*, unpag.), **68** (reprinted from BSHC, *Biennial Report* [1919], 22), **70b**, **76–77**, **82** (reprinted from BSHC, *Biennial Report* [1941], 29), **98l**, **100tr**, **108**, **110**, **111**, **122–123**, **124** (reprinted from BSHC, *Biennial Report* [1910], after 38), **128bl** (reprinted from BSHC, *Biennial Report* [1910], 20), **128br** (reprinted from BSHC, *Biennial Report* [1913], 20), **129** (reprinted from BSHC, *Biennial Report* [1913], 40), **130**, **131t** (reprinted from BSHC, *Biennial Report* [1910], 32), **131b** (reprinted

from BSHC, *Biennial Report* [1910], 26), **132t** (reprinted from BSHC, *Biennial Report* [1931], 20), **132b** (reprinted from BSHC, *Biennial Report* [1931], 24), **133**, **136tr** (reprinted from BSHC, *Biennial Report* [1910], 10), **137**, **138**, **139**, **140t** (reprinted from BSHC, *Biennial Report* [1916], 32), **143**, **144–145**, **146**, **147**, **148**, **156–157**, **157b** (reprinted from BSHC, *Biennial Report* [1914], 34), **158t** (reprinted from BSHC, *Biennial Report* [1913], 36), **160r** (reprinted from BSHC, *Biennial Report* [1931], 34), **174–175** (reprinted from BSHC, *Biennial Report* [1926]), **176–177**, **180t**, **180bl** (reprinted from BSHC, *Biennial Report* [1926], 60), **180br** (reprinted from BSHC, *Biennial Report* [1932], 44), **181t** (reprinted from BSHC, *Biennial Report* [1921], 46), **181b** (reprinted from BSHC, *Biennial Report* [1919], 45), **182l** (reprinted from BSHC, *Biennial Report* [1938], 34), **183t** (reprinted from BSHC, *Biennial Report* [1921], 62), **185b** (reprinted from BSHC, *Biennial Report* [1932], 40), **186r**, **187b** (reprinted from BSHC, *Biennial Report* [1921], 8), **188tr**, **189**, **190tl** (reprinted from BSHC, *Biennial Report* [1923], 12), **191l** (reprinted from BSHC, *Biennial Report* [1932], 26), **193tl** (reprinted from BSHC, *Biennial Report* [1938], 44), **193b**, **198**, **200tl** (reprinted from BSHC, *Biennial Report* [1916], 42), **206l** (reprinted from BSHC, *Biennial Report* [1910], 6), **209t**, **209b**, **213t**

Photograph by Rafael Rivera: **22r**

Courtesy David Rumsey: **65** (reprinted from Auguste Chevalier, *The Chevalier Commercial, Pictorial, and Tourist Map of San Francisco from the Latest U.S. Government and Official Surveys*, detail), **83t**, **m**, **b** (reprinted from E. S. Glover, *The Illustrated Directory*)

Collection of San Francisco Airport Museums: **104**

Courtesy San Francisco Architectural Heritage **14**, **47**, **97t**, **184l**, **216**

San Francisco Chamber of Commerce: **72–73** (reprinted from *The Golden Gate, San Francisco*, unpag.)

San Francisco History Center, San Francisco Public Library: **1** (AAC-2400), **2–3** (AAB-3539), **6–7** (AAC-2417), **31** (AAC-2070), **38r** (reprinted from *Harper's Weekly*, December 31, 1881), **40b** (AAB-6704), **41** (AAC-1841), **42m** (AAC-8270), **44** (AAC-0526), **46tl** (AAC-5033), **46tr** (AAC-4751), **46bl** (AAB-3073), **46bm** (AAB-3086), **46br** (AAB-3097), **48** (reprinted from *Architect and Engineer* 51, no. 2 [November 1917]: 60), **49** (AA1-0187), **52** (AAD-5684), **53** (AAE-1051), **54–55** (A11.17,510n), **62t** (reprinted from *Langley's San Francisco Directory*, 44), **73tr** (AAC-2325), **73br** (AAC-2248), **88r** (AAB-6682), **89** (AAC-2182), **91** (AAB-3535), **94t** (AAD-6279), **94b** (AAF-0647), **97b** (AAC-8174), **100tl** (AAC-2302), **100b** (AAC-2324), **102** (AAC-2173), **103** (AAC-2010), **105tl** (Ferry Building, Park Proposal), **105tr** (Ferry Building, Park Proposal), **109r** (AAC-2203), **112b** (AAC-2236), **115** (AAD-5653), **116** (AAD-4954), **117** (AAD-5021), **121** (AAD-4949), **128tl** (AAB-6699), **128tr** (AAH-0283), **136tl** (AAC-1971), **149b** (AAK-0678), **151–152** (reprinted from Daniel H. Burnham, assisted by Edward H. Bennett, *Report on a Plan for San Francisco*), **154**, **158b** (AAC-2343), **160l** (AAC-2427), **161** (Ferry Building, Park Proposal), **164b** (AAC-2198), **167** (reprinted from San Francisco Port Commission, *Multiport*), **169tr** (AAC-2368), **170t** (San Francisco Freeways, Embarcadero), **179br** (AAC-4696), **182r** (Drawing by Henry Hill, reprinted from "The Longshoremen Build a Monu-

Pier 28

Pages 2–3: Aerial view south of the Ferry Building to Pier 26, 1932
Page 4: Pier 28
Pages 6–7: Aftermath of an accident at Pier 45, April 4, 1929

Published in 2010 by
San Francisco Architectural Heritage
San Francisco, CA 94109
www.sfheritage.org

Compilation © 2010 San Francisco
  Architectural Heritage
Text © 2010 Michael R. Corbett

978-0-615-39831-0

Printed and bound in Singapore

Editor and Project Manager: Elisa Urbanelli
Designer: Robin Weiss
Photographer:
Ezra Cattan, Urban-Eyes Industries
Rights and Reproductions:
Leiasa Beckham and Leslie Ann Dutcher
Proofreader: Mark Woodworth
Indexer: Susan Burke
Printer: CS Graphics Pte Ltd., Singapore